Invitation to Mathematics

L. Carey Bolster
Supervisor of Mathematics
Baltimore County Public Schools
Towson, Maryland

Warren Crown
Assistant Professor of Mathematics Education
Rutgers University
New Brunswick, New Jersey

Mary Montgomery Lindquist
Professor of Mathematics Education
National College of Education
Evanston, Illinois

Charles McNerney
Professor of Mathematics
University of Northern Colorado
Greeley, Colorado

William Nibbelink
Professor and Chairman
Elementary Education
University of Iowa
Iowa City, Iowa

Glenn Prigge
Professor of Mathematics
University of North Dakota
Grand Forks, North Dakota

Cathy Rahlfs
Math Consultant
Region IV Education Service Center
Houston, Texas

David Robitaille
Head, Department of Mathematics
and Science Education
University of British Columbia
Vancouver, British Columbia, Canada

James Schultz
Associate Professor of Mathematics
The Ohio State University
Columbus, Ohio

Jane Swafford
Professor of Mathematics
Northern Michigan University
Marquette, Michigan

Irvin Vance
Professor of Mathematical Sciences
New Mexico State University
Las Cruces, New Mexico

James Wilson
Professor of Mathematics Education
University of Georgia
Athens, Georgia

Robert Wisner
Professor of Mathematical Sciences
New Mexico State University
Las Cruces, New Mexico

Scott, Foresman and Company

Editorial Offices: Glenview, Illinois

Regional Offices: Palo Alto, California •
Tucker, Georgia • Glenview, Illinois •
Oakland, New Jersey • Dallas, Texas

Advisors

Robert Hamada
Supervisor of Mathematics
Los Angeles Unified School District
Los Angeles, California

Viggo Hansen
Professor, Mathematics Education
California State University
Northridge, California

David E. Williams
Assistant Director
Division of Education
School District of Philadelphia
Philadelphia, Pennsylvania

Teacher Consultants for Grade 6

Maxine Blackmon
Wilkins Elementary School
1970 Castle Hill Drive
Jackson, Mississippi

Wiona Mitchell
Frick Middle School
10 Thrackey Street
Pittsburgh, Pennsylvania

Acknowledgments

For permission to reproduce indicated information on the following pages, acknowledgment is made to:

Ranger Rick magazines shown on page 54 are a publication of the National Wildlife Federation.

References

Data on world clock on pages 102 and 103, *Jens Olsen's World Clock*, 2nd Department of the City Administration Executive of Copenhagen. Castle construction on page 282 is made from LEGO® brand building bricks.

For permission to reproduce photographs on the following pages, acknowledgment is made to:

2 Courtesy NASA   **38** Gerald Jarosz   **48** Courtesy NASA   **68** Baseball cards, AU Sports Memorabilia, Skokie, Ill.   **68–69** UPI Photo   **92** *Civil War Drum*; Index of American Design; National Gallery of Art, Washington   **102** James Schultz   **157** Timothy Eagan/WOODFIN CAMP   **158** Beatrice Flesch/STOCK BOSTON, INC.   **216–217** Phillip A. Harrington/PETER ARNOLD, INC.   **244** Robert Lightfoot II right   **254** Library of Congress   bkg. and left   **254** U.S. Air Force Photo   **256** Rick Smolan/LEO DE WYS   **270** *Reicher Haffen*, Paul Klee, 1938. Oeffentliche Kunstsammlung, Basel   **272** *Broadway Boogie Woogie,* Piet Mondrian, Collection Museum of Modern Art, New York   **292–293** Adam Woolfitt/WOODFIN CAMP   **340–341** Tiffany Chin/FOCUS ON SPORTS   **342–343** Randy Hufford/TOM STACK AND ASSOCIATES   **352** Courtesy NASA   **357** Elliott Erwitt/MAGNUM

Editorial development, design, art and photography by: Scott, Foresman staff, Norman Perman, Inc., William A. Seabright

Ballard, James L.; Cochran, Bobbye; Csicsko, David; Drehobl Bros. Art Glass Co.; Dypold, Pat; Herbert Gotsch Studio, Inc.; Hoffman, Cynthia; Kock, Carl; Lazar, Arthur; Lightfoot III, Robert M.; O'Donnell Studio, Prokos, Nick; Ralph Cowan, Inc.; Renaud, Phil; Seabright, David; Seabright, Jeanne; Signorino, Slug; Sumichrast, Jozef; Zielinski, John

vii

Addition and Subtraction of Whole Numbers

1,500 revolutions per minute

12 inches

Naming Whole Numbers

The distance around the earth at the equator is about 40,075 kilometers.

hundred-thousands	ten-thousands	thousands	hundreds	tens	ones
	4	0	0	7	5

40,075

forty thousand, seventy-five

Standard form

40,075

Expanded form

40,000 + 70 + 5

Try

a. Write 3,638 in words.   **b.** Write 4,326 in expanded form.

c. Write 500,000 + 20,000 + 7,000 + 300 + 40 + 1 in standard form.

Practice   Write each number in words.

1. 1,828   **2.** 4,026   **3.** 38,056   **4.** 26,518   **5.** 128,682   **6.** 402,605

Write each number in expanded form.

7. 2,186   **8.** 7,042   **9.** 58,061   **10.** 12,637   **11.** 429,135   **12.** 503,806

Write each number in standard form.

13. 3,000 + 700 + 30 + 2

14. 6,000 + 800 + 60 + 1

15. 50,000 + 8,000 + 700 + 80 + 8

16. 80,000 + 7,000 + 600 + 90 + 5

17. 60,000 + 300 + 30 + 2

18. 10,000 + 5,000 + 10 + 8

19. 300,000 + 40,000 + 3,000 + 40

20. 300,000 + 300 + 4

21. Two thousand, five hundred fourteen

22. Nine thousand, four hundred seventy-five

23. Forty-two thousand, eight hundred sixty-three

24. Ninety-eight thousand, two hundred thirty-seven

25. Five hundred twenty-one thousand, eighty-three

26. Four hundred thousand, one hundred three

Apply   Give the answer to each problem.

27. The diameter of the earth at the equator is twelve thousand, seven hundred fifty-six kilometers. Write this number in standard form.

28. The distance around the earth through the North Pole and the South Pole is forty thousand, eight kilometers. Write this number in standard form.

Large Numbers

The volume of the earth is about
1,086,230,300,000 cubic kilometers.
The commas separate 1,086,230,300,000
into *periods.*

trillions period			billions period			millions period			thousands period			ones period		
hundred-trillions	ten-trillions	trillions	hundred-billions	ten-billions	billions	hundred-millions	ten-millions	millions	hundred-thousands	ten-thousands	thousands	hundreds	tens	ones
		1	0	8	6	2	3	0	3	0	0	0	0	0

1,086,230,300,000

1 trillion, 86 billion, 230 million, 300 thousand

one trillion, eighty-six billion, two hundred thirty million, three hundred thousand

Try

a. Tell which digits are in the billions period in the number 4,323,782,182,155.

b. Tell what the 6 means in the number 5,651,182,000,000.

c. Write the number 9,105,607,040 in words.

d. Write 78 billions, 425 million, 256 thousand, 9 in standard form.

Practice Tell which digits are in the millions period in each number.

1. 46,284,321
2. 157,325,000
3. 4,751,323,000

4. 8,121,215,390
5. 14,288,683,221,739
6. 27,459,048,902,130

Tell what each 8 in each number means.

7. 9,158,325
8. 8,325,492
9. 3,211,814,000

10. 21,112,386,000
11. 8,211,502,114,600
★12. 4,128,033,214,118

Write each number in words.

13. 8,400,218
14. 300,000,000
15. 2,300,601,000,008

Write each number in standard form.

16. 14 million, 105 thousand, 828
17. 518 million, 605 thousand, 801

18. 3 billion, 215 thousand
19. 8 trillion, 65 million, 650

Apply Give the answer for each problem.

20. The area of the surface of the earth is about 510,945,000 square kilometers. What does the 1 mean?

21. The water surface of the earth is about 362 million, 33 thousand, 993 square kilometers. Write this number in standard form.

22. The total land area of the earth is about one hundred forty-eight million, nine hundred eleven thousand, sixty-seven square kilometers. Write this number in standard form.

★23. The periods to the left of trillions are quadrillions, quintillions, and sextillions. The weight of the earth is 6 sextillion metric tons. Write this number in standard form.

Comparing and Ordering Whole Numbers

A. The area of Lake Huron is 59,699 square kilometers and the area of Lake Michigan is 57,757 square kilometers. Which lake is larger?

Compare 59,699 and 57,757.

The ten-thousands are the same. Compare the thousands. 9 thousands is greater than 7 thousands.

59,699 ● 57,757

> means "is greater than."
59,699 is greater than 57,757.

59,699 > 57,757

Lake Huron is larger.

Discuss If you were asked which lake was smaller, how would you write the numbers using the "is less than" symbol?

Try Compare. Use <, >, or =.

a. 8,214 ● 8,321

b. 56,391 ● 56,385

List these numbers in order from the least to the greatest.

c. 5,382   8,524   3,852

d. 47,394   47,402   47,264

B. List these numbers in order from the least to the greatest.

58,560   58,216   58,876

The ten-thousands and the thousands are the same. Compare the hundreds.

58,560   58,216   58,876

58,216 < 58,560
58,560 < 58,876

The numbers in order from least to greatest are:

58,216   58,560   58,876

Practice Compare. Use <, >, or =.

1. 3,435 ○ 3,589

2. 2,102 ● 1,657

3. 18,453 ● 17,653

4. 35,628 ○ 35,268

5. 58,274 ● 71,015

6. 81,372 ● 81,367

7. 476,144 ○ 97,698

8. 69,305 ● 69,305

9. 268,272 ● 285,253

10. 10,000 ○ 9,999

11. 99,999 ● 100,000

12. 201,100 ● 189,879

13. 100,312 ○ 100,312

14. 33,333 ● 222,222

15. 540,682 ● 540,268

List these numbers in order from the least to the greatest.

16. 4,678   3,615   4,238

17. 1,211   2,111   333

18. 8,283   5,681   3,892

19. 10,000   9,999   10,100

20. 32,183   32,615   32,419

21. 65,184   65,814   65,481

22. 500,555   501,000   500,000

★23. 1,435   1,345   1,543   1,453

Apply Solve each problem.

24. Lake Ontario has an area of 19,554 square kilometers and Lake Erie has an area of 25,667 square kilometers. Which lake is larger?

★25. The depths of the Great Lakes are as follows: Superior, 406 meters; Michigan, 281 meters; Huron, 229 meters; Erie, 64 meters; and Ontario, 244 meters. List these numbers in order, starting with the smallest depth.

CHALLENGE

A boat can carry only 150 pounds. How could a man, weighing 150 pounds, and two children, each weighing 75 pounds, use the boat to cross the lake?

Each person can row the boat.

Rounding Whole Numbers

A. The diameter of the earth is about 7,913 miles. Round 7,913 to the nearest thousand.

```
←•————————————•—————————•————————→
7,000              7,500         7,913
                               8,000
```

7,913 is between 7,000 and 8,000. Since 7,913 is closer to 8,000 than to 7,000, round to 8,000.

The diameter of the earth to the nearest thousand is 8,000 miles.

B. Round these numbers to the nearest hundred.

624   782   2,453

Look at the hundreds place. The digit to the right is less than 5. The hundreds digit stays the same.

624
↓
600

The digit next to the hundreds digit is greater than 5. Add 1 to the hundreds digit.

782
↓
800

The digit next to the hundreds digit is 5. Add 1 to the hundreds digit.

2,453
↓
2,500

Try   Round to the nearest hundred.

a. 382
400

b. 1,241
1,200

Round to the nearest thousand.

c. 7,385
7,000

d. 7,538
8,000

Add or subtract.

1. $6 + 3$　　2. $8 + 4$

3. $9 - 7$　　4. $7 + 6$

5. $8 + 9$　　6. $11 - 4$

7. $14 - 7$　8. $3 + 7$

9. $12 - 3$　10. $4 + 9$

11. $13 - 6$　12. $15 - 6$

13. $5 + 4$　14. $10 - 4$

15. $11 - 3$　16. $4 + 7$

17. $7 + 7$　18. $15 - 9$

19. $8 + 3$　20. $6 + 5$

21. $10 - 5$　22. $7 + 5$

23. $13 - 9$　24. $12 - 6$

25. $9 + 6$　26. $18 - 9$

27. $15 - 7$　28. $6 + 8$

29. $5 + 8$　30. $6 + 4$

31. $16 - 9$　32. $9 + 5$

33. $12 - 9$　34. $13 - 4$

35. $7 + 8$　36. $9 + 7$

37. $17 - 9$　38. $8 + 8$

39. $15 - 8$　40. $9 + 9$

41. $12 - 5$　42. $14 - 8$

Practice　Round to the nearest hundred.

1. 439　　　　2. 682　　　　3. 3,450

4. 2,080　　　5. 2,286　　　6. 3,981

Round to the nearest thousand.

7. 5,283　　　8. 8,453　　　9. 61,845

10. 28,865　　11. 48,500　　12. 409,607

Round to the nearest ten-thousand.

13. 58,655　　14. 38,405　　15. 437,159

16. 293,426　　17. 109,592　　18. 9,581

Apply　The diameters of some of the other planets in our solar system are given. Round each number to the nearest thousand and nearest hundred.

Planet	Diameter (miles)	Thousand	Hundred
Mercury	3,031	19.	20.
Venus	7,527	21.	22.
Jupiter	88,720	23.	24.

Estimating Sums and Differences

A. A 4-day hike was scheduled as follows:

1st day   7,580 meters
2nd day   8,320 meters
3rd day   9,680 meters
4th day   6,470 meters

Estimate the total length of the hike.

Estimate 7,580 + 8,320 + 9,680 + 6,470.

To estimate, round each addend to the nearest thousand.

$$7{,}580 + 8{,}320 + 9{,}680 + 6{,}470$$
$$\downarrow \qquad \downarrow \qquad \downarrow \qquad \downarrow$$
$$8{,}000 + 8{,}000 + 10{,}000 + 6{,}000 = 32{,}000$$

The hike was about 32,000 meters long.

B. Estimate 624 − 198.

Round each number to the nearest hundred.

$$624 - 198$$
$$\downarrow \qquad \downarrow$$
$$600 - 200 = 400$$

Try *Estimation* Estimate each sum or difference. First round each number to the nearest hundred.

a. 437 + 283   **b.** 742 − 138

Estimation Estimate each sum or difference. First round each number to the nearest thousand.

c. 3,643 + 2,315   **d.** 8,765 − 5,729

Practice *Estimation* Estimate each sum or difference. First round each number to the nearest hundred.

1. 375 + 219   **2.** 835 − 427   **3.** 418 + 576

4. 382 − 196   **5.** 642 − 198   **6.** 487 + 932

7. 985 − 621   **8.** 1,238 + 466   **9.** 2,634 − 243

Estimation Estimate each sum or difference. First round each number to the nearest thousand.

10. 2,381 + 6,902   **11.** 6,321 − 3,137   **12.** 3,558 − 1,726

13. 7,263 − 5,139   **14.** 6,821 + 2,168   **15.** 3,487 + 4,932

16. 24,830 + 6,324   **17.** 19,965 + 2,202   **18.** 3,001 − 2,978

Apply Solve each problem. Use the information given in Example A.

19. *Estimation* Estimate how many more meters were hiked on the third day than on the first day. Round each number to the nearest thousand.

20. *Estimation* Estimate the distance hiked on the first three days of the hike. Round each number to the nearest thousand.

21. Put the number of meters hiked each day in order from the least to the greatest.

★22. *Estimation* Estimate how many meters of the hike were left after two days of hiking were completed.

Adding with One Renaming

Mary's backpack weighs 1,360 grams and its contents weigh 2,924 grams. Find the total weight.

Estimate:
1,000 + 3,000 = 4,000

Find 1,360 + 2,924.

Add the ones.
Add the tens.

```
  1,3 6 0
+ 2,9 2 4
─────────
      8 4
```

Add the hundreds.
12 hundreds =
1 thousand 2 hundreds

```
      1
  1,3 6 0
+ 2,9 2 4
─────────
    2 8 4
```

Add the thousands.

```
      1
  1,3 6 0
+ 2,9 2 4
─────────
  4,2 8 4
```

The total weight is 4,284 grams.

Try   Add.

a.   25
   + 48

b.   482
   + 93

c.   437
   + 457

d.   1,557
   + 3,271

e. 5 + 7 + 3 + 6

Practice Add.

1. 36
   + 59

2. 54
   + 29

3. 58
   + 17

4. 34
   + 29

5. 43
   + 37

6. 29
   + 58

7. 53
   + 82

8. 24
   + 66

9. 36
   + 45

10. 68
    + 22

11. 153
    + 39

12. 247
    + 18

13. 271
    + 84

14. 274
    + 75

15. 356
    + 37

16. 583
    + 245

17. 762
    + 194

18. 237
    + 458

19. 124
    + 547

20. 425
    + 439

21. 382
    + 284

22. 375
    + 341

23. 319
    + 476

24. 328
    + 458

25. 395
    + 574

26. 6,832
    + 2,742

27. 2,627
    + 3,149

28. 5,251
    + 3,197

29. 2,815
    + 6,240

30. 2,272
    + 5,564

31. 3 + 6 + 7

32. 6 + 9 + 5 + 4

33. 5 + 8 + 2 + 7

34. 61 + 34 + 42

35. 45 + 21 + 27

36. 58 + 17 + 24

Apply   Solve each problem.

37. Mary bought a sleeping bag for $75 and boots for $42. What was the total cost of her purchases?

38. Lupi's backpack with its contents weigh 3,652 grams. What will be the weight if he adds a camp stove that weighs 824 grams?

39. *Estimation* A backpack weighs 2,924 grams with a frying pan and 2,470 grams without it. Estimate the weight of the frying pan.

★40. Which weighs more: a backpack that weighs 973 grams with contents that weigh 2,624 grams, or a backpack that weighs 1,043 grams with contents that weigh 2,827 grams?

Adding with Two or More Renamings

The lengths of three trails are 5,224 meters, 6,435 meters, and 4,927 meters. What is the total length of a hike along these trails?

Find 5,224 + 6,435 + 4,927.

Add the ones.
16 ones = 1 ten 6 ones

```
    1
  5,224
  6,435
+ 4,927
───────
      6
```

Add the tens.
Add the hundreds.
15 hundreds =
1 thousand 5 hundred

```
   1  1
  5,224
  6,435
+ 4,927
───────
    586
```

Add the thousands.

```
   1  1
  5,224
  6,435
+ 4,927
───────
 16,586
```

The total length is 16,586 meters.

Try Add.

a. 1,856
    + 367

b. 8,946
    + 4,265

c. 4,678
       3,895
    +   468

d. 5,674 + 4,287

Practice Add.

1. 1,527
    + 565

2. 1,936
    + 827

3. 3,745
    + 782

4. 7,394
    + 568

5. 6,487
    + 269

6. 6,487
    + 269

7. 5,694
    + 2,748

8. 4,753
    + 3,898

9. 6,874
    + 2,579

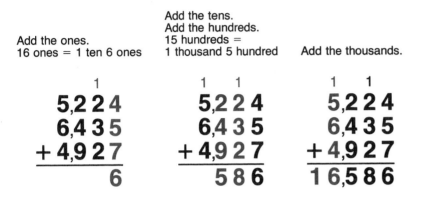

10. 28,315
+ 48,298

11. 35,357
+ 16,358

12. 56,387
+ 76,296

13. 264,545
+ 329,693

14. 450,543
+ 578,798

15. 549
372
+ 457

16. 286
193
+ 345

17. 57,193
4,621
+ 3,127

18. 3,946
65,278
+ 937

19. 1,858
12,401
+ 456,823

20. 3,648 + 4,974

21. 6,976 + 3,279

22. 8,963 + 4,547

23. 907,321 + 33,548

24. 84,295 + 979,657

25. 792,869 + 484,967

Apply Solve each problem.

26. Find the total length of a hike along trails of the following lengths: 8,856 meters, 7,475 meters, 7,850 meters, and 6,721 meters.

27. A side trail leads 1,875 meters to a dead end and then hikers must go back on the same trail. How long is a hike along the side trail and back?

CALCULATOR

Use your calculator to find each sum. Study the answers to each pair of exercises.

1. 696 + 3,875
2. 3,875 + 696

3. 64,836 + 7,619
4. 7,619 + 64,836

5. 853,809 + 2,536,675
6. 2,536,675 + 853,809

Commutative Property: You can change the order of the addends. The sum is the same.

Use your calculator to find each sum. Add the numbers in parentheses first. Study the answers to each pair of exercises.

7. 7,556 + (1,642 + 3,869)
8. (7,556 + 1,642) + 3,869

9. (218,497 + 53,281) + 416,759
10. 218,497 + (53,281 + 416,759)

Associative Property: You can change the grouping of the addends. The sum is the same.

Subtracting with One Renaming

An airplane was flying at an altitude of 9,156 meters. The pilot decreased the altitude by 1,322 meters. At what altitude was the plane then flying?

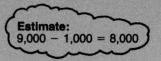

Estimate:
9,000 − 1,000 = 8,000

Find 9,156 − 1,322.

Subtract ones. Subtract tens.	You need more hundreds. Rename to get 10 more hundreds.	Subtract hundreds. Subtract thousands.
9,1 5 6 − 1,3 2 2 —— 3 4	8 11 9̸,1̸ 5 6 − 1,3 2 2 —— 3 4	8 11 9̸,1̸ 5 6 − 1,3 2 2 —— 7,8 3 4

The airplane was flying at an altitude of 7,834 meters.

You can check your work by addition.

```
  9,156          7,834
− 1,322        + 1,322
 _____         _____
  7,834          9,156
```

Try Subtract.

a. 82
−15

b. 706
−473

c. 8,326
− 814

d. 9,839
−4,765

e. 7,284 − 159

Practice Subtract.

1. 68
−29

2. 72
−58

3. 56
−29

4. 97
−38

5. 48
−19

6. 248
−229

7. 539
−278

8. 362
− 49

9. 674
− 67

10. 465
−239

11. 508
−272

12. 607
−425

13. 536
−228

14. 5,407
− 182

15. 3,608
− 346

16. 2,780
−2,329

17. 6,093
−5,682

18. 3,591
−2,479

19. 5,708
−1,265

20. 3,902
−1,872

21. 317 − 193

22. 408 − 295

23. 549 − 87

24. 672 − 56

25. 4,462 − 380

26. 3,990 − 576

27. 2,070 − 27

28. 5,073 − 66

29. 5,079 − 438

30. 4,308 − 94

31. 3,893 − 589

32. 5,090 − 88

Apply Solve each problem.

33. A plane has 340 seats. 326 of the seats are filled. How many seats are empty?

34. Of the 340 seats, 30 are first class and the rest are coach. How many seats are in the coach section?

35. An airplane made an 851-kilometer trip from Montreal to Detroit and then went 378 kilometers to Chicago. What was the total length of the trip?

★36. When a plane carries 94,000 kilograms of fuel, 45,000 kilograms of human cargo, and 13,000 kilograms of luggage, it weighs 322,000 kilograms. How much does it weigh empty?

Subtracting with Two or More Renamings

An airplane used 9,064 gallons of fuel flying from San Francisco to Denver. A train used 2,426 gallons of fuel to make the same trip. How many more gallons of fuel did the airplane use?

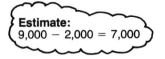

Estimate:
9,000 − 2,000 = 7,000

Find 9,064 − 2,426.

You need more ones. Rename to get 10 more ones.

$$\begin{array}{r} \overset{\scriptstyle 5\ 14}{9{,}0\cancel{6}\cancel{4}} \\ -\ 2{,}4\ 2\ 6 \\ \hline \end{array}$$

Subtract ones. Subtract tens.

$$\begin{array}{r} \overset{\scriptstyle 5\ 14}{9{,}0\cancel{6}\cancel{4}} \\ -\ 2{,}4\ 2\ 6 \\ \hline 3\ 8 \end{array}$$

You need more hundreds. Rename to get 10 more hundreds.

$$\begin{array}{r} \overset{\scriptstyle 8\ 10\ 5\ 14}{9{,}0\cancel{6}\cancel{4}} \\ -\ 2{,}4\ 2\ 6 \\ \hline 3\ 8 \end{array}$$

Subtract hundreds. Subtract thousands.

$$\begin{array}{r} \overset{\scriptstyle 8\ 10\ 5\ 14}{9{,}0\cancel{6}\cancel{4}} \\ -\ 2{,}4\ 2\ 6 \\ \hline 6{,}6\ 3\ 8 \end{array}$$

The airplane used 6,638 more gallons of fuel.

Try   Subtract.

a. $\begin{array}{r} 633 \\ -286 \\ \hline \end{array}$

b. $\begin{array}{r} 503 \\ -146 \\ \hline \end{array}$

c. $\begin{array}{r} 5{,}356 \\ -3{,}979 \\ \hline \end{array}$

d. $\begin{array}{r} 48{,}000 \\ -\ 4{,}683 \\ \hline \end{array}$

e. 3,700 − 1,467

Practice   Subtract.

1. $\begin{array}{r} 542 \\ -197 \\ \hline \end{array}$

2. $\begin{array}{r} 723 \\ -286 \\ \hline \end{array}$

3. $\begin{array}{r} 342 \\ -174 \\ \hline \end{array}$

4. $\begin{array}{r} 621 \\ -358 \\ \hline \end{array}$

5. $\begin{array}{r} 506 \\ -327 \\ \hline \end{array}$

6. $\begin{array}{r} 2{,}703 \\ -1{,}285 \\ \hline \end{array}$

7. $\begin{array}{r} 3{,}186 \\ -2{,}947 \\ \hline \end{array}$

8. $\begin{array}{r} 8{,}327 \\ -1{,}654 \\ \hline \end{array}$

9. $\begin{array}{r} 53{,}903 \\ -\ 1{,}668 \\ \hline \end{array}$

10. $\begin{array}{r} 68{,}508 \\ -\ 3{,}457 \\ \hline \end{array}$

11. 80,507 − 34,684	12. 97,600 − 56,047	13. 53,900 − 47,059	14. 523,716 − 485,937	15. 433,725 − 361,807

16. 600 − 257

17. 900 − 194

18. 6,235 − 4,657

19. 3,107 − 498

20. 5,076 − 894

21. 5,600 − 2,443

22. 6,040 − 2,569

23. 3,020 − 1,643

24. 3,000 − 1,946

Apply Solve each problem.

25. A train has 520 passengers and a plane has 385. How many more passengers are on the train?

26. A plane needs 1,900 meters of runway for a takeoff. 450 meters more than this are needed for a landing. What is the distance needed for a landing?

27. *Estimation* There were 24,967 gallons of fuel on board a plane. After a coast-to-coast flight, 5,567 gallons were left. Round to the nearest thousand to estimate the amount of fuel used for the flight.

★28. A plane has 4 main gas tanks and 2 reserve tanks. Two of the main tanks hold 4,069 gallons each, the other two main tanks each hold 2,323 gallons, and each reserve tank holds 439 gallons. What is the total capacity of the tanks?

Problem Solving: Choose the Operation

Read — Read the problem. What is known? What is the question?

About 1,700 million tons of oil are transported by tanker ships each year. Another 1,000 million tons of oil are transported by other methods. How many million tons of oil are transported each year?

Plan — What should you do to solve the problem?

Since two groups are joined, add to solve the problem.

Solve — Do the work.

$$\begin{array}{r} 1,700 \\ +\,1,000 \\ \hline 2,700 \end{array}$$

Answer — Answer the question.

2,700 million tons of oil are transported each year.

Look Back — Does the answer make sense?

Two groups are joined, which shows addition. The answer is larger than either addend.

Try Tell what operation you would use to solve the problem. Then solve it.

a. A supertanker can carry 2,000,000 barrels of oil. A small tanker can carry 330,000 barrels. How much more oil can a supertanker carry?

Apply Tell what operation you would use to solve each problem.

1. A supertanker weighed ● tons when empty. It carried ● tons of oil. How much did it weigh when it was full of oil?

2. A supertanker is ● feet long. A small tanker is ● feet long. How much longer is a supertanker than a small tanker?

Tell what operation you would use to solve each problem. Then solve each problem.

3. There are about 7,000 ships in the world tanker fleet. 600 of these are supertankers. How many ships in the fleet are not supertankers?

4. Pipelines pump oil from a tanker to a platform 15 miles away. The oil is then pumped 21 miles to storage tanks. What is the total distance the oil is pumped?

5. The distance by tanker from Alaska to oil refineries is 4,500 miles. The distance by way of the Alaskan pipeline is 789 miles. How many fewer miles would oil travel by pipeline?

6. The Big Inch pipeline from Texas to Pennsylvania is 1,476 miles long. The Little Big Inch pipeline is 238 miles longer. How long is the Little Big Inch pipeline?

7. A supertanker is 1,094 feet long. The tank car of a train is 50 feet long. How much longer is a supertanker than a tank car?

8. A train without a locomotive is 648 feet long. The locomotive is 68 feet long. How long is the train with the locomotive?

9. A freight train can carry 1,800 tons of cargo. A large plane can carry 130 tons. How much more can a train carry?

10. A truck weighs 26,000 pounds when empty. What does it weigh when carrying 94,000 pounds of cargo?

11. An oil truck started its run with 7,900 gallons of gasoline. It delivered 1,765 gallons to a gas station. How much gasoline was still in the truck?

*12. In the United States 115,173 million gallons of fuel were used for highway driving. 3,595 million gallons were used for city driving. 22,000 million gallons of the total were used by trucks. How many gallons were used by cars?

Practice: Addition and Subtraction

Estimation Estimate each sum or difference.
First round each number to the nearest hundred.

1. 867 + 193

2. 458 − 169

3. 290 + 228

4. 387 − 242

5. 586 − 416

6. 357 + 128

Estimation Estimate each sum or difference.
First round each number to the nearest thousand.

7. 3,986 − 2,104

8. 2,976 + 3,058

9. 9,173 + 7,625

10. 1,732 − 987

11. 4,682 − 2,114

12. 8,456 + 9,732

Add or subtract.

13. 63 + 28	**14.** 7,624 − 852	**15.** 6,108 − 2,619	**16.** 3,865 + 429	**17.** 33 − 16
18. 68,123 + 57,984	**19.** 3,852 − 627	**20.** 81 + 42	**21.** 7,493 + 595	**22.** 57 − 38
23. 147 + 37	**24.** 268 − 129	**25.** 136 + 705	**26.** 5,379 − 1,402	**27.** 2,406 + 3,279
28. 7,516 + 2,894	**29.** 6,382 + 9,354	**30.** 256 + 72	**31.** 436 − 209	**32.** 5,426 + 3,482
33. 31,087 + 79,522	**34.** 414 + 279	**35.** 950 − 584	**36.** 5,616 + 1,508	**37.** 854 − 257

38. 54 + 27 + 12

39. 9,505 − 84

40. 265,357 + 281,874

41. 600 − 109

42. 28 + 84 + 96

43. 29 + 46 + 34

44. 1,096 − 27

45. 386,431 + 857,890

46. 800 − 584

Apply Solve each problem.

47. On a busy day at O'Hare Airport, 1,557 planes landed and 1,569 planes took off. What was the total number of takeoffs and landings?

48. The pilot checks 250 items in preparation for takeoff. He has checked 180 items. How many items are still to be checked?

49. A four-engine plane weighs about 775,000 pounds. It weighs how much more than a two-engine plane that weighs 114,000 pounds?

50. A new plane weighed 95,250 pounds. After ten years, the weight of the plane had increased 300 pounds due to painting. What was the weight of the plane after ten years?

51. Bill hiked 3,140 meters on Thursday and 2,925 meters on Friday. How much farther did he hike on Thursday than Friday?

52. Jim's backpack contains a sweater weighing 295 grams and a parka weighing 681 grams. What is the total weight of these two items?

53. Yuki hiked 25 kilometers on Monday, 17 on Tuesday, and 18 on Wednesday. Find the total distance he hiked.

COMPUTER

Flow Charts

A flow chart shows the steps to use to solve a problem. This flow chart shows the steps used to fill a pail with water.

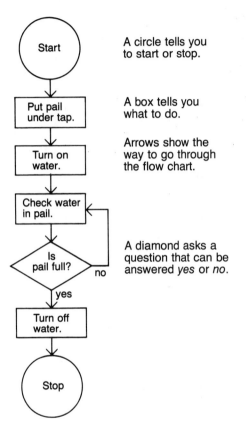

A circle tells you to start or stop.

A box tells you what to do.

Arrows show the way to go through the flow chart.

A diamond asks a question that can be answered *yes* or *no*.

For each activity, make a flow chart that shows the steps in order.

1. Is there more to read?
Get a book.
Read.
Look at where you are in the book.

2. Pay for the item.
Is the item too expensive?
Look at the price.
Find an item.

Missing-Addend Equations

A. The swim team has 30 members. 16 were members last year. How many members joined the team this year?

Number from last year		Number joined this year		Total number

$$16 \;+\; n \;=\; 30 \qquad \text{Write an equation.}$$

$$n \;=\; 30 - 16 \qquad \begin{array}{l}\text{Subtract to find}\\ \text{the missing addend.}\end{array}$$

$$n \;=\; 14$$

14 members joined the team this year.

B. Find n.

$$50 = 38 + n$$
$$50 - 38 = n$$
$$12 = n$$

Try Find n.

a. $n + 25 = 50$

b. $125 + n = 200$

c. $3{,}625 = 1{,}625 + n$

d. $217 = n + 53$

Practice Find n.

1. $37 + n = 94$

2. $n + 25 = 63$

3. $66 = 57 + n$

4. $58 + n = 89$

5. $n + 63 = 84$

6. $48 = 39 + n$

7. $193 = 146 + n$

8. $157 + n = 305$

9. $n + 642 = 931$

10. $851 = 178 + n$

11. $n + 300 = 566$

12. $216 + n = 500$

13. $7,061 = 1,873 + n$

14. $3,465 + n = 7,261$

15. $1,000 = n + 976$

Apply Solve each problem.

16. The swim team added 7 extra practices to their schedule. This brought the total number of practices up to 45. How many practices are in a regular schedule?
(HINT: $n + 7 = 45$)

17. The 30 members of the swim team formed two squads for practice. Squad A has 12 members. How many members are in squad B?
(HINT: $12 + n = 30$)

18. At one swim meet, 24 members of the swim team participated. In addition some members went to the meet as substitutes. In all, 28 members went to the meet. How many substitutes were there? (HINT: $24 + n = 28$)

19. The 30 members of the Knapp School swim team had a meet with the swim team from Gifford School. In all, there were 55 swimmers. How many swimmers were from Gifford School? (HINT: $30 + n = 55$)

Problem Solving: Write an Equation

A useful plan for solving some problems is to write an equation.

Read   20 students tried out for the school play on Monday. More students tried out on Tuesday. In all, 48 students tried out on the two days. How many tried out on Tuesday?

Plan   Write an equation that shows that if you combine the number of students who tried out on Monday with the number on Tuesday, you get 48.

Number on Monday	Number on Tuesday	Total number
20	$+ \quad n \quad =$	48

Solve

$$20 + n = 48$$
$$n = 48 - 20$$
$$n = 28$$

Answer   28 students tried out on Tuesday.

Look Back   Since $20 + 28 = 48$, the answer checks.

Discuss Could you have written a different equation? Would it have given you the same answer?

Try Write an equation. Then find the answer.

a. Of the 48 students who tried out for the play, 21 were boys. How many were girls?

b. There were 15 sixth graders in the play and 3 fifth graders. How many students were in the play?

Apply Write an equation. Then find the answer.

1. The number of rehearsals was increased by 5. This brought the total to 42. How many rehearsals were originally scheduled?

2. At first, 16 students were on the stage crew. Later, 3 others joined it. How many students were then on the stage crew?

3. Debbie missed 4 of the 42 rehearsals. How many rehearsals did she attend?

4. Rosa found 12 props and David found the rest, bringing the total to 19. How many props did David find?

5. The first act of the play lasts 45 minutes and the second act lasts 32 minutes. How long do these two acts last?

6. Kathy sold 7 tickets to her family. This brought the total she sold to her family and friends to 32. How many tickets did she sell to her friends?

7. Thursday, 96 people attended the play. Friday, 126 people attended. How many people attended these two nights?

8. Allen had 65 lines in the play and Sue had 42. How many more lines did Allen have than Sue?

9. Wilma sold 23 tickets. Steve sold 17. How many more tickets did Wilma sell than Steve?

10. Along with Mrs. Finney's class, 32 students in Mr. Adams's class saw the play. There were 59 students. How many students were from Mrs. Finney's class?

Chapter 1 Test

1. Write 8,572 in expanded form.

Write each number in standard form.

2. 700,000 + 40,000 + 3,000 + 200 + 60 + 8

3. 93 billion, 682 million, 385 thousand, 7

4. Tell what the 3 means in the number 7,832,546,000.

Compare. Use <, >, or =.

5. 8,271 ● 8,732

6. 48,276 ● 48,265

7. List these numbers in order from least to greatest.

   58,265   58,371   58,107

Round to the nearest thousand.

8. 8,465   9. 6,543   10. 3,752

Estimate each sum or difference. First round each number to the nearest hundred.

11. 647 + 392   12. 831 − 227

Add.

13. 624
   + 358

14. 3,749
   + 538

15. 6,857
   + 5,483

16. 3,694
   5,768
   + 589

Subtract.

17. 673
   − 249

18. 524
   − 187

19. 7,362
   − 2,638

20. 60,029
   − 25,464

Find n.

21. $42 + n = 85$ 22. $743 = 295 + n$

Tell what operation you would use to solve each problem. Then solve it.

23. Of the 735 runners who began a marathon, only 546 finished the race. How many dropped out along the way?

24. There are 2,456 fiction books and 1,897 nonfiction books in the library. What is the total number of books in the library?

Write an equation. Then find the answer.

25. Gwen had 78 coins in her collection. She was given more coins for her birthday. Then she had 112 coins. How many coins was Gwen given for her birthday?

CHALLENGE
Roman Numerals

The ancient Romans used the letters
I, V, X, L, C, D, and M to form numerals.

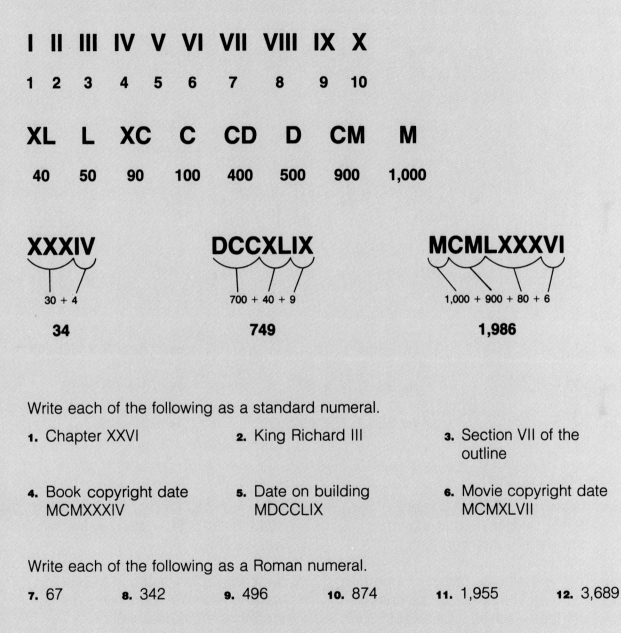

I	II	III	IV	V	VI	VII	VIII	IX	X
1	2	3	4	5	6	7	8	9	10

XL	L	XC	C	CD	D	CM	M
40	50	90	100	400	500	900	1,000

XXXIV
30 + 4
34

DCCXLIX
700 + 40 + 9
749

MCMLXXXVI
1,000 + 900 + 80 + 6
1,986

Write each of the following as a standard numeral.

1. Chapter XXVI

2. King Richard III

3. Section VII of the outline

4. Book copyright date MCMXXXIV

5. Date on building MDCCLIX

6. Movie copyright date MCMXLVII

Write each of the following as a Roman numeral.

7. 67   8. 342   9. 496   10. 874   11. 1,955   12. 3,689

MAINTENANCE

Add or subtract.

1. 54
   + 29

2. 6,703
   − 641

3. 8,437
   − 4,619

4. 5,627
   + 846

5. 42
   − 25

6. 75,246
   + 84,836

7. 4,773
   − 348

8. 72
   + 51

9. 6,362
   + 794

10. 65
    − 46

11. 453
    + 28

12. 326
    − 143

13. 208
    + 675

14. 4,487
    − 2,761

15. 4,327
    + 2,435

16. 3,559
    + 3,473

17. 4,173
    + 8,396

18. 374
    + 42

19. 582
    − 168

20. 7,346
    + 2,158

21. 45,728
    + 79,664

22. 253
    + 314

23. 329
    − 286

24. 2,518
    + 3,747

25. 342
    − 265

26. 32 + 49 + 71

27. 6,856 − 82

28. 279,565 + 375,836

29. 400 − 159

30. 26 + 12 + 87

31. 76 + 58 + 19

32. 2,703 − 24

33. 824,117 + 692,539

34. 900 − 563

Solve each problem.

35. A stadium has 30,000 seats. 19,437 people were at a game. How many seats were empty?

36. Louis XIV was King of France from 1643 to 1715. How many years was he king?

37. The height of the Statue of Liberty is 151 feet. The height of the base is 154 feet. Find the total height.

38. Jack worked 24 hours in the library. Karla worked 19 hours. How many more hours did Jack work?

39. There are 35 dancers and 18 actors in the play. How many more dancers are there?

40. What is the total weight of a canteen that weighs 142 grams and a first-aid kit that weighs 255 grams?

$$\begin{array}{r} 12 \\ \times\ 10 \\ \hline 120 \end{array}$$

Meaning of Multiplication

A. Andy is stacking firewood for a wood-burning stove. He carries 4 pieces of wood on each trip. How much wood does he carry in 5 trips?

You can solve the problem using repeated addition.

$4 + 4 + 4 + 4 + 4 = 20$

Since there are 5 groups and 4 pieces of wood in each group, you can also multiply to find the answer.

$5 \times 4 = 20$

Andy carries 20 pieces of wood.

B. Write two multiplication equations with these numbers.

18 6 3

$3 \times 6 = 18$

$6 \times 3 = 18$

Try Complete the table.

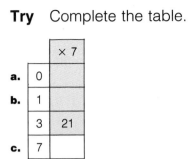

		× 7
a.	0	
b.	1	
	3	21
c.	7	

d. Write two multiplication equations with these numbers.

6   5   30

Practice Complete each table.

		× 3
1.	1	
2.	2	
3.	3	
4.	4	

		× 5
5.	0	
6.	2	
7.	4	
8.	5	

		× 8
9.	3	
10.	5	
11.	7	
12.	9	

		× 6
13.	1	
14.	2	
15.	3	
16.	5	

		× 2
17.	7	
18.	1	
19.	9	
20.	2	

		× 4
21.	9	
22.	4	
23.	7	
24.	0	

		× 9
25.	9	
26.	0	
27.	1	
28.	5	

		× 8
29.	1	
30.	6	
31.	2	
32.	4	

Write two multiplication equations for each set of numbers.

33. 3   7   21

34. 24   3   8

35. 63   7   9

36. 72   8   9

37. 9   36   4

38. 2   18   9

39. 7   4   28

40. 6   8   48

Apply Solve each problem.

41. Each round piece of firewood can be split into 4 smaller pieces. How many smaller pieces can Andy make from 9 round pieces?

42. Andy's family uses about 6 pieces of firewood a day in their wood-burning stove. How much do they use in a week?

Multiplying Multiples of 10, 100, and 1,000

A. A BTU is the amount of heat needed to raise the temperature of one pound of water by one degree Fahrenheit. How many BTUs does it take to make 300 pounds of water 5° hotter?

It takes 300 BTUs to raise 300 pounds of water 1°, so you can add.

300 + 300 + 300 + 300 + 300 = 1,500

Or you can multiply.

5 × 300 = 1,500

1,500 BTUs are needed.

Notice that there are a total of two ending zeros in the *factors* 5 and 300. There are also two ending zeros in the *product* 1,500.

To multiply numbers that end in zeros, first multiply without considering ending zeros. Then write as many zeros in the product as there are in all the factors.

B. Find 100 × 10,000.

Count the ending zeros.

100 × 10,000 = 1,000,000

2 zeros   4 zeros   6 zeros

Try Multiply.

a. 80 × 800   **b.** 53 × 1,000   **c.** 600 × 50

Practice Multiply.

1. 10 × 10   **2.** 100 × 10   **3.** 1,000 × 100   **4.** 1,000 × 1,000

5. 100 × 8   **6.** 4 × 1,000   **7.** 10 × 24   **8.** 38 × 100

9. 8 × 30   **10.** 70 × 5   **11.** 600 × 8   **12.** 6 × 900

13. 7 × 4,000   **14.** 2,000 × 9   **15.** 20 × 600   **16.** 700 × 60

17. 400 × 800   **18.** 600 × 200   **19.** 5 × 40   **20.** 20 × 50

21. 60 × 500   **22.** 800 × 500   **23.** 90 × 8,000   **24.** 4,000 × 70

25. 900 × 6,000   **26.** 8,000 × 700   **27.** 5,000 × 3,000   **28.** 7,000 × 9,000

★29. 20 × 3 × 600   **★30.** 800 × 100 × 70   **★31.** 40 × 2,000 × 90

Apply Solve each problem.

32. A pound of dry firewood produces about 5,000 BTUs. How much heat is produced if 30 pounds of wood are burned overnight in a stove?

★33. A pot holds about 10 pounds of water. How many BTUs does it take to raise the temperature from 62° to 212°?

Estimating Products

A. In Laura Ingalls Wilder's book, *The Long Winter*, Almanzo Wilder and Cap Garland saved their town from starvation by bringing 30 sacks of wheat to it. Each sack weighed 125 pounds. Estimate how much the wheat weighed in all.

Estimate 30 × 125.

30 × 125

30 × 100 = 3,000   Round each number so only the first digit is not zero.

30 × 125 ≈ 3,000   ≈ means is approximately equal to.

The wheat weighed about 3,000 pounds.

B. Estimate 311 × 48.

311 × 48
↓   ↓
300 × 50 = 15,000

Try *Estimation*
Estimate each product.

a. 39 × 42

b. 307 × 612

c. 79 × 11 × 91

Practice _Estimation_ Estimate each product.

1. 65 × 32
2. 72 × 49
3. 43 × 75
4. 45 × 82

5. 32 × 76
6. 28 × 51
7. 83 × 58
8. 41 × 21

9. 33 × 468
10. 75 × 321
11. 84 × 756
12. 62 × 874

13. 287 × 412
14. 475 × 728
15. 629 × 861
16. 524 × 587

17. 73 × 18 × 62
18. 37 × 22 × 27
19. 19 × 32 × 77

Apply _Estimation_ Estimate the answer to each problem.

20. The regular price for wheat was 82¢ a bushel. Estimate how much 60 bushels of wheat would have cost at the regular price.

21. The farmer who sold the wheat to Almanzo and Cap charged 43¢ a bushel over the regular price. Estimate how much extra the boys paid for the 60 bushels of wheat.

★22. Estimate how much Almanzo and Cap paid for the 60 bushels of wheat.

Multiplying by a One-Digit Multiplier

In Sid Fleischman's book, *By the Great Horn Spoon!*, Jack and Praiseworthy had to sell cats after they lost their gold. How much did they get for their first 8 cats if they sold them for $15 each?

Find 8 × 15.

$$
\begin{array}{r}
\overset{4}{1\,5} \\
\times\ \ \ 8 \\
\hline
0
\end{array}
$$
8 × 5 = 40 = 4 tens 0 ones

$$
\begin{array}{r}
\overset{4}{1\,5} \\
\times\ \ \ 8 \\
\hline
1\,2\,0
\end{array}
$$
8 × 1 ten = 8 tens
8 tens + 4 tens = 12 tens

Jack and Praiseworthy got $120 for their first 8 cats.

Try Multiply.

a. 829
× 6

b. 6,305
× 7

c. 3 × 56

d. 8 × 29

Practice Multiply.

1. 17
× 4

2. 37
× 8

3. 83
× 9

4. 36
× 5

5. 325
× 3

6. 361
× 7

7. 683
× 8

8. 247
× 2

9. 230
× 7

10. 470
× 9

11. 709
× 6

12. 208
× 9

13. 820
× 5

14. 360
× 5

15. 4,123
× 3

16. 3,569
× 7

17. 3,218
× 5

18. 4,275
× 6

19. 7,590
× 7

20. 6,230
× 9

21. 4,076
× 7

22. 6,208
× 4

23. 5,007
× 6

24. 4,006
× 9

25. 1,070
× 7

26. 4,300
× 6

27. 4,506
× 8

28. 7 × 26

29. 9 × 38

30. 6 × 402

31. 8 × 704

32. 2 × 3,241

33. 6 × 1,815

34. 4 × 13,072

35. 9 × 680,507

Apply   Solve each problem.

36. At the Empire Hotel in Hangtown, a slice of buttered bread cost $2. How much would a 24-slice loaf of buttered bread cost?

37. Riverboat fare from San Francisco to Sacramento City was $25 per person. How much did Jack and Praiseworthy spend altogether for their 2 tickets?

38. Hay to feed the burro named Stubb cost 8¢ a pound. How much would 32 pounds of hay have cost?

★39. Gold was worth $16 an ounce in San Francisco, but only $4 an ounce in Hangtown. How much was 12 ounces of gold worth in Hangtown?

There are three houses in a row: a log cabin, a cottage, and a ranch house. Each house is a different color, and a different animal lives in each.

The red house is next door to the green house.

The gerbil lives in the cottage.

The ranch house is not green.

The dog's house is red.

The rabbit lives in the middle house.

One of the houses is blue.

Which animal lives in the log cabin?

Multiplying by a Multiple of 10

A roofer earns $393 a week. How much does the roofer earn in 50 weeks?

Find 50 × 393.   Estimate: 50 × 400 = 20,000

$$\begin{array}{r} 393 \\ \times\ \ 50 \\ \hline 0 \end{array}$$

Write 0 in the ones place.

$$\begin{array}{r} 393 \\ \times\ \ 50 \\ \hline 19{,}650 \end{array}$$

Multiply 393 by 5.

The roofer earns $19,650 in 50 weeks.

Try Multiply.

a.
$$\begin{array}{r} 36 \\ \times\ 20 \\ \hline \end{array}$$

b.
$$\begin{array}{r} 215 \\ \times\ \ 40 \\ \hline \end{array}$$

c.
$$\begin{array}{r} 602 \\ \times\ \ 70 \\ \hline \end{array}$$

d. 3,456 × 70   **e.** 3,006 × 80

Practice Multiply.

1. 36×7	**2.** 36×70	**3.** 79×8	**4.** 79×80	**5.** 87×4
6. 87×40	**7.** 53×10	**8.** 38×20	**9.** 76×50	**10.** 85×20
11. 794×60	**12.** 492×30	**13.** 708×20	**14.** 305×10	**15.** 207×80
16. $6,503 \times 70$	**17.** $6,048 \times 30$	**18.** $2,004 \times 60$	**19.** $6,007 \times 40$	**20.** $3,294 \times 70$

21. 39×40 **22.** 47×30 **23.** 502×60 **24.** 107×40

25. 956×50 **26.** 885×80 **27.** $2,045 \times 80$ **28.** $7,205 \times 60$

Apply Solve each problem.

29. A programmer earns $624 a week. How much does the programmer earn in 50 weeks?

30. A security guard is paid $262 a week. How much does he earn in 50 weeks?

31. An attorney bills her clients $55 for each hour of her time. How much does she earn on a 40-hour case?

32. *Estimation* A moving company has 30 truck drivers who each earn about $26,500 a year. Estimate how much this company spends each year for drivers' salaries.

Multiplying by a Two-Digit Multiplier

A. The Lees are building a house. They are using Spanish-style red tiles for the roof. One section of the roof is 29 tiles long and 18 tiles wide. How many tiles will the Lees need for this section of the roof?

Find 18 × 29. (Estimate: 20 × 30 = 600)

$$
\begin{array}{r}
29 \\
\times 18 \\
\hline
232 \\
290 \\
\hline
522
\end{array}
$$

18 = 10 + 8

8 × 29

10 × 29

The Lees need 522 tiles for this section of the roof.

B. Find 47 × 5,096.

$$
\begin{array}{r}
5{,}096 \\
\times 47 \\
\hline
35672 \\
203840 \\
\hline
239{,}512
\end{array}
$$

7 × 5,096

40 × 5,096

Try Multiply.

a. $\begin{array}{r} 67 \\ \times 38 \\ \hline \end{array}$

b. $\begin{array}{r} 318 \\ \times 62 \\ \hline \end{array}$

c. $\begin{array}{r} 306 \\ \times 42 \\ \hline \end{array}$

d. $\begin{array}{r} 5{,}136 \\ \times 21 \\ \hline \end{array}$

e. 52 × 86 × 65

Practice Multiply.

1. $\begin{array}{r} 32 \\ \times 23 \\ \hline \end{array}$

2. $\begin{array}{r} 43 \\ \times 12 \\ \hline \end{array}$

3. $\begin{array}{r} 46 \\ \times 32 \\ \hline \end{array}$

4. $\begin{array}{r} 52 \\ \times 47 \\ \hline \end{array}$

5. $\begin{array}{r} 36 \\ \times 54 \\ \hline \end{array}$

6. $\begin{array}{r} 85 \\ \times 35 \\ \hline \end{array}$

7. $\begin{array}{r} 90 \\ \times 27 \\ \hline \end{array}$

8. $\begin{array}{r} 70 \\ \times 48 \\ \hline \end{array}$

9. $\begin{array}{r} 723 \\ \times 43 \\ \hline \end{array}$

10. $\begin{array}{r} 576 \\ \times 68 \\ \hline \end{array}$

11. 464
× 92

12. 345
× 87

13. 580
× 71

14. 270
× 63

15. 603
× 72

16. 205
× 34

17. 3,516
× 34

18. 7,435
× 52

19. 5,795
× 67

20. 6,528
× 79

21. 3,840
× 64

22. 2,940
× 57

23. 7,054
× 78

24. 3,508
× 54

25. 8,002
× 43

26. 47 × 96

27. 71 × 42

28. 34 × 682

29. 29 × 478

30. 74 × 106

31. 83 × 305

32. 46 × 6,407

33. 49 × 5,006

34. 46 × 28,743

35. 65 × 34,789

36. 54 × 80,705

37. 39 × 90,009

38. 34 × 13 × 11

39. 23 × 98 × 44

40. 47 × 73 × 14

41. 76 × 81 × 36

Apply Solve each problem.

42. Tiles are ordered in "squares" that contain about 171 tiles in each square. The Lees need 21 squares for the entire roof. How many tiles do they need?

43. Each square of tiles weighs about 900 pounds. How much do the 21 squares for the Lees' roof weigh?

★44. *Estimation* Estimate the number of tiles in 27 squares of Spanish tile.

★45. *Estimation* Estimate the weight of 27 squares of Spanish tile.

Multiplying by a Three-Digit Multiplier

A farmer's orchard has 268 apple trees. A typical tree produces 352 pounds of apples. How many pounds of apples does the orchard produce in all?

Find 268 × 352.

Estimate:
300 × 400 = 120,000

```
    3 5 2
  × 2 6 8        268 = 200 + 60 + 8
  2 8 1 6        8 × 352
2 1 1 2 0        60 × 352
7 0 4 0 0        200 × 352
9 4,3 3 6
```

The orchard produces 94,336 pounds of apples.

Try Multiply.

a. 314
× 428

b. 819
× 406

c. 861
× 280

d. 129 × 6,382

Practice   Multiply.

1. 754 $\times\,400$	**2.** 836 $\times\,600$	**3.** 754 $\times\,430$
4. 836 $\times\,640$	**5.** 754 $\times\,432$	**6.** 836 $\times\,641$
7. 793 $\times\,408$	**8.** 637 $\times\,905$	**9.** 507 $\times\,486$
10. 705 $\times\,835$	**11.** 5,317 $\times\ \ \,128$	**12.** 2,813 $\times\ \ \,212$
13. 2,643 $\times\ \ \,203$	**14.** 9,698 $\times\ \ \,301$	**15.** 6,057 $\times\ \ \,387$
16. 4,609 $\times\ \ \,617$	**17.** 5,046 $\times\ \ \,806$	**18.** 4,609 $\times\ \ \,607$

19. 480 × 906   **20.** 832 × 409

21. 2,814 × 197   **22.** 3,619 × 419

Apply   Solve each problem.

23. The farmer increased the yield to 380 pounds of apples per tree. What was the yield for the 268 trees then?

24. *Estimation* Another orchard with 510 trees produces 318 pounds of apples per tree. Estimate the total yield.

Problem Solving: Choose the Operation

Read   The McDades have an orchard with 14 rows of pecan trees. Each row contains 25 trees. How many trees are there in the orchard?

Plan   Think of each row of trees as a group of trees. To find the number of trees, multiply the number of groups by the number in each group.

Solve   Find 14×25.

$$
\begin{array}{r}
25 \\
\times\,14 \\
\hline
100 \\
250 \\
\hline
350
\end{array}
$$

Answer   There are 350 pecan trees in the McDades' orchard.

Look Back   An estimate is 10×30, or 300 trees. The answer is reasonable.

Try Tell what operation you would use to solve the problem. Then find the answer.

a. One year, each of the 350 trees in the McDades' orchard produced about 16 pounds of nuts. How many pounds did the trees produce altogether that year?

Apply Tell what operation you would use to solve the problem.

1. The Bullocks have ▩ trees in their orchard, while the Juarez family has ▩ trees. How many more trees do the Bullocks have?

2. A pound of pecans contains about ▩ nuts. Each tree produces about ▩ pounds of pecans. How many nuts does each tree produce?

Tell what operation you would use to solve the problem. Then find the answer.

3. The Bullocks received $5,812 for their pecan harvest one year. They received $920 more than this for the second year's harvest. How much were they paid for the second year's harvest?

4. The McDades' orchard produced 6,487 pounds of pecans one year. Some trees were damaged the next year so that only 4,129 pounds were produced. How many pounds of pecans were lost due to the damage?

5. If pecans sold for $2 a pound, how much did the McDades receive for their harvest of 6,487 pounds?

6. In an eight-acre orchard, 35 trees were planted on each acre. How many trees were planted in all?

7. _Estimation_ An orchard of 380 trees yields about 21 pounds of pecans per tree. Estimate the total weight of the pecans from this orchard.

*8. At the price of $2 per pound, how much money did the McDades lose because of the tree damage?

MAINTENANCE

Write each number in expanded form.

1. 3,297   2. 8,103   3. 67,032   4. 23,748   5. 503,246

Write each number in standard form.

6. 4,000 + 800 + 20 + 7

7. 60,000 + 900 + 40 + 9

8. Five thousand, eight hundred twenty-one

9. Forty-six thousand, nine hundred five

Practice: Multiplication

Scavenger Hunt There is a number, a letter, and a multiplication exercise on each section of this space shuttle. Begin at section number 1 and find the product. The answer tells you which section to go to next.

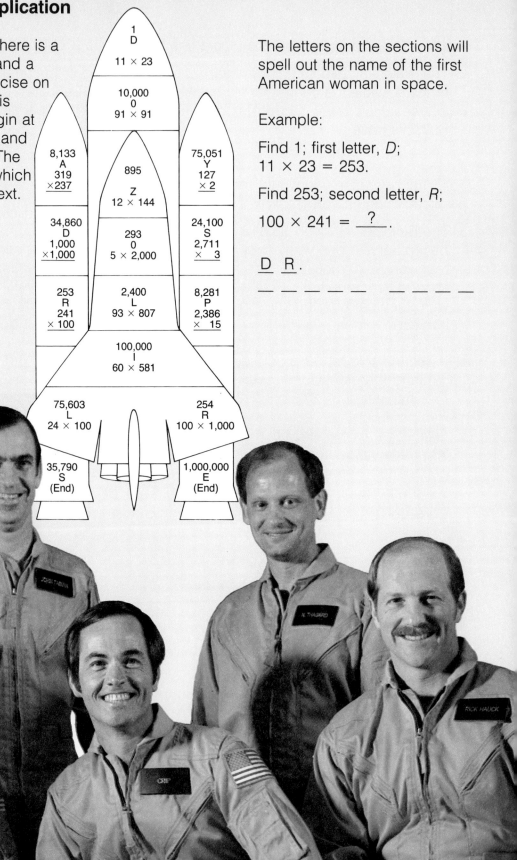

The letters on the sections will spell out the name of the first American woman in space.

Example:

Find 1; first letter, *D*;

$11 \times 23 = 253$.

Find 253; second letter, *R*;

$100 \times 241 = \underline{\ \ ?\ \ }$.

$\underline{D}\ \underline{R}$.

$\underline{\ \ }\ \underline{\ \ }\ \underline{\ \ }\ \underline{\ \ }\ \underline{\ \ }\ \ \ \underline{\ \ }\ \underline{\ \ }\ \underline{\ \ }\ \underline{\ \ }$

Shuttle section labels:

1
D
11×23

10,000
O
91×91

8,133
A
319
$\times 237$

895
Z
12×144

75,051
Y
127
$\times 2$

34,860
D
1,000
$\times 1,000$

293
O
$5 \times 2,000$

24,100
S
2,711
$\times\ 3$

253
R
241
$\times 100$

2,400
L
93×807

8,281
P
2,386
$\times\ 15$

100,000
I
60×581

75,603
L
24×100

254
R
$100 \times 1,000$

35,790
S
(End)

1,000,000
E
(End)

Estimation Estimate each product.

1. 63×42
2. 18×31
3. 113×56
4. 398×11
5. 395×869
6. 305×486

Multiply.

7. $\begin{array}{r} 86 \\ \times\ 5 \\ \hline \end{array}$
8. $\begin{array}{r} 93 \\ \times\ 7 \\ \hline \end{array}$
9. $\begin{array}{r} 51 \\ \times\ 9 \\ \hline \end{array}$

10. $\begin{array}{r} 57 \\ \times 14 \\ \hline \end{array}$
11. $\begin{array}{r} 48 \\ \times 32 \\ \hline \end{array}$
12. $\begin{array}{r} 215 \\ \times\ 86 \\ \hline \end{array}$

13. $\begin{array}{r} 332 \\ \times 128 \\ \hline \end{array}$
14. $\begin{array}{r} 562 \\ \times 306 \\ \hline \end{array}$
15. $\begin{array}{r} 6{,}405 \\ \times\ \ 417 \\ \hline \end{array}$

Apply Solve each problem.

16. An orchard produced 7,890 pounds of pecans one year. The owner expects it to produce 250 pounds more the next year from new trees. What should next year's yield be?

17. A section of a roof is 14 shingles wide and 36 shingles high. How many shingles are needed for this section?

18. A car salesman earns $430 a week. How much does the salesman earn in 50 weeks?

19. Kinuke's gym class meets 40 minutes a day, 3 days a week. How many minutes does Kinuke spend in gym each week?

COMPUTER

BASIC: PRINT Statements

This is a computer program.

```
10 PRINT "THIS PROGRAM IS"
20 PRINT "WRITTEN IN BASIC."
30 END
```

Program statements are numbered to show the order to follow. When quotation marks are used with PRINT, the computer will print whatever is inside the quotation marks.

When the above program is run on a computer, this is printed.

```
THIS PROGRAM IS
WRITTEN IN BASIC.
```

In BASIC, + means add, − means subtract, and * means multiply. For these PRINT statements, only the answer is printed.

```
                        This is printed
10 PRINT 32+18          50
20 PRINT 35-7           28
30 PRINT 5*23           115
40 END
```

Tell what would be printed for each program.

1.
```
10 PRINT "THE PRODUCT IS"
20 PRINT 27*53
30 END
```

2.
```
10 PRINT 325+679
20 PRINT 208*43
30 PRINT 6813-786
40 END
```

49

Problem Solving: Use a Diagram

Read Mary is lending part of her doll collection to the library for a display. Mary has 3 rag dolls, 2 antique dolls, and 2 storybook dolls. The librarian would like one of each of these types. In how many ways can Mary choose 3 dolls, one from each type?

Plan Look at the three decisions one by one. Draw a *tree diagram* and count.

Solve

1. Choose a rag doll.	2. Choose an antique doll.	3. Choose a storybook doll.	Result

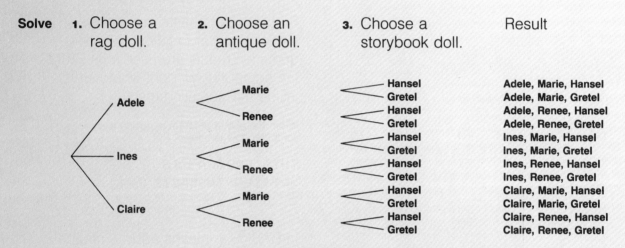

	Marie	Hansel	Adele, Marie, Hansel
Adele	Marie	Gretel	Adele, Marie, Gretel
	Renee	Hansel	Adele, Renee, Hansel
	Renee	Gretel	Adele, Renee, Gretel
	Marie	Hansel	Ines, Marie, Hansel
Ines	Marie	Gretel	Ines, Marie, Gretel
	Renee	Hansel	Ines, Renee, Hansel
	Renee	Gretel	Ines, Renee, Gretel
	Marie	Hansel	Claire, Marie, Hansel
Claire	Marie	Gretel	Claire, Marie, Gretel
	Renee	Hansel	Claire, Renee, Hansel
	Renee	Gretel	Claire, Renee, Gretel

Answer Mary has 12 ways to choose the three dolls.

Look Back Are all the choices different? Were any combinations missed?

50

Try Use a tree diagram to solve the problem.

a. Al has 5 pennies and 4 dimes to trade in his coin collection. How many different ways can he choose one penny and one dime? (HINT: Let P1 represent the first penny, P2 the second penny, and so on.)

Apply Use a tree diagram to solve each problem.

1. Mary has 3 cornhusk dolls and 4 china dolls. In how many ways could she lend the library one cornhusk doll and one china doll?

2. Anita has 3 cornhusk dolls, 3 rag dolls, and 2 antique dolls. In how many ways could she choose one cornhusk doll, one rag doll, and one antique doll?

3. Kim has one of every kind of nickel made in 1942 and 1943. Each of these years, nickels were marked with a P, an S, or a D. In how many ways could Kim choose two nickels, one from each year?

4. Yvonne saves campaign buttons. In one election, each of the 2 candidates had 4 kinds of buttons. In how many ways could she choose one button from each candidate?

5. Larry collects stories about animals. He has 5 books by Walter Farley, 3 by Marguerite Henry, and 2 by James Kjelgaard. In how many ways could he choose a book by each author?

*6. How could you solve Problem 5 without drawing a diagram? What operation would you use?

Exponents

A. The checkerboard has 8 rows of 8 squares each. It has 8×8 squares. We can write 8×8 as 8^2. The 2 is an *exponent*. It tells how many times 8 is used as a factor. 8^2 is read "8 to the second power," or "8 squared."

B. Write 5^3 in standard form.

5 is used as a factor three times.

$$5^3 = 5 \times 5 \times 5 = 125$$

5^3 is read "5 to the third power," or "5 cubed."

C. Write $2^4 \times 3^2$ in standard form.

$$2^4 \times 3^2 = 2 \times 2 \times 2 \times 2 \times 3 \times 3 = 144$$

2^4 is read "2 to the fourth power."

Try Write each number in standard form.

a. 8^3 **b.** 2^6 **c.** $2^3 \times 5^2$

d. Write $7 \times 7 \times 3 \times 3 \times 3$ with exponents.

Practice Write each number in standard form.

1. 3^2 **2.** 2^3 **3.** 6^2

4. 8^2 **5.** 3^3 **6.** 4^3

7. 9^2 **8.** 3^4 **9.** 2^4

10. 10^2 11. 10^3

12. 10^4 13. 10^5

14. 2×3^2 15. $3^2 \times 5$

16. $2^2 \times 3^3$ 17. $3^3 \times 5^2$

Write each product with exponents.

18. 3×3

19. $3 \times 3 \times 3$

20. $5 \times 5 \times 5 \times 5$

21. $2 \times 2 \times 3 \times 3$

22. $4 \times 4 \times 5 \times 5$

23. $7 \times 7 \times 7 \times 8 \times 8$

Apply Solve each problem.

24. In a backgammon tournament, a "doubling cube" can be used to keep track of the number of points that a game is worth. If the cube is used 5 times, the game is worth 2^5 points. Write 2^5 in standard form.

25. In chess, there are 20^2 ways for the two players to make their first moves. Write 20^2 in standard form.

1. Copy and complete the table.

Exponent	Number	Standard form
—	9	9
2	9^2	81
3	9^3	729
4	9^4	6,561
5	▦	▦
6	▦	▦
7	▦	▦
8	▦	▦

2. Look at the pattern in the ones digits. What is the ones digit of 9^9?

3. Make a similar table for powers of 4. What is the ones digit of 4^7?

4. Predict what the ones digit of 4^{14} will be.

5. Make another table for powers of 3. What will the ones digit of 3^{17} be?

6. What is the ones digit of 7^{10}?

7. What is the tens digit of 7^{10}?

8. What is the tens digit of 6^{22}?

9. What are the last two digits of 5^{12}?

10. What are the last four digits of 5^{15}?

11. *Estimation* Estimate the number of digits in the standard form of 2^{18}.

Multiples and Least Common Multiple

Wei's mother told him to box up part of his magazine collection and stack the boxes on shelves. The boxes are about 20 cm high and the holes for the shelf brackets are 6 cm apart. How far apart should Wei put the brackets and shelves if he wants to waste no space?

List the numbers that you can get by multiplying 20 and 6 by counting numbers. These are the *multiples* of 20 and of 6.

20 40 60 80 100 120

6 12 18 24 30 36 42 48 54 60 66

The number 60 is a *common multiple* of 20 and 60. So, if Wei puts the shelves 60 cm apart, he can stack three boxes and use all 60 cm of space.

Other common multiples of the two numbers 20 and 6 are 120, 180, and 360. The *least common multiple* of the two numbers is 60.

Zero and all multiples of 2 are called *even numbers*. Counting numbers that are not multiples of 2 are called *odd numbers*.

Try

a. List the first 6 multiples of 3.

b. Find 2 common multiples of 2 and 6.

c. Find the least common multiple of 3 and 5.

Practice List the first 8 multiples of each number.

1. 5   **2.** 7   **3.** 9   **4.** 8   **5.** 12   **6.** 15   **7.** 20   **8.** 25

Find two common multiples of each pair of numbers.

9. 4 and 6   **10.** 6 and 9   **11.** 4 and 8   **12.** 3 and 6

13. 6 and 10   **14.** 4 and 10   **15.** 2 and 5   **16.** 3 and 5

Find the least common multiple for each pair of numbers.

17. 5 and 7   **18.** 3 and 8   **19.** 3 and 9   **20.** 4 and 12

21. 8 and 10   **22.** 9 and 12   **23.** 15 and 30   **24.** 12 and 24

Tell whether the answer is even or odd in each case.

25. The sum of two even numbers

26. The product of two odd numbers

27. The sum of one even and one odd number

28. The product of one even and one odd number

Apply Solve each problem. Remember that the holes for the shelf brackets are 6 cm apart.

29. How far apart should Wei put shelves for boxes that are 21 cm high?

30. How many boxes could Wei stack on one shelf in Problem 29?

★31. One clock chimes every 30 minutes. Another clock runs fast and chimes every 14 minutes. If the clocks chime together once, how many minutes before they will chime together again?

Problem Solving: Find a Pattern

Read   In a round-robin tournament, each team plays against each of the other teams once. If there are 5 teams, how many games will there be?

Plan   Try solving easier, related problems. Put the results in a table to help you find a pattern.

Solve   If there were 2 teams, A and B, there would be just 1 game (A vs. B).

2 teams
1 game

If there were 3 teams, A, B, and C, there would be 3 games (A vs. B, A vs. C, and B vs. C). A would play 2 games.

3 teams
3 games

If there were 4 teams, A, B, C, and D, there would be 6 games. A would play 3 games.

4 teams
6 games

Put the results in a table and continue the pattern.

Answer   A round-robin tournament with 5 teams has 10 games.

How many teams?	How many games for team A?	How many other games?	Total
2	1	0	1
3	2	1	3
4	3	2 + 1	6
5	4	3 + 2 + 1	10

Look Back   Look for another way to count all the games. There are 5 teams and each team plays 4 games. There should be 5 × 4, or 20 games, then, but that counts each game twice. 2 × 10 = 20, so the answer is correct.

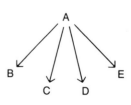

56

Try Solve the problem.

a. How many games are there in a round-robin tournament with 8 teams?

Apply Solve each problem.

1. There are 7 people in a room. Each person shakes hands with each of the other people in the room. How many handshakes are there in all?

2. The dot patterns at the right show the first four triangular numbers. What is the fifth one?

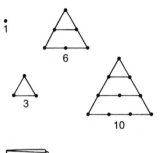

3. What is the ninth triangular number?

★4. What is the 100th triangular number?

5. Four toothpicks can be used to make one small 1-by-1 square. Twelve toothpicks are needed for a complete 2-by-2 square. How many toothpicks are needed for the 3-by-3 square?

6. Copy and fill in the table. Draw toothpick squares to help.

How wide?	How many toothpicks on outside?	How many toothpicks on inside?	How many toothpicks in all?
1	4	0	4
2	8	4	12
3	12	12	▓
4	▓	▓	▓
5	▓	▓	▓

7. Predict the number of toothpicks in a 6-by-6 square and check.

★8. Compare the column of the number of toothpicks in all to the first six triangular numbers. How are these numbers related?

Chapter 2 Test

1. Write two multiplication equations with these numbers.

4 7 28

Estimate each product.

2. 48×51

3. 602×416

4. $88 \times 21 \times 73$

Multiply.

5. 6×5

6. 8×9

7. 0×4

8. 60×200

9. $82 \times 1{,}000$

10. 700×30

11.
$$\begin{array}{r} 637 \\ \times \quad 5 \\ \hline \end{array}$$

12.
$$\begin{array}{r} 5{,}406 \\ \times \quad\quad 8 \\ \hline \end{array}$$

13.
$$\begin{array}{r} 380 \\ \times \quad 9 \\ \hline \end{array}$$

14.
$$\begin{array}{r} 27 \\ \times 30 \\ \hline \end{array}$$

15.
$$\begin{array}{r} 327 \\ \times \quad 60 \\ \hline \end{array}$$

16.
$$\begin{array}{r} 5{,}007 \\ \times \quad\quad 40 \\ \hline \end{array}$$

17.
$$\begin{array}{r} 78 \\ \times 46 \\ \hline \end{array}$$

18.
$$\begin{array}{r} 327 \\ \times \quad 54 \\ \hline \end{array}$$

19.
$$\begin{array}{r} 7{,}247 \\ \times \quad\quad 23 \\ \hline \end{array}$$

20.
$$\begin{array}{r} 425 \\ \times 317 \\ \hline \end{array}$$

21.
$$\begin{array}{r} 926 \\ \times 503 \\ \hline \end{array}$$

22.
$$\begin{array}{r} 6{,}491 \\ \times \quad\quad 417 \\ \hline \end{array}$$

Write each number in standard form.

23. 6^3

24. $2^2 \times 3^4$

25. Write $2 \times 2 \times 2 \times 2 \times 5 \times 5$ with exponents.

26. List the first 6 multiples of 8.

27. Find the least common multiple of 4 and 10.

Tell what operation you would use to solve the problem. Then find the answer.

28. If pecans sold for $2 a pound, how much did the Simpsons receive for their harvest of 7,263 pounds?

Use a tree diagram to solve the problem.

29. Vicente has 3 ski badges from Vail, 2 from Aspen, and 4 from Squaw Valley. In how many ways can he choose one from each place?

Solve the problem.

30. There are 9 people in a room. Each person shakes hands with each of the other people in the room. How many handshakes are there in all?

Properties of Multiplication

When you multiply numbers, you can change the order of the factors and get the same product. This is the *commutative property of multiplication*.

$$\begin{array}{r} 36 \\ \times 123 \\ \hline 108 \\ 720 \\ 3600 \\ \hline 4{,}428 \end{array} \qquad \begin{array}{r} 123 \\ \times\ \ 36 \\ \hline 738 \\ 3690 \\ \hline 4{,}428 \end{array}$$

When you multiply numbers, you can change the grouping of the factors and get the same product. This is the *associative property of multiplication*.

$(18 \times 5) \times 2 \qquad 18 \times (5 \times 2)$

$90 \times 2 \qquad\qquad 18 \times 10$

$180 \qquad\qquad\quad 180$

When you add first then multiply, as in $8 \times (10 + 4)$, you can write $(8 \times 10) + (8 \times 4)$ instead and get the same answer. This is the *distributive property*.

$8 \times (10 + 4) \qquad (8 \times 10) + (8 \times 4)$

$8 \times 14 \qquad\qquad 80 + 32$

$112 \qquad\qquad\quad 112$

These properties can be used to make your work easier.

$(500 \times 96) \times 2 = (96 \times 500) \times 2 = 96 \times (500 \times 2)$

Can you simplify $96 \times (500 \times 2)$ mentally?

Find the missing number and tell which property is used.

1. $(37 \times 8) \times 5 = 37 \times (\blacksquare \times 5)$

2. $5 \times (62 \times 20) = 5 \times (\blacksquare \times 62)$

3. $3 \times (10 + 4) = (3 \times 10) + (3 \times \blacksquare)$

4. $6 \times (20 + 5) = (6 \times 20) + (\blacksquare \times 5)$

Find each answer. Use the three properties to make your work easier.

5. $(13 \times 5) \times 2$ **6.** $(35 \times 4) \times 5$ **7.** $25 \times (9 \times 40)$ **8.** $8 \times (67 \times 50)$

9. $5 \times (10 + 6)$ **10.** $9 \times (10 + 5)$ **11.** $8 \times (100 + 6)$ **12.** $4 \times (200 + 9)$

MAINTENANCE

Find each answer.

1.
$$218 \times 4$$

2.
$$49,000 - 34,486$$

3.
$$51 - 28$$

4.
$$15 + 27$$

5.
$$85 \times 30$$

6.
$$8,002 \times 8$$

7.
$$6,391 + 728$$

8.
$$412 - 243$$

9.
$$8,265 \times 97$$

10.
$$476 - 67$$

11.
$$75,353 + 83,561$$

12.
$$395 \times 62$$

13.
$$354 + 87$$

14.
$$9,823 - 4,671$$

15.
$$6,183 - 4,249$$

16.
$$705 \times 684$$

17.
$$3,472 + 5,815$$

18.
$$182 + 365$$

19.
$$80,304 - 392$$

20.
$$328,654 \\ 8,581 \\ + 10,421$$

21. $7,300 - 641$

22. $500 - 211$

23. $16 + 43 + 24$

24. $5,402 \times 80$

25. $10,000 \times 92$

26. 600×600

27. $8,271 + 719$

28. $11 \times 36 \times 49$

Solve each problem.

29. To play a math game in class, each of the 25 students needs 20 markers. How many markers are needed in all?

30. The Cinellis drove 1,422 miles on their vacation. They also drove 591 miles to go to a family reunion. How many miles did they drive on the two trips?

31. The goal of the Hill City United Fund is $85,000. The town has pledges for $62,520 so far. How much more money does the town need to raise to meet the goal?

32. Monroe School has 283 students. Kelly School has 225 students. If the schools are combined, how many students will the combined school have?

33. Miguel has read 281 pages in a book with 335 pages. How many pages are there left for him to read?

34. *Estimation* Each shelf of books in a library has about 35 books. The library has 2,160 shelves. Estimate the number of books in the library.

Division of Whole Numbers

150 days

3,000 miles

6 days

Introduction to Division

A. The sixth-graders at Jefferson School are making a yearbook. They have 27 pictures for the book. If they put 4 pictures on a page, how many pictures will be on the page that is not completely filled?

Find 27 ÷ 4.

$$\begin{array}{r} 6\text{ R}3 \\ 4\overline{)27} \\ 24 \\ \hline 3 \end{array}$$

Divide.
How many 4s in 27? *6*

Multiply.
Subtract and compare.
3 is less than 4.

The remainder is 3. The remainder must be less than the divisor.

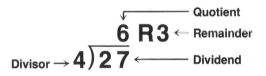

6 pages will be completely filled, and 3 pictures will be on the page that is not completely filled.

Check
$$\begin{array}{r} 6 \leftarrow \text{Quotient} \\ \times 4 \\ \hline 24 \\ +\ \ 3 \leftarrow \text{Remainder} \\ \hline 27 \leftarrow \text{Dividend} \end{array}$$

Practice Divide.

1. $6\overline{)54}$ 2. $9\overline{)18}$ 3. $8\overline{)15}$

4. $5\overline{)47}$ 5. $7\overline{)40}$ 6. $9\overline{)63}$

7. $4\overline{)27}$ 8. $6\overline{)16}$ 9. $5\overline{)18}$

10. $7\overline{)33}$ 11. $8\overline{)68}$ 12. $6\overline{)31}$

13. $29 \div 3$ 14. $73 \div 9$

15. $75 \div 8$ 16. $22 \div 7$

17. $26 \div 3$ 18. $35 \div 6$

19. $26 \div 8$ 20. $48 \div 5$

21. $60 \div 9$ 22. $13 \div 2$

B. Find $36 \div 9$.

$$9\overline{)36}$$
$$\underline{3\,6}$$
$$0$$
quotient 4

The remainder is 0, so 9 is a divisor of 36, and 36 is **divisible** by 9.

Discuss Is 36 divisible by 4? Is 27 divisible by 4? Name a divisor of 27.

Try Divide.

a. $9\overline{)54}$ b. $3\overline{)22}$ c. $43 \div 5$

d. List four divisors of 24.

e. List four numbers that are divisible by 6.

List two divisors of each number.

23. 32 24. 21 25. 16

26. 63 27. 35 28. 42

List four numbers that are divisible by each number.

29. 8 30. 4 31. 7 32. 9

Apply Solve each problem.

Fifteen students are working on the yearbook.

33. How many groups of 6 are there? How many are left over?

34. How can they separate into groups of equal size?

One-Digit Divisors

A. There are 143 students in the sixth-grade classes at Jefferson School. They are having their pictures taken for the yearbook in groups of 6. How many groups of 6 will there be? How many students will be in the group of fewer than 6?

Find 143 ÷ 6.

```
    2
6)143      Divide.
  12       How many 6s in 14? 2
   2       Multiply.
           Subtract and compare.
           2 is less than 6.
```

```
   23 R5
6)143
  12↓      Bring down.
   23      Divide.
   18      How many 6s in 23? 3
           Multiply.
    5      Subtract and compare.
           5 is less than 6.

           There are no more digits to
           bring down. The remainder is 5.
```

There will be 23 groups of 6.
5 students will be in the group
with fewer than 6.

```
Check     23
        ×  6
         138
        +  5
         143
```

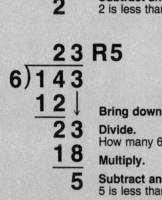

B. Find 744 ÷ 4.

```
    186
4)744
  4
  34
  32
   24
   24
    0
```

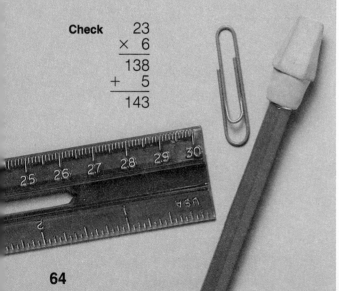

64

Try Divide.

a. $8\overline{)184}$ **b.** $6\overline{)1,279}$ **c.** $8,758 \div 3$

Practice Divide.

1. $3\overline{)89}$ **2.** $5\overline{)95}$ **3.** $2\overline{)35}$ **4.** $6\overline{)93}$ **5.** $4\overline{)96}$

6. $5\overline{)413}$ **7.** $7\overline{)291}$ **8.** $4\overline{)204}$ **9.** $9\overline{)828}$ **10.** $6\overline{)109}$

11. $8\overline{)597}$ **12.** $7\overline{)849}$ **13.** $2\overline{)684}$ **14.** $3\overline{)892}$ **15.** $7\overline{)957}$

16. $5\overline{)849}$ **17.** $8\overline{)2,650}$ **18.** $7\overline{)6,775}$ **19.** $6\overline{)3,937}$ **20.** $9\overline{)2,799}$

21. $910 \div 8$ **22.** $754 \div 6$ **23.** $689 \div 8$

24. $5,930 \div 9$ **25.** $8,440 \div 3$ **26.** $9,865 \div 5$

27. $8,862 \div 6$ **28.** $9,404 \div 3$ **29.** $7,000 \div 6$

30. $12,396 \div 5$ **★31.** $558,945 \div 4$ **★32.** $1,271,866 \div 8$

Apply Solve each problem.

33. Each yearbook contained 18 sheets of paper. How many sheets of paper were used for 150 books?

34. The students collected $372 for the sale of the yearbooks. If each book sold for $3, how many books were sold?

35. The yearbook committee has $75 to buy film. How many $7 film packs can they buy? How much money will they have left?

36. Each day the students attend classes for 300 minutes. This time is separated into 6 class periods, each the same length. How long is each period?

★37. The sixth-grade students attended classes for 5 hours a day, 182 days a year, for 6 years. How many hours of class is this?

One-Digit Divisors: Zeros in the Quotient

A. Ross earns money by picking up golf balls around the course and selling them. If he has 875 golf balls, how many packages of 8 can he make? How many golf balls will be left over?

Find 875 ÷ 8.

```
    1
8)875     Divide.
  8       How many 8s in 8? 1
  ─       Multiply.
  0       Subtract and compare.
```

```
   10
8)875
  8 ↓      Bring down.
  ──
  07      Divide.
          There are zero 8s in 7.
          Write 0 in the quotient.
```

```
  109 R3
8)875
  8  ↓     Bring down.
  ───
  075     Divide.
          How many 8s in 75? 9
  72      Multiply.
  ──
   3      Subtract and compare.
          The remainder is 3.
```

Ross can make
109 packages of 8.
3 golf balls will
be left over.

Every time you bring down a digit in division computation, you must write a digit in the quotient. Sometimes that digit is zero.

B. Find 1,650 ÷ 3.

```
     550
3)1,650
  15 ↓
  ──
   15
   15 ↓
   ──
    00
```

C. Find 7,205 ÷ 9.

```
    800 R5
9)7,205
  72 ↓↓
  ──
   005
```

Try   Divide.

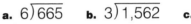

a. 6)665   **b.** 3)1,562   **c.** 3,200 ÷ 8

66

Practice   Divide.

1. $3\overline{)152}$ 2. $2\overline{)161}$

3. $4\overline{)424}$ 4. $7\overline{)739}$

5. $3\overline{)692}$ 6. $6\overline{)965}$

7. $8\overline{)2,416}$ 8. $7\overline{)2,841}$

9. $6\overline{)3,606}$ 10. $2\overline{)1,418}$

11. $5\overline{)4,504}$ 12. $8\overline{)3,206}$

13. $5,229 \div 4$ 14. $6,311 \div 3$

15. $7,503 \div 5$ 16. $9,600 \div 8$

17. $6,183 \div 6$ 18. $8,041 \div 4$

19. $8,064 \div 8$ 20. $6,030 \div 6$

21. $14,636 \div 7$ 22. $24,050 \div 6$

★23. $250,453 \div 5$ ★24. $1,230,078 \div 6$

Apply   Solve each problem.

25. Golf lessons cost $6 for each half-hour lesson. Karen saved $65. How many lessons can she take? How much money will she have left?

26. During a tournament, 83 golfers were put into groups of 4. How many players were not in a group of 4?

More Practice Set 27, page 380

CHALLENGE

Find $1,235 \div 4$.

When you divide by a one-digit number, you can save time and space by using short division.

Short form

$$4\overline{)1,2\,^03\ 5}^{\ 3}$$

Long form

$$\begin{array}{r} 3 \\ 4\overline{)1,235} \\ \underline{12} \\ 0 \end{array}$$

$$4\overline{)1,2\,^03\,^35}^{\ 3\ 0}$$

$$\begin{array}{r} 30 \\ 4\overline{)1,235} \\ \underline{12} \\ 03 \end{array}$$

$$4\overline{)1,2\,^03\,^35}^{\ 3\ 0\ 8\ R3}$$

$$\begin{array}{r} 308\ R3 \\ 4\overline{)1,235} \\ \underline{12} \\ 035 \\ \underline{32} \\ 3 \end{array}$$

Divide. Use short division.

1. $4\overline{)236}$ 2. $5\overline{)361}$

3. $3\overline{)714}$ 4. $7\overline{)759}$

5. $4\overline{)3,592}$ 6. $2\overline{)4,896}$

7. $5\overline{)9,836}$ 8. $6\overline{)9,879}$

9. $8\overline{)70,998}$ 10. $9\overline{)68,029}$

11. $7\overline{)27,070}$ 12. $5\overline{)61,002}$

13. $6\overline{)2,710,564}$ 14. $4\overline{)127,893,106}$

Averages

In the nine years from 1924 to 1932, Babe Ruth hit the following numbers of home runs.

46 25 47 60 54 46 49 46 41

What was the average number of home runs that he hit per year?

To find the *average* number of home runs he hit per year, add to find the total number. Then divide that sum by the number of years.

Add the number of home runs.

Divide by the number of years.

```
 46
 25
 47              4 6  ← Average
 60         9)4 1 4
 54           3 6
 46           ‾‾‾‾
 49            5 4
 46            5 4
+41            ‾‾‾‾
‾‾‾‾             0
414
```

During these nine years, Babe Ruth hit an average of 46 home runs per year.

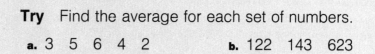

Try Find the average for each set of numbers.

a. 3 5 6 4 2   **b.** 122 143 623

Practice Find the average for each set of numbers.

1. 5 9

2. 2 6 7 8 11 14

3. 11 12 13 14 15

4. 5 5 5 5 5

5. 13 39 41 79

6. 101 201

7. 211 411 611 811

8. 948 1,250 1,426

9. 11 15 4 8 9 3 6 7 18

10. 2 4 6 8 10 12 14 16 18

11. 92 93 91 92 98 99 100

12. 147 96 257 318 142

Apply Solve each problem.

13. In the years 1963 through 1967, Willie Mays came to bat the following numbers of times.

596 578 558 552 486

Find the average number of times he came to bat per year.

★14. In the 1983 NBA championship games, the following numbers of points were scored.

Game 1: Philadelphia—113; Los Angeles—107
Game 2: Philadelphia—103; Los Angeles—93
Game 3: Philadelphia—111; Los Angeles—94
Game 4: Philadelphia—115; Los Angeles—108

Find the average number of points scored per game.

Problem Solving:
Interpret the Remainder

Read Each of the 1,277 players in the Park Ridge Youth Soccer League gets a league patch. If the patches come in packages of 8, how many packages are needed?

Plan Divide to find the number of groups of 8 in 1,277. Then decide how the remainder affects the answer.

Solve

$$8)\overline{1,277} = 159 \text{ R}5$$

The quotient tells that 159 packages of 8 are needed.

The remainder tells that 5 more patches are needed besides the 159 packages of 8.

Therefore, another package is needed.

Answer 160 packages of patches are needed.

Look Back 159 packages are not enough because 159 × 8 = 1,272. Since 160 × 8 = 1,280, 160 packages are enough.

Try Solve each problem.

a. A hockey team has $75 to spend for hockey sticks. How many $4 sticks can they buy?

b. 4 people play in a doubles tennis match. 150 people signed up for doubles matches. How many players will be left over?

Apply Solve each problem.

1. The tennis coaches need 100 tennis balls. How many packages of 3 balls must they buy?

2. The cheerleaders have $100 to buy sweatshirts. How many $9 sweatshirts can they buy?

3. Ann bought as many $4 baseballs as she could with $15. How much money did she have left?

4. There are 31 students in a gym class. How many basketball teams of 5 each can be made?

5. Grace saved $40 for swimming lessons. How many $7 lessons can she take?

6. Marta can save $6 a week. How many weeks will it take her to save $75 for hockey equipment?

7. The Pep Club is selling T-shirts. Shirts come in boxes of 6. How many boxes will the club have to buy if 250 shirts are needed?

8. Each cabin at a volleyball camp houses 9 girls. If 125 girls go to camp, how many would be in a cabin that is not completely filled?

9. A soccer banquet is planned for 140 people. How many tables of 8 will need to be set?

10. Each box seat at the stadium holds 7 people. How many boxes will be needed for 220 people?

11. Members of the band plan to cut lawns to earn money to go to the basketball tournament. How many lawns, at $6 each, will they have to cut to earn at least $500?

★12. The 52 students in the intramural program are separated into teams. Write a division problem that uses this information and that has 4 as the answer.

Two-Digit Divisors: One-Digit Quotients

A. In June, 1983, the space shuttle *Challenger* was in space for about 146 hours. How many days and hours is this? (1 day = 24 hours)

Find 146 ÷ 24.

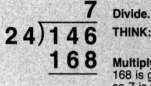

$$\begin{array}{r} 7 \\ 24)\overline{146} \\ \underline{168} \end{array}$$

Divide.

THINK: How many 2s in 14? 7
Write 7 above the 6.

Multiply.
168 is greater than 146,
so 7 is too big.

$$\begin{array}{r} 6 \ \text{R2} \\ 24)\overline{146} \\ \underline{144} \\ 2 \end{array}$$

Try 6.

Multiply.
Subtract and compare.
The remainder is 2.

146 hours is 6 days and 2 hours.

Check
$$\begin{array}{r} 24 \\ \times 6 \\ \hline 144 \\ + \ \ 2 \\ \hline 146 \end{array}$$

B. Find 603 ÷ 93.

$$\begin{array}{r} 6 \ \text{R45} \\ 93)\overline{603} \\ \underline{558} \\ 45 \end{array}$$

Divide.

THINK: How many 9s
in 60? *6*

Multiply.
Subtract and compare.
The remainder is 45.

Try Divide.

a. $52\overline{)486}$ **b.** $47\overline{)358}$ **c.** $120 \div 15$

Round each number to the nearest ten.

1. 63   **2.** 48

Practice Divide.

3. 91   **4.** 60

1. $24\overline{)98}$ **2.** $22\overline{)77}$ **3.** $13\overline{)58}$

5. 97   **6.** 75

4. $14\overline{)68}$ **5.** $30\overline{)158}$ **6.** $40\overline{)329}$

7. 153   **8.** 535

7. $60\overline{)372}$ **8.** $50\overline{)217}$ **9.** $70\overline{)384}$

9. 398   **10.** 201

10. $90\overline{)373}$ **11.** $41\overline{)378}$ **12.** $52\overline{)435}$

13. $44\overline{)264}$ **14.** $57\overline{)285}$ **15.** $55\overline{)246}$

Round each number to the nearest hundred.

16. $25\overline{)179}$ **17.** $58\overline{)164}$ **18.** $36\overline{)234}$

11. 432   **12.** 551

19. $23\overline{)192}$ **20.** $56\overline{)200}$ **21.** $64\overline{)300}$

13. 549   **14.** 389

22. $62\overline{)615}$ **23.** $24\overline{)236}$ **24.** $39\overline{)312}$

15. 825   **16.** 750

25. $203 \div 29$ **26.** $150 \div 17$ **27.** $122 \div 13$

17. 3,412   **18.** 4,375

28. $139 \div 15$ **29.** $103 \div 14$ **30.** $116 \div 18$

19. 1,652   **20.** 1,397

31. $566 \div 74$ **32.** $674 \div 86$ **33.** $315 \div 63$

Round each number to the nearest thousand.

Apply Solve each problem.

34. In 1962, John Glenn was in space for about 295 minutes. How many hours and minutes is this? (1 hour = 60 minutes)

21. 3,610   **22.** 8,511

23. 3,500   **24.** 3,499

35. During the *Apollo 17* mission in 1972, Astronauts Cernan and Schmitt stayed on the moon for about 75 hours. How many days and hours is this?

25. 9,800   **26.** 9,990

27. 19,700   **28.** 30,480

36. The *Apollo 10* space mission in 1969 lasted for about 8 days. How many hours is this?

29. 40,000   **30.** 59,500

Making Better Estimates in Division

A. South Dakota is about 400 miles wide. At an average speed of 49 miles per hour, how long would it take to drive across the state?

Find 400 ÷ 49.

$$\begin{array}{r} 9 \\ 49\overline{)400} \\ 441 \end{array}$$

Divide.
THINK: How many 4s are there in 40? *10*
$10 \times 49 = 490$, so there are fewer than ten 49s.

Multiply.
441 is greater than 400, so 9 is too big.

When you divide, the estimate you choose may be too big or too small. Sometimes you can make a better estimate.

$$\begin{array}{r} 8 \text{ R8} \\ 49\overline{)400} \\ 392 \\ \hline 8 \end{array}$$

Divide.
THINK: 49 rounds to 50. How many 5s in 40? *8*

Multiply.
Subtract and compare.
The remainder is 8.

The trip would take about 8 hours.

B. Find 693 ÷ 86.

$$\begin{array}{r} 7 \\ 86\overline{)693} \\ 602 \\ \hline 91 \end{array}$$

Divide.
THINK: 86 rounds to 90. How many 9s in 69? 7

Multiply.
Subtract and compare.
91 is greater than 86, so 7 is too small.

$$\begin{array}{r} 8 \text{ R5} \\ 86\overline{)693} \\ 688 \\ \hline 5 \end{array}$$

Try 8.

Multiply.
Subtract and compare.
The remainder is 5.

Try Divide.

a. $19\overline{)134}$ **b.** $87\overline{)542}$ **c.** $469 \div 58$

74

Practice Divide.

1. $35\overline{)136}$
2. $47\overline{)212}$
3. $18\overline{)148}$
4. $19\overline{)127}$
5. $56\overline{)392}$

6. $77\overline{)385}$
7. $38\overline{)295}$
8. $57\overline{)548}$
9. $46\overline{)315}$
10. $68\overline{)571}$

11. $17\overline{)143}$
12. $19\overline{)105}$
13. $19\overline{)130}$
14. $16\overline{)103}$
15. $26\overline{)139}$

16. $27\overline{)169}$
17. $38\overline{)316}$
18. $28\overline{)239}$
19. $57\overline{)189}$
20. $67\overline{)227}$

21. $85\overline{)363}$
22. $75\overline{)484}$
23. $18\overline{)151}$
24. $17\overline{)104}$
25. $78\overline{)390}$

26. $549 \div 88$
27. $541 \div 59$
28. $314 \div 78$
29. $240 \div 48$

30. $840 \div 89$
31. $644 \div 78$
32. $813 \div 98$
33. $741 \div 97$

34. $85 \div 16$
35. $94 \div 15$
36. $130 \div 15$
37. $118 \div 16$

Apply Solve each problem.

38. Kiyo's car gets about 31 miles to the gallon. How many gallons of gasoline would she use going from Toronto to Ottawa, a distance of 248 miles?

39. The Sievers averaged 48 miles an hour on a trip from Albany to Baltimore, a distance of about 336 miles. How long did the trip take?

40. The Palsons drove from Houston to Los Angeles. They drove 625 miles the first day, 490 miles the second day, and 427 miles the third day. Find the average number of miles they drove each day.

★41. The Hyans drive a camper from Detroit to Atlanta in 2 days. They averaged 387 miles a day, and they used 86 gallons of gasoline. How many miles per gallon did they get on this trip?

Two-Digit Divisors: Two-Digit Quotients

A. It is about 3,009 km from Sydney, Australia, to Alice Springs, Australia. If a train averaged 59 km per hour, how long would the trip take by train?

Find 3,009 ÷ 59.

```
      5
59)3,009
  2 9 5
  ─────
      5
```

Divide.

THINK: 59 rounds to 60.
How many 6s in 30? 5

Multiply.
Subtract and compare.

```
     5 1
59)3,009
  2 9 5↓
  ─────
      5 9
      5 9
      ───
        0
```

Bring down.
Divide.

There is one 59 in 59.

Multiply.
Subtract and compare.

The trip would take about 51 hours.

B. Find 844 ÷ 43.

```
      2
43)844
  86
```

Divide.

THINK: 43 rounds to 40.
How many 4s in 8? 2

Multiply.
86 is greater than 84, so 2 is too big.

```
     1
43)844
  43
  ──
  41
```

Try 1.

Multiply.
Subtract and compare.

```
    1 9 R27
43)844
  43↓
  ───
  414
  387
  ───
   27
```

Bring down.
Divide.

THINK: How many 4s in 41? 10
Since 10 cannot be a digit in the quotient, try 9.

Multiply.
Subtract and compare.
The remainder is 27.

Try Divide.

a. $32\overline{)1{,}696}$ b. $5{,}351 \div 77$

Practice Divide.

1. $31\overline{)824}$ 2. $22\overline{)794}$ 3. $47\overline{)997}$ 4. $38\overline{)461}$ 5. $54\overline{)837}$

6. $63\overline{)915}$ 7. $29\overline{)958}$ 8. $28\overline{)617}$ 9. $46\overline{)982}$ 10. $26\overline{)850}$

11. $62\overline{)4{,}486}$ 12. $71\overline{)3{,}889}$ 13. $47\overline{)2{,}176}$ 14. $58\overline{)2{,}735}$

15. $1{,}421 \div 49$ 16. $1{,}917 \div 32$ 17. $1{,}271 \div 43$ 18. $1{,}723 \div 18$

19. $1{,}482 \div 17$ 20. $2{,}378 \div 26$ 21. $3{,}156 \div 37$ 22. $4{,}045 \div 54$

Apply Solve each problem.

23. It is about 812 km from Sydney to Brisbane, Australia. If a bus averages 58 km per hour, how long does the bus trip take?

24. The air distance between Sydney and Perth is about 3,300 km. If it takes an airplane 5 hours to make the trip, what is the average speed of the plane?

25. The population of Sydney is about 3,095,000, and the population of Perth is about 825,000. How many more people live in Sydney?

★26. The train trip between Sydney and Perth takes about 64 hours. How many days and hours is this?

Three- and Four-Digit Quotients

Career Dick Damoski uses a word processor. He has typed 69,564 lines of manuscript into the computer. The material will be printed 51 lines on a page. How many pages of manuscript will be printed?

Find 69,564 ÷ 51.

```
        1 3 6 4
51)6 9,5 6 4
   5 1↓
   1 8 5
   1 5 3↓
       3 2 6
       3 0 6↓
           2 0 4
           2 0 4
               0
```

Divide.
THINK: 51 rounds to 50.
How many 5s in 6? *1*
Multiply.
Subtract and compare.

Bring down.
Divide.
THINK: How many 5s in 18? *3*
Multiply.
Subtract and compare.

Bring down.
Divide.
THINK: How many 5s in 32? *6*
Multiply.
Subtract and compare.

Bring down.
Divide.
THINK: How many 5s in 20? *4*
Multiply.
Subtract and compare.

There will be 1,364 pages of manuscript.

Try Divide.

a. 22)3,850
b. 60)88,545

c. 48)29,472

Practice Divide.

1. 50)7,382
2. 80)9,973
3. 30)8,585
4. 20)7,167
5. 33)8,585
6. 24)5,544
7. 33)5,346
8. 51)8,900
9. 27)8,764
10. 28)9,457
11. 19)9,180
12. 18)9,690
13. 40)28,581
14. 50)31,565

15. $80\overline{)27,647}$ **16.** $70\overline{)29,662}$ **17.** $62\overline{)16,205}$ **18.** $81\overline{)31,712}$

19. $78\overline{)24,336}$ **20.** $65\overline{)26,975}$ **21.** $30\overline{)76,967}$ **22.** $20\overline{)67,714}$

23. $50\overline{)87,161}$ **24.** $60\overline{)93,750}$ **25.** $13\overline{)69,454}$ **26.** $14\overline{)87,747}$

27. $43\overline{)69,584}$ **28.** $41\overline{)87,187}$ **★29.** $21\overline{)286,461}$ **★30.** $60\overline{)6,857,174}$

Apply   Solve each problem.

A *character* in word processing is a space, letter, digit, or symbol. A manuscript contains 25,000 characters. How many lines long will it be, if it is printed with the following number of characters per line?

31. 36 per line   **32.** 45 per line

33. 60 per line   **34.** 75 per line

★35. Another manuscript contains 50,000 characters. How many pages will it take if it is printed with 48 characters per line and 55 lines per page?

Two-Digit Divisors: Zeros in the Quotient

A. *Career* Dianne Roth is a computer operator. She put 6,754 cards into a card reader that can read 22 cards per second. How long will it take for the cards to be read?

Find 6,754 ÷ 22.

```
      3
22)6,754        Divide.
   66           Multiply.
   ──           Subtract and compare.
    1
```

```
     30
22)6,754
   66↓
   ──
    15          Bring down.
     0          Divide.
   ──           How many 22s in 15? 0
    15          Multiply.
                Subtract and compare.
```

```
    307
22)6,754
   66 │
   ── │
   15 │
    0↓
   ──
   154          Bring down.
   154          Divide.
   ───          Multiply.
     0          Subtract and compare.
                The remainder is 0.
```

It will take 307 seconds to read the cards.

Remember, each time you bring down a digit in division computation, you must write a digit in the quotient. Sometimes that digit is 0.

B. Find 7,215 ÷ 24.

```
      3
24)7,215        Divide.
   72           Multiply.
   ──           Subtract and compare.
    0
```

```
     30
24)7,215
   72↓
   ──
   01           Bring down.
                Divide.
    0           How many 24s in 1? 0
   ──           Multiply.
    1           Subtract and compare.
```

```
    300 R15
24)7,215
   72 │
   ── │
   01 │
    0↓
   ──
   15           Bring down.
    0           Divide.
   ──           How many 24s in 15? 0
   15           Multiply.
                Subtract and compare.
                The remainder is 15.
```

C. Find 10,680 ÷ 89.

```
     120
89)10,680
   89↓
   ──
   178│
   178↓
   ───
    00
```

Try Divide.

a. $54\overline{)3,240}$ **b.** $29\overline{)6,055}$ **c.** $73\overline{)64,995}$

Practice Divide.

1. $22\overline{)1,339}$ **2.** $41\overline{)3,316}$ **3.** $93\overline{)2,794}$ **4.** $84\overline{)4,209}$

5. $59\overline{)7,697}$ **6.** $68\overline{)8,218}$ **7.** $23\overline{)9,217}$ **8.** $34\overline{)6,829}$

9. $71\overline{)7,560}$ **10.** $62\overline{)6,530}$ **11.** $28\overline{)10,925}$ **12.** $39\overline{)10,528}$

13. $18\overline{)12,960}$ **14.** $19\overline{)11,590}$ **15.** $70\overline{)49,063}$ **16.** $80\overline{)48,054}$

17. $60\overline{)18,566}$ **18.** $90\overline{)18,573}$ **19.** $83\overline{)29,907}$ **20.** $72\overline{)41,801}$

21. $26\overline{)18,218}$ **22.** $37\overline{)14,814}$ **23.** $12\overline{)10,860}$ **24.** $14\overline{)12,180}$

★25. $54\overline{)108,046}$ **★26.** $82\overline{)114,000}$ **★27.** $24\overline{)72,183}$ **★28.** $67\overline{)282,002}$

Apply Solve each problem.

Punched cards are used to put information into large computers.

29. A punched card has 12 rows of 80 columns for holes. How many positions for holes are on the card?

30. A key-punch machine punched 35,600 holes a minute into cards. If 80 holes were punched in each card, how many cards were punched?

31. Electro-mechanical card readers can read 32,400 cards a minute. How many cards can be read in a second? (1 minute = 60 seconds)

32. A key-punch operator can punch 15,000 holes per hour. How many holes can be punched per minute? (1 hour = 60 minutes)

More Practice Set 34, page 382

Problem Solving: Choose the Operation

Read A floppy disk is divided into 40 tracks. Each track holds 2,304 *bytes* of information. How many bytes of information can be put onto a disk?

Plan The disk has 40 tracks with 2,304 bytes on each track. Multiply to find the total number of bytes.

Solve

$$
\begin{array}{r}
2{,}3\,0\,4 \\
\times \quad 4\,0 \\
\hline
9\,2{,}1\,6\,0
\end{array}
$$

Answer 92,160 bytes of information can be put onto a disk.

Look Back $2{,}000 \times 40 = 80{,}000$, so the answer is reasonable.

Try Tell what operation you would use to solve the problem. Then solve the problem.

a. Each track of a floppy disk holds 2,304 bytes of information and is divided into 9 equal sectors. How many bytes can be held in each sector?

Apply Tell what operation you would use to solve each problem. Then solve each problem.

1. A printer for Computer MAX costs $875 plus $75 sales tax. What is the total cost including tax?

2. Ms. Karlson ordered 24 boxes of floppy disks for a total cost of $456. What was the cost of each box?

3. How many characters can be printed on a page if there are 65 characters per line and 55 lines per page?

4. Some electrostatic printers can print 15,000 lines per minute. How many lines per second is this? (1 minute = 60 seconds)

5. A system of punched cards was used to speed the handling of data in the 1890 United States census. How many years ago was this?

6. A microcomputer with 8K memory can store 8,192 bytes of information. A computer with 64K memory can store 8 times this amount. How many bytes can a computer with 64K memory store?

7. Personal Computer MAX costs $535 more than Computer MIN. MIN costs $995. How much does MAX cost?

8. Blaise Pascal invented a calculating machine in 1642. If he was 19 years old at that time, in what year was he born?

9. A computer with 32K memory can store 32,768 bytes of information. This is 2 times the amount a computer with 16K memory can store. How many bytes can a computer with 16K memory store?

10. In 1981, there were 18,000 robots in the United States, Europe, and Japan. There were 6,500 robots in the United States and Europe. How many were in Japan?

More Practice Set 35, page 382

Practice: Division

Find the average for each set of numbers.

1. 6 8 3 2 5 7 9 4 1

2. 321 518 263 483 455

3. 432 456 444 468

4. 3,214 2,948 3,105

5. List four divisors of 48.

6. List four divisors of 64.

7. List four numbers that are divisible by 6.

8. List four numbers that are divisible by 10.

What is a computer's favorite sport?

To answer the riddle, find each answer. Then write, in order, the letters for exercises that have a remainder of zero.

9. 3)1,423 (B)

10. 6)1,032 (R)

11. 41)3,446 (H)

12. 32)2,948 (S)

13. 27)2,230 (Q)

14. 29)1,788 (Y)

15. 12)540 (U)

16. 15)785 (A)

17. 53)5,569 (M)

18. 44)9,025 (F)

19. 87)9,883 (V)

20. 68)9,631 (J)

21. 5)5,125 (N)

22. 7)8,415 (A)

23. 6)4,324 (K)

24. 9)8,820 (N)

25. 43)9,015 (C)

26. 52)5,393 (L)

27. 25)5,275 (I)

28. 35)5,316 (M)

29. 67)26,811 (W)

30. 94)2,810 (R)

31. 83)3,237 (N)

32. 49)34,315 (M)

33. 77)68,615 (Z)

34. 58)90,084 (E)

35. 13)28,574 (G)

Apply   Solve each problem.

36. Some magnetic tape for a computer is 2,400 feet long. If information can be stored on the tape at a rate of 15 feet per second, how many seconds does it take to fill the tape?

37. Jean's bowling scores for four games were 131, 158, 141, and 142. What was her average score?

38. There are 36 pictures on a roll of film. A photographer will take 1,250 school pictures. How many rolls of film will the photographer need?

39. The 6th graders were selling denim book bags for $2.95 a bag. 42 bags were sold. How much money did the 6th graders earn?

40. On a solo flight from Newfoundland to Ireland, Amelia Earhart flew 2,025 miles in about 15 hours. What was the average number of miles per hour for the flight?

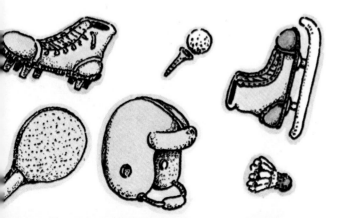

BASIC: INPUT Statements

In BASIC, / means divide.

In this program, an INPUT statement is used to enter the divisor (D). While the program is running, a ? will appear on the screen when the computer reads INPUT. The computer will wait for a number to be typed in before it continues the program.

4 is typed for D.

```
10 PRINT "WHAT IS D"     WHAT IS D
20 INPUT D               ? 4
30 PRINT 36/D            9
40 END
```

Tell what is printed in line 30 for the program above when the following numbers are typed in for D.

1. 2   **2.** 6   **3.** 36   **4.** 9

Tell what is printed for the following programs when 96 is typed in for A.

5.
```
10 PRINT "WHAT IS A"
20 INPUT A
30 PRINT A+28
40 PRINT A/4
50 END
```

6.
```
10 PRINT "WHAT IS A"
20 INPUT A
30 PRINT "THE QUOTIENT IS"
40 PRINT A/8
50 END
```

7. Which line would be changed in Exercise 6 to divide by 12?

Missing-Factor Equations

The gold rush in California resulted in a rapid increase in the population of the area. To help bring faster mail service to these people, the Pony Express was established in 1860. The riders carried the mail from St. Joseph, Missouri, to Sacramento, California, in about 8 days.

A. When the Pony Express was established in 1860, the postage rate was $160 a pound. When the service ended in 1861, the rate had dropped to $32 a pound. The 1860 rate was how many times the 1861 rate?

Number of times →   1861 rate →   1860 rate →

$$n \times 32 = 160 \qquad \text{Use this equation.}$$

$$n = 160 \div 32 \qquad \text{Divide to find the missing factor.}$$

$$n = 5$$

The 1860 rate was 5 times the 1861 rate.

B. Find n.

$$3{,}600 = 15 \times n$$

$$3{,}600 \div 15 = n$$

$$240 = n$$

Try Find n.

a. $n \times 11 = 55$ **b.** $3 \times n = 381$ **c.** $n \times 30 = 930$

Practice Find n.

1. $9 \times n = 135$ **2.** $6 \times n = 150$ **3.** $n \times 4 = 868$

4. $n \times 3 = 582$ **5.** $2{,}185 = n \times 5$ **6.** $2{,}496 = n \times 8$

7. $1{,}938 = 6 \times n$ **8.** $1{,}380 = 5 \times n$ **9.** $42 \times n = 294$

10. $51 \times n = 408$ **11.** $120 = 15 \times n$ **12.** $126 = 18 \times n$

13. $n \times 34 = 544$ **14.** $n \times 63 = 882$ **15.** $4{,}680 = 78 \times n$

16. $4{,}300 = 86 \times n$ **17.** $1{,}974 = n \times 94$ **18.** $2{,}211 = n \times 67$

19. $3{,}760 = 94 \times n$ **20.** $1{,}827 = n \times 87$ **21.** $2{,}244 = n \times 68$

Apply Solve each problem.

22. Some Pony-Express riders earned $120 a day. This was 9 times the amount a cowboy might have earned. How much might a cowboy have earned? (HINT: $9 \times n = 120$)

23. A letter that cost $5.00 (500¢) to send by Pony Express in 1860 cost 20¢ to send in 1980. The postage rate in 1860 was how many times the rate in 1980? (HINT: $n \times 20 = 500$)

24. The Pony-Express route covered about 1,960 miles. Sometimes the trip took only 8 days. What was the average number of miles per day?

25. Horses used for the Pony Express could carry 165 pounds, including the rider. If a rider's supplies and mail weighed 45 pounds, how much could the rider weigh?

Problem Solving: Write an Equation

Read In 1850, it took a stagecoach about 600 hours to travel from St. Louis to San Francisco. Today, the same trip would take about 40 hours by car. How many times as many hours did it take in 1850 as it takes today?

Plan Find the number that 40 is multiplied by to get 600. Use *n* for this number and write an equation.

Number of times	Hours now	Hours in 1850
↓	↓	↓

$$n \times 40 = 600$$

Solve

$$n \times 40 = 600$$
$$n = 600 \div 40$$
$$n = 15$$

Answer The trip in 1850 took 15 times the number of hours it takes today.

Look Back Since $15 \times 40 = 600$, the answer checks.

Discuss Could you have written a different equation? Would it have given you the same answer?

Try Write an equation. Then find the answer.

a. How many days would the 600-hour stagecoach trip from St. Louis to San Francisco take? (1 day = 24 hours)

b. There were about 800 people living in San Francisco in 1848. Because of the gold rush, the population grew to 25,000 in 1849. How many people came to San Francisco during 1848 and 1849?

Apply Write an equation. Then find the answer.

1. A covered-wagon trip across the United States often took about 150 days. After 1869, the same trip could be made by train in 6 days. How many times as many days was the wagon trip as the train trip?

2. Between 1840 and 1860, the number of miles of railroad track in the United States increased from 3,300 miles to 30,000 miles. How many miles of track were added between 1840 and 1860?

3. The 1849 gold rush in California resulted in a rapid increase in prices. In 1849, one egg cost about 84¢. This is 12 times the cost of an egg today. How much does an egg cost today?

4. A piece of land in San Francisco that sold for $17 before the gold rush sold for $6,000 in 1849. How much more did the piece of land cost in 1849?

5. A piece of land that cost $6,000 in 1849 cost 8 times that amount in 1850. How much did the land cost in 1850?

6. In 1850, about 91,000 people came to California by land or by sea. About 55,000 of them came by land. How many came by sea?

7. One of the first gold mines yielded its owners $75,000 in 3 months. How much money did the gold mine average per month?

8. In 1849, it was common for a miner to find a pound of gold a day. At $15 an ounce, how much was the pound of gold worth? (1 pound = 16 ounces)

9. After 1850, a miner who found $5 worth of gold a day was doing well. At this rate, how many days would it take a miner to find $1,000 worth of gold?

10. In 1848, $5,000,000 worth of gold was mined in California. In 1849, $40,000,000 worth of gold was mined. What was the difference in these amounts?

Factors and Greatest Common Factor

A. Six Royal Trumpeters are going to march in rows, with the same number in each row. The ways they can do this are given below.

1 row of 6 $1 \times 6 = 6$ 6 rows of 1 $6 \times 1 = 6$

2 rows of 3 $2 \times 3 = 6$ 3 rows of 2 $3 \times 2 = 6$

The products show all the *factors*, or divisors, of 6.
The factors of 6 are 1, 2, 3, and 6.

When 6 is divided by any of its factors, the remainder is 0.

B. These products show all the factors of 16.

1 × 16
2 × 8
4 × 4

The factors of 16 are 1, 2, 4, 8, and 16.

C. The *common factors* of 16 and 24 are shown in color.

Factors of 16: 1, 2, 4, 8, 16

Factors of 24: 1, 2, 3, 4, 6, 8, 12, 24

The common factors of 16 and 24 are 1, 2, 4, and 8.

The *greatest common factor* of 16 and 24 is 8.

Try

a. Is 8 a factor of 30? Write *yes* or *no*.

b. List all the factors of 36.

c. Find the common factors of 20 and 28.
Then name the greatest common factor.

Practice   Write *yes* or *no*.

1. Is 6 a factor of 42?

2. Is 9 a factor of 50?

3. Is 8 a factor of 4?

4. Is 7 a factor of 7?

5. Is 4 a factor of 46?

6. Is 1 a factor of 13?

List all the factors of each number.

7. 8   **8.** 10   **9.** 13   **10.** 11   **11.** 15   **12.** 14   **13.** 7

14. 2   **15.** 50   **16.** 35   **17.** 28   **18.** 32   **19.** 30   **20.** 20

21. 12   **22.** 18   **23.** 42   **24.** 48   **25.** 72   **26.** 64   **27.** 100

Find the common factors of each pair of numbers.
Then name the greatest common factor.

28. 9; 12   **29.** 12; 15   **30.** 21; 28   **31.** 8; 12   **32.** 20; 25

33. 5; 7   **34.** 7; 11   **35.** 5; 15   **36.** 8; 16   **37.** 18; 30

38. 6; 13   **39.** 12; 17   **40.** 9; 9   *41. 48; 72   *42. 96; 144

Apply   The members of the Royal Band are arranged in rows,
with the same number in each row. How many possible
arrangements are there if there are

43. 25 members?   **44.** 24 members?   **45.** 64 members?   **46.** 81 members?

Prime and Composite Numbers

A. Three Royal Drummers are going to march in rows, with the same number in each row. They can march in 1 row of 3 or in 3 rows of 1.

These products show all the factors of 3.

1×3 and 3×1

The factors of 3 are 1 and 3. A number with exactly two factors is a *prime number*. 3 is a prime number.

B. Suppose another Royal Drummer joined the march. The four drummers can march in 1 row of 4, 4 rows of 1, or 2 rows of 2.

These products show all the factors of 4.

1×4, 4×1, and 2×2

The factors of 4 are 1, 2, and 4. A number with more than two factors is a *composite number*. 4 is a composite number.

Every whole number greater than 1 is either prime or composite. 0 and 1 are neither prime nor composite.

Discuss Describe the two factors of a prime number. Name the only even number that is prime.

Try List all the factors of each number. Then tell if the number is prime, or composite, or neither.

a. 2   **b.** 5   **c.** 8   **d.** 9

Practice List all the factors of each number. Then tell if the number is prime, or composite, or neither.

1. 18   **2.** 27   **3.** 11   **4.** 30

5. 14   **6.** 17   **7.** 49   **8.** 21

9. 38   **10.** 56   **11.** 41   **12.** 23

Here is a way to find all the prime numbers less than 100. List the whole numbers from 1 through 100. Then follow these steps.

13. Cross out 1 because it is neither prime nor composite.

14. Circle 2 because it is prime. Cross out all numbers that have 2 as a factor.

15. Circle 3 because it is prime. Cross out all numbers that have 3 as a factor.

16. Circle 5. Cross out all numbers that have 5 as a factor.

17. Circle 7. Cross out all numbers that have 7 as a factor.

★18. After you have crossed out all the numbers that have 7 as a factor, how do you know that all the remaining numbers are prime numbers?

19. List the prime numbers less than 100.

You can use your calculator to see if one number is a factor of another.

A. Is 127 a factor of 5,789?

Press: 5789 $\div$ 127

Display: *45.582677*

This display tells you that when 5,789 is divided by 127, there is a remainder. 127 is not a factor of 5,789.

B. Is 7 a factor of 5,789?

Press: 5789 $\div$ 7

Display: *827*

This display tells you that the remainder is zero. 7 is a factor of 5,789. 827 is also a factor of 5,789.

Each number is a composite number. Find a factor of the number other than 1 and the number itself.

1. 105   **2.** 346

3. 417   **4.** 169

5. 343   **6.** 143

7. 581   **8.** 361

9. 1,067   **10.** 931

Chapter 3 Test

Divide.

1. $8\overline{)40}$ 2. $7\overline{)61}$

3. $4\overline{)984}$ 4. $8\overline{)9{,}893}$

5. $9\overline{)2{,}738}$ 6. $6\overline{)7{,}792}$

7. $52\overline{)327}$ 8. $73\overline{)628}$

9. $19\overline{)161}$ 10. $48\overline{)347}$

11. $27\overline{)962}$ 12. $62\overline{)4{,}647}$

13. $81\overline{)9{,}978}$ 14. $35\overline{)29{,}606}$

15. $24\overline{)9{,}619}$ 16. $93\overline{)28{,}746}$

Find the average for each set of numbers.

17. 4 7 6 3 5

18. 157 360 224

Find n.

19. $n \times 12 = 72$ 20. $40 \times n = 880$

21. List all the factors of 40.

Find the common factors of each pair of numbers. Then name the greatest common factor.

22. 6; 10   23. 24; 28

List all the factors of each number. Then tell if the number is prime, composite, or neither.

24. 39   25. 37

Solve the problem.

26. It takes 52 centimeters of canvas to make a book bag. How many book bags can be made from 340 centimeters of canvas?

27. Pedro needs 195 tiles for the floor of the family room. There are 8 tiles in each carton. How many cartons should Pedro buy?

Tell what operation you would use to solve each problem. Then solve each problem.

28. *Sputnik I* circled the earth every 90 minutes. How many times did it circle the earth in one day? (1 day = 1,440 minutes)

29. The band bought 7 new trombones. Each trombone cost $150. What was the total cost of the trombones?

Write an equation. Then find the answer.

30. A bear weighs about 20 times the weight of a cub. The bear weighs 360 kilograms. How much does the cub weigh?

CHALLENGE

Divisibility Rules

Here are ways you can tell if a whole number is divisible by 2, 3, 5, 9, or 10.

 The number is divisible by 2 if the ones digit is 0, 2, 4, 6, or 8.

76 is divisible by 2 because the ones digit is 6.

 The number is divisible by 3 if the sum of the digits is divisible by 3.

786 is divisible by 3 because 7 + 8 + 6 = 21, and 21 is divisible by 3.

The number is divisible by 5 if the ones digit is 5 or 0.

605 is divisible by 5 because the ones digit is 5.

The number is divisible by 9 if the sum of the digits is divisible by 9.

288 is divisible by 9 because 2 + 8 + 8 = 18, and 18 is divisible by 9.

A number is divisible by 10 if the ones digit is 0.

700 is divisible by 10 because the ones digit is 0.

Copy and complete the table. The check marks show that 3,285 is divisible by 3, 5, and 9.

	Number	2	Divisible by 3	5	9	10
	3,285		✓	✓	✓	
1.	630					
2.	762					
3.	856					
4.	810					
5.	2,685					
6.	5,814					
7.	32,004					
8.	74,010					
9.	431,204					
10.	602,265					
11.	4,277,133					
12.	5,009,407					
13.	7,961,590					
14.	9,951,413					

15. If a number is divisible by 6, it is divisible by both 2 and 3. Give a test for divisibility by 6.

16. Tell which of the numbers in Exercises 1–14 are divisible by 6.

MAINTENANCE

Compare. Use $<$, $>$, or $=$.

1. 6,123 ● 6,286

2. 96,153 ● 91,027

3. 10,100 ● 10,001

4. 42,390 ● 42,185

5. 875,255 ● 99,789

6. 65,491 ● 65,492

7. 4,103 ● 5,645

8. 99,999 ● 100,000

9. 1,000 ● 999

10. 2,000 ● 199,999

11. 89,406 ● 89,406

12. 33,333 ● 333,333

List the numbers in order from least to greatest.

13. 4,372   5,816   3,204

14. 2,222   2,111   2,000

15. 6,493   6,512   6,399   6,284

16. 6,700   6,791   6,750   6,718

17. 10,900   9,999   19,100

18. 500,000   500,500   500,005

19. 327,902   327,892   372,219

20. 76,822   76,191   76,533

Solve each problem.

21. An African elephant eats about 775 pounds of food a day. How much food does the elephant eat in one week? (1 week = 7 days)

22. The Mann School basketball team played 32 games last season. 2,304 points were scored by the team. How many points did the team average per game?

23. A queen honeybee can live about 43 times as long as a worker honeybee. If the queen can live 1,892 days, how long can a worker live?

24. A river hippopotamus weighs about 1,125 kilograms more than a pygmy hippopotamus. If a pygmy hippo weighs 225 kilograms, how much does a river hippo weigh?

25. The Green Bay Packers play some home games at Lambeau Field, which contains 56,267 seats. They play other home games at County Stadium in Milwaukee, which has 55,898 seats. How many more seats are in Lambeau Field than in County Stadium?

26. *Estimation* An airline had 26 flights between Toronto and London last month. Each flight carried an average of 196 passengers. Estimate the total number of passengers on the 26 flights.

Cumulative Test, Chapters 1-3

Give the letter for the correct answer.

1. What is 2,046 in expanded form?

   A 2,000 + 400 + 60
   B 2,000 + 40 + 6
   C 2 + 4 + 6
   D 200 + 40 + 6

2. Which numbers are written in order from least to greatest?

   A 12,506   12,078   12,320
   B 12,078   12,506   12,320
   C 12,078   12,320   12,506
   D 12,320   12,078   12,506

3. Round 4,628 to the nearest thousand.

   A 4,000   C 5,600
   B 4,700   D 5,000

4. Estimate the sum. First round both numbers to the nearest hundred.

   538 + 261

   A 800   C 700
   B 900   D 600

5. Add.

   4,763
   + 5,856

   A 9,519
   B 9,619
   C 10,619
   D 10,519

6. Subtract.

   8,237
   − 4,562

   A 4,775
   B 4,675
   C 3,775
   D 3,675

7. Choose the operation that should be used to solve this problem. Then solve the problem.

   Ms. Fraser's factory produced 2,487 computers in January and 3,129 computers in March. How many computers were produced in these two months?

   A Addition; 5,616 computers
   B Subtraction; 642 computers
   C Addition; 5,606 computers
   D Subtraction; 742 computers

8. Choose the equation that should be used to solve this problem. Then solve the problem.

   The store had 123 cartons of milk at the start of the day. When the store closed, there were 47 cartons of milk. How many cartons of milk were sold?

   A $123 + 47 = n$; 170 cartons
   B $123 − 47 = n$; 76 cartons
   C $170 − 123 = n$; 47 cartons
   D $n + 47 = 76$; 29 cartons

9. Multiply.

   27 × 100

   A 27,000
   B 270
   C 2,700
   D 270,000

10. Estimate the product.

37 × 43

A 1,200   **C** 160
B 120   **D** 1,600

11. Multiply.

39
× 43

A 1,326
B 1,677
C 1,357
D 1,096

12. Choose the operation that should be used to solve this problem. Then solve the problem.

If corn sold for $3 per bushel, how much did the Williamses receive for their harvest of 4,267 bushels?

A Multiplication; $12,801
B Division; $1,422.33
C Addition; $4,270
D Subtraction; $4,264

13. What is the least common multiple of 6 and 8?

A 14   **B** 48   **C** 36   **D** 24

14. Divide.

4)138

A 32
B 37
C 34 R2
D 33 R3

15. Divide.

3)1,521

A 507
B 57
C 570
D 500 R7

16. What is the average for this set of numbers?

36   45   26   41

A 32   **C** 148
B 37   **D** 40

17. Divide.

124 ÷ 19

A 6
B 5 R14
C 5 R4
D 6 R10

18. Divide.

80)36,572

A 432 R82
B 457 R12
C 407 R82
D 456 R92

19. Divide.

25)7,538

A 310 R13
B 300 R13
C 301 R13
D 31 R13

20. Choose the equation that should be used to solve this problem. Then solve the problem.

King School purchased 18 desks. The total cost was $2,052. How much did each desk cost?

A $2,052 + 18 = n; $2,070
B $2,052 − 18 = n; $2,034
C $2,052 ÷ 18 = n; $114
D $2,052 × 18 = n; $36,936

Addition and Subtraction of Decimals

$0.10 + $0.75 + $1.75 = $2.60

Meaning of Decimals

Clocks have become more accurate over the centuries.

Type of clock	Gain or loss per day
First pendulum (1656)	Ten seconds
Temperature pendulum (1726)	One second
Barometric pendulum (1835)	One-tenth second
Improved pendulum (1893)	One-hundredth second
Free pendulum (1924)	One-thousandth second
Atomic (1952)	One-millionth second

A. If 1 one is divided into 10 equal parts, each part is 1 *tenth*.

The *decimal* for 1 tenth is 0.1.

1 one = 10 tenths

1 tenth ⟶ 0.1

B. If 1 tenth is divided into 10 equal parts, each part is 1 *hundredth*.

1 tenth = 10 hundredths
1 one = 100 hundredths

1 hundredth ⟶ 0.01

C. If 1 hundredth is divided into 10 equal parts, each part is 1 *thousandth*.

1 hundredth = 10 thousandths
1 one = 1,000 thousandths

1 thousandth ⟶ 0.001

D.

thousands	hundreds	tens	ones	tenths	hundredths	thousandths
			0	0	3	2

0.032
thirty-two thousandths

Try

a. Write 0.913 in words.

b. Give the missing number.

1 one = ▨ hundredths

c. Write the decimal for one hundred three thousandths.

Practice   Write each decimal in words.

1. 0.05   **2.** 0.5   **3.** 0.005   **4.** 0.37   **5.** 0.895   **6.** 0.046

Write the decimal.

7. seven tenths

8. nine tenths

9. fifty-eight hundredths

10. nineteen hundredths

11. one hundred sixty-one thousandths

12. nine hundred five thousandths

13. two thousandths

14. six hundredths

15. twelve thousandths

16. seventy-nine hundredths

Give each missing number.

17. 1 one = ▨ tenths

18. 1 tenth = ▨ hundredths

19. 1 one = ▨ thousandths

20. 1 hundredth = ▨ thousandths

★21. 1 hundred = ▨ thousandths

★22. 1 thousand = ▨ thousandths

Apply   Solve each problem.

23. Juanita's watch lost three thousandths second a day. Write this as a decimal.

24. The Sanders' grandfather clock loses 0.35 second a day. Write this decimal in words.

Numeration

The World Clock of Jens Olsen gives the time everywhere in the world, important dates, and information about the planets and stars.

One of the hands on this clock moves around once every 6,798.361524 days. This number is shown in the place-value chart.

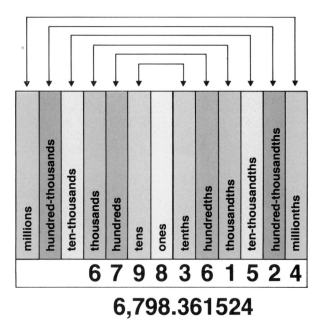

millions	hundred-thousands	ten-thousands	thousands	hundreds	tens	ones	tenths	hundredths	thousandths	ten-thousandths	hundred-thousandths	millionths
6	7	9	8	3	6	1	5	2	4

6,798.361524

six thousand seven hundred ninety-eight and three hundred sixty-one thousand five hundred twenty-four millionths

6,798.361524 has six decimal places.

The digit 5 is in the ten-thousandths place.

Try

a. Write the decimal for 2 tens 2 hundredths.

b. Write the decimal for forty-two and sixteen hundred-thousandths.

c. Count the number of decimal places in 6.100.

d. Tell what the 4 means in 207.00843.

Practice Tell what each 8 means.

1. 1.84   **2.** 3.0018   **3.** 2.08   **4.** 0.00008   **5.** 480.011

Tell how many decimal places are in each number.

6. 3.14   **7.** 61.0903   **8.** 1.941   **9.** 100.0   **10.** 0.670

In each exercise, place a decimal point to show 3 decimal places.

11. 562   **12.** 137   **13.** 8430   **14.** 64328   **15.** 4000

Write each decimal.

16. 8 ones 7 hundredths

17. 5 tens 3 ones 8 thousandths

18. 6 hundreds 3 thousandths

19. 7 thousands 7 thousandths

20. 6 tenths 4 hundredths
5 thousandths 3 ten-thousandths

21. 2 tenths 2 thousandths
2 hundred-thousandths

22. twenty-seven ten-thousandths

23. sixty-five millionths

24. one and eighteen thousandths

25. seventy-six and twelve hundredths

26. eighty-five and five hundred
seventy-one thousandths

27. six thousand four and six hundred
ninety-four ten-thousandths

Apply Solve each problem.

28. One of the hands on the World Clock comes to a standstill every 173.31001 days. Write the decimal in words.

29. The World Clock loses 0.0013 second every year. Tell what the 1 means in this number.

30. Leap years are shown on the calendar of the World Clock. If the number of a year like 1492 is divisible by 4, it is a leap year. Was 1492 a leap year?

31. An exception to the rule in Problem 30 is that years divisible by 100 must also be divisible by 400 to be leap years. Will 2000 be a leap year?

Comparing and Ordering Decimals

A. The stopwatch shows
90 hundredths of a second.

90 hundredths = 9 tenths

0.90 = 0.9

These decimals are *equal decimals*.

0.90 = 0.90 = 0.900 = 0.9000

B. Compare the numbers.

0.825 ● 0.82

↓ ↓   Write with the same number of decimal places.

0.825 ● 0.820

0.825 > 0.820   Compare as with whole numbers. 825 > 820

↓ ↓

0.825 > 0.82

C. Order the numbers from least to greatest.

0.44	0.4	0.404	
↓	↓	↓	Write with the same number of decimal places.
0.440	0.400	0.404	

0.400	0.404	0.440	Order as with whole numbers.
↓	↓	↓	
0.4	0.404	0.44	

Try

a. Write 15.6 in hundredths.

b. Write 6.70 in tenths.

c. Compare. Use <, >, or =.

1.23 ● 1.3

d. List 0.2, 0.22, and 0.202 in order from least to greatest.

e. Give a number for the lettered point on the number line.

```
      0.7              1.2
  <----•--•--•--•--•--•--•--•--•--•---->
           X
```

Practice Write each number in hundredths.

1. 0.7 **2.** 0.1 **3.** 9.9 **4.** 7.3 **5.** 6 **6.** 12.200

Write each number in thousandths.

7. 0.16 **8.** 0.59 **9.** 1.3 **10.** 15.06 **11.** 8 **12.** 0.0090

Compare. Use <, >, or =.

13. 0.6 ● 0.8 **14.** 0.54 ● 0.37 **15.** 0.50 ● 0.5

16. 0.84 ● 0.829 **17.** 0.737 ● 0.733 **18.** 4.89 ● 4.88

19. 5.091 ● 5.09 **20.** 4.1 ● 4.011 **21.** 6.4 ● 6.359

22. 6.29 ● 9 **23.** 3 ● 3.89 **24.** 200.8 ● 200.80

List these numbers in order from least to greatest.

25. 0.67 0.6 0.7 **26.** 0.25 0.52 0.052 **27.** 3.48 4.2 3.8

28. 6.8 8.66 8.06 **29.** 0.8 0.88 0.808 **30.** 4.0 3.44 4.044

Give a number for each letter point.

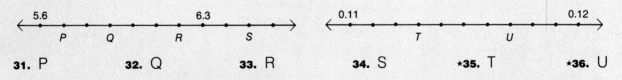

31. P **32.** Q **33.** R **34.** S **★35.** T **★36.** U

Apply The chart gives the top runners of the 100-yard dash.

37. Who came in first?

38. Who came in last?

★39. List the names in order, beginning with the person who was first.

100-Yard Dash	
Ron Jensen	16.21 seconds
Alice Pajac	16.10 seconds
Marí Tomas	16.15 seconds
Alex Reed	16.09 seconds

Rounding Decimals

A. In Norway, there is an average of 36.7 people per square mile. Round this to the nearest one.

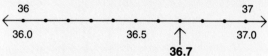

The number line shows that 36.7 is between 36 and 37. It is closer to 37.

36.7
↓
37

Notice that the digit to the right of the ones digit is greater than 5, so 1 is added to the ones digit.

There are about 37 people per square mile in Norway.

B. Round each number to the nearest hundredth.

4.152
↓
4.15

The digit to the right of the hundredths digit is less than 5. The hundredths digit stays the same.

0.588
↓
0.59

The digit to the right of the hundredths digit is greater than 5. Add 1 to the hundredths digit.

1.035
↓
1.04

The digit to the right of the hundredths digit is 5. Add 1 to the hundredths digit.

Try Round to the nearest one.

a. 9.43   **b.** 6.0   **c.** $9.98

Round to the nearest tenth.

d. 1.058   **e.** 21.7   **f.** 0.99

Practice Round to the nearest one.

1. 7.2

2. 3.8

3. 9.5

4. 98.5

5. 39.6

6. 8.87

7. $4.39

8. $6.48

9. $0.82

Round to the nearest tenth.

10. 0.68

11. 0.81

12. 0.35

13. 3.97

14. 8.99

15. 0.519

Round to the nearest hundredth.

16. 0.548

17. 2.341

18. 7.498

19. 6.399

20. 0.005

21. 0.06

Round to the nearest thousandth.

22. 6.3045

23. 9.7165

24. 0.00318

25. 0.00573

26. 0.4693

27. 0.0095

Apply Round each number to the nearest one.

	Country	People per Square Mile
28.	India	519.13
29.	United States	62.43
30.	Indonesia	206.65
31.	Australia	4.93

★32. List Norway and the countries in Problems 28–31 in order, beginning with the country with the least number of people per square mile.

To use your calculator to round to the nearest one, add 0.5 to the number to be rounded. The rounded number is the whole-number part of the display.

Round 2.3 to the nearest one.

Press: 2.3 [+] 0.5 [=]

Display: *2.8*

2.3 rounds to 2.

Round 5.812 to the nearest one.

Press: 5.812 [+] 0.5 [=]

Display: *6.312*

5.812 rounds to 6.

Use your calculator to round each number to the nearest one.

1. 8.1

2. 8.6

3. 9.8

4. 9.5

5. 11.5

6. 11.2

7. 7.83

8. 3.704

9. Explain how you would use your calculator to round 31.781 to the nearest tenth.

Estimating Sums and Differences

Past records show that the monthly rainfall in Jakarta, Indonesia, is as follows.

Jan. 11.81	Feb. 11.81	Mar. 8.31	Apr. 5.79	May 4.49	June 3.82
July 2.52	Aug. 1.69	Sept. 2.60	Oct. 4.41	Nov. 5.59	Dec. 7.99

A. Estimate the number of inches of rain that can be expected to fall in October, November, and December.

Estimate 4.41 + 5.59 + 7.99.

4.41 + 5.59 + 7.99   Round each number to the nearest one.

↓   ↓   ↓

4   **+ 6**   **+ 8**   **= 18**   Then add.

About 18 inches of rain can be expected.

B. Estimate 11.81 − 7.99.

11.81 − 7.99   Round each number to the nearest one.

↓   ↓

12   **− 8**   **= 4**   Subtract.

Try *Estimation* Estimate each sum or difference. Round to the nearest one.

a. 8.6 + 7.2   **b.** $25.18 + $21 + $6.92

c. 9.8 − 2.3   **d.** $51.91 − $18.49

Practice *Estimation* Estimate each sum or difference.
Round to the nearest one.

1. $2.3 + 6.8$ **2.** $5.8 + 7.9$ **3.** $30.2 + 15.1$ **4.** $99.7 + 60.2$

5. $4.216 + 8.19$ **6.** $9.02 + 4.796$ **7.** $8.7 - 4.1$ **8.** $7.2 - 5.8$

9. $20.3 - 14.9$ **10.** $159.1 - 99.8$ **11.** $19.1 - 4.093$ **12.** $7.998 - 4.5$

13. $\$1.98 + \$2.32$ **14.** $\$3.25 + \$4.67$ **15.** $\$4.16 + \$6.23$

16. $\$19.95 + \$6.85$ **17.** $\$49.50 + \$20.48$ **18.** $\$99.99 + \$69.85$

19. $\$8.42 - \$6.13$ **20.** $\$78.53 - \$5.19$ **21.** $\$10.15 - \$9.97$

22. $\$100 - \$4.54$ **23.** $\$10 - \$0.89$ **24.** $\$50 - \$7.98$

25. $\$31.83 + \$24.59 + \$1.98$ **26.** $\$218 + \$253.69 + \$37.25$

Apply *Estimation* Use the table on page 108.

For each exercise, estimate the total number of inches of
rain that can be expected to fall in the given months.

27. June, July, August   **28.** January, February   ★**29.** Entire year

For each exercise, estimate the difference in rainfall for
the two months.

30. February and June   **31.** April and August   **32.** May and September

MAINTENANCE

Add or subtract.

1. $287 + 39$ **2.** $376 - 62$ **3.** $1,271 - 552$

4. $3,741 + 688$ **5.** $1,826 + 2,938$ **6.** $17,620 - 8,957$

7. $6,000 - 1,379$ **8.** $38,062 + 27,879$ **9.** $20,001 - 11,982$

10. $12,630 + 8,497 + 23,200$ **11.** $6,400 + 75,630 + 124,752$

Adding Decimals

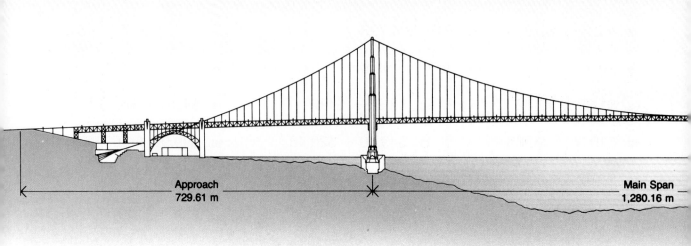

Approach
729.61 m

Main Span
1,280.16 m

A. The picture shows the Golden Gate Bridge in San Francisco. What is the total length of the bridge?

Find 729.61 + 1,280.16 + 779.63.

```
  1 1  1 1 1
    7 2 9.6 1
  1,2 8 0.1 6
+   7 7 9.6 3
  ─────────────
  2,7 8 9.4 0
```

The bridge is 2,789.4 meters long.

B. Find 8 + 0.8 + 0.808.

```
  1
    8.0 0 0     Write each decimal with the same
    0.8 0 0     number of decimal places.
+   0.8 0 8     Line up the decimal points and add.
  ─────────
    9.6 0 8     Put the decimal point in the answer.
```

Try Add.

a. 8.42
      + 9.39

b. 8.61
       0.403
      + 5.9

c. 28.3 + 5.062 + 4

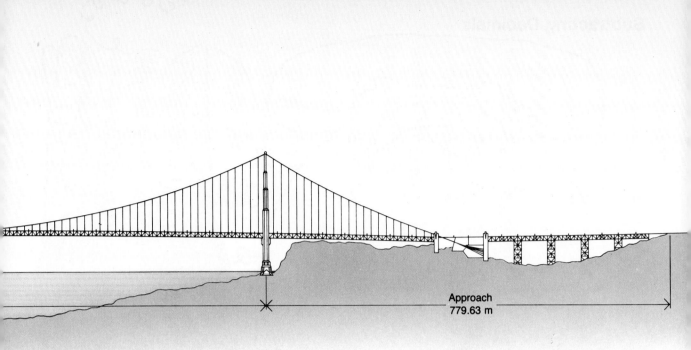

Approach
779.63 m

Practice Add.

1. 3.7
  + 8.9

2. 4.5
  + 6.8

3. 48.7
  + 5.3

4.   3.9
  + 28.1

5. 6.75
  + 5.48

6. 3.741
  + 9.688

7. 38.062
  + 27.879

8.   5.634
   78.95
  + 2.4

9. 82.74
   8.904
  + 6.5

10. 72.63
   8.497
  + 23.2

11. 29.6 + 13.62

12. 15.68 + 37.4

13. 85.5 + 2.638

14. 1.073 + 772

15. 12.5 + 6 + 9.08

16. 29.34 + 8.67 + 7

Apply Solve each problem.

17. The main span of the Mackinac Bridge is 1,158.24 meters long. Each of the two approaches is 548.84 meters long. What is the length of the bridge?

★18. The total length of the Ponte 25 deAbril is 1,960 meters. Each of the two approaches is 483.5 meters long. How long is the main span?

Subtracting Decimals

Telephones per 100 people

Australia........39.43	Norway........38.37
Ecuador.........2.71	United States....73.47
Indonesia........0.23	Zaire...........0.17

A. How many more telephones per 100 people are there in the United States than in Australia?

Find 73.47 − 39.43.

```
  6 13
 7 3.4 7     Line up the decimal points and
-3 9.4 3     subtract as with whole numbers.
 3 4.0 4     Put the decimal point in the answer.
```

There are 34.04 more telephones per 100 people in the United States than in Australia.

B. Find 1 − 0.681.

```
 1.0 0 0     Write 1 as       9 9
-0.6 8 1     1.000 so you    1010 10
             can subtract.    1.0 0 0
                             -0.6 8 1
                              0.3 1 9
```

Try Subtract.

a. 4.26   **b.** 9.201   **c.** 80.2 − 9.815   **d.** 26 − 3.001
      − 2.36   − 2.8

112

Practice   Subtract.

1. 3.76
   − 0.62

2. 8.23
   − 4.95

3. 12.71
   − 5.52

4. 18.26
   − 9.38

5. 33.42
   − 19.12

6. 65.37
   − 24.18

7. 83.74
   − 2.567

8. 97.35
   − 4.365

9. 26.7
   − 12.426

10. 23.41
    − 11.606

11. 35.371
    − 17.4

12. 51.208
    − 27.7

13. 98.5
    − 0.634

14. 23.4
    − 0.768

15. 32
    − 18.62

16. 0.756 − 0.384

17. 0.857 − 0.242

18. 0.6 − 0.379

19. 0.2 − 0.184

20. 78 − 24.321

21. 145 − 98.643

22. 15 − 0.416

23. 23 − 0.983

What did the woman say when she looked into the flower?

Write the answers to the problems below in order, from least to greatest. The letters will give you the answer.

567 × 36   (A)

567 − 63   (I)

567 ÷ 63   (O)

567 × 63   (B)

567 + 63   (C)

Apply   Solve each problem. Use the table on page 112.

24. The number of telephones per 100 people is how much greater in Australia than in Norway?

25. In Monaco there are 87.23 more telephones per 100 people than in the United States. How many telephones are there per 100 people in Monaco?

26. Which of the six countries in the table has the greatest number of telephones per person?

Problem Solving: Use a Table

Read   The Booster Club is selling hot dogs, tacos, and juice at the fun fair. If tacos cost $0.75 each and juice costs $0.35 a cup, what is the most that Ralph can buy with $2.50?

Plan   Make a table showing the cost of each combination of juice and tacos. Stop when the total cost is more than $2.50.

Solve   Make the table. Fill in the first row to show the cost of 0 tacos and cups of juice. Fill in the second row to show the cost of 1 taco and cups of juice, and so on.

Cups of Juice

	0	1	2	3	4	5	6	7	8
0	0	0.35	0.70	1.05	1.40	1.75	2.10	2.45	2.80
1	0.75	1.10	1.45	1.80	2.15	2.50	2.85		
2	1.50	1.85	2.20	2.55					
3	2.25	2.60							
4	3.00								

Tacos

Answer   Ralph can buy 7 cups of juice, or 1 taco and 5 cups of juice, or 2 tacos and 2 cups of juice, or 3 tacos.

Look Back There are 4 possible combinations given in the answer and in the table.

Try Use the table on page 114 to solve each problem.

a. What is the most that Terry can buy with $1.75?

b. Larry had $2.25 and wants 2 cups of juice. How many tacos can he also buy?

Apply Solve each problem.

1. Two kinds of fun-fair tickets are sold. Red tickets cost $0.25 each and blue tickets cost $0.15 each. Make a table showing the total cost of all combinations of red tickets and blue tickets costing $1.25 or less.

2. Irene has $1.25 to spend. How many blue tickets can she buy if she buys 1 red ticket?

3. Irene has $1.25 to spend. How many blue tickets can she buy if she buys 4 red tickets?

4. The Booster Club can buy hot dogs in packages of 32 and in packages of 48. Make a table showing the total number of hot dogs in all combinations of packages of 32 and packages of 48 totaling 200 hot dogs or fewer.

5. The club plans to buy 200 hot dogs. How many packages of 32 should the club buy if it buys 1 package of 48?

∗6. Suppose packages of 32 hot dogs cost $7 and packages of 48 hot dogs cost $10. Which combination gives 200 hot dogs at the cheapest price?

Practice: Adding and Subtracting Decimals

Estimation Estimate each sum or difference.
Round to the nearest one.

1. 4.2 + 8.6

2. 9.4 + 4.6

3. 26.2 − 14.8

4. 19.1 − 12.9

5. 19.14 + 18.92

6. 24.27 − 13.81

7. $6.25 + $9.50

8. $20.73 + $52.08

9. $26.50 − $19.11

10. $47.13 − $24.07

11. $10 − $1.13

12. $14.56 − $9

Add or subtract.

13. 9.2
    + 8.7

14. 47.6
    + 82.9

15. 9.812
    + 5.97

16. 9.6
    + 84.21

17. 7.4
    − 3.5

18. 8.6
    − 4.9

19. 12.34
    − 5.12

20. 46.93
    − 5.41

21. 9.61
    + 8.49

22. 11.8
    + 4.92

23. 21.6
    − 5.87

24. 93.1
    − 4.79

25. 3.28
    + 8.57

26. 4.812
    − 3.11

27. 62
    − 43.47

28. 4.3 − 3.777

29. 5.29 + 1.82 + 8.5

30. 49.2 − 8.42

31. 1.52 + 9.21

32. 26.82 + 41.93

33. 8.15 − 3.87

34. 5.6 − 2.88

35. 8.6 + 5.21 + 0.912

36. 23.4 + 8.21 + 9

37. 21.8 + 1.42

38. 100 − 0.57

39. 127.81 + 0.6 + 92

Solve each problem.

After the fun fair, the Booster Club found that they took in this amount of money:

Hot dogs	$98.50
Caramel apples	$71.55
Juice	$78.05
Popcorn	$47.25

40. _Estimation_ Estimate the total amount the Booster Club took in. Round each number to the nearest one.

41. The juice cost the club $44.77. How much did the Booster Club make on the sale of the juice?

42. The hot dogs cost the club $41.37 and the buns cost $12.08. How much did the Booster Club pay for hot dogs and buns?

43. How much more did the Booster Club take in from the sale of caramel apples than from the sale of popcorn?

44. Brian went to the fun fair with $5. He left with $0.85. How much did Brian spend at the fair?

COMPUTER

BASIC: REM Statements

REM statements are remarks in a program. They give information to someone reading the program. They are ignored by the computer and are not part of the output. Output is what the computer prints. A REM statement can be anywhere in the program before end.

```
10 REM ADDING DECIMALS
20 PRINT "THE ANSWER IS"
30 PRINT 32.17 + 5.875
40 END
```
Output
```
THE ANSWER IS
38.045
```

1. Write a program that will print your favorite book and movie. Use a REM statement before each PRINT statement.

2. Give the output for the program that you wrote for Exercise 1.

3. Write a program using only PRINT statements that will give the answers to the following exercises as output. Use a REM statement to give a brief description of the program.

$$23.7 - 9.85$$
$$7.19 - 3$$
$$1.02 - 0.75$$

4. Give the output for the program that you wrote for Exercise 3.

Problem Solving: Try and Check

Read   Together Mauricio and Frances spent $9 at the fun fair. Mauricio spent $4 more than Frances. How much did Frances spend?

Plan   Choose a number for the amount Frances spent. Then add $4 to find the amount Mauricio would have spent. Add the two amounts together, and if the sum is $9, your choice is correct. Otherwise, choose again.

Solve   First choice: $3

$ 3   Frances
+   7   Mauricio ($3 + $4 = $7)
$10   The total spent is more than $9, so the choice of $3 is too high.

Second choice: $2

$2   Frances
+ 6   Mauricio
$8   The total spent is less than $9, so the choice of $2 is too low.

Since $3 is too high, and $2 is too low, choose a number between $2 and $3. Choose $2.50.

$2.50   Frances
+ 6.50   Mauricio
$9.00   The total is $9.

Answer   Frances spent $2.50.

Look Back $6.50 − 2.50 = $4, so Mauricio spent $4 more than Frances, and together they spent $9.

118

Try Try and check to solve the problem.

a. The sum of two numbers is 23 and their difference is 4. What are the two numbers?

Practice Try and check to solve each problem.

1. Tricia bought 19 fun-fair tickets. If she bought 5 more red tickets than blue tickets, how many of each kind did she buy?

2. Don spent $5 for fun-fair tickets. If he spent $2 more for red tickets than for blue tickets, how much did he spend for each kind of ticket?

3. Ruth sold 112 cups of orange and grape juice. If she sold 18 more cups of orange juice than grape juice, how many cups of each kind did she sell?

4. The Witching-Pond game earned $17 less than the Spook House. Together these two attractions earned $142. How much did the Spook House earn?

5. The sum of two numbers is 38 and their difference is 4. Find each number.

6. The sum of two numbers is 12. One number is 2 times the other. What are the two numbers?

7. One number is 3.5 more than another number. The sum of the two numbers is 10.5. What are the two numbers?

8. The difference of two numbers is 2.8 and their sum is 6.2. What are the two numbers?

9. Fill in the circles at the right with these numbers so that the sum of the numbers in each row is the same. Use each number once.

   6.35 8 9.65 11.3 12.95

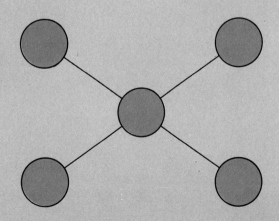

*10. Find another solution to Problem 9, using a different number in the center circle.

*11. Find still another solution to Problem 9.

Chapter 4 Test

1. Write 0.873 in words.

2. Give the missing number.

   1 one = ▧ thousandths

3. Write the decimal for three hundred six thousandths.

4. Write the decimal for 6 tens 6 hundredths.

5. Write the decimal for fifty-two and eighteen hundred-thousandths.

6. Count the number of decimal places in 6.40.

7. Tell what the 6 means in 528.00026.

8. Write 7.9 in hundredths.

9. Write 18.20 in tenths.

10. Compare. Use <, >, or =.

    1.47 ● 1.5

11. List 0.9, 0.09, and 0.909 in order from least to greatest.

Round to the nearest one.

12. 6.72   13. 4.2   14. $7.53

Round to the nearest tenth.

15. 2.468   16. 3.03   17. 7.96

Estimate each sum or difference. Round to the nearest one.

18. 7.2 + 3.8   19. 9.3 − 3.5

20. $17.25 + $34 + $4.89

21. $52.38 − $20.05

Add.

22. $\begin{array}{r} 6.78 \\ + 8.36 \\ \hline \end{array}$ 23. $\begin{array}{r} 4.8 \\ + 0.039 \\ \hline \end{array}$

24. 42.7 + 4.036 + 8

Subtract.

25. $\begin{array}{r} 5.32 \\ - 2.46 \\ \hline \end{array}$ 26. $\begin{array}{r} 8.3 \\ - 2.47 \\ \hline \end{array}$

27. 52.3 − 4.32   28. 38 − 6.056

Solve the problem.

29. Donna can buy rolls in packages of 10 and in packages of 12. Make a table showing the total number of rolls in all combinations of packages of 10 and packages of 12. Stop when the total number of rolls is more than 50.

Try and check to solve the problem.

30. The sum of two numbers is 6.2 and their difference is 2.4. Find the numbers.

CHALLENGE

Density of Numbers

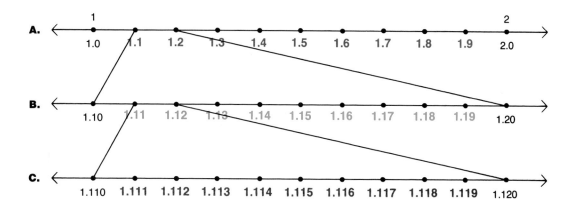

A.
1   2
1.0   1.1   1.2   1.3   1.4   1.5   1.6   1.7   1.8   1.9   2.0

B.
1.10   1.11   1.12   1.13   1.14   1.15   1.16   1.17   1.18   1.19   1.20

C.
1.110   1.111   1.112   1.113   1.114   1.115   1.116   1.117   1.118   1.119   1.120

There are no whole numbers between 1 and 2, but there are other numbers.

A. Find numbers between 1 and 2.

Write 1 and 2 in tenths. Number line A shows some numbers between 1 and 2.

B. Find numbers between 1.1 and 1.2.

Write 1.1 and 1.2 in hundredths. Number line B shows some numbers between 1.1 and 1.2. These numbers are also between 1 and 2.

C. Find numbers between 1.11 and 1.12.

Write 1.11 and 1.12 in thousandths. Number line C shows some numbers between 1.11 and 1.12. These numbers are also between 1.1 and 1.2 and between 1 and 2.

D. Find a number between 1.999 and 2.

$1.999 \rightarrow 1.9990 \qquad 2 \rightarrow 2.0000$

1.9991 is between 1.9990 and 2.0000, so 1.9991 is between 1.999 and 2.

Find a number between the given numbers.

1. 5 and 6

2. 10 and 11

3. 4.2 and 4.3

4. 3.7 and 3.8

5. 1.99 and 2

6. 4.99 and 5

7. 0.001 and 0.002

8. 0 and 0.000001

9. Find 20 different numbers between 1.999 and 2.

10. Are there any numbers between 0.5 and 0.50? Explain your answer.

121

MAINTENANCE

Find n.

1. $68 + n = 93$

2. $n + 64 = 103$

3. $6 \times n = 252$

4. $n \times 9 = 162$

5. $73 + n = 136$

6. $5 \times n = 455$

7. $4 \times n = 268$

8. $89 = 46 + n$

9. $135 = n + 25$

10. $172 = n + 148$

11. $n + 53 = 200$

12. $931 = 278 + n$

13. $1,500 = n \times 60$

14. $40 \times n = 1,800$

15. $42 \times n = 882$

16. $n \times 78 = 936$

17. $1,972 = 1,250 + n$

18. $n + 792 = 2,343$

19. $n + 540 = 782$

20. $932 = 278 + n$

21. $6 \times n = 348$

22. $4,680 = 36 \times n$

23. $192 = n + 25$

24. $42 \times n = 3,738$

25. $5 \times n = 130,000$

26. $n + 53 = 100$

27. $4,481 = 1,572 + n$

Solve each problem.

28. The population of Ridgeville is 8,279. 3,115 of these people are under age 18. How many are 18 or over?

29. A hummingbird's heart beats about 900 times per minute. How many times does it beat per second? (1 minute = 60 seconds)

30. After Milly spent $2.84 for a book, she had $1.95 left. How much money did she have before she bought the book?

31. George Washington was born in 1732. How many years ago was he born?

32. The air distance between New York and Paris is 5,854 kilometers. A pilot made 8 one-way trips. How many kilometers did the pilot travel?

33. A queen honeybee can live about 43 times as long as a worker honeybee. If a worker can live for 45 days, how long can a queen honeybee live?

★34. The elevators to the top of the Sears Tower each hold 40 people. One day 3,288 people visited the tower. What was the fewest number of elevator trips needed?

35. *Estimation* Suppose 3,288 people visit the Sears Tower each day. Estimate how many people visit the tower each month. Use 30 days for one month.

Multiplication and Division of Decimals

chapter 5

31 g protein
638 mg calcium
0.75 mg niacin
66 mg vitamin C

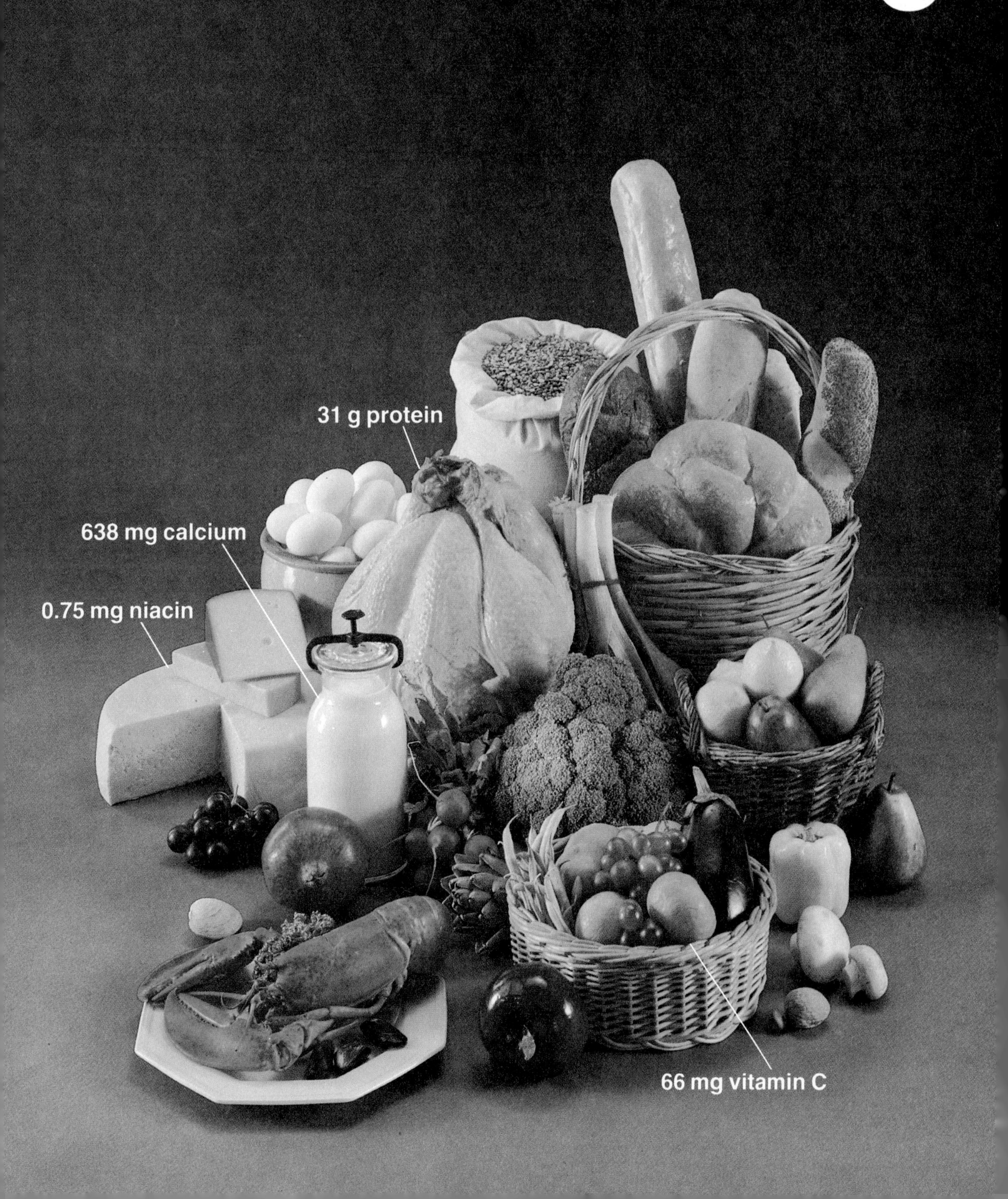

Multiplying Decimals

A. Del Medico's Pizzeria offers a pizza buffet for $4.05 for adults. For children under twelve, the charge is 30 cents times their age. Tanya is 11 years old. How much will her meal cost?

Find 0.30 × 11.

```
     1 1  ← 0 decimal places
  × 0.3 0  ← 2 decimal places
    3.3 0  ← 0 + 2, or 2, decimal places
```

Tanya's meal will cost $3.30.

To multiply decimals, first multiply as with whole numbers. Then count the total number of decimal places in the factors. Show that number of decimal places in the product.

B. Find 1.2 × 3.64.

```
    3.6 4  ← 2 decimal places
  ×   1.2  ← 1 decimal place
    7 2 8
  3 6 4 0
  4.3 6 8  ← 2 + 1, or 3, decimal places
```

Try Place a decimal point correctly in each circled number.

a. 8.16 × 3.002 = (2449632)

b. 215 × 0.688 = (147920)

Multiply.

c. 18 × 0.43   **d.** 0.45 × 3.6

e. 79.1 × 60.4

Practice   Place a decimal point correctly in each circled number.

1. $3.1 \times 56 = \boxed{1736}$ 2. $0.87 \times 2.09 = \boxed{18183}$ 3. $2.6 \times 7.22 = \boxed{18772}$

4. $4.6 \times 2.9 = \boxed{1334}$ 5. $6.008 \times 1.4 = \boxed{84112}$ 6. $3 \times 1.1101 = \boxed{33303}$

★7. $0.8 \times \boxed{6154} = 4.9232$ ★8. $\boxed{4} \times 1.23 = 0.492$ ★9. $\boxed{5} \times 6.73 = 0.3365$

Multiply.

10. $\begin{array}{r} 14.8 \\ \times\ \ \ 7 \\ \hline \end{array}$
11. $\begin{array}{r} 1.48 \\ \times\ \ \ 7 \\ \hline \end{array}$
12. $\begin{array}{r} 1.48 \\ \times\ 0.7 \\ \hline \end{array}$
13. $\begin{array}{r} 24.6 \\ \times\ \ \ 8 \\ \hline \end{array}$
14. $\begin{array}{r} 0.246 \\ \times\ \ 0.8 \\ \hline \end{array}$
15. $\begin{array}{r} 24.6 \\ \times 0.08 \\ \hline \end{array}$

16. $\begin{array}{r} 4.15 \\ \times\ 0.5 \\ \hline \end{array}$
17. $\begin{array}{r} 235 \\ \times 0.05 \\ \hline \end{array}$
18. $\begin{array}{r} 307 \\ \times\ 2.5 \\ \hline \end{array}$
19. $\begin{array}{r} 6.17 \\ \times\ 1.3 \\ \hline \end{array}$
20. $\begin{array}{r} 8,099 \\ \times\ 0.25 \\ \hline \end{array}$
21. $\begin{array}{r} 7.25 \\ \times\ 6.4 \\ \hline \end{array}$

22. 0.7×9.3 23. 0.09×2.13 24. 0.04×22.13 25. 16×7.4

26. 4.5×6.12 27. 7.04×342 28. 8.15×0.794 29. 3.14×0.302

Apply   Solve each problem.

30. Find the cost of the pizza buffet for Tanya's 9-year-old brother, Tim.

★31. Find the cost of the pizza buffet for a party of 7 adults and two 8-year-old children.

Multiplying Decimals: Zeros in the Product

A. *Career* Mrs. Del Medico owns the pizzeria. She listed her costs for toppings on a small deluxe pizza. Find the cost of the onions.

Item	Cost per pound (lb)	Amount used
Pepperoni	$2.95	0.25 lb
Green peppers	$0.60	0.15 lb
Onions	$0.32	0.12 lb
Mushrooms	$1.78	0.16 lb

Find 0.32 × 0.12.

```
0.12  ← 2 decimal places        0.12
×0.32 ← 2 decimal places       ×0.32
  24                             24
 360                            360       To show 4 decimal
 384                         0.00384      places in the product,
                                          you need to write an
                                          extra 0.
```

To the nearest cent, the onions cost $0.04.

B. Find 0.013 × 0.65.

```
   0.65
 ×0.013
    195     To show 5 decimal
    650     places in the product,
0.00845     you need to write
            2 extra zeros.
```

Try Multiply.

a. 0.2
       ×0.4

b. 0.046
       × 0.14

c. 0.7 × 0.9 × 0.11

Practice Multiply.

1. 0.5
    × 0.7

2. 0.05
    × 0.7

3. 0.005
    × 0.7

4. 0.304
    × 0.6

5. 0.603
    × 0.05

6. 0.09
    × 0.6

7. 0.04
    × 0.08

8. 0.903
    × 0.04

9. 2.05
    × 0.03

10. 7.08
    × 9

11. 0.063
    × 0.48

12. 0.0218
    × 0.17

13. 0.0055
    × 9.2

14. 0.183
    × 0.602

15. 0.073
    × 0.84

16. 0.5 × 0.07 × 0.03

17. 0.004 × 0.83 × 0.9

18. 6 × 0.001 × 5.8

19. 0.004 × 0.014 × 36

20. 0.05 × 0.008 × 0.51

21. 0.017 × 9 × 0.066

Apply Find the cost of each topping for a small vegetable pizza.

Item	Cost per pound (lb)	Amount used	Cost of topping
Black olives	$0.80	0.10 lb.	**22.**
Green peppers	$0.60	0.25 lb.	**23.**
Onions	$0.32	0.20 lb.	**24.**
Mushrooms	$1.78	0.40 lb.	**25.**

Solve each problem.

★26. Use the table on page 126. Find the total cost of the 4 toppings on a small deluxe pizza.

★27. Use the table above. Find the total cost of the 4 toppings on a small vegetable pizza.

Multiplying Decimals by 10, 100, and 1,000

A. The pizza oven at Del Medico's Pizzeria uses about 10 *therms* of natural gas per day. If the gas rate is $0.4712 per therm, how much does it cost to operate the oven for one day?

Find 10 × 0.4712.

$$
\begin{array}{r}
0.4712 \\
\times \quad 10 \\
\hline
4.7120
\end{array}
$$

It costs about $4.71 to operate the oven for one day.

B. Look for a pattern.

10 × 6.823 = 68.23

100 × 6.823 = 682.3

1,000 × 6.823 = 6,823

10 × 49.1 = 491

100 × 49.1 = 4,910

1,000 × 49.1 = 49,100

To multiply a decimal by 10, 100, or 1,000, move the decimal point one place to the right for each zero in 10, 100, or 1,000.

Try Multiply.

a. 10 × 3.9   **b.** 81.4 × 100   **c.** 1,000 × 0.6

Practice Multiply.

1. 10 × 0.9

2. 100 × 0.9

3. 1,000 × 0.9

4. 0.36 × 10

5. 0.36 × 100

6. 0.36 × 1,000

7. 6.02 × 10

8. 7.04 × 100

9. 1.53 × 1,000

10. 10 × 0.003

11. 100 × 0.065

12. 1,000 × 0.008

13. 8.304 × 10

14. 71.984 × 10

15. 6.992 × 1,000

16. 73.4 × 100

17. 0.853 × 100

18. 2.405 × 100

19. 3.2 × 1,000

20. 521.64 × 1,000

21. 0.0062 × 1,000

22. 611.08 × 1,000

23. 0.0061 × 10

24. 100 × 521.9928

★25. 0.00059 × 10,000

★26. 7.92 × 10,000

★27. 10,000 × 81.4

Apply Solve each problem.

28. In one month, about 1,000 therms of gas were used to heat Del Medico's Pizzeria. At $0.4712 per therm, how much was paid for heat for the month?

29. It costs about $0.38 per day to operate a refrigerator. How much does it cost to operate the refrigerator for 100 days?

★30. It costs $0.12 per day to operate one light bulb. How much does it cost to operate 10 light bulbs for 10 days?

★31. One therm of gas provides about 100,000 BTUs of heat for an hour. How many BTUs of heat for an hour are provided by 8.61 therms?

CALCULATOR

Jeffry multiplies 0.00018 × 0.0009. How many decimal places should there be in the answer? The display shows only 0.0000001 because the calculator has an 8-digit display. Here is a way to get the correct answer.

First multiply 18 × 9 on a calculator. Then correctly place the decimal point to get the product 0.000000162.

Use this technique to find each product.

1. 0.0008 × 0.00017

2. 0.00006 × 0.0000512

3. 0.0004 × 2.6644

4. 0.0531 × 1.0087

5. 0.1111 × 0.000099

6. 9.8789 × 0.00012

7. 0.1234 × 0.56789

8. 0.00027^2

9. 0.000087^2

Dividing a Decimal by a Whole Number

The low density of spruce wood makes it suitable for making violins. To find the *density* of a substance, divide its weight by its volume. 16 cubic centimeters (cm³) of spruce has a weight of 6.72 grams (g). Find the density of spruce in grams per cubic centimeter.

Find 6.72 ÷ 16.

$$16\overline{)6.72}$$

The divisor is a whole number. Place the decimal point in the quotient directly above the decimal point in the dividend.

$$
\begin{array}{r}
0.4\,2 \\
16\overline{)6.7\,2} \\
6\,4 \\
\hline
3\,2 \\
3\,2 \\
\hline
0
\end{array}
$$

Then divide the same way you divide whole numbers.

The density of spruce is 0.42 grams per cubic centimeter.

Check

$$
\begin{array}{r}
0.4\,2 \leftarrow \text{Quotient}\\
\times\quad 1\,6 \leftarrow \text{Divisor}\\
\hline
2\,5\,2\\
4\,2\,0\\
\hline
6.7\,2 \leftarrow \text{Dividend}
\end{array}
$$

Try Divide.

a. $8 \overline{)5.6}$

b. $13 \overline{)5.33}$

c. $6.592 \div 64$

d. $772.8 \div 56$

Practice Divide.

1. $7 \overline{)6.3}$

2. $9 \overline{)4.5}$

3. $3 \overline{)0.72}$

4. $8 \overline{)0.96}$

5. $2 \overline{)8.0}$

6. $6 \overline{)9.0}$

7. $7 \overline{)7.56}$

8. $5 \overline{)5.35}$

9. $4 \overline{)37.2}$

10. $4 \overline{)25.6}$

11. $6 \overline{)0.672}$

12. $3 \overline{)0.777}$

13. $5.04 \div 9$

14. $4.50 \div 6$

15. $9.92 \div 8$

16. $8.54 \div 7$

17. $1.827 \div 9$

18. $2.121 \div 7$

19. $87 \overline{)43.5}$

20. $76 \overline{)30.4}$

21. $38 \overline{)60.8}$

22. $23 \overline{)64.4}$

23. $23 \overline{)747.5}$

24. $44 \overline{)963.6}$

25. $8.17 \div 43$

26. $7.35 \div 35$

27. $51.50 \div 25$

28. $13.3 \div 19$

29. $13.5 \div 15$

30. $89.28 \div 62$

Apply Solve each problem.

31. A piece of balsa wood with a volume of 54 cm³ weighs 8.64 g. Find the density of balsa in grams per cubic centimeter.

32. A piece of oak with a volume of 63 cm³ weighs 44.73 g. Find the density of oak.

33. The density of spruce wood is 0.42 grams per cubic centimeter and of pine wood is 0.69 grams per cubic centimeter. What is the difference of their densities?

★34. What is the weight of a piece of spruce if its volume is 1,000 cm³?

★35. A piece of spruce and a piece of pine each have a volume of 1,000 cm³. Which piece of wood is heavier?

Writing Zeros in the Quotient

A. The sound energy from musical instruments is measured in *watts*. A large orchestra playing very loudly produces only enough energy to light a 60-watt bulb.

A piano produces 8 times as much energy as a flute when they are played at their loudest. The energy output of a piano is 0.440 watts. What is the energy output of a flute?

Find 0.440 ÷ 8.

$$\begin{array}{r} 0.0 \\ 8\overline{)0.4\,4\,0} \end{array}$$

There are no 8s in 4. Write a zero above the 4.

$$\begin{array}{r} 0.0\,5\,5 \\ 8\overline{)0.4\,4\,0} \\ 4\,0 \\ \hline 4\,0 \\ 4\,0 \\ \hline 0 \end{array}$$

Then continue to divide.

The energy output of a flute is 0.055 watts.

Check
$$\begin{array}{r} 0.0\,5\,5 \\ \times\,8 \\ \hline 0.4\,4\,0 \end{array}$$

B. Find 0.092 ÷ 23.

$$\begin{array}{r} 0.0\,0\,4 \\ 23\overline{)0.0\,9\,2} \\ 9\,2 \\ \hline 0 \end{array}$$

There are no 23s in 0 or in 9, so you need to write two zeros in the quotient.

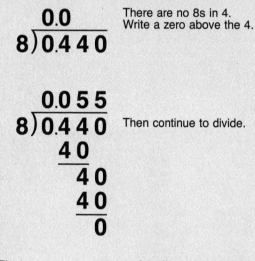

Try Divide.

a. $9\overline{)0.36}$　　　　**b.** $52\overline{)0.364}$　　　　**c.** $0.1554 \div 37$

Practice Divide.

1. $3\overline{)0.09}$　　　**2.** $6\overline{)0.42}$　　　**3.** $7\overline{)0.49}$

4. $9\overline{)0.72}$　　　**5.** $8\overline{)0.64}$　　　**6.** $6\overline{)0.024}$

7. $8\overline{)0.048}$　　　**8.** $31\overline{)2.17}$　　　**9.** $44\overline{)3.96}$

10. $71\overline{)5.68}$　　　**11.** $57\overline{)1.71}$　　　**12.** $78\overline{)4.056}$

13. $73\overline{)4.526}$　　　**14.** $56\overline{)1.1368}$　　　**15.** $41\overline{)1.6687}$

16. $39\overline{)0.0117}$　　　**17.** $84\overline{)0.0672}$　　　**18.** $78\overline{)0.0468}$

19. $3.034 \div 74$　　　　**20.** $1.105 \div 85$

21. $0.234 \div 26$　　　　**22.** $0.185 \div 37$

Apply Solve each problem.

23. A trumpet produces 6 times as much energy as a clarinet when played at their loudest. The energy output of a trumpet is 0.300 watt. What is the energy output of a clarinet?

24. When played loudly a trombone produces 80 times as much energy as a piccolo. The energy output of a trombone is 6.40 watts. What is the energy output of a piccolo?

★25. The energy output of a normal speaking voice is 0.000024 watt. 1,000,000 voices produce twice as much energy as a snare drum played loudly. What is the energy output of a snare drum?

Round to the nearest one.

1. 8.1

2. 8.6

3. 12.09

4. 29.56

5. 124.5

Round to the nearest tenth.

6. 0.46

7. 5.62

8. 0.98

9. 3.449

10. 7.306

Round to the nearest hundredth.

11. 0.068

12. 4.103

13. 9.007

14. 3.0963

15. 8.0814

More Practice Set 53, page 388

133

Problem Solving: Multiple-Step Problems

Read To raise money for charity, Todd took pledges from people who promised to give him money for every mile he ran. He listed these amounts on his sheet. What was the average pledge?

Pledge Sheet	
Name	Amount per mile
1. Mrs. Phillips	$0.10
2. Dr. Krause	$0.15
3. Ms. Wong	$0.30
4. Mr. Miller	$0.15
5. Mr. Dunn	$0.25

Plan Add the pledges. Then divide by the number of pledges to find the average.

Solve Add the pledges.   Divide by 5.

```
  0.1 0            0.1 9
  0.1 5         5)0.9 5
  0.3 0            5
  0.1 5           45
+ 0.2 5           45
  0.9 5            0
```

Answer The average pledge was $0.19 per mile.

Look Back The average pledge is greater than the smallest pledge and less than the largest pledge.

134

Try Use the pledge sheet on page 134 to solve each problem.

a. If Todd runs 8 miles, how much money will he raise for charity?

b. If Todd runs 8 miles, what is the average amount of money he will collect from each person?

Apply Solve each problem.

Phil ran 10 miles in a charity race. He took pledges of $0.05, $0.12, $0.25, $0.15, $0.10, $0.20, and $0.25 per mile.

1. Find the average pledge.

2. How much money did Phil raise for charity?

3. What is the average amount of money Phil collected from each person?

4. Rita ran in four marathons. She completed distances of 8.2 miles, 6.5 miles, 10.0 miles, and 6.1 miles. What is the average distance she ran per marathon?

5. Luis received a pledge from his mother of $0.15 per mile plus a bonus of $5.00 for running at least 10 miles. Luis ran 13 miles. How much did his mother pay?

Glynnis took pledges of $0.20, $0.45, $0.25, and $0.15 per mile. Margo took pledges of $0.30, $0.30, $0.10, $0.25, and $0.15 per mile. Suppose Glynnis runs 9 miles and Margo runs 7 miles.

★6. How much more money would Glynnis raise than Margo?

★7. If Margo took a sixth pledge, what amount would it have to be so that both girls would raise the same amount of money?

Dividing Decimals

A. Iron is a mineral needed to form *hemoglobin* in the blood. A glass of apple juice contains 1.5 milligrams (mg) of iron. A glass of prune juice contains 10.5 mg of iron. The prune juice contains how many times as much iron as the apple juice?

Find 10.5 ÷ 1.5.

$$1.5\overline{)1\,0.5}$$

So that you can divide by a whole number, multiply both the divisor and the dividend by 10. Place the decimal point in the quotient.

$$
\begin{array}{r}
7. \\
1.5\overline{)1\,0.5} \\
\underline{1\,0\,5} \\
0
\end{array}
$$

Divide 105 by 15.

The prune juice contains 7 times as much iron as the apple juice.

Check
$$
\begin{array}{r}
7 \\
\times\,1.5 \\
\hline
1\,0.5
\end{array}
$$

B. Find 0.893 ÷ 0.47.

$$0.47\overline{)0.893}$$

So that you can divide by a whole number, multiply both the divisor and the dividend by 100.

$$
\begin{array}{r}
1.9 \\
0.47\overline{)0.893} \\
\underline{47} \\
4\,2\,3 \\
\underline{4\,2\,3} \\
0
\end{array}
$$

Divide 89.3 by 47.

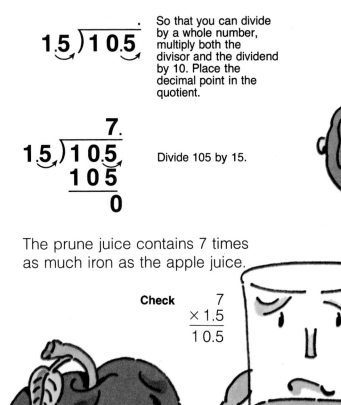

136

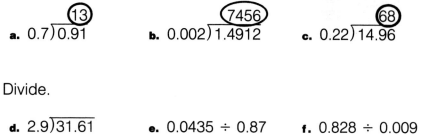

Try   Place the decimal point correctly in each circled number.

          ⑬

a. 0.7)0.91

          ⑦④⑤⑥

b. 0.002)1.4912

          ⑥⑧

c. 0.22)14.96

Divide.

d. 2.9)31.61

e. 0.0435 ÷ 0.87

f. 0.828 ÷ 0.009

Practice   Place the decimal point correctly in each circled number.

          ⑫

1. 0.7)0.84

          ⑥③

2. 0.09)5.67

          ①③⑤

3. 0.07)0.945

Divide.

4. 0.4)3.2

5. 0.4)0.32

6. 0.4)0.032

7. 0.08)0.56

8. 0.07)0.056

9. 0.05)0.0055

10. 0.04)4.04

11. 0.07)0.434

12. 0.09)0.0558

13. 0.005)0.465

14. 0.008)4.984

15. 0.043)0.645

16. 0.031)0.837

17. 0.68)1.972

18. 0.81)5.265

19. 6.5)287.95

20. 6.2)1.0788

21. 0.027)2.2248

22. 6.24 ÷ 1.3

23. 9.36 ÷ 2.4

24. 17.34 ÷ 0.51

25. 3.96 ÷ 0.18

26. 0.086 ÷ 4.3

27. 0.084 ÷ 2.1

Apply   Solve this problem.

28. One glass of milk contains 0.4 mg of *riboflavin*. An 11-year-old boy needs 1.6 mg of riboflavin each day. How many glasses of milk supply the 1.6 mg of riboflavin?

Dividing Decimals: Zeros in the Dividend

A. A 12-year-old girl needs 1.1 mg of *thiamine* each day. A lean pork chop has 0.55 mg of thiamine. How many pork chops supply the 1.1 mg of thiamine?

Find 1.1 ÷ 0.55.

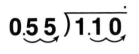

Multiply the divisor and the dividend by 100. Place the decimal point in the quotient.

$$\begin{array}{r} 2. \\ 0.55\overline{)1.10} \\ \underline{110} \\ 0 \end{array}$$

Divide 110 by 55.

2 pork chops supply 1.1 mg of thiamine.

B. Find 24 ÷ 4.8.

Multiply the divisor and the dividend by 10.

$$\begin{array}{r} 5. \\ 4.8\overline{)240.} \\ \underline{240} \\ 0 \end{array}$$

Divide 240 by 48.

Try Divide.

a. $0.18\overline{)4.5}$ **b.** $0.2\overline{)92}$

c. 20 ÷ 0.125

138

Practice Divide.

1. $0.7\overline{)0.35}$ 2. $0.7\overline{)3.5}$ 3. $0.7\overline{)35}$ 4. $0.7\overline{)350}$

5. $1.6\overline{)0.48}$ 6. $1.6\overline{)4.8}$ 7. $1.6\overline{)48}$ 8. $1.6\overline{)480}$

9. $0.05\overline{)0.085}$ 10. $0.06\overline{)0.096}$ 11. $0.08\overline{)6.4}$ 12. $0.05\overline{)75}$

13. $1.2\overline{)4.08}$ 14. $2.4\overline{)40.8}$ 15. $1.2\overline{)576}$ 16. $3.2\overline{)608}$

17. $0.6\overline{)78}$ 18. $0.2\overline{)74}$ 19. $3.5\overline{)245}$ 20. $6.2\overline{)248}$

21. $0.018\overline{)0.09}$ 22. $0.022\overline{)0.11}$ 23. $0.38\overline{)17.1}$ 24. $0.72\overline{)46.8}$

25. $0.75\overline{)70.5}$ 26. $0.62\overline{)52.7}$ 27. $0.025\overline{)87.5}$ 28. $0.054\overline{)70.2}$

29. $15 \div 0.6$ 30. $27 \div 0.5$ 31. $12.6 \div 0.84$ 32. $10.5 \div 0.75$

33. $2,040 \div 1.6$ 34. $3,650 \div 2.5$ 35. $15.345 \div 0.45$ 36. $11.752 \div 0.26$

Apply   Solve each problem.

37. A chicken potpie contains 3 mg of iron and 0.25 mg of thiamine. The iron content is how many times the thiamine content?

*38. Helene's intake of iron for one day was 6 mg at breakfast, 10 mg at lunch, and 11 mg at supper. Her total intake was 1.5 times the amount needed at her age. How much iron does Helene need each day?

*39. Mrs. Floyd took in 1.3 mg of thiamine on Monday, 0.9 mg on Tuesday, and 1.4 mg on Wednesday. Her average daily intake was 1.2 times as much as she needs each day. How much thiamine does Mrs. Floyd need each day?

CHALLENGE

Four small squares are formed by these 12 crayons. Try to reposition just 3 of the crayons so that 3 squares are formed in all.

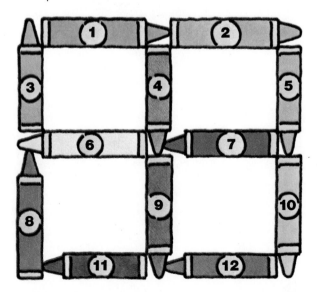

Rounding Quotients

A. A male African elephant is about 1.2 times as tall as a male Asian elephant. The African elephant is about 3.2 meters tall. Find the height of the Asian elephant to the nearest meter.

Find 3.2 ÷ 1.2.

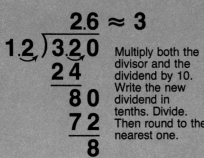

$$\begin{array}{r} 2.6 \approx 3 \\ 1.2\overline{)3.2\,0} \\ 2\,4 \\ \hline 8\,0 \\ 7\,2 \\ \hline 8 \end{array}$$

Multiply both the divisor and the dividend by 10. Write the new dividend in tenths. Divide. Then round to the nearest one.

The Asian elephant is about 3 meters tall.

B. Find 7 ÷ 19. Round the quotient to the nearest hundredth.

$$\begin{array}{r} 0.3\,6\,8 \approx 0.37 \\ 19\overline{)7.0\,0\,0} \\ 5\,7 \\ \hline 1\,3\,0 \\ 1\,1\,4 \\ \hline 1\,6\,0 \\ 1\,5\,2 \\ \hline 8 \end{array}$$

Write the dividend in thousandths. Divide. Then round to the nearest hundredth.

Try Divide.

a. Find $2 \div 7$ to the nearest hundredth.

b. Find $72.66 \div 9.5$ to the nearest tenth.

c. Find $6,456 \div 4.5$ to the nearest one.

Practice Divide. Round each quotient to the nearest one.

1. $7\overline{)170}$
2. $4\overline{)763}$
3. $1.3\overline{)56}$
4. $5.1\overline{)91}$

5. $1,074 \div 5$
6. $4,772 \div 3$
7. $2,683 \div 4.2$
8. $8,656 \div 5.3$

Divide. Round each quotient to the nearest tenth.

9. $6\overline{)2.95}$
10. $3\overline{)0.5}$
11. $6\overline{)43}$
12. $8\overline{)27}$

13. $5 \div 6$
14. $1 \div 3$
15. $3.023 \div 5.5$
16. $1.89 \div 0.46$

Divide. Round each quotient to the nearest hundredth.

17. $9.3 \div 4$
18. $5.8 \div 7$
19. $0.311 \div 0.6$
20. $1.45 \div 0.9$

21. $7 \div 22$
22. $5 \div 17$
23. $62 \div 24$
24. $97 \div 11$

Apply Solve each problem. Round each answer to the nearest tenth.

25. Asian elephants live about 1.3 times as long as African elephants. The life span of an Asian elephant is 80 years. What is the life span of an African elephant?

26. At birth, an elephant calf weighs about 90 kilograms (kg). At nine months, it weighs about 340 kg. The calf's weight at nine months is how many times its birth weight?

27. The adult African elephant weighs about 5,500 kg. How many times its birth weight of 90 kg is this?

*28. In the wild, an African elephant consumes about 50,000 kg of food each year. How much food does it consume each day?

Dividing Decimals by 10, 100, and 1,000

A. *Career* Ms. Ogutu is a park ranger in Kenya, Africa. To determine the running speeds of various wild animals, she recorded the distances they traveled in 10 seconds.

Find the speed of the lion in meters per second.

Find $220 \div 10$.

$$
\begin{array}{r}
22 \\
10\overline{)220} \\
\underline{20} \\
20 \\
\underline{20} \\
0
\end{array}
$$

The speed of the lion is 22 meters per second.

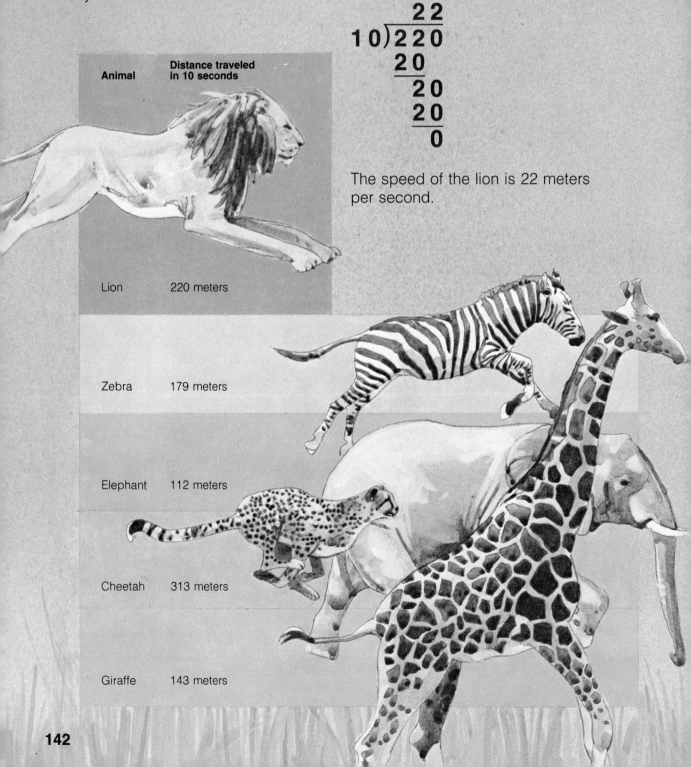

Animal	Distance traveled in 10 seconds
Lion	220 meters
Zebra	179 meters
Elephant	112 meters
Cheetah	313 meters
Giraffe	143 meters

B. Look for a pattern.

285.9 ÷ 10 = 28.59

285.9 ÷ 100 = 2.859

285.9 ÷ 1,000 = 0.2859

3.7 ÷ 10 = 0.37

3.7 ÷ 100 = 0.037

3.7 ÷ 1,000 = 0.0037

To divide a decimal by 10, 100, or 1,000, move the decimal point one place to the left for each zero in 10, 100, or 1,000.

Try Divide.

a. 8.65 ÷ 10   **b.** 8.65 ÷ 100

c. 8.65 ÷ 1,000   **d.** 452 ÷ 1,000

Practice Divide.

1. 387 ÷ 10   **2.** 387 ÷ 100   **3.** 387 ÷ 1,000   **4.** 63.4 ÷ 10

5. 63.4 ÷ 100   **6.** 63.4 ÷ 1,000   **7.** 7.1 ÷ 10   **8.** 7.1 ÷ 100

9. 7.1 ÷ 1,000   **10.** 0.5 ÷ 10   **11.** 0.5 ÷ 100   **12.** 0.5 ÷ 1,000

13. 74 ÷ 10   **14.** 5 ÷ 10   **15.** 1.3 ÷ 10   **16.** 5.2 ÷ 10

17. 0.6 ÷ 10   **18.** 0.17 ÷ 10   **19.** 43 ÷ 10   **20.** 875 ÷ 100

21. 27.4 ÷ 100   **22.** 30.4 ÷ 100   **23.** 0.91 ÷ 100   **24.** 1.3 ÷ 100

25. 699 ÷ 1,000   **26.** 1,234 ÷ 1,000   **27.** 800 ÷ 1,000   **28.** 400 ÷ 1,000

29. 0.03 ÷ 100   **30.** 0.041 ÷ 10   **31.** 0.008 ÷ 100   **32.** 5 ÷ 1,000

33. 0.064 ÷ 10   **34.** 0.007 ÷ 100   **★35.** 5.4 ÷ 10,000   **★36.** 6 ÷ 10,000

Apply Solve each problem. Use the table on page 142.
Round each answer to the nearest tenth.

37. Find the speed of the zebra.

38. Find the speed of the elephant.

39. Find the speed of the cheetah.

40. Find the speed of the giraffe.

★41. Find the average speed of all 5 animals.

★42. The cheetah is how many times as fast as the elephant?

Practice: Multiplying and Dividing Decimals

Place a decimal point correctly in each circled number.

1. $6.1 \times 7.64 =$ ⟨46604⟩

2. $7.3 \times 4.25 =$ ⟨31025⟩

3. $1.25 \times 0.82 =$ ⟨10250⟩

4. $3.56 \times 0.71 =$ ⟨25276⟩

5. $53 \times 9.71 =$ ⟨51463⟩

6. $92 \times 8.53 =$ ⟨78476⟩

7. $0.09\overline{)6.498}$ ⟨722⟩

8. $0.08\overline{)1.856}$ ⟨232⟩

9. $7.1\overline{)69.58}$ ⟨98⟩

10. $4.7\overline{)38.54}$ ⟨82⟩

11. $0.063\overline{)0.882}$ ⟨14⟩

12. $0.043\overline{)1.247}$ ⟨29⟩

Multiply or divide.

13. 5.14×8.2

14. 0.92×0.14

15. $21.15 \div 9$

16. $45.794 \div 7$

17. 4.2×85

18. $143.07 \div 1.9$

19. $53.32 \div 6.2$

20. 42×0.35

21. 100×8.61

22. 10×0.36

23. $0.0444 \div 6$

24. $0.448 \div 8$

25. $4 \div 10$

26. 0.03×0.06

27. 0.02×0.13

28. $53 \div 100$

29. $7 \div 0.25$

30. $8 \div 0.16$

31. 0.15×0.09

32. 0.05×0.13

33. $2.64 \div 100$

34. $46.3 \div 1,000$

35. 0.5×10

36. $1,000 \times 3.06$

37. $0.1722 \div 2.1$

38. $0.2145 \div 3.9$

39. $0.4 \times 0.2 \times 0.06$

40. $0.09 \times 1.1 \times 0.03$

41. $10.148 \div 0.086$

42. $1.909 \div 0.023$

43. $1,000 \times 0.0034$

44. 9.4×100

45. 0.293×0.16

46. 0.14×0.188

47. $731 \div 0.17$

48. $840 \div 0.24$

49. $1.189 \div 0.058$

50. $0.7878 \div 0.39$

51. Find $180 \div 14$ to the nearest one.

52. Find $84 \div 1.9$ to the nearest one.

53. Find $7.8 \div 24$ to the nearest hundredth.

54. Find $7 \div 12$ to the nearest tenth.

144

Apply Solve each problem.

55. In captivity, a hippopotamus lives about 1.7 times as long as a zebra. If the life span of a hippopotamus is 25 years, what is the life span of a zebra to the nearest whole year?

56. At Nelsons', the cost of the dinner buffet for children under 12 years old is 35 cents times their age in years. Mike is 11 years old. How much will his meal cost?

57. Molly ran in five marathons. She completed distances of 4.6 miles, 7.5 miles, 8.0 miles, 6.4 miles, and 8.0 miles. What is the average distance she ran per marathon?

58. Find the cost of 0.08 pounds of grapes at $0.79 per pound.

59. Find the cost of 100 cans of cat food at $0.44 per can.

60. What is the cost of one pencil if a package of 15 pencils costs $1.20?

61. Ned needs 1.6 milligrams of riboflavin each day. This is ten times the amount provided by a serving of ham. How much riboflavin does the ham provide?

62. A chicken drumstick has 5 times as much riboflavin as thiamine. It has 0.15 mg of riboflavin. How much thiamine does it have?

COMPUTER

BASIC: GO TO Statements

An INPUT statement can accept more than one number. When the computer reads INPUT in line 20, it waits for three numbers to be typed. A GO TO statement sends the computer to another line in a program. Line 50 in this program causes the question in line 10 to be asked over and over.

```
10 PRINT "GIVE THREE DECIMALS"
20 INPUT X,Y,Z
30 PRINT "THE PRODUCT IS"
40 PRINT X*Y*Z
50 GO TO 10
60 END
```

When this program is run and 9.3, 3, and 2.68 are typed, you will see this.
Output

```
GIVE THREE DECIMALS
? 9.3, 3, 2.68
THE PRODUCT IS
74.772
GIVE THREE DECIMALS
?
```

1. Give the output for the program above when 7, 5.07, and 12.3 are entered for X, Y, and Z.

2. Change lines 20 and 40 in the program above so that it finds the product for four numbers.

3. Write a program to find the quotient when the dividend and divisor are entered. Make it a program that repeats.

Chapter 5 Test

Multiply.

1. 0.54
     $\times$ 29

2. 0.36
     $\times$ 2.7

3. 0.3
    $\times$ 0.2

4. 0.037
     $\times$ 0.25

5. 80.2×59.3

6. 0.05×0.07

7. 10×2.8

8. 72.3×100

9. $1{,}000 \times 0.7$

Divide.

10. $9)\overline{5.4}$

11. $12)\overline{4.44}$

12. $7)\overline{0.35}$

13. $48)\overline{0.144}$

14. $0.7)\overline{0.028}$

15. $0.43)\overline{0.645}$

16. $0.4)\overline{72}$

17. $0.16)\overline{4}$

18. $7.124 \div 52$

19. $0.1591 \div 43$

20. $9.36 \div 2.4$

21. $11.7 \div 0.26$

22. $9.56 \div 10$

23. $18.9 \div 100$

24. $88.2 \div 1{,}000$

25. Find $3 \div 7$ to the nearest hundredth.

26. Find $4.7 \div 33$ to the nearest tenth.

27. Find $3{,}175 \div 5.5$ to the nearest one.

Solve each problem.

28. Juan ran 10 miles in a charity race. He took pledges of $0.10, $0.10, $0.15, $0.25, and $0.20 per mile. Find the average pledge per mile.

29. Nancy ran in four marathons. She completed distances of 6.4 miles, 12.5 miles, 10.6 miles, and 9.3 miles. What is the average distance she ran per marathon?

30. Danny received a pledge from his father of $0.20 per mile plus a bonus of $5.00 for running at least 10 miles. Danny ran 14 miles. How much did his father pay?

CHALLENGE

Estimating Products and Quotients of Decimals

Suki's doctor gave her a chart that shows how many Calories Suki uses in certain activities. Even when she is totally inactive, she uses about 0.9 Calories per minute just to keep her body functioning.

Activity	Calories expended per minute
Sitting at rest	1.4
Typing	2.0
Walking slowly	2.9
Walking downstairs	6.1
Exercising vigorously	6.4
Swimming	7.3
Jogging	8.3
Walking upstairs	15.8

A. Estimate the number of Calories Suki uses walking slowly for 45 minutes.

Find 2.9×45.

$$
\begin{array}{r}
45 \\
\times 2.9 \\
\end{array}
\rightarrow
\begin{array}{r}
45 \\
\times 3 \\
\hline
135
\end{array}
$$
Round 2.9 to the nearest one. Then multiply.

Suki uses about 135 Calories.

B. Estimate the number of minutes Suki would need to swim to use 350 Calories.

Find $350 \div 7.3$.

$$
7.3\overline{)350} \rightarrow 7\overline{)350}^{\,50}
$$
Round 7.3 to the nearest one. Then divide.

Suki would need to swim for about 50 minutes.

Estimation Estimate the number of Calories Suki uses for each activity.

1. Jogging, 25 minutes

2. Sitting, 90 minutes

3. Typing, 40 minutes

4. Swimming, 35 minutes

5. Walking, 2 hours

6. Walking upstairs, 6 minutes, and then downstairs, 4 minutes

Estimation Estimate the number of minutes Suki would need to do each activity to use 600 Calories.

7. Exercising

8. Jogging

9. Walking

10. Typing

11. **Estimation** Estimate the number of Calories Suki uses in 24 hours.

MAINTENANCE

Tell what each 7 means.

1. 9.07 **2.** 8.72 **3.** 6.007 **4.** 8.1107 **5.** 71.319 **6.** 7.002

Write each decimal.

7. 6 tens 5 tenths

8. 4 ones 6 hundredths

9. 3 tenths 2 thousandths 5 millionths

10. twenty-nine ten-thousandths

Compare. Use <, >, or =.

11. 8.1 ● 8.0

12. 9.0 ● 9.1

13. 3.8 ● 8.3

14. 5.8 ● 5.800

15. 9.00 ● 9

16. 0.9 ● 0.78

List these numbers in order from least to greatest.

17. 3.2   3.02   3.002

18. 5.76   6.3   5.8

19. 6.44   6.404   6.044

Solve each problem.

20. There are 3,279 automobiles in Creston. 1,408 of them are less than 10 years old. How many of them are 10 or more years old?

21. Jim drove 162 miles Monday, 238 miles Tuesday, and 423 miles Wednesday. How many miles did he drive in all?

22. After Kevin paid $6.94 for a calculator, he had $2.88 left. How much money did he have before buying the calculator?

23. A *milla* is a unit of length in Honduras that is equivalent to 1.1493 miles. How many miles is 214 millas?

24. A *libra* is a unit of weight in Mexico that is equivalent to 1.01467 pounds. How many pounds is 23 libras?

25. An author wrote a 434-page novel in 124 days. On the average, how many pages did she write each day?

Measurement

chapter 6

33 mm

45 mm

51 mm

Metric Units of Length

a. A 10-speed bicycle is about one *meter* (1 m) high.

B. A link in the chain is about one *centimeter* (1 cm) long.

100 cm = 1 m

Try

a. *Estimation* To measure the diameter of a tennis ball, would you use millimeters, centimeters, meters, or kilometers?

b. *Estimation* Choose the best measurement for the length of a baseball bat.

1 km   1 m   1 cm

Practice

Estimation Would you use millimeters, centimeters, meters, or kilometers to measure the

1. width of home plate?

2. length of a soccer field?

3. distance of a sailboat race?

4. length of a stitch on a baseball?

c. The width of a spoke is about one *millimeter* (1 mm).

10 mm = 1 cm

1,000 mm = 1 m

D. It takes about four minutes to ride a bicycle one *kilometer* (1 km).

1 km = 1,000 m

Estimation Choose the best measurement.

5. Length of a golf club

1 km   1 m   1 cm

6. Diameter of a golf ball

4 m   4 cm   4 mm

7. Height of a basketball hoop

3 km   3 m   3 cm

8. Distance walked in ten minutes

1 km   1 m   1 cm

Apply _Estimation_ Solve each problem.

9. Name some lengths or distances in your classroom that you would measure in centimeters.

10. Name some lengths or distances in your classroom that you would measure in meters.

Equal Metric Measures

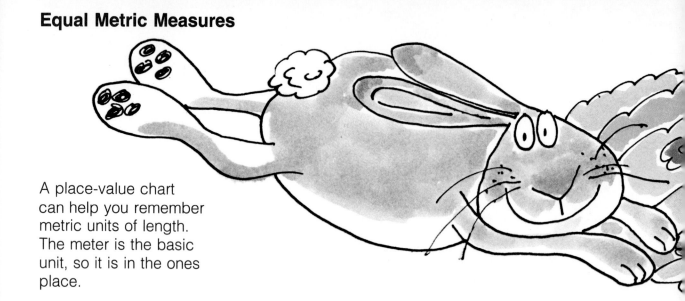

A place-value chart can help you remember metric units of length. The meter is the basic unit, so it is in the ones place.

thousands	hundreds	tens	ones	tenths	hundredths	thousandths
1,000 meters kilometer km 1 m = 0.001 km	100 meters hectometer hm 1 m = 0.01 hm	10 meters dekameter dam 1 m = 0.1 dam	1 meter meter m	0.1 meter decimeter dm 1 m = 10 dm	0.01 meter centimeter cm 1 m = 100 cm	0.001 meter millimeter mm 1 m = 1,000 mm

A. A rabbit's hop is 2 m long. How many centimeters long is a rabbit's hop?

1 m = 100 cm

To change meters to centimeters, multiply by 100.

2 × 100 = 200

A rabbit's hop is 200 cm long.

To change from a larger unit to a smaller one, multiply.

B. Give 400 mm in centimeters.

To change millimeters to centimeters, divide by 10.

400 ÷ 10 = 40

400 mm = 40 cm

To change from a smaller unit to a larger one, divide.

a. 52 km   **b.** 6.1 cm   **c.** 4 dm

Practice Give each measure in meters.

1. 3 km   **2.** 8 hm

3. 600 cm   **4.** 3,150 mm

5. 850 dm   **6.** 42 cm

7. 38 km   **8.** 922 cm

9. 8.3 cm   **10.** 4.2 km

Give each measure in centimeters.

11. 2 m   **12.** 40 mm   **13.** 8 km   **14.** 23 mm   **15.** 43 dm

16. 63 mm   **17.** 29 m   **18.** 35 km   **19.** 7.1 m   **20.** 0.3 km

Give each measure in millimeters.

21. 4 m   **22.** 7 cm   **23.** 2 km   **24.** 4.3 m   **25.** 7.8 cm

Give each measure in kilometers.

26. 3,000 m   **27.** 400 cm   **28.** 5,237 m   **29.** 820 hm   **30.** 38.6 m

Apply Give each measure in meters.

31. Otter

← 38 cm →

32. Mink

← 28 cm →

★33. A raccoon's strides are 68 cm long. About how many strides does a raccoon take to travel 1 m?

★34. A deer's strides are 35 dm long. About how many strides does a deer take to travel 1 km?

Measuring with Metric Units of Length

A. Rosalia collected insects for a science project. To the nearest millimeter, what is the length of this beetle?

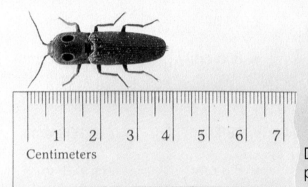

The beetle is 39 mm.

B. Draw a segment 4.5 cm long.

Put a point at the zero mark of the ruler and another point at the mark for 4.5 cm.

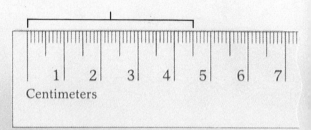

Draw a segment to connect the points.

Try

a. Give the length of this segment to the nearest centimeter.

b. Draw a segment 67 mm long.

Practice Give the length of each segment to the nearest millimeter.

1. ├───────────┤ 2. ├───────────────┤ 3. ├──────┤

4. ├────┤ 5. ├───────────┤ 6. ├──────────────────┤

Give the length of each segment to the nearest centimeter.

7. ├──────────────────┤ 8. ├───────────┤

9. ├───────────────┤ 10. ├──────────────────┤

11. ├───────────────┤ 12. ├──────────────────────┤

Draw a segment for each of the following lengths.

13. 3 cm 14. 9 mm 15. 52 mm 16. 2.6 cm 17. 8.5 cm 18. 80 mm

Apply Give each measurement to the nearest millimeter.

19. Stink bug

20. Ladybird beetle

21. Coral moth

22. Robber fly

23. Pinching beetle

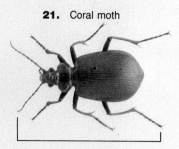

24. Caterpiller hunter

Draw a segment to show the length of a

25. 6-cm lanternfly.

27. 1.9-cm shield bug.

29. 8-mm silverfish.

26. 2-cm firefly.

28. 7.5-cm dragonfly.

30. 1.6-cm tiger beetle.

Metric Units of Area

Pat is making a model of the White House. What is the area of the Green Room in Pat's model?

Area is measured in square units.

1 square centimeter

1 cm^2

Green Room

You can count the squares to find the area.

The area of the Green Room in Pat's model is 6 cm^2.

Try Find the area of each figure by counting. Each square is 1 cm^2.

a.
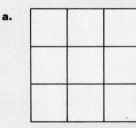

b.
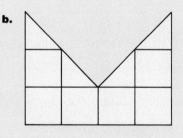

c. *Estimation* Would you use square millimeters, square centimeters, or square meters to measure the area of the school playground?

Practice Find the area of each figure by counting. Each square is 1 cm^2.

1.
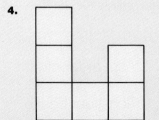

2.
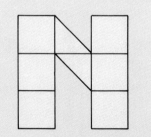

3.
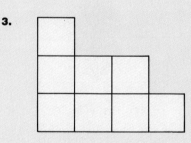

4.
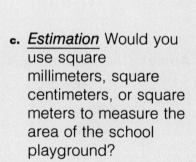

5.

6.
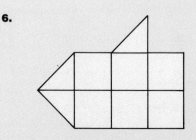

156

Estimation Would you use square millimeters, square centimeters, or square meters to measure the area of a

7. page in a book?

8. postage stamp?

9. soccer field?

10. locket?

11. living-room carpet?

12. postcard?

Apply   Count to find the area of the model of each room of the White House. Each square is 1 cm².

13. State Dining Room

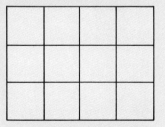

14. East Room

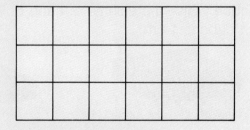

★15. Entrance Hall

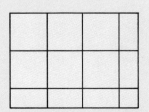

★16. *Estimation* Blue Room

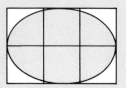

Metric Units of Volume

This is a model of the base of the Washington Monument. What is the volume of the model?

Each edge of this cube is 1 cm. The volume of the cube is 1 *cubic centimeter* (1 cm³).

There are 9 cubes in the model.

The volume of the model is 9 cm³.

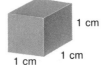

Try

a. Give the volume of the box. The volume of each cube is 1 cm³.

b. *Estimation* Would you use cubic centimeters or cubic meters to measure the volume of a moving van?

Practice Give the volume of each box. The volume of each cube is 1 cm³.

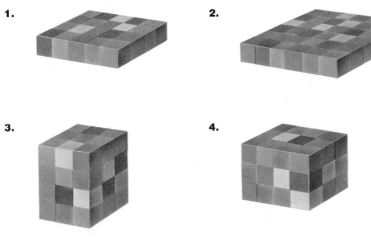

1.

2.

3.

4.

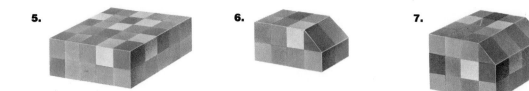

5.   **6.**   **7.**

Estimation Would you use cubic centimeters or cubic meters to measure the volume of a

8. briefcase?   **9.** safe-deposit box?   **10.** garage?

11. silo?   **12.** toy chest?   **13.** classroom?

Tell whether you would use area or volume to find which is larger.

14. Two different sized refrigerators   **15.** Two different sized parking lots

Apply Solve each problem.

16. _Estimation_ Which is the better estimate for the volume of the Washington Monument?

30,000 m³   30 m³

★17. The Capitol is about 85 m high. The Eiffel tower is 4 times as high as the Capitol and twice as high as the Washington Monument. What is the height of the Washington Monument?

MAINTENANCE

Find each answer.

1. 5.3
       + 7.8

2.   2 6.3
      ×   7

3.   7.3 5
      − 4.8 8

4. 7)6.3

5.   0.0 4
      ×   0.3

6.   4.3 5
       + 7 6.8

7. 0.6)1.9 8

8.   4 1
      − 2 7.3 9

9.   0.3 5 6
       × 0.1 2 4

10.   7.4 9 3
       + 3.4 8 5

11. 23.6 + 8.45   **12.** 56.3 − 17.82   **13.** 16.3 × 7.49

Metric Units of Capacity and Mass

A. Terry had lunch at Potomac Park. His thermos holds 1 *liter* (1 L).

His spoon holds about 15 **milliliters** (15 mL).

1,000 mL = 1 L

1 mL = 0.001 L

B. The mass of a bunch of bananas is about 1 *kilogram* (1 kg).

An olive has a mass of about 1 *gram* (1 g).

1,000 g = 1 kg

1 g = 0.001 kg

Several grains of salt have a mass of 1 *milligram* (1 mg).

1,000 mg = 1 g

1 mg = 0.001 g

Try *Estimation* Choose the better measure.

a. Bucket

   8 mL   8 L

b. Pencil

   6 g   6 kg

c. Write 2.2 L as milliliters. **d.** Write 400 g as kilograms.

Practice _Estimation_ Choose the better measure.

1. Aquarium
   40 mL   40 L

2. Steam iron
   180 mL   180 L

3. Washing machine
   80 mL   80 L

4. Paper clip
   500 mg   500 g

5. Bowling ball
   7 mg   7 kg

6. Egg
   50 g   50 kg

Give each measure in liters.

7. 3,000 mL

8. 11,000 mL

9. 783 mL

10. 310 mL

Give each measure in milliliters.

11. 5 L

12. 9 L

13. 11 L

14. 2.36 L

Give each measure in grams.

15. 5 kg

16. 35 kg

17. 4.7 kg

18. 2,400 mg

Give each measure in milligrams.

19. 4 g

20. 80 g

21. 0.25 g

22. 6 kg

Give each measure in kilograms.

23. 8,000 g

24. 4,700 g

25. 600 g

26. 56,000 mg

Apply Solve each problem.

27. Does a loaf of bread weigh 500 g or 500 kg?

28. The mass of a melon is 340 g. How many milligrams is that?

★29. Which has a greater mass, 3 kg of apples or 2,900 g of apples?

★30. Which is more, 2,500 mL of water or 2.5 L of water?

More Practice Set 64, page 390

Practice: Metric Measures

Give each measure in meters.

1. 5 km **2.** 6 hm **3.** 400 cm **4.** 4,260 mm

5. 720 dm **6.** 28 cm **7.** 53 km **8.** 763 cm

Give each measure in centimeters.

9. 4 m **10.** 80 mm **11.** 9 km **12.** 63 mm

Give each measure in millimeters.

13. 8 m **14.** 6 cm **15.** 3 km **16.** 2.6 m

Give each measure in kilometers.

17. 5,000 m **18.** 600 cm **19.** 2,482 m **20.** 780 hm

Give each measure in liters.

21. 8,000 mL **22.** 22,000 mL **23.** 476 mL **24.** 420 mL

Give each measure in milliliters.

25. 6 L **26.** 8 L **27.** 42 L **28.** 3.47 L

Give each measure in grams.

29. 3 kg **30.** 47 kg **31.** 5.3 kg **32.** 6,900 mg

33. 840 mg **34.** 0.5 kg **35.** 42 mg **36.** 67.3 mg

Give each measure in milligrams.

37. 6 g **38.** 30 g **39.** 0.75 g **40.** 8 kg

Give each measure in kilograms.

41. 4,000 g **42.** 3,200 g **43.** 400 g **44.** 82,000 mg

Why did George Washington chop down the cherry tree?

To find the answer, write the letter of the measure that is equal to each measure below.

□ 1 m
E 1,000 m
ı 0.005 m
M 5 m
P 5,000 m
s 0.07 m
T 7 m
U 700 m

45. 5 mm   **46.** 0.007 km   **47.** 100 cm

48. 7 cm   **49.** 700 cm   **50.** 7 hm

51. 5,000 mm   **52.** 5 km   **53.** 70 mm

54. 1,000 mm   **55.** 500 cm   **56.** 1 km

Apply   Solve each problem.

57. Does a lemon weigh 110 g or 110 kg?

58. A paint can holds 4 L. How many milliliters is that?

59. *Estimation* Would you use millimeters or meters to measure the length of a car?

★60. The diameter of a button is 13 mm. Will it fit through a buttonhole that is 1.5 cm long?

CHALLENGE

In 1842, Louis Braille, a blind Frenchman, invented a pattern of raised dots that enabled people to read and write by touch.

These are the digits 1 through 9 written in Braille symbols.

Find the sum of these numbers. Give your answers in Braille.

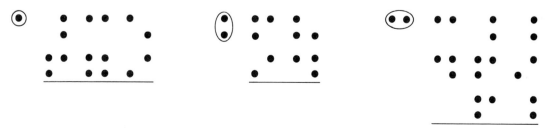

Customary Units of Length

A. The bean seeds in Ruth's garden are 1 *inch* (1 in.) apart.

The cabbage plants are 1 *foot* (1 ft.) apart.

1 ft. = 12 in.

Rows of cabbage plants are 1 *yard* (1 yd.) apart.

1 yd. = 3 ft.

1 yd. = 36 in.

Ruth drove 1 *mile* (1 mi.) to buy seeds.

1 mi. = 5,280 ft.

B. Write 3 ft. as inches.

To change feet to inches, multiply by 12.

3 × 12 = 36

3 ft. = 36 in.

C. Write 7 ft. as yards, feet.

To change feet to yards, divide by 3.

7 ÷ 3 = 2 R1

7 ft. = 2 yd. 1 ft.

Try

a. *Estimation* Choose the best measure for the length of a broom.

56 in.   2 ft.   6 yd.

b. Write 2 yd. as inches.

c. Write 15 in. as feet, inches.

Practice _Estimation_ Choose the best measure.

1. Height of a man

  27 in.   6 ft.   4 yd.

2. Width of a doorway

  17 in.   8 ft.   1 yd.

3. Length of an envelope

  6 in.   2 ft.   3 yd.

4. Length of a railroad train

  20 ft.   5 yd.   1 mi.

5. Length of a car

  32 in.   10 ft.   19 yd.

6. Length of a potato

  5 in.   2 ft.   7 yd.

Give each measure as inches.

7. 2 ft.   **8.** 4 yd.   **9.** 16 ft.   **10.** 1 ft. 4 in.   **11.** 1 yd. 2 ft.

Give each measure as feet, inches.

12. 17 in.   **13.** 41 in.   **14.** 64 in.   **15.** 3 yd.   **16.** 2 mi.

Give each measure as yards, feet, inches.

17. 7 ft. 2 in.   **18.** 9 ft. 5 in.   ★**19.** 88 in.   ★**20.** 135 in.   ★**21.** 168 in.

Apply Solve each problem.

22. Squash plants are 2 ft. apart. Write this as inches.

23. Broccoli plants are 15 in. apart. Write this as feet, inches.

24. Tomato plants are 30 in. apart. Write this as feet, inches.

★**25.** If pepper plants are 22 in. apart, how many plants are in a row that is 6 ft. long?

Customary Units of Area and Volume

A. This is a drawing of Ruth's garden. Each square represents 1 *square foot* (1 sq. ft.). What is the area of the garden?

Count the squares to find the area.

The area of Ruth's garden is 72 sq. ft.

Other customary units of area are the *square inch* (sq. in.), the *square yard* (sq. yd.), and the *square mile* (sq. mi.).

B. Find the volume of the box. Each cube represents 1 *cubic foot* (1 cu. ft.).

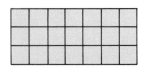

The volume of the box is 24 cu. ft.

Other customary units of volume are the *cubic inch* (cu. in.) and the *cubic yard* (cu. yd.).

Try

a. Find the area of the figure. Each square represents 1 sq. in.

b. Find the volume of the box. Each cube represents 1 cu. in.

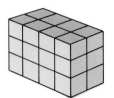

Practice Find the area of each figure. Each square represents 1 sq. in.

1.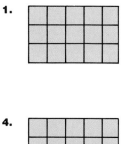

2.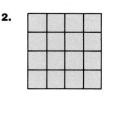

3.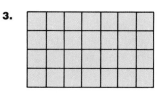

4.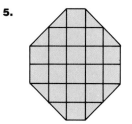

5.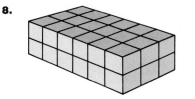

6.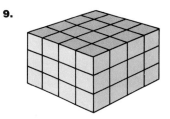

Find the volume of each box. Each cube represents 1 cu. in.

7.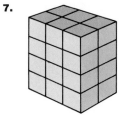

8.

9.

10.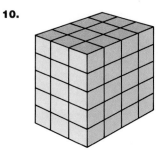

11.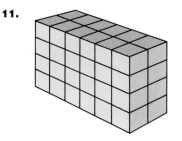

12.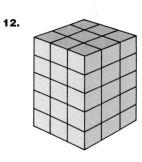

Apply Find the area of each flower garden. Each square represents 1 sq. ft.

13.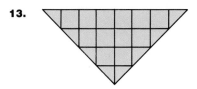

*14. _Estimation_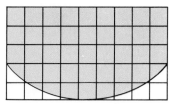

Customary Units of Capacity and Weight

A. Ruth canned tomato sauce. Her measuring cup holds 1 *cup* (1 c.).

A jar holds 1 *pint* (1 pt.).

1 pt. = 2 c.

A saucepan holds 1 *quart* (1 qt.).

1 qt. = 2 pt.

A pressure cooker holds 1 *gallon* (1 gal.).

1 gal. = 4 qt.

B. A cherry tomato weighs about 1 *ounce* (1 oz.).

16 cherry tomatoes weigh about 1 *pound* (1 lb.).

1 lb. = 16 oz.

Another customary unit of weight is the *ton* (T.).

1 T. = 2,000 lb.

C. Write 36 oz. as pounds, ounces.

To change ounces to pounds, divide by 16.

36 ÷ 16 = 2 R4

36 oz. = 2 lb. 4 oz.

Try *Estimation* Choose the better measure.

a. Watering can
  1 c.   1 gal.

b. Bicycle
  18 oz.   18 lb.

c. Give 3 qt. 1 pt. as pints.

d. Give 68 oz. as pounds, ounces.

Practice *Estimation* Choose the better measure.

1. Soup bowl
  1 c.   1 gal.

2. Can of motor oil
  1 c.   1 qt.

3. Carton of cream
  1 pt.   1 gal.

4. Brick
  2 oz.   2 lb.

5. Dime
  1 oz.   1 lb.

6. Car
  200 lb.   1 T.

Give each measure as pints.

7. 1 qt.   **8.** 1 gal.   **9.** 2 qt.   **10.** 10 c.   **11.** 5 qt. 1 pt.

Give each measure as quarts, pints.

12. 2 gal.   **13.** 6 gal.   **14.** 12 c.   **15.** 18 c.   **16.** 11 pt.

Give each measure as gallons, quarts, pints.

17. 12 qt.   **18.** 16 pt.   **19.** 15 qt.   **★20.** 23 pt.   **★21.** 35 pt.

Give each measure as ounces.

22. 3 lb.   **23.** 5 lb.   **24.** 1 T.   **25.** 4 T.   **26.** 2 lb. 3 oz.

Give each measure as pounds, ounces.

27. 3 T.   **28.** 7 T.   **29.** 80 oz.   **30.** 53 oz.   **31.** 72 oz.

Apply Solve each problem.

32. Ruth made 2 gal. of sauce. How many pint jars will this fill?

★33. How many quart jars are needed for 15 pt. of squash?

Practice: Customary Measures

Give each measure as inches.

1. 2 yd.   **2.** 1 ft. 8 in.   **3.** 18 ft.   **4.** 4 ft.

5. 2 ft. 7 in.   **6.** 5 yd.   **7.** 2 yd. 2 ft.   **8.** 8 ft.

Give each measure as feet, inches.

9. 4 yd.   **10.** 52 in.   **11.** 3 mi.   **12.** 19 in.

13. 75 in.   **14.** 2 yd.   **15.** 66 in.   **16.** 23 in.

Give each measure as yards, feet, inches.

17. 9 ft. 5 in.   **18.** 8 ft. 4 in.   **19.** 10 ft. 2 in.   **20.** 6 ft. 7 in.

Give each measure as pints.

21. 16 c.   **22.** 2 gal.   **23.** 4 qt. 1 pt.   **24.** 3 qt.

25. 7 qt. 1 pt.   **26.** 5 qt.   **27.** 10 c.   **28.** 6 gal.

Give each measure as quarts, pints.

29. 9 pt.   **30.** 5 gal.   **31.** 22 c.   **32.** 15 pt.

33. 8 c.   **34.** 10 c.   **35.** 3 gal.   **36.** 6 gal.

Give each measure as gallons, quarts, pints.

37. 17 qt.   **38.** 20 pt.   **39.** 12 pt.   **40.** 8 qt.

Give each measure as ounces.

41. 3 lb. 4 oz.   **42.** 7 lb.   **43.** 6 lb. 2 oz.   **44.** 4 lb.

Give each measure as pounds, ounces.

45. 60 oz.   **46.** 2 T.   **47.** 57 oz.   **48.** 5 T.

Apply Solve each problem.

49. How many quart bottles would be needed for 20 pt. of beets?

50. Fence posts are 38 in. apart. How many feet, inches is this?

51. A recipe calls for 4 c. of milk. How many pints is this?

52. Paul made 1 qt. of soup. How many cups is this?

53. Gina bought 3 lb. 4 oz. of apples. How many ounces is this?

54. Lin jumped 4 ft. 7 in. Emilio jumped 50 in. Who jumped higher?

55. Which weighs more, 2 lb. of apples or 35 oz. of apples?

BASIC: LET Statements

A LET statement puts a number into a memory location. Letters are used to label these locations. In line 30, a value is put into a memory location labeled I. In line 50, the value currently stored in location I is referred to and printed.

This program changes feet to inches.

```
10 PRINT "FEET ="          Output
20 INPUT F
30 LET I=F*12              FEET =
40 PRINT "INCHES ="        ? 4
50 PRINT I                 INCHES =
60 END                     48
```

Give the output for the program above when the following numbers are entered for F.

1. 2   **2.** 6   **3.** 10   **4.** 15

5. Give the output for the following program when 2 is entered for Y.

```
10 PRINT "YARDS ="
20 INPUT Y
30 LET F=Y*3
40 LET I=Y*36
50 PRINT "FEET ="
60 PRINT F
70 PRINT "INCHES ="
80 PRINT I
90 END
```

6. Give the output for the program in Exercise 5 when 7 is entered.

Adding and Subtracting Customary Units

A. *Career* Kit Donaldson is a contractor. He needs 3 ft. 8 in. and 5 ft. 9 in. of pipe. How much pipe should he buy?

Add the like units.

$$
\begin{array}{r}
3 \text{ ft.} \quad 8 \text{ in.} \\
+\, 5 \text{ ft.} \quad 9 \text{ in.} \\
\hline
8 \text{ ft.} \; 17 \text{ in.}
\end{array}
$$

Rename 8 ft. 17 in.
17 in. = 1 ft. 5 in.

8 ft. 17 in. = 9 ft. 5 in.

He should buy 9 ft. 5 in. of pipe.

B. Find 7 lb. 3 oz. − 2 lb. 10 oz.

You cannot subtract 10 oz. from 3 oz.
Rename 7 lb. 3 oz.

$$
\begin{array}{r}
7 \text{ lb.} \quad 3 \text{ oz.} \\
-\, 2 \text{ lb.} \; 10 \text{ oz.}
\end{array}
\longrightarrow
\begin{array}{r}
\overset{6}{\cancel{7}} \text{ lb.} \; \overset{19}{\cancel{3}} \text{ oz.} \\
-\, 2 \text{ lb.} \; 10 \text{ oz.} \\
\hline
4 \text{ lb.} \quad 9 \text{ oz.}
\end{array}
$$

172

Try Add or subtract.

a. 3 gal. 2 qt.
$\underline{+ 5 \text{ gal. } 1 \text{ qt.}}$

b. 3 lb. 9 oz.
$\underline{+ 4 \text{ lb. } 8 \text{ oz.}}$

c. 5 qt.
$\underline{- 2 \text{ qt. } 1 \text{ pt.}}$

Practice Add or subtract.

1. 6 lb. 4 oz.
$\underline{+ 7 \text{ lb. } 2 \text{ oz.}}$

2. 7 gal. 3 qt.
$\underline{- 4 \text{ gal. } 1 \text{ qt.}}$

3. 4 ft. 8 in.
$\underline{+ 3 \text{ ft. } 2 \text{ in.}}$

4. 20 lb. 7 oz.
$\underline{- 15 \text{ lb. } 3 \text{ oz.}}$

5. 2 yd. 1 ft. 3 in.
$\underline{+ \phantom{2 \text{ yd. }} 1 \text{ ft. } 4 \text{ in.}}$

6. 2 gal. 1 qt.
$\underline{+ \phantom{2 \text{ gal. }} 1 \text{ qt. } 1 \text{ pt.}}$

7. 5 ft. 6 in.
$\underline{+ 6 \text{ ft. } 9 \text{ in.}}$

8. 10 lb. 5 oz.
$\underline{- 6 \text{ lb. } 8 \text{ oz.}}$

9. 5 gal. 1 qt.
$\underline{- 2 \text{ gal. } 3 \text{ qt.}}$

10. 22 lb. 12 oz.
$\underline{+ 18 \text{ lb. } 10 \text{ oz.}}$

11. 9 ft. 3 in.
$\underline{- 6 \text{ ft. } 8 \text{ in.}}$

12. 5 qt. 1 pt.
$\underline{+ 4 \text{ qt. } 1 \text{ pt.}}$

13. 7 lb.
$\underline{- \phantom{7 \text{ lb. }} 2 \text{ oz.}}$

14. 7 yd. 2 ft. 8 in.
$\underline{+ 3 \text{ yd. } 2 \text{ ft. } 7 \text{ in.}}$

15. 8 gal. 1 qt.
$\underline{- 4 \text{ gal. } 3 \text{ qt. } 1 \text{ pt.}}$

16. 8 ft. 7 in.
5 ft. 8 in.
$\underline{+ 7 \text{ ft. } 9 \text{ in.}}$

17. 3 lb. 10 oz.
9 lb. 14 oz.
$\underline{+ 6 \text{ lb. } 9 \text{ oz.}}$

18. 12 gal. 3 qt. 1 pt.
7 gal. 2 qt.
$\underline{+ 9 \text{ gal. } 3 \text{ qt. } 1 \text{ pt.}}$

Apply Solve each problem.

19. An air-conditioning duct is to be 45 ft. 10 in. long. Kit has completed 23 ft. 8 in. How much is left to complete?

20. Kit had 50 ft. of air-conditioning duct. If he uses 45 ft. 10 in., how much duct will he have left?

★21. What is the total length of 5 pieces of wire if each piece is 9 ft. 10 in. long?

★22. Kit bought 2 rolls of electrical tape. Each roll of tape was 50 ft. long. He used 72 ft. 8 in. How much tape was left?

Problem Solving: Give Sensible Answers

Read   Kit is buying oak flooring for a house. Which of the following is the most sensible answer for the amount of flooring he should buy?

528 ft.   528 sq. ft.   528 cu. ft.

Plan   The choices include a measurement of length, a measurement of area, and a measurement of volume.

Solve   Since flooring will cover area, the answer should be square units.

Answer   Kit should buy 528 sq. ft. of flooring.

Look Back   528 ft. and 528 cu. ft. can be eliminated as answers because they are not units of area.

Try *Estimation* Choose the most sensible measure.

a. Kit had 8,496 ft. of baseboard. How much baseboard did he use for one house?

3,256 ft.   3,256 yd.   3,256 sq. ft.

Apply *Estimation* From the following list of amounts, choose the most sensible answer for each problem.

$5.89 $325 $600 $2,657.20

2 in.   8 ft.   200 ft.   1,500 ft.

4 sq. in.   30 sq. in.   30 sq. ft.   140 sq. ft.

4 gal.   50 gal.   16 cu. in.   16 cu. ft.

1. Carpeting costs $18.98 a square yard. What was the cost of living-room carpeting?

2. A door costs $85. What was the cost of 7 doors?

3. What was the area of the living room?

4. What was the height of a door?

5. What was the area of the counter top in the kitchen?

6. Was was the thickness of the counter top?

7. What was the area of a tile in the kitchen floor?

8. How much water will the kitchen sink hold?

9. How much water will a bathtub hold?

10. What was the volume of the cabinet below the kitchen sink?

11. Kit bought 3 spools of wire. How much wire did he buy?

12. What was the cost of a spool of wire?

Time Zones

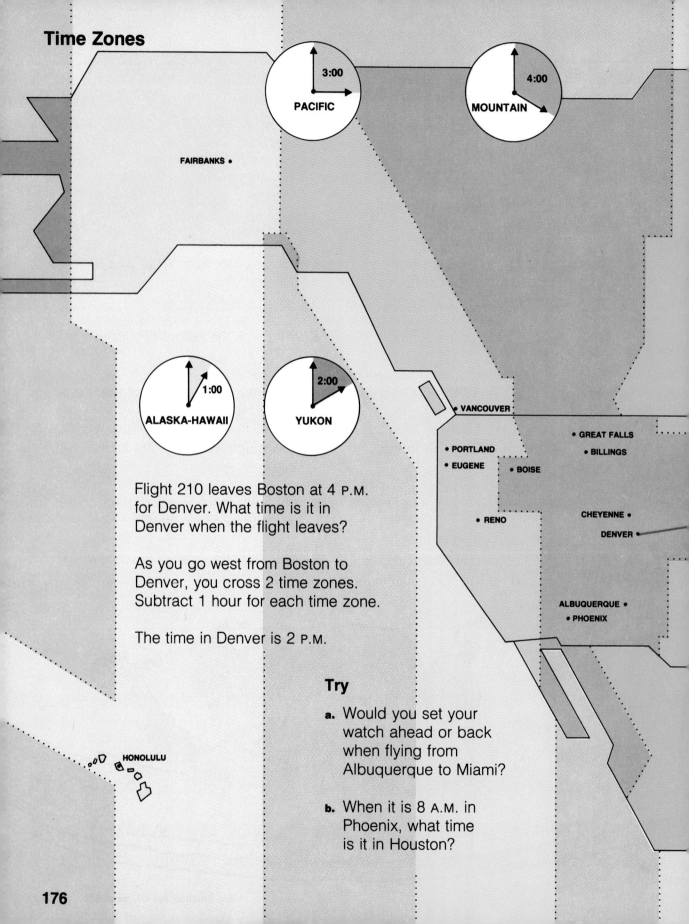

PACIFIC 3:00

MOUNTAIN 4:00

FAIRBANKS •

ALASKA-HAWAII 1:00

YUKON 2:00

• VANCOUVER

• GREAT FALLS
• BILLINGS

• PORTLAND
• EUGENE
• BOISE

• RENO

CHEYENNE •
DENVER •

ALBUQUERQUE •
• PHOENIX

Flight 210 leaves Boston at 4 P.M. for Denver. What time is it in Denver when the flight leaves?

As you go west from Boston to Denver, you cross 2 time zones. Subtract 1 hour for each time zone.

The time in Denver is 2 P.M.

HONOLULU

Try

a. Would you set your watch ahead or back when flying from Albuquerque to Miami?

b. When it is 8 A.M. in Phoenix, what time is it in Houston?

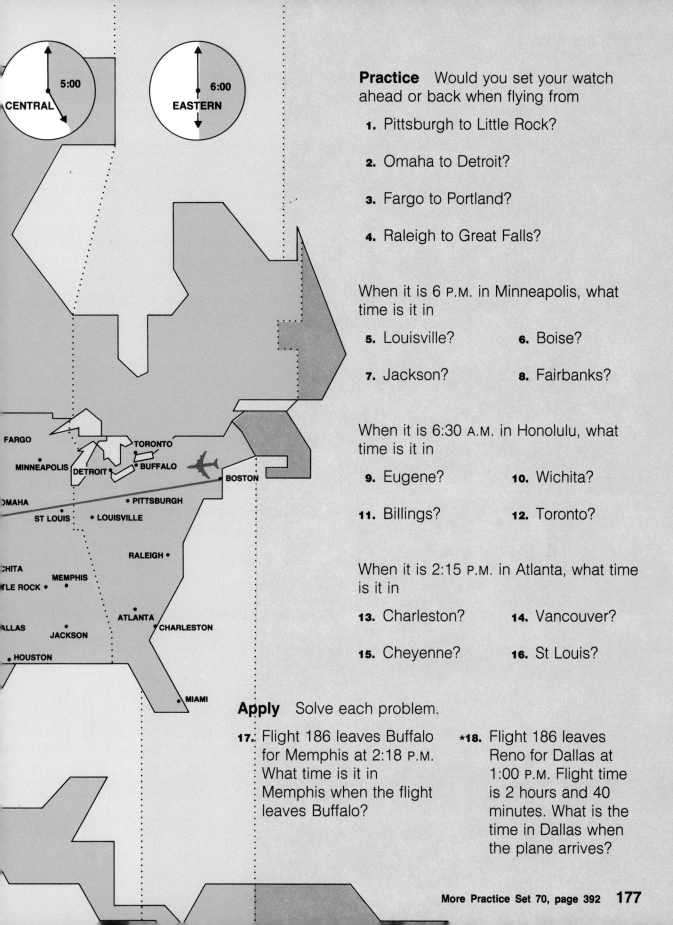

Practice Would you set your watch ahead or back when flying from

1. Pittsburgh to Little Rock?

2. Omaha to Detroit?

3. Fargo to Portland?

4. Raleigh to Great Falls?

When it is 6 P.M. in Minneapolis, what time is it in

5. Louisville? 6. Boise?

7. Jackson? 8. Fairbanks?

When it is 6:30 A.M. in Honolulu, what time is it in

9. Eugene? 10. Wichita?

11. Billings? 12. Toronto?

When it is 2:15 P.M. in Atlanta, what time is it in

13. Charleston? 14. Vancouver?

15. Cheyenne? 16. St Louis?

Apply Solve each problem.

17. Flight 186 leaves Buffalo for Memphis at 2:18 P.M. What time is it in Memphis when the flight leaves Buffalo?

*18. Flight 186 leaves Reno for Dallas at 1:00 P.M. Flight time is 2 hours and 40 minutes. What is the time in Dallas when the plane arrives?

Temperature

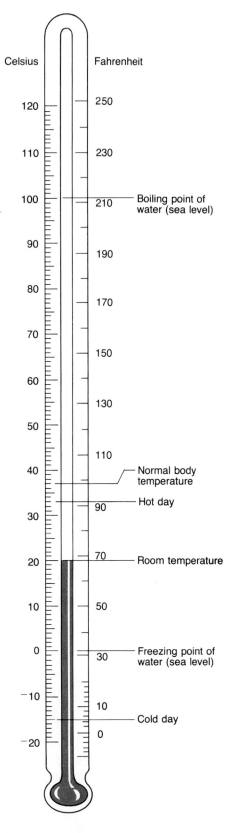

Celsius   Fahrenheit

120 — 250
110 — 230
100 — 210 — Boiling point of water (sea level)
90 — 190
80 — 170
70 — 150
60 — 130
50 — 110
40 — Normal body temperature
    — 90 — Hot day
30 — 70 — Room temperature
20 — 70 — Room temperature
10 — 50
0 — 30 — Freezing point of water (sea level)
−10 — 10
    — Cold day
−20 — 0

Mr. Carletti, the plant engineer at Loch Raven High School, uses a computer to regulate the temperature of the building.

A. This thermometer shows a room temperature of 20 degrees *Celsius* (20°C).

B. Is the more sensible temperature for cold milk 40°F or 80°F?

40°F is more sensible, since 80°F is above room temperature.

Try

a. Give the Celsius temperature shown on the thermometer.

50
40

b. *Estimation* Choose the more sensible temperature for hot soup.

20°C   80°C

Practice   Give the Celsius temperature shown on each thermometer.

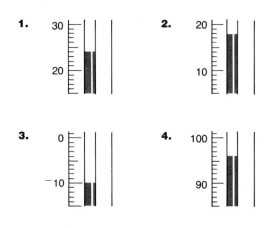

1. 30
    20

2. 20
    10

3. 0
    −10

4. 100
    90

Estimation Choose the more sensible temperature.

5. Warm day

  5°C   30°C

6. Grilled steak

  3°C   60°C

7. Rainy day

  7°C   −17°C

8. Hot drink

  82°C   18°C

9. Boiling water

  100°C   212°C

10. Hot bath

  43°C   11°C

11. Melted butter

  38°F   88°F

12. Refrigerator

  40°F   70°F

13. Snowy day

  −5°F   55°F

Apply Solve each problem.

14. Hot air leaves the coil at 21°C and arrives at the room at 18.5°C. What is the difference in temperature?

15. The temperature in the hallway is 68°F. Due to body heat, the temperature in the classroom is 8° warmer. What is the temperature in the classroom?

16. When the outside temperature falls below 29°F the computer switches from gas to oil heat. The temperature was 34°F at 3:00 P.M. and fell 1 degree each hour. At what time was the oil heat started?

★17. During winter vacations the temperature is set at 56°F. When school reopens at 7:00 A.M., the temperature should be 68°F. It takes 1 hour to raise the temperature 4°. At what time should the heat be turned up?

CALCULATOR

We can change Fahrenheit readings to Celsius using the formula $C = \frac{5}{9} \times (F - 32)$.

Use the key sequence F $\boxed{-}$ 32 $\boxed{=}$ $\boxed{\times}$ 5 $\boxed{\div}$ 9 $\boxed{=}$ C.

Change the following readings to Celsius. Round to the nearest whole number.

1. 200°F   **2.** 97°F   **3.** 85°F   **4.** 320°F   **5.** 45°F   **6.** 60°F

7. 72°F   **8.** 122°F   **9.** 55°F   **10.** 174°F   **11.** 32°F   **12.** 38°F

Chapter 6 Test

1. Choose the best measure for the length of a carrot.

   20 mm   20 cm   20 m

Give each measure in meters.

2. 43 km   3. 5.6 cm   4. 2 dm

5. Give the length of this segment to the nearest centimeter.

   _____

6. Find the area of the figure by counting. The area of each square is 1 cm².

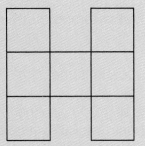

7. Give the volume of the box. The volume of each cube is 1 cm³.

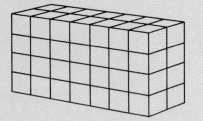

Choose the better measure.

8. Paint can   9. Dime

   4 mL 4 L   4 g 4 kg

10. Write 3.6 L as milliliters.

11. Choose the best measure for the length of a broomstick.

    14 in. 4 ft. 6 yd.

12. Write 22 in. as feet, inches.

13. Find the area of the figure. Each square represents 1 sq. in.

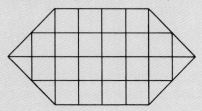

Choose the better measure.

14. Teakettle   15. Pliers

    1 c. 1 qt.   9 oz. 9 lb.

Add or subtract.

16.   5 lb. 9 oz.   17.   5 ft. 4 in.
    + 3 lb. 8 oz.   −   7 in.

18. Use the map on page 176. When it is 7:00 A.M. in Dallas, what time is it in Reno?

19. Choose the more sensible temperature for an icicle.

    0°C 20°C

20. Choose the most sensible measure.

    What is the area of a bathroom floor?

    28 ft. 28 sq. ft. 28 cu. ft.

CHALLENGE

Metric Measures of Land Area

A. A *hectare* is used to measure land area, like the area of a farm. A square whose sides are 100 m long has an area of 1 hectare.

1 hectare = 10,000 m²

B. Very large areas, like the area of a state, are measured using *square kilometers*.

1 km² = 100 hectares

Estimation Would you use square meters, hectares, or square kilometers to measure the area of

1. a forest?   **2.** a country?   **3.** a kitchen?

4. a shopping center?   **5.** an airport?   **6.** a schoolyard?

Give each measure in square meters.

7. 2 hectares   **8.** 5 hectares   **9.** 12 hectares

10. 22 hectares   **11.** 4.7 hectares   **12.** 0.65 hectares

Give each measure in hectares.

13. 40,000 m²   **14.** 70,000 m²   **15.** 150,000 m²

16. 6,550,000 m²   **17.** 892 m²   **18.** 37.2 m²

19. 5 km²   **20.** 56 km²   **21.** 0.96 km²

Give each measure in square kilometers.

22. 300 hectares   **23.** 80,000 hectares   **24.** 17 hectares

25. 2,374 hectares   **26.** 5.8 hectares   **27.** 29.3 hectares

28. 0.8 hectares   **29.** 796,400 hectares   **30.** 673.4 hectares

MAINTENANCE

Find the least common multiple for each pair of numbers.

1. 2 and 3   **2.** 3 and 4   **3.** 3 and 6   **4.** 4 and 8

5. 5 and 2   **6.** 5 and 3   **7.** 4 and 10   **8.** 6 and 8

9. 15 and 10   **10.** 25 and 10   **11.** 25 and 20   **12.** 18 and 20

Find the greatest common factor for each pair of numbers.

13. 9 and 12   **14.** 12 and 15   **15.** 14 and 21   **16.** 22 and 33

17. 45 and 27   **18.** 63 and 45   **19.** 40 and 24   **20.** 56 and 40

21. 13 and 6   **22.** 24 and 16   **23.** 40 and 16   **24.** 6 and 12

Solve each problem.

25. The library can seat 64 people. When 9 of the chairs are empty, how many people are sitting in the library?

26. The band bought 7 new trombones. Each trombone cost $150. What was the total cost of the trombones?

27. Jim has dimes in one pocket and quarters in the other. He has the same amount of money in each. What is the smallest amount he can have in each pocket?

28. Tammy has 5 skirts, 8 blouses, and 3 sweaters. How many different outfits can she make each having a skirt, a blouse, and a sweater?

29. One box of oatmeal makes 42 servings. How many boxes of oatmeal are needed to make 336 servings?

30. A movie camera with sound runs 1,440 frames per minute. How many frames are used in an 18-minute film?

31. Rhonda is putting boxes 20 cm high in one stack and boxes 25 cm high in another stack. How high must the stacks be to come out even on top?

32. *Estimation* An airline has 28 flights between Toronto and Vancouver each week. Each flight carries about 214 passengers. Estimate the number of passengers each week.

Cumulative Test, Chapters 1–6

Give the letter for the correct answer.

1. Round 13,628 to the nearest thousand.

   A 13,000   **c** 10,000
   B 14,000   **D** 13,600

2. Add.

     4,687
  +   369

   A 5,046
   B 5,056
   c 4,956
   D 4,946

3. Subtract.

    7,348
  − 2,653

   A 4,795
   B 5,695
   c 5,795
   D 4,695

4. Choose the equation that should be used to solve this problem. Then solve the problem.

The bakery has 2,538 loaves of bread. A shipment of 836 loaves of bread is received. How many loaves does the bakery have now?

   A 2,538 + 836 = n; 3,374 loaves
   B 2,538 − 836 = n; 1,702 loaves
   c 2,538 − 1,702 = n; 836 loaves
   D n + 836 = 2,538; 1,702 loaves

5. Estimate the product.

  63 × 58

   A 3,000   **c** 360
   B 30   **D** 3,600

6. Multiply.

  307 × 90

   A 2,763
   B 28,530
   c 27,630
   D 24,540

7. Multiply.

    343
  × 46

   A 15,778
   B 21,952
   c 19,742
   D 14,468

8. Divide.

  13)‾10,579

   A 806 R1
   B 813 R10
   c 713 R10
   D 926 R1

9. What is the greatest common factor of 8 and 20?

   A 8   **B** 4   **c** 2   **D** 5

10. What is three hundredths written as a decimal?

   A 0.3   **c** 0.03
   B 0.003 **D** 300.0

11. What does the 7 mean in 14.2376?

   A 7 hundredths
   B 7 tenths
   c 7 hundreds
   D 7 thousandths

12. Which statement is true?

- **A** 1.06 > 1.60
- **B** 1.06 < 1.061
- **C** 1.06 > 1.08
- **D** 1.06 < 1.006

13. Round 16.271 to the nearest tenth.

- **A** 16.3
- **C** 20
- **B** 16.27
- **D** 16.2

14. Add.

$$13.45$$
$$+ 24.86$$

- **A** 38.21
- **B** 38.41
- **C** 38.11
- **D** 38.31

15. Subtract.

$$36.73$$
$$- 12.96$$

- **A** 24.87
- **B** 24.23
- **C** 23.77
- **D** 23.23

16. Multiply.

$$0.42$$
$$\times \quad 37$$

- **A** 15.54
- **B** 30.66
- **C** 15.44
- **D** 29.76

17. Multiply.

$$0.03$$
$$\times \quad 0.4$$

- **A** 0.12
- **B** 0.012
- **C** 1.2
- **D** 12

18. Multiply.

$$9.426 \times 1,000$$

- **A** 9,426
- **B** 94,260
- **C** 942.60
- **D** 94.260

19. Divide.

$$8.82 \div 9$$

- **A** 0.098
- **B** 9.8
- **C** 98
- **D** 0.98

20. Divide.

$$0.08\overline{)0.032}$$

- **A** 4
- **B** 0.4
- **C** 0.04
- **D** 12

21. Write 35 m as centimeters.

- **A** 0.35 cm
- **C** 3,500 cm
- **B** 3.50 cm
- **D** 35,000 cm

22. Write 2 lb. as ounces.

- **A** 24 oz.
- **C** 16 oz.
- **B** 32 oz.
- **D** 20 oz.

23. Subtract.

$$5 \text{ ft. } 3 \text{ in.}$$
$$- 1 \text{ ft. } 9 \text{ in.}$$

- **A** 4 ft. 6 in.
- **B** 3 ft. 4 in.
- **C** 3 ft. 6 in.
- **D** 4 ft. 4 in.

24. Choose the most sensible measure for the area of a living room floor.

- **A** 96 cu. ft.
- **C** 96 sq. ft.
- **B** 96 ft.
- **D** 96 sq. mi.

$7\frac{7}{8}$ inches

$16\frac{1}{2}$ inches —

— $1\frac{1}{8}$ inches

A. The Taylor children are shopping. The front of the store has four equal panels. Three panels are glass.

Fractions may name part of an object.

Numerator ⟶ **3** Number of glass parts
Denominator ⟶ **4** Number of equal parts

three fourths

$\frac{3}{4}$ of the front is glass.

B. Fractions may name part of a group.

$\frac{3}{4}$ Number of girls
  Number of children

$\frac{3}{4}$ of the Taylor children are girls.

Try

a. What is the numerator of $\frac{5}{7}$?

b. Write three eighths as a fraction.

What fraction of the spinner is

c. blue?

d. red?

e. blue or white?

Practice Complete the table.

Numerator	4	3	7	1	**4.**	2	**6.**	0
Denominator	5	8	10	**3.**	6	**5.**	12	5
Fraction	$\frac{4}{5}$	**1.**	**2.**	$\frac{1}{2}$	$\frac{5}{6}$	$\frac{2}{3}$	$\frac{7}{12}$	**7.**

Write each fraction.

8. one fourth

9. two thirds

10. four fifths

11. five eighths

12. three sevenths

13. eight ninths

14. three tenths

15. one twelfth

16. nine tenths

17. five twelfths

18. zero tenths

19. six sixths

What fraction of the squares on top of the cube are

20. red?

21. white?

22. yellow or green?

23. white or green?

★24. orange?

★25. not brown?

What fraction of the game markers are

26. white?

27. orange?

28. not orange?

29. brown?

30. not brown?

31. large?

Apply Give each fraction.

32. There are 5 parking spaces in front of the store. 3 of them are taken. What fraction of the spaces are taken?

★33. There were 5 shoppers who made purchases at the store and 4 who did not. What fraction of the shoppers made purchases?

Finding Equal Fractions

The Taylors are buying a new television set. They saw this display in the store. What fraction of the sets are on?

Teresa said $\frac{2}{3}$ of the sets are on.   Mark said $\frac{8}{12}$ of the sets are on.

$$\frac{2}{3} = \frac{8}{12}$$

$\frac{2}{3}$ and $\frac{8}{12}$ are *equal fractions*.

You can multiply the numerator and the denominator of a fraction by the same nonzero number to find an equal fraction.

$$\frac{2}{3} = \frac{8}{12}$$

2×4

3×4

Try Give the missing numbers.

a. $\frac{2}{3} = \frac{\blacksquare}{21}$ **b.** $\frac{5}{8} = \frac{20}{\blacksquare}$ **c.** $\frac{5}{6} = \frac{\blacksquare}{12} = \frac{\blacksquare}{18} = \frac{20}{\blacksquare}$

Practice Use the pictures. Give the missing numerators.

1. $\frac{2}{5} = \frac{\blacksquare}{10}$ **2.** $\frac{2}{5} = \frac{\blacksquare}{15}$ **3.** $\frac{3}{5} = \frac{\blacksquare}{20}$

4. $\frac{6}{10} = \frac{\blacksquare}{20}$ **5.** $\frac{4}{10} = \frac{\blacksquare}{20}$ **6.** $\frac{6}{15} = \frac{\blacksquare}{20}$

Use the number lines.
Give the missing numbers.

7. $\frac{1}{4} = \frac{\blacksquare}{8}$ **8.** $\frac{3}{4} = \frac{9}{\blacksquare}$

9. $\frac{0}{2} = \frac{\blacksquare}{12}$ **10.** $\frac{1}{2} = \frac{\blacksquare}{4} = \frac{\blacksquare}{8} = \frac{6}{\blacksquare}$

Give the missing numbers.

11. $\frac{2}{3} = \frac{\blacksquare}{6}$ **12.** $\frac{1}{5} = \frac{\blacksquare}{15}$ **13.** $\frac{1}{2} = \frac{4}{\blacksquare}$ **14.** $\frac{5}{6} = \frac{10}{\blacksquare}$ **15.** $\frac{3}{4} = \frac{\blacksquare}{16}$

16. $\frac{2}{7} = \frac{\blacksquare}{14}$ **17.** $\frac{1}{6} = \frac{\blacksquare}{18}$ **18.** $\frac{3}{8} = \frac{\blacksquare}{24}$ **19.** $\frac{3}{5} = \frac{\blacksquare}{10}$ **20.** $\frac{1}{3} = \frac{4}{\blacksquare}$

21. $\frac{4}{7} = \frac{8}{\blacksquare}$ **22.** $\frac{1}{2} = \frac{\blacksquare}{6}$ **23.** $\frac{2}{5} = \frac{\blacksquare}{20}$ **24.** $\frac{3}{8} = \frac{\blacksquare}{16}$ **25.** $\frac{3}{7} = \frac{\blacksquare}{21}$

26. $\frac{2}{3} = \frac{\blacksquare}{6} = \frac{\blacksquare}{9} = \frac{8}{\blacksquare}$ **27.** $\frac{3}{4} = \frac{\blacksquare}{8} = \frac{9}{\blacksquare} = \frac{12}{\blacksquare}$ **28.** $\frac{5}{8} = \frac{10}{\blacksquare} = \frac{\blacksquare}{24} = \frac{20}{\blacksquare}$

Apply Solve each problem.

In another display, 8 of 24 television sets are portable. Write this as a fraction with a denominator of 24.

Of the 24 sets, 12 are color. Write this as a fraction with a denominator of 2.

30. Three of the 24 television sets have a remote control. Write this as a fraction.

★32. Three fourths of the 24 sets sell for over $400. How many sell for $400 or less?

Writing Fractions in Lowest Terms

Batteries come in different sizes. Before buying a new one, Judy measured the battery for her camera. What is the diameter of the battery?

The diameter of the battery is $\frac{12}{16}$ inch, or $\frac{3}{4}$ inch.

$$\frac{12}{16} = \frac{3}{4}$$

$\frac{12}{16}$ and $\frac{3}{4}$ are equal fractions. $\frac{3}{4}$ is in *lowest terms*.

You can divide the numerator and the denominator of a fraction by the same nonzero number to find an equal fraction in lowest terms.

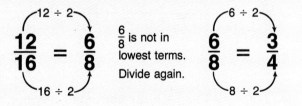

$$\overset{12 \div 2}{\frac{12}{16}} = \frac{6}{8} \qquad \begin{array}{l}\frac{6}{8}\text{ is not in}\\ \text{lowest terms.}\\ \text{Divide again.}\end{array} \qquad \overset{6 \div 2}{\frac{6}{8}} = \frac{3}{4}$$

$\frac{3}{4}$ is in lowest terms because the greatest number that divides both 3 and 4 is 1.

A fraction is in lowest terms when the greatest number that divides both the numerator and the denominator is 1.

Try Tell whether the fraction is in lowest terms. Write *yes* or *no*.

a. $\frac{3}{5}$ **b.** $\frac{5}{15}$

Write each fraction in lowest terms.

c. $\frac{7}{21}$ **d.** $\frac{8}{10}$

e. $\frac{12}{16}$ **f.** $\frac{6}{9}$

Practice Tell whether the fraction is in lowest terms.
Write *yes* or *no*.

1. $\frac{2}{4}$ 2. $\frac{2}{3}$ 3. $\frac{1}{5}$ 4. $\frac{1}{2}$ 5. $\frac{6}{8}$

6. $\frac{4}{9}$ 7. $\frac{4}{10}$ 8. $\frac{8}{12}$ 9. $\frac{5}{6}$ 10. $\frac{7}{12}$

11. $\frac{10}{15}$ 12. $\frac{3}{5}$ 13. $\frac{7}{8}$ 14. $\frac{9}{12}$ 15. $\frac{5}{10}$

Write each fraction in lowest terms.

16. $\frac{3}{6}$ 17. $\frac{4}{12}$ 18. $\frac{6}{8}$ 19. $\frac{4}{10}$ 20. $\frac{14}{16}$

21. $\frac{10}{12}$ 22. $\frac{2}{6}$ 23. $\frac{2}{4}$ 24. $\frac{4}{8}$ 25. $\frac{3}{9}$

26. $\frac{6}{10}$ 27. $\frac{6}{16}$ 28. $\frac{9}{12}$ 29. $\frac{8}{14}$ 30. $\frac{8}{12}$

31. $\frac{5}{15}$ 32. $\frac{15}{27}$ 33. $\frac{30}{60}$ 34. $\frac{20}{50}$ 35. $\frac{15}{21}$

36. $\frac{18}{30}$ 37. $\frac{18}{24}$ 38. $\frac{24}{36}$ 39. $\frac{50}{60}$ 40. $\frac{35}{45}$

Apply Solve each problem. Give each answer in lowest terms.

41. Judy took 8 of the 12 pictures on a roll of film. What fraction of the roll did she use?

42. Mark had a roll of 24 pictures developed. 20 of the pictures were good. What fraction of the pictures were good?

43. Judy paid $24.72 to have 4 rolls of film developed. What was the cost per roll?

*44. On a roll of 24 pictures, 8 were taken in Wisconsin, 4 in Illinois, and 6 in Iowa. The rest of the roll was taken in Indiana. What fraction of the pictures were taken in Indiana?

More Practice Set 74, page 393

MAINTENANCE

Add or subtract.

1. 2,265 + 12,948

2. 9.7 − 6.47

3. 2.4 + 7 + 0.75

4. 58 + 37

5. 8,002 − 2,896

6. 12.6 + 4.782

7. 9.3 − 7.433

8. 537 − 358

9. 8.2 + 5.93

10. 83 − 49

11. 6.82 + 18.3 + 9.39

12. 35 − 8.62

13. 82.9 − 7.64

14. 3.7 + 9.6

15. 2.81 + 4.59

16. 5.78 − 3.94

17. 74.97 − 32.6

18. 1,694 + 209

19. 8.45 − 4.59

20. 5.089 + 6.3

Common Denominators

| $\frac{0}{4}$ | | $\frac{1}{4}$ | | $\frac{2}{4}$ | | $\frac{3}{4}$ | | $\frac{4}{4}$ |

| $\frac{0}{8}$ | $\frac{1}{8}$ | $\frac{2}{8}$ | $\frac{3}{8}$ | $\frac{4}{8}$ | $\frac{5}{8}$ | $\frac{6}{8}$ | $\frac{7}{8}$ | $\frac{8}{8}$ |

Sometimes you need to write fractions with a common denominator.

A. The picture shows that a turkey can run $\frac{1}{4}$ of a mile and a lion can run $\frac{7}{8}$ of a mile in one minute. Write $\frac{1}{4}$ and $\frac{7}{8}$ with a common denominator.

Look at the number lines.

$$\frac{1}{4} \qquad \frac{7}{8}$$
$$\downarrow \qquad \downarrow$$
$$\frac{2}{8} \qquad \frac{7}{8}$$

B. Write $\frac{3}{4}$ and $\frac{5}{6}$ with a common denominator.

A common denominator of these fractions is a common multiple of 4 and 6. List the multiples of 4 and 6 until you find a common multiple.

4   8   12

6   12

The least common multiple of 4 and 6 is 12.

The *least common denominator* of $\frac{3}{4}$ and $\frac{5}{6}$ is 12.

Write $\frac{3}{4}$ and $\frac{5}{6}$ with a denominator of 12.

$$\frac{3}{4} = \frac{9}{12} \qquad \frac{5}{6} = \frac{10}{12}$$

Try For each exercise, give the least common denominator.

For each exercise, write the fractions with the least common denominator.

a. $\frac{1}{2}$ $\frac{2}{3}$ **b.** $\frac{1}{4}$ $\frac{5}{6}$

c. $\frac{3}{8}$ $\frac{7}{10}$ **d.** $\frac{1}{4}$ $\frac{2}{5}$ $\frac{9}{20}$

Practice For each exercise, give the least common denominator.

1. $\frac{2}{3}$ $\frac{1}{6}$ **2.** $\frac{3}{7}$ $\frac{5}{14}$ **3.** $\frac{2}{5}$ $\frac{2}{3}$ **4.** $\frac{1}{3}$ $\frac{3}{4}$ **5.** $\frac{5}{6}$ $\frac{3}{8}$

6. $\frac{7}{10}$ $\frac{3}{4}$ **7.** $\frac{5}{12}$ $\frac{1}{8}$ **8.** $\frac{11}{15}$ $\frac{5}{6}$ **9.** $\frac{1}{2}$ $\frac{4}{7}$ $\frac{13}{14}$ **10.** $\frac{2}{3}$ $\frac{11}{18}$ $\frac{5}{6}$

For each exercise, write the fractions with the least common denominator.

11. $\frac{1}{3}$ $\frac{1}{9}$ **12.** $\frac{1}{4}$ $\frac{1}{12}$ **13.** $\frac{3}{16}$ $\frac{5}{8}$ **14.** $\frac{5}{21}$ $\frac{2}{7}$ **15.** $\frac{5}{6}$ $\frac{11}{24}$

16. $\frac{4}{9}$ $\frac{7}{36}$ **17.** $\frac{1}{2}$ $\frac{4}{7}$ **18.** $\frac{2}{3}$ $\frac{1}{5}$ **19.** $\frac{3}{4}$ $\frac{5}{6}$ **20.** $\frac{1}{6}$ $\frac{5}{8}$

21. $\frac{3}{10}$ $\frac{1}{6}$ **22.** $\frac{5}{8}$ $\frac{5}{6}$ **23.** $\frac{1}{4}$ $\frac{3}{14}$ **24.** $\frac{1}{2}$ $\frac{1}{6}$ $\frac{2}{3}$ **25.** $\frac{1}{5}$ $\frac{1}{2}$ $\frac{3}{10}$

26. $\frac{5}{6}$ $\frac{2}{15}$ **27.** $\frac{1}{8}$ $\frac{7}{10}$ **28.** $\frac{5}{8}$ $\frac{1}{12}$ **29.** $\frac{4}{9}$ $\frac{5}{6}$ $\frac{1}{2}$ **30.** $\frac{5}{12}$ $\frac{1}{3}$ $\frac{1}{8}$

Apply The distances certain animals can run in one minute are given. For each problem, write the fractions with the least common denominator.

31. Hunting dog: $\frac{3}{4}$ mile
Zebra: $\frac{2}{3}$ mile

32. Giraffe: $\frac{8}{15}$ mile
Rabbit: $\frac{3}{5}$ mile

33. Squirrel: $\frac{1}{5}$ mile
Snake: $\frac{1}{3}$ mile
Cat: $\frac{1}{2}$ mile

More Practice Set 75, page 393

Comparing and Ordering Fractions

$\frac{0}{2}$ $\frac{1}{2}$

$\frac{0}{8}$ $\frac{1}{8}$ $\frac{2}{8}$ $\frac{3}{8}$ $\frac{4}{8}$

A. In the race between the tortoise and the hare, the tortoise has gone $\frac{3}{8}$ mile and the hare has gone $\frac{7}{8}$ mile. Which animal has gone farther?

Compare $\frac{3}{8}$ and $\frac{7}{8}$.

$$3 < 7, \text{ so } \frac{3}{8} < \frac{7}{8}, \text{ or } \frac{7}{8} > \frac{3}{8}$$ When fractions have the same denominator, compare numerators.

The hare has gone farther than the tortoise.

B. Compare $\frac{3}{4}$ and $\frac{5}{8}$.

$\frac{3}{4}$ ● $\frac{5}{8}$

$\frac{6}{8}$ ● $\frac{5}{8}$ Write the fractions with a common denominator.

$\frac{6}{8} > \frac{5}{8}$ Compare the numerators. 6 > 5

$\frac{3}{4} > \frac{5}{8}$ Write the original fractions.

C. List the fractions $\frac{3}{4}$, $\frac{7}{8}$, and $\frac{1}{2}$ in order from least to greatest.

$\frac{3}{4}$ $\frac{7}{8}$ $\frac{1}{2}$
↓   ↓   ↓
$\frac{6}{8}$ $\frac{7}{8}$ $\frac{4}{8}$ Write the fractions with a common denominator.

$\frac{4}{8}$ $\frac{6}{8}$ $\frac{7}{8}$ Order the numerators.
↓   ↓   ↓
$\frac{1}{2}$ $\frac{3}{4}$ $\frac{7}{8}$ Write the original fractions.

194

$$\frac{5}{8} \qquad \frac{6}{8} \qquad \frac{7}{8} \qquad \frac{2}{2} \qquad \frac{8}{8}$$

Try Compare the fractions. Use <, >, or =.

a. $\frac{7}{10}$ ● $\frac{3}{4}$ **b.** $\frac{1}{4}$ ● $\frac{4}{16}$

List the fractions in order from least to greatest.

c. $\frac{7}{12}$ $\frac{3}{4}$ $\frac{2}{3}$ **d.** $\frac{3}{4}$ $\frac{1}{2}$ $\frac{0}{3}$

Practice Compare the fractions. Use <, >, or =.

1. $\frac{5}{8}$ ● $\frac{7}{8}$ **2.** $\frac{9}{10}$ ● $\frac{7}{10}$ **3.** $\frac{4}{5}$ ● $\frac{4}{5}$ **4.** $\frac{3}{5}$ ● $\frac{1}{3}$ **5.** $\frac{1}{2}$ ● $\frac{3}{7}$

6. $\frac{2}{3}$ ● $\frac{3}{4}$ **7.** $\frac{2}{5}$ ● $\frac{1}{2}$ **8.** $\frac{2}{3}$ ● $\frac{5}{6}$ **9.** $\frac{3}{4}$ ● $\frac{4}{5}$ **10.** $\frac{3}{12}$ ● $\frac{1}{4}$

List the fractions in order from least to greatest.

11. $\frac{5}{9}$ $\frac{7}{9}$ $\frac{2}{9}$ **12.** $\frac{5}{8}$ $\frac{7}{8}$ $\frac{3}{8}$ **13.** $\frac{4}{5}$ $\frac{2}{5}$ $\frac{1}{2}$ **14.** $\frac{2}{7}$ $\frac{4}{7}$ $\frac{1}{3}$

15. $\frac{5}{8}$ $\frac{3}{4}$ $\frac{1}{2}$ **16.** $\frac{5}{6}$ $\frac{1}{2}$ $\frac{2}{3}$ **17.** $\frac{3}{4}$ $\frac{4}{5}$ $\frac{1}{2}$ **18.** $\frac{2}{3}$ $\frac{5}{6}$ $\frac{4}{9}$

Apply Solve each problem.

19. In one minute, a coyote ran $\frac{7}{10}$ mile and a lion ran $\frac{5}{6}$ mile. Which animal ran farther?

20. In one minute, an elk ran $\frac{3}{4}$ mile and a reindeer ran $\frac{8}{15}$ mile. Which animal ran farther?

Mixed Numbers

A. Rafael filled his bird feeder with this much birdseed.

2 cups . $\frac{1}{2}$ cup

$$2\frac{1}{2}$$

two and one half

Numbers like $2\frac{1}{2}$, $1\frac{7}{8}$, and $15\frac{3}{4}$ are mixed numbers. A mixed number has a whole-number part and a fraction part.

B. Compare $2\frac{1}{2}$ and $2\frac{5}{8}$.

$2\frac{1}{2} \bullet 2\frac{5}{8}$ The whole numbers are the same.

$2\frac{4}{8} \bullet 2\frac{5}{8}$ Write the fractions with a common denominator.

$2\frac{4}{8} < 2\frac{5}{8}$ Compare the fractions.

$2\frac{1}{2} < 2\frac{5}{8}$

Try

a. Give a mixed number for the following amount.

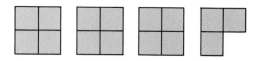

b. Write seven and four fifths as a mixed number.

Compare the numbers. Use <, >, or =.

c. $3\frac{1}{6} \bullet 2\frac{9}{10}$ **d.** $5\frac{3}{7} \bullet 5\frac{4}{7}$ **e.** $7\frac{4}{12} \bullet 7\frac{1}{3}$ **f.** $1\frac{2}{3} \bullet 1\frac{7}{8}$

Practice Give a mixed number for each amount.

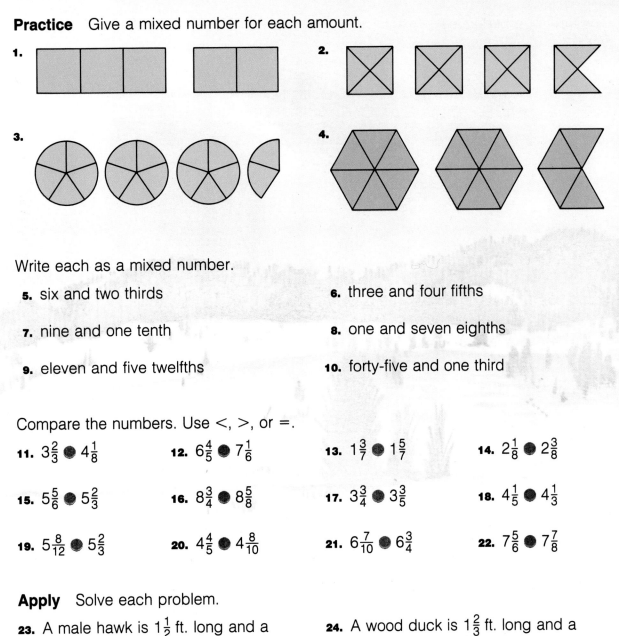

1.

2.

3.

4.

Write each as a mixed number.

5. six and two thirds

6. three and four fifths

7. nine and one tenth

8. one and seven eighths

9. eleven and five twelfths

10. forty-five and one third

Compare the numbers. Use <, >, or =.

11. $3\frac{2}{3}$ ● $4\frac{1}{8}$

12. $6\frac{4}{5}$ ● $7\frac{1}{6}$

13. $1\frac{3}{7}$ ● $1\frac{5}{7}$

14. $2\frac{1}{8}$ ● $2\frac{3}{8}$

15. $5\frac{5}{6}$ ● $5\frac{2}{3}$

16. $8\frac{3}{4}$ ● $8\frac{5}{8}$

17. $3\frac{3}{4}$ ● $3\frac{3}{5}$

18. $4\frac{1}{5}$ ● $4\frac{1}{3}$

19. $5\frac{8}{12}$ ● $5\frac{2}{3}$

20. $4\frac{4}{5}$ ● $4\frac{8}{10}$

21. $6\frac{7}{10}$ ● $6\frac{3}{4}$

22. $7\frac{5}{6}$ ● $7\frac{7}{8}$

Apply Solve each problem.

23. A male hawk is $1\frac{1}{2}$ ft. long and a female is $1\frac{2}{3}$ ft. long. Which is longer?

24. A wood duck is $1\frac{2}{3}$ ft. long and a mallard duck is $1\frac{5}{6}$ ft. long. Which is longer?

★25. List these hummingbirds in order from the shortest to the longest.

Black-Chinned: $3\frac{3}{4}$ in.
Ruby-Throated: $3\frac{1}{4}$ in.
Rufous: $3\frac{7}{10}$ in.
Anna's: $3\frac{1}{2}$ in.
Blue-Throated: $5\frac{1}{4}$ in.

Mixed Numbers in Measurement

The front of a birdhouse is shown in actual size.

Door

Perch

Ledge

1   2   3   4   5   6

How wide is the birdhouse, to the nearest eighth inch?

The ruler is marked in eighths of an inch. Look at the mark by the birdhouse. To the nearest eighth, the width is $5\frac{6}{8}$ inches.

Try

a. Give the length of the segment to the nearest $\frac{1}{8}$ inch.

b. Draw a segment to show $3\frac{3}{4}$ inches.

Practice Give the length of each segment to the nearest $\frac{1}{8}$ inch.

1. _____

2. _____

3. _____

4. _____

5. _____

6. _____

7. _____

8. _____

Draw a segment to show each length.

9. $1\frac{1}{2}$ inches

10. $1\frac{1}{8}$ inches

11. $1\frac{3}{4}$ inches

12. $\frac{2}{8}$ inches

13. $1\frac{7}{8}$ inches

14. $\frac{6}{8}$ inch

15. $1\frac{2}{4}$ inches

16. $1\frac{3}{8}$ inches

Apply Give the length of each part of the birdhouse on page 198 to the nearest $\frac{1}{8}$ inch.

17. Height of the birdhouse from the base to the top of the roof

18. Distance from the top of the door to the top of the roof

19. Distance from the bottom of the door to the perch

20. Length of the slanted roof

21. Height of a side

22. Length of the ledge

★23. Width of the door

★24. Height of the door

Quotients as Fractions and Mixed Numbers

A. Kathy used 5 yd. of braid to make 8 tiebacks for drapes. What fraction of a yard was each tieback?

Find 5 ÷ 8.

$$5 \div 8 = \frac{5}{8}$$

Each tieback was $\frac{5}{8}$ yd.

B. Find 77 ÷ 12.

$$
\begin{array}{r}
6\frac{5}{12} \\
12\overline{)77} \\
72 \\
\hline
5
\end{array}
$$

5 ← Remainder
12 ← Divisor

Try Divide. Give each answer as a fraction in lowest terms.

a. 8 ÷ 10   **b.** 14 ÷ 42

Divide. Give each answer as a mixed number.

c. 4)29   **d.** 15)265

Practice Divide. Give each answer as a fraction in lowest terms.

1. 6 ÷ 12   **2.** 5 ÷ 15

3. 8 ÷ 20   **4.** 24 ÷ 42

5. 18 ÷ 21   **6.** 21 ÷ 30

7. 25 ÷ 65   **8.** 18 ÷ 32

9. 45 ÷ 90   **10.** 72 ÷ 99

200

Divide. Give each answer as a mixed number.

11. $4\overline{)67}$ 12. $3\overline{)94}$ 13. $2\overline{)89}$

14. $5\overline{)77}$ 15. $3\overline{)97}$ 16. $4\overline{)63}$

17. $7\overline{)263}$ 18. $9\overline{)257}$ 19. $6\overline{)488}$

20. $8\overline{)338}$ 21. $4\overline{)995}$ 22. $5\overline{)829}$

23. $12\overline{)186}$ 24. $10\overline{)573}$ 25. $15\overline{)275}$

26. $25\overline{)515}$ 27. $35\overline{)602}$ 28. $10\overline{)779}$

29. $16\overline{)492}$ 30. $21\overline{)434}$ 31. $36\overline{)549}$

32. $24\overline{)448}$ 33. $25\overline{)780}$ 34. $15\overline{)260}$

35. $21\overline{)707}$ 36. $16\overline{)622}$ 37. $35\overline{)637}$

Apply   Solve each problem.

38. Each drapery is 7 ft. How many yards is 7 ft.?

39. Kathy used 82 drapery hooks. 82 objects is how many dozen? (12 objects = 1 dozen)

40. It took 75 minutes to install the drapery rods. How many hours is 75 minutes?

★41. The DeMotts bought a carpet runner $12\frac{1}{2}$ ft. long. $12\frac{1}{2}$ ft. is how many yards?

CHALLENGE

Think of a number less than 100. Add 3. Double your answer. Then subtract 4 and divide by 2. Now subtract the first number. What is your answer?

Try this trick with some other numbers. What is your answer each time?

Problem Solving: Interpret the Remainder

When you solve a problem, you may need to decide whether a mixed number is a sensible answer.

Read   Kathy has 14 yd. of fabric to make 6 pillows. If she makes each pillow the same size, how many yards can she use for each?

Plan   Divide 14 by 6.

Solve
$$2\frac{2}{6} = 2\frac{1}{3}$$
$$6\overline{)14}$$
$$\underline{12}$$
$$2$$

A fraction of a yard makes sense. Write the answer as a mixed number.

Answer   Kathy can use $2\frac{1}{3}$ yd. for each pillow.

Look Back   It is possible to cut $2\frac{1}{3}$ yd. of fabric. 6 pillows, with about 2 yd. of fabric for each, would be 12 yd., which is close to 14 yd.

Try   Solve each problem.

Kathy needs 27 yd. of fringe to decorate the pillows. The fringe is sold in 4-yd. packages.

a. How many packages should she buy?

b. How many complete packages will she use?

c. What fraction of the last package will she use?

Apply Solve each problem.

1. How many $32 light fixtures can the DeMotts buy with $100?

2. How many 4-ft. shelves can Kathy cut from a 10-ft. board?

3. Kathy used 15 lb. of cotton to fill 6 pillows. She used the same amount for each pillow. How many pounds did she use for each pillow?

4. The DeMotts need 580 tiles to cover a floor. The tiles are sold in boxes of 24 each. How many boxes should they buy?

5. Hank needs a carpet runner 156 in. long. How many yards of carpet runner does he need?

6. Kathy bought 30 skeins of yarn for an afghan. How many dozen skeins did she buy?

7. Kathy cut yarn into 15-ft. pieces for a wall hanging. How many pieces could she cut from a 250-ft. ball of yarn?

8. Kathy needs 48 beads for the wall hanging. The beads come in packages of 10. How many packages should she buy?

★9. Hank cut 45 yd. of curtain fabric into as many 6-ft. lengths as he could. How many feet of fabric were left over?

★10. One quart of paint covers 80 sq. ft. Hank bought 5 qt. to cover 360 sq. ft. What fraction of a quart was left over?

To solve a problem, Kathy and Hank divided 30 by 12. Write a problem for each of the following answers.

★11. 2 ft.   ★12. 3 packages   ★13. 2 pieces

Mixed Numbers and Improper Fractions

A. Each row of this piece of needlepoint is $\frac{1}{8}$ in. wide.

Sixteen rows are how many inches?
Twenty-six rows are how many inches?

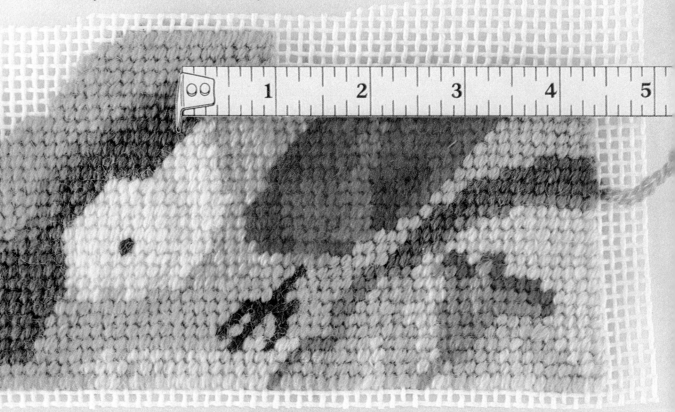

Fractions like $\frac{16}{8}$ and $\frac{26}{8}$ are *improper fractions*.

The numerator of an improper fraction is greater than or equal to the denominator.

B. Write 3 as an improper fraction with a denominator of 4.

$3 = \frac{3}{1} = \frac{12}{4} \leftarrow \begin{array}{l} 3 \times 4 \\ 1 \times 4 \end{array}$

C. Write $2\frac{3}{4}$ as an improper fraction.

$2\frac{3}{4} = \frac{11}{4} \leftarrow \begin{bmatrix} 2 \times 4 = 8 \\ 8 + 3 = 11 \end{bmatrix}$

D. Write $\frac{6}{4}$ as a mixed number.

$\frac{6}{4} = 6 \div 4$

$\begin{array}{r} 1\frac{2}{4} = 1\frac{1}{2} \\ 4\overline{)6} \\ \underline{4} \\ 2 \end{array}$

$\frac{6}{4} = 1\frac{1}{2}$

Try Give each missing number.

Give a fraction for each mixed number.

Give a mixed or whole number for each fraction.

a. $2 = \frac{\blacksquare}{4}$ **b.** $6 = \frac{\blacksquare}{3}$ **c.** $1\frac{2}{3}$ **d.** $8\frac{2}{7}$ **e.** $\frac{14}{4}$ **f.** $\frac{40}{8}$

Practice Give each missing number.

1. $4 = \frac{\blacksquare}{3}$ **2.** $7 = \frac{\blacksquare}{2}$ **3.** $2 = \frac{\blacksquare}{4}$ **4.** $3 = \frac{\blacksquare}{6}$ **5.** $1 = \frac{\blacksquare}{4}$

6. $4 = \frac{\blacksquare}{10}$ **7.** $6 = \frac{\blacksquare}{5}$ **8.** $9 = \frac{\blacksquare}{3}$ **9.** $0 = \frac{\blacksquare}{6}$ **10.** $10 = \frac{\blacksquare}{1}$

Give a fraction for each mixed number.

11. $1\frac{1}{3}$ **12.** $2\frac{1}{2}$ **13.** $4\frac{2}{5}$ **14.** $3\frac{3}{4}$ **15.** $2\frac{3}{8}$ **16.** $4\frac{2}{7}$ **17.** $3\frac{4}{9}$

18. $7\frac{2}{5}$ **19.** $5\frac{3}{4}$ **20.** $6\frac{3}{8}$ **21.** $6\frac{2}{3}$ **22.** $8\frac{3}{4}$ **23.** $9\frac{5}{7}$ **24.** $7\frac{4}{5}$

Give a mixed number or a whole number for each fraction.

25. $\frac{5}{4}$ **26.** $\frac{4}{3}$ **27.** $\frac{14}{5}$ **28.** $\frac{22}{7}$ **29.** $\frac{52}{8}$ **30.** $\frac{34}{4}$ **31.** $\frac{18}{2}$

32. $\frac{13}{7}$ **33.** $\frac{27}{8}$ **34.** $\frac{21}{3}$ **35.** $\frac{40}{6}$ **36.** $\frac{48}{9}$ **37.** $\frac{85}{10}$ **38.** $\frac{72}{10}$

Apply Solve each problem.

39. Each row of a piece of knitting is $\frac{1}{3}$ in. wide. 20 rows are how many inches wide?

40. Each row of a quilt is $\frac{1}{2}$ ft. wide. 12 rows are how many feet wide?

41. Fifteen rows of a hooked rug are $3\frac{3}{4}$ in. wide. Write $3\frac{3}{4}$ as an improper fraction.

★42. Each row on a piece of needlepoint is $\frac{1}{8}$ in. wide. How many rows make $4\frac{1}{2}$ in.?

Practice: Fractions and Mixed Numbers

Write each fraction in lowest terms.

1. $\frac{5}{10}$ 2. $\frac{4}{6}$ 3. $\frac{9}{15}$ 4. $\frac{4}{8}$ 5. $\frac{8}{10}$ 6. $\frac{3}{12}$ 7. $\frac{3}{9}$

8. $\frac{9}{12}$ 9. $\frac{6}{21}$ 10. $\frac{12}{20}$ 11. $\frac{12}{18}$ 12. $\frac{12}{32}$ 13. $\frac{20}{36}$ 14. $\frac{18}{27}$

For each exercise, write the fractions with the least common denominator.

15. $\frac{1}{2}$ $\frac{3}{8}$ 16. $\frac{1}{3}$ $\frac{2}{9}$ 17. $\frac{1}{4}$ $\frac{2}{3}$ 18. $\frac{1}{2}$ $\frac{4}{5}$ 19. $\frac{1}{8}$ $\frac{2}{3}$

20. $\frac{2}{5}$ $\frac{1}{4}$ 21. $\frac{1}{3}$ $\frac{3}{10}$ 22. $\frac{5}{6}$ $\frac{1}{8}$ 23. $\frac{1}{5}$ $\frac{1}{2}$ $\frac{1}{10}$ 24. $\frac{1}{4}$ $\frac{2}{3}$ $\frac{3}{8}$

Compare the numbers. Use <, >, or =.

25. $\frac{9}{10}$ ● $\frac{7}{10}$ 26. $\frac{5}{7}$ ● $\frac{6}{7}$ 27. $\frac{3}{4}$ ● $\frac{7}{8}$ 28. $\frac{2}{3}$ ● $\frac{5}{9}$

29. $2\frac{1}{3}$ ● $2\frac{1}{2}$ 30. $1\frac{5}{6}$ ● $1\frac{11}{12}$ 31. $3\frac{1}{4}$ ● $3\frac{1}{5}$ 32. $4\frac{2}{3}$ ● $4\frac{6}{9}$

What did one rug say to the other?

To answer the riddle, match each fraction with a mixed or whole number below. Some letters are used twice.

33. K $\frac{5}{3}$ 34. Y $\frac{9}{4}$ 35. M $\frac{6}{2}$ 36. U $\frac{10}{5}$ 37. N $\frac{8}{7}$ 38. I $\frac{19}{10}$

39. D $\frac{11}{3}$ 40. O $\frac{16}{5}$ 41. E $\frac{43}{5}$ 42. O $\frac{16}{10}$ 43. H $\frac{28}{8}$ 44. O $\frac{16}{6}$

$\frac{}{1\frac{9}{10}}$, $\frac{}{3}$ $\frac{}{3\frac{1}{2}}$ $\frac{}{2\frac{4}{6}}$ $\frac{}{2\frac{2}{3}}$ $\frac{}{1\frac{2}{3}}$ $\frac{}{8\frac{3}{5}}$ $\frac{}{3\frac{2}{3}}$ $\frac{}{3\frac{1}{5}}$ $\frac{}{1\frac{1}{7}}$ $\frac{}{2\frac{1}{4}}$ $\frac{}{1\frac{3}{5}}$ $\frac{}{2}$!

Apply   Solve each problem. Give each answer as a fraction or a mixed number.

45. It took the DeMotts 90 days to build their addition. 90 days is how many weeks?

46. In 1973 teen-ager Lynne Cox swam the English Channel in 576 minutes. How many hours was this?

47. An average sixth grader is 64 in. tall. How many feet is this?

48. A chimpanzee spends about 18 hours a day in trees. What fraction of a day is this?

49. Sound travels 1,087 feet per second. How many yards per second does it travel?

50. Rosa used 27 in. of material for a skirt. What fraction of a yard is this?

51. How many quarts of water are contained in a 5-pt. pitcher?

52. A large truck weighs 5,750 lb. What is its weight in tons?

53. The weight of a package is 26 oz. Find this weight in pounds.

54. A movie lasts 100 minutes. How many hours is this?

★55. The clearance under a bridge is $15\frac{1}{2}$ ft. Can a truck that is 190 in. high pass under it?

BASIC: IF . . . THEN Statements

An IF . . . THEN statement is used in a program when there is a decision to be made. In line 40, when 0 is entered for N, the program will go to line 80 and end. If 0 is not entered for N, the instructions in line 50 will be followed.

```
10 REM FRACTIONS TO DECIMALS
20 PRINT "NUMERATOR, DENOMINATOR"
30 INPUT N,D
40 IF N=0 THEN 80
50 PRINT "THE DECIMAL IS"
60 PRINT N/D
70 GO TO 10
80 END
```

For the fraction $\frac{1}{4}$, 1 is entered for N and 4 is entered for D.

Output

```
NUMERATOR, DENOMINATOR
? 1,4
THE DECIMAL IS
.25
NUMERATOR, DENOMINATOR
?
```

Give the output for the program above.

1. 3,5   **2.** 5,8   **3.** 7,16

Use the program above to change the following fractions to decimals.

4. $\frac{9}{10}$ **5.** $5\frac{4}{5}$ **6.** $\frac{7}{8}$ **7.** $\frac{3}{16}$

8. What numbers should you enter for N and D to end the program?

207

Decimals and Fractions

A. About three tenths of the earth's surface is land.

You can write three tenths as a fraction or a decimal.

$0.3 = \frac{3}{10}$

water

land

B. Write 0.62 as a fraction.

0.62 is 62 hundredths.

$0.62 = \frac{62}{100}$, or $\frac{31}{50}$

C. Write $\frac{73}{1,000}$ as a decimal.

$\frac{73}{1,000}$ is 73 thousandths.

$\frac{73}{1,000} = 0.073$

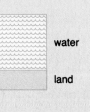

D. Write $\frac{3}{4}$ as a decimal.

$\frac{3}{4} = 3 \div 4$

$$\begin{array}{r} 0.75 \\ 4\overline{)3.00} \\ \underline{28} \\ 20 \\ \underline{20} \\ 0 \end{array}$$

Add zeros in the dividend and divide until the remainder is zero.

$\frac{3}{4} = 0.75$

Try Write each decimal as a fraction.   Write each fraction as a decimal.

a. 0.9   **b.** 0.45   **c.** 0.056   **d.** $\frac{28}{100}$ **e.** $\frac{33}{1,000}$ **f.** $\frac{1}{2}$

Practice Write each decimal as a fraction.

1. 0.3   **2.** 0.1   **3.** 0.43   **4.** 0.89   **5.** 0.07   **6.** 0.03

7. 0.8   **8.** 0.54   **9.** 0.86   **10.** 0.225   **11.** 0.675   **★12.** 17.58

Write each fraction as a decimal.

13. $\frac{7}{10}$ **14.** $\frac{19}{100}$ **15.** $\frac{427}{1,000}$ **16.** $\frac{89}{1,000}$ **17.** $\frac{1}{4}$ **18.** $\frac{2}{5}$ **19.** $\frac{4}{5}$

20. $\frac{3}{8}$ **21.** $\frac{7}{8}$ **22.** $\frac{5}{16}$ **23.** $\frac{13}{25}$ **24.** $\frac{2}{50}$ **25.** $\frac{9}{20}$ **★26.** $1\frac{3}{4}$

Apply South America makes up about $\frac{1}{8}$ of the earth's total land area. Tell if these continents are larger or smaller than South America.

27. Asia: 0.3 of all land area

28. Antarctica: 0.1 of all land area

29. Africa: 0.2 of all land area

Repeating Decimals

A. North America makes up about $\frac{1}{6}$ of the earth's land area. Write the fraction as a decimal.

Find $1 \div 6$.

```
    0.1 6 6 6
6)1.0 0 0 0
    6
    4 0
    3 6
      4 0
      3 6
        4 0
        3 6
          4
```

If you continue to divide, the remainder will always be 4, and you will continue to get 6s in the quotient.

$\frac{1}{6} = 0.1666\ldots$

This decimal is a *repeating* decimal. To write the decimal, put a bar over the digit that repeats.

$\frac{1}{6} = 0.1\overline{6}$

B. Write $\frac{3}{11}$ as a repeating decimal.

Find $3 \div 11$.

```
    0.2 7 2 7
11)3.0 0 0 0
    2 2
      8 0
      7 7
        3 0
        2 2
          8 0
          7 7
            3
```

If you continue, the remainder will always be 8 or 3, and you will continue to get 27s in the quotient.

To write the decimal, put a bar over the digits that repeat.

$\frac{3}{11} = 0.\overline{27}$

Try

a. Write the first 6 digits of $0.\overline{12}$.

b. Write the first 6 digits of $0.1\overline{2}$.

c. Write $0.8777\ldots$ using a bar over the digit that repeats.

Write each fraction as a repeating decimal.

d. $\frac{1}{3}$ **e.** $\frac{5}{12}$

Practice Write 6 digits of each decimal.

1. $0.\overline{7}$ 2. $0.\overline{70}$ 3. $0.\overline{23}$

4. $0.2\overline{3}$ 5. $0.9\overline{32}$ 6. $0.\overline{932}$

Write each decimal with a bar over the digit or digits that repeat.

7. $0.999\ldots$ 8. $0.7111\ldots$

9. $0.818181\ldots$ 10. $0.00323232\ldots$

Write each fraction as a repeating decimal. Use a bar over the digit or digits that repeat.

11. $\frac{2}{3}$ 12. $\frac{4}{9}$ 13. $\frac{5}{6}$

14. $\frac{7}{15}$ 15. $\frac{11}{15}$ 16. $\frac{4}{11}$

17. $\frac{11}{18}$ 18. $\frac{13}{18}$ 19. $\frac{10}{12}$

20. $\frac{11}{12}$ 21. $\frac{10}{33}$ 22. $\frac{13}{22}$

23. $\frac{17}{22}$ ★24. $\frac{3}{7}$ ★25. $\frac{8}{13}$

Apply Antarctica contains 0.1 of the earth's total land area. Tell if each of these continents is larger or smaller than Antarctica.

26. North America: $\frac{1}{6}$ of all land area

27. Europe: $\frac{1}{15}$ of all land area

28. Australia: $\frac{1}{18}$ of all land area

Write each fraction as a repeating decimal. Use your calculator to divide.

1. $\frac{1}{9}$ 2. $\frac{2}{9}$ 3. $\frac{3}{9}$ 4. $\frac{4}{9}$

Use the pattern in Exercises 1–4 and write each fraction as a repeating decimal. Then use your calculator to check.

5. $\frac{5}{9}$ 6. $\frac{6}{9}$ 7. $\frac{7}{9}$ 8. $\frac{8}{9}$

Write each fraction as a repeating decimal. Use your calculator to divide until you see a pattern. Then use the pattern to complete the exercises.

9. $\frac{1}{11}$ 10. $\frac{2}{11}$ 11. $\frac{3}{11}$ 12. $\frac{4}{11}$

13. $\frac{5}{11}$ 14. $\frac{6}{11}$ 15. $\frac{7}{11}$ 16. $\frac{8}{11}$

17. $\frac{9}{11}$ 18. $\frac{10}{11}$ 19. $\frac{11}{11}$ 20. $\frac{12}{11}$

21. $\frac{13}{11}$ 22. $\frac{14}{11}$ 23. $\frac{15}{11}$ 24. $\frac{16}{11}$

Write each fraction as a repeating decimal. Use your calculator to divide until you see a pattern. Then use the pattern to complete the exercises.

25. $\frac{1}{111}$ 26. $\frac{2}{111}$ 27. $\frac{3}{111}$

28. $\frac{4}{111}$ 29. $\frac{5}{111}$ 30. $\frac{6}{111}$

31. $\frac{7}{111}$ 32. $\frac{8}{111}$ 33. $\frac{9}{111}$

Chapter 7 Test

1. Write seven ninths as a fraction.

2. What fraction of the game board is white?

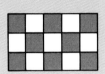

Give the missing numbers.

3. $\frac{1}{5} = \frac{\blacksquare}{20}$ 4. $\frac{3}{8} = \frac{6}{\blacksquare}$

Write each fraction in lowest terms.

5. $\frac{3}{6}$ 6. $\frac{8}{12}$ 7. $\frac{30}{36}$

Write the fractions with the least common denominator.

8. $\frac{2}{9}$ $\frac{1}{3}$ 9. $\frac{2}{5}$ $\frac{1}{4}$

Compare. Use <, >, or =.

10. $\frac{4}{7} \bullet \frac{5}{7}$ 11. $\frac{2}{3} \bullet \frac{5}{8}$

12. $6\frac{1}{4} \bullet 5\frac{1}{2}$ 13. $1\frac{1}{2} \bullet 1\frac{2}{3}$

14. How many squares are shaded? Give a mixed number.

15. Write three and five eighths as a mixed number.

16. Give the length of the segment to the nearest $\frac{1}{8}$ inch.

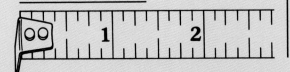

Divide. Give each answer as a mixed number.

17. $5\overline{)83}$ 18. $12\overline{)183}$

Give a fraction for each mixed number.

19. $2\frac{1}{3}$ 20. $4\frac{3}{8}$ 21. $6\frac{3}{5}$

Give a mixed or whole number for each fraction.

22. $\frac{23}{7}$ 23. $\frac{52}{8}$ 24. $\frac{14}{2}$

Write each decimal as a fraction.

25. 0.9 26. 0.16 27. 0.04

Write each fraction as a decimal.

28. $\frac{3}{10}$ 29. $\frac{8}{100}$ 30. $\frac{1}{4}$

Write each fraction as a repeating decimal.

31. $\frac{1}{6}$ 32. $\frac{4}{9}$ 33. $\frac{5}{11}$

Solve each problem.

34. There are 23 students on the track team. They traveled to their last meet in cars. If each car held 5 students, how many cars were needed?

35. A swimming pool 50 ft. wide is separated into 4 sections, each section the same width. How wide is each section?

CHALLENGE
Terminating and Repeating Decimals

How can you tell whether a fraction will result in a terminating decimal or a repeating decimal?

Each of these fractions can be written as a terminating decimal. Write each decimal.

1. $\frac{1}{2}$
2. $\frac{3}{4}$
3. $\frac{5}{8}$
4. $\frac{3}{10}$
5. $\frac{9}{16}$
6. $\frac{11}{20}$
7. $\frac{6}{25}$

8. $\frac{1}{32}$
9. $\frac{7}{40}$
10. $\frac{13}{50}$
11. $\frac{27}{100}$
12. $\frac{31}{125}$
13. $\frac{17}{200}$
14. $\frac{183}{500}$

Each of these fractions can be written as a repeating decimal. Write each decimal.

15. $\frac{1}{3}$
16. $\frac{5}{6}$
17. $\frac{2}{7}$
18. $\frac{4}{9}$
19. $\frac{2}{11}$
20. $\frac{11}{12}$
21. $\frac{4}{13}$

22. $\frac{8}{15}$
23. $\frac{1}{18}$
24. $\frac{13}{24}$
25. $\frac{9}{37}$
26. $\frac{13}{54}$
27. $\frac{17}{60}$
28. $\frac{19}{75}$

29. Write each denominator in Exercises 1–14 as the product of prime factors. What do you notice about the factors?

30. Write each denominator in Exercises 15–28 as the product of prime factors. What do you notice about the factors?

If, when a fraction is written in lowest terms, the only prime factors of the denominator are 2 or 5, then that fraction will result in a terminating decimal. Otherwise, it will result in a repeating decimal.

Tell if the fraction will result in a terminating decimal or a repeating decimal.

31. $\frac{7}{8}$
32. $\frac{2}{3}$
33. $\frac{3}{7}$
34. $\frac{1}{4}$
35. $\frac{7}{20}$
36. $\frac{9}{50}$
37. $\frac{8}{9}$

38. $\frac{5}{11}$
39. $\frac{21}{25}$
40. $\frac{5}{14}$
41. $\frac{8}{21}$
42. $\frac{11}{80}$
43. $\frac{9}{400}$
44. $\frac{237}{600}$

MAINTENANCE

Find n.

1. $542 + n = 830$

2. $n \times 4 = 460$

3. $n + 37 = 62$

4. $n + 365 = 583$

5. $n \times 24 = 312$

6. $93 \times n = 3{,}720$

7. $182 = 136 + n$

8. $357 = 7 \times n$

9. $48 + n = 83$

10. $n \times 61 = 488$

11. $6 \times n = 120$

12. $407 = 247 + n$

13. $87 = 58 + n$

14. $47 \times n = 2{,}961$

15. $n + 74 = 132$

16. $15 \times n = 405$

17. $n + 146 = 931$

18. $8 \times n = 272$

19. $896 = n \times 2$

20. $n + 1{,}136 = 3{,}000$

21. $32 \times n = 416$

Solve each problem.

22. A package of 4 tulip bulbs costs $0.75. What is the price per bulb to the nearest cent?

23. Lin needs 780 beads. How many packages of 25 should he buy?

24. Russ needs enough grass sod to cover 200 sq. ft. Each roll will cover 6 sq. ft. How many rolls of sod should he buy?

25. Wendell wants to cut 50 ft. of fencing into 4 equal sections. How long should he make each section?

26. A book has 12 sections with 64 pages in each section. How many pages are in the book?

27. 15 sheets of paper in a dictionary are 1 mm thick. What is the thickness of 1,350 sheets?

28. A hummingbird can fly 96 km per hour. It flies 4 times as fast as a bat. How fast can a bat fly?

29. A chicken egg weighs about 0.15 lb. An ostrich egg weighs 24 times as much. How much does an ostrich egg weigh?

30. To restore some forest land, 5 students planted 270 trees. What was the average number of trees planted per person?

31. Green Thumb Garden Store received 25 bags of weed killer. Each bag weighed 6.82 kg. What was the total weight of the shipment?

Multiplication and Division of Fractions

$1\frac{1}{4}$ c. carrots

$1\frac{2}{3}$ c. potatoes

$1\frac{1}{2}$ lb. beef

Multiplying Fractions

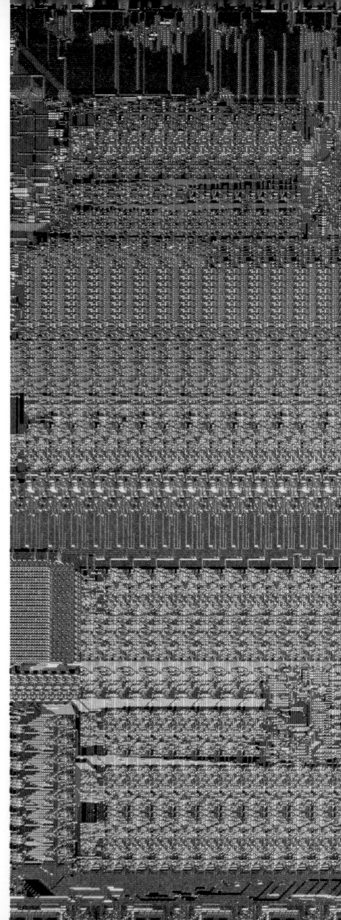

This is a chip, an electronic circuit, from a microcomputer. It is $\frac{3}{4}$ inch long. The width is $\frac{1}{3}$ of its length. Find the width of the chip.

$\frac{3}{4}$ of an inch on the ruler is dotted.

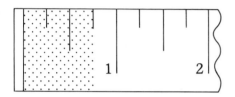

$\frac{1}{3}$ of the dotted part is shaded.

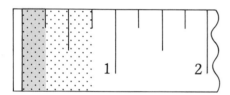

You can see that $\frac{1}{4}$ of the whole inch is dotted and shaded. $\frac{1}{3}$ of $\frac{3}{4}$ is $\frac{1}{4}$.

You can also find the answer by multiplying.

$$\frac{1}{3} \times \frac{3}{4} = \frac{1 \times 3}{3 \times 4} = \frac{3}{12} = \frac{1}{4}$$

Write the answer in lowest terms.

The width of the chip is $\frac{1}{4}$ inch.

To multiply fractions, multiply the numerators and multiply the denominators.

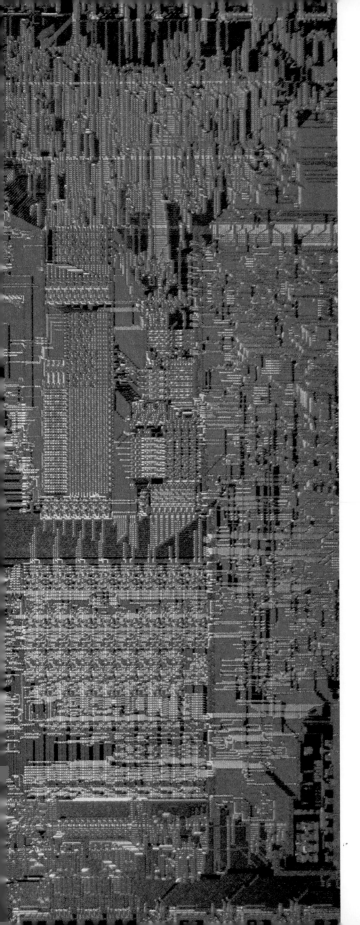

Try Multiply.

a. $\frac{5}{6} \times \frac{3}{4}$ b. $\frac{5}{6} \times \frac{2}{3} \times \frac{1}{2}$

Practice Multiply.

1. $\frac{1}{2} \times \frac{1}{5}$ 2. $\frac{2}{3} \times \frac{1}{3}$

3. $\frac{1}{4} \times \frac{5}{6}$ 4. $\frac{2}{3} \times \frac{4}{5}$

5. $\frac{3}{10} \times \frac{3}{5}$ 6. $\frac{5}{8} \times \frac{3}{4}$

7. $\frac{1}{4} \times \frac{4}{5}$ 8. $\frac{1}{6} \times \frac{6}{7}$

9. $\frac{5}{6} \times \frac{2}{3}$ 10. $\frac{3}{4} \times \frac{5}{9}$

11. $\frac{3}{4} \times \frac{4}{9}$ 12. $\frac{3}{10} \times \frac{5}{9}$

13. $\frac{1}{4} \times \frac{1}{5} \times \frac{3}{7}$ 14. $\frac{1}{3} \times \frac{2}{5} \times \frac{4}{7}$

15. $\frac{2}{5} \times \frac{3}{7} \times \frac{5}{6}$ 16. $\frac{3}{4} \times \frac{2}{7} \times \frac{2}{5}$

Apply Solve each problem.

17. A chip that is $\frac{3}{4}$ inch long is $\frac{3}{4}$ as thick as it is long. How thick is the chip?

18. A circuit in a large computer system is $\frac{1}{8}$ inch long. The width is $\frac{9}{10}$ its length. What is the width of the circuit?

19. Yesterday, Maria worked at the microcomputer for $\frac{3}{4}$ hour. Jane worked $\frac{2}{3}$ as long. How long did Jane work?

Multiplying Fractions and Whole Numbers

A. George and Carla are learning to type with a drill-and-practice program on the school's microcomputer. Carla's typing speed is 40 words per minute. George's typing speed is $\frac{3}{4}$ as fast as Carla's. What is George's typing speed?

Find $\frac{3}{4}$ of 40.

$\frac{3}{4} \times 40$ Write 40 as a fraction and multiply.

$\frac{3}{4} \times \frac{40}{1} = \frac{3 \times 40}{4 \times 1} = \frac{120}{4} = 30$

George's typing speed is 30 words per minute.

B. Find $10 \times \frac{2}{3}$

$10 \times \frac{2}{3}$

$\frac{10}{1} \times \frac{2}{3} = \frac{10 \times 2}{1 \times 3} = \frac{20}{3} = 6\frac{2}{3}$

Try Multiply.

a. $12 \times \frac{3}{8}$

b. $25 \times \frac{4}{5}$

Practice Multiply.

1. $\frac{1}{2} \times 8$ 2. $\frac{1}{3} \times 15$ 3. $\frac{1}{3} \times 10$ 4. $\frac{1}{4} \times 9$ 5. $\frac{1}{7} \times 15$

6. $\frac{2}{3} \times 2$ 7. $\frac{5}{6} \times 3$ 8. $\frac{3}{4} \times 4$ 9. $\frac{3}{4} \times 12$ 10. $\frac{3}{5} \times 15$

11. $\frac{3}{8} \times 24$ 12. $\frac{7}{8} \times 16$ 13. $\frac{2}{3} \times 23$ 14. $\frac{3}{5} \times 17$ 15. $\frac{3}{4} \times 21$

16. $\frac{8}{9} \times 63$ 17. $\frac{7}{8} \times 64$ 18. $\frac{5}{6} \times 20$ 19. $\frac{3}{8} \times 30$ 20. $\frac{3}{10} \times 24$

21. $62 \times \frac{1}{8}$ 22. $54 \times \frac{1}{5}$ 23. $93 \times \frac{2}{3}$ 24. $64 \times \frac{3}{4}$ 25. $63 \times \frac{4}{7}$

26. $27 \times \frac{5}{9}$ 27. $24 \times \frac{3}{8}$ 28. $26 \times \frac{1}{2}$ 29. $54 \times \frac{5}{6}$ 30. $48 \times \frac{7}{8}$

31. $328 \times \frac{3}{5}$ 32. $427 \times \frac{7}{8}$ 33. $532 \times \frac{5}{6}$ 34. $285 \times \frac{9}{10}$ 35. $486 \times \frac{3}{4}$

Apply   Solve each problem.

36. Juan's typing speed is 50 words per minute. Heather's typing speed is $\frac{3}{5}$ as fast as Juan's. What is Heather's typing speed?

37. Donna's typing speed is 48 words per minute. Last month, it was 16 words less. What was her typing speed last month?

38. The manual for the typing drill is $\frac{3}{4}$ inch thick. How high is a stack of 10 manuals?

39. The TV monitor for the microcomputer weighs about 9 pounds. The central processing unit weighs about $\frac{2}{3}$ as much. How much does the central processing unit weigh?

More Practice Set 85, page 396

Multiplying Mixed Numbers

The printer for the school's microcomputer prints $2\frac{1}{2}$ lines per second. How many lines can it print in 5 seconds?

Find $5 \times 2\frac{1}{2}$.

$5 \times 2\frac{1}{2}$ Write 5 and $2\frac{1}{2}$ as fractions. Then multiply.

$$\frac{5}{1} \times \frac{5}{2} = \frac{5 \times 5}{1 \times 2} = \frac{25}{2} = 12\frac{1}{2}$$

The printer can print $12\frac{1}{2}$ lines in 5 seconds.

Try   Multiply.

a. $10 \times 1\frac{2}{3}$ **b.** $\frac{1}{2} \times 1\frac{3}{4}$

c. $1\frac{7}{8} \times 3\frac{4}{5}$

Practice Multiply.

1. $3 \times 2\frac{1}{4}$

2. $2 \times 1\frac{3}{5}$

3. $\frac{2}{3} \times 3\frac{1}{3}$

4. $\frac{3}{4} \times 5\frac{1}{2}$

5. $\frac{5}{6} \times 2\frac{1}{3}$

6. $3\frac{1}{2} \times 4\frac{1}{3}$

7. $2\frac{1}{4} \times 1\frac{2}{5}$

8. $5 \times 1\frac{3}{8}$

9. $4 \times 3\frac{2}{5}$

10. $3 \times 2\frac{3}{4}$

11. $\frac{3}{4} \times 2\frac{1}{3}$

12. $\frac{2}{3} \times 5\frac{3}{4}$

13. $1\frac{3}{8} \times 2\frac{2}{3}$

14. $3\frac{1}{4} \times 2\frac{2}{3}$

15. $2\frac{5}{6} \times 3\frac{3}{4}$

16. $2\frac{3}{4} \times 6$

17. $4\frac{2}{5} \times 10$

18. $2\frac{5}{6} \times \frac{3}{4}$

19. $3\frac{3}{8} \times \frac{4}{5}$

20. $5\frac{2}{3} \times \frac{6}{7}$

21. $2\frac{1}{8} \times 4\frac{4}{5}$

22. $2\frac{1}{2} \times 1\frac{1}{4}$

23. $1\frac{1}{4} \times 1\frac{4}{5}$

24. $1\frac{5}{9} \times 1\frac{1}{2}$

25. $9\frac{2}{3} \times 8\frac{1}{2}$

26. $3\frac{1}{5} \times 2$

27. $4\frac{2}{5} \times 3$

28. $\frac{3}{7} \times 2\frac{1}{6}$

29. $\frac{3}{8} \times 4\frac{8}{9}$

30. $\frac{3}{4} \times 1\frac{1}{5}$

Apply Solve each problem. Use the information given for the school's printer.

31. How many lines can the printer print in 1 minute?

32. It took the printer 48 seconds to print the output from a job. How many lines did it print?

33. Rosa heard of a printer that was $1\frac{1}{2}$ times as fast as the school's printer. How many lines could that printer print in 1 second?

★34. How many lines could the printer in Problem 33 print in 1 minute?

Using a Shortcut When Multiplying

A. Some computer systems use magnetic tape to store large quantities of information. Large computer systems use reels of tape that is $\frac{9}{16}$ inch wide. Microcomputer systems use cassette tape that is $\frac{1}{3}$ as wide as the tape used on large computer systems. How wide is the cassette tape?

Find $\frac{1}{3} \times \frac{9}{16}$.

You already know how to multiply fractions and then write your answer in lowest terms.

$$\frac{1}{3} \times \frac{9}{16} = \frac{1 \times 9}{3 \times 16} = \frac{9}{48} = \frac{3}{16}$$

Here is a shortcut.

$$\frac{1}{3} \times \frac{9}{16} = \frac{1 \times \overset{3}{\cancel{9}}}{\underset{1}{\cancel{3}} \times 16} = \frac{3}{16}$$

$9 \div 3 = 3$

$3 \div 3 = 1$

Divide numerator and denominator by a common factor.

The cassette tape is $\frac{3}{16}$ inch wide.

B. Find $1\frac{3}{5} \times \frac{5}{6}$.

$1\frac{3}{5} \times \frac{5}{6}$

$$\frac{8}{5} \times \frac{5}{6} = \frac{\overset{4}{\cancel{8}} \times \overset{1}{\cancel{5}}}{\underset{1}{\cancel{5}} \times \underset{3}{\cancel{6}}} = \frac{4}{3} = 1\frac{1}{3}$$

Sometimes you can use the shortcut more than once.

Try Multiply.

a. $\frac{3}{8} \times \frac{4}{5}$　　**b.** $2\frac{2}{5} \times 3\frac{1}{3}$　　**c.** $6 \times 1\frac{2}{3} \times \frac{4}{5}$

Practice   Multiply.

1. $\frac{1}{2} \times \frac{2}{3}$

2. $\frac{1}{3} \times \frac{3}{4}$

3. $\frac{2}{3} \times \frac{3}{5}$

4. $\frac{3}{4} \times \frac{4}{5}$

5. $\frac{5}{8} \times \frac{2}{3}$

6. $\frac{3}{4} \times \frac{5}{6}$

7. $2\frac{1}{2} \times \frac{2}{3}$

8. $3\frac{1}{3} \times \frac{9}{10}$

9. $4 \times 1\frac{5}{6}$

10. $6 \times 2\frac{2}{3}$

11. $2\frac{2}{3} \times 1\frac{3}{4}$

12. $1\frac{2}{5} \times 3\frac{1}{3}$

13. $\frac{9}{12} \times \frac{7}{8}$

14. $\frac{5}{10} \times \frac{3}{4}$

15. $3\frac{3}{5} \times 2\frac{2}{9}$

16. $3\frac{3}{4} \times 5\frac{1}{3}$

17. $\frac{7}{10} \times 6\frac{1}{4}$

18. $\frac{5}{6} \times 2\frac{5}{8}$

19. $2\frac{4}{5} \times 4\frac{3}{8}$

20. $6\frac{2}{3} \times 3\frac{5}{8}$

21. $3\frac{1}{8} \times 1\frac{1}{5}$

22. $3\frac{1}{9} \times 1\frac{1}{5}$

23. $4\frac{2}{3} \times 1\frac{1}{2}$

24. $2\frac{1}{2} \times 4\frac{4}{5}$

25. $6\frac{1}{3} \times 2\frac{1}{4}$

26. $6\frac{2}{5} \times 1\frac{1}{2}$

27. $3\frac{3}{4} \times 2\frac{4}{10}$

28. $5\frac{1}{3} \times 1\frac{1}{8}$

29. $\frac{5}{8} \times 3\frac{1}{5} \times \frac{1}{2}$

30. $4\frac{4}{5} \times \frac{3}{8} \times 3\frac{3}{4}$

31. $4 \times 3\frac{1}{2} \times 1\frac{4}{7}$

32. $2\frac{1}{12} \times 1\frac{4}{5} \times 5\frac{1}{3}$

Apply   Solve each problem.

33. At one computer installation, 1,000 characters can be stored on $\frac{5}{8}$ inch of tape. At a second installation, 4 times as much tape is needed to store the same information. How much tape is needed to store 1,000 characters at the second installation?

34. Reels of computer tape come in different sizes. One size is $10\frac{7}{8}$ inches in diameter and another is $\frac{2}{3}$ that size. What is the diameter of the smaller reel?

35. One reel of computer tape can hold 25,000 words that are each 80 characters long. How many characters can this reel of tape hold?

★36. At a third installation, 8 times as much tape is needed to store 1,000 characters as the second installation in Problem 35. How much tape is needed to store 1,000 characters at the third installation?

Problem Solving: Too Much or Too Little Information

A. Read   Sue pays $6.50 for a $\frac{1}{2}$-hour piano lesson. How much does she pay for 3 lessons?

Plan   To find the cost of 3 lessons, multiply the cost of one lesson by 3. *Do not* use the $\frac{1}{2}$.

Solve $3 \times 6.50 = 19.50$

Answer   Sue paid $19.50 for 3 lessons.

Look Back   The fact that these are $\frac{1}{2}$-hour lessons is extra information. Sue estimated that the lessons cost about $21 ($3 \times \$7$), so the answer is reasonable.

B. Read   Sue has taken piano lessons for the last 10 months. Each lesson costs $6.50. How much has she spent on piano lessons?

Plan   To find the answer, you need to know the number of lessons that she had each month. There is not enough information to solve the problem.

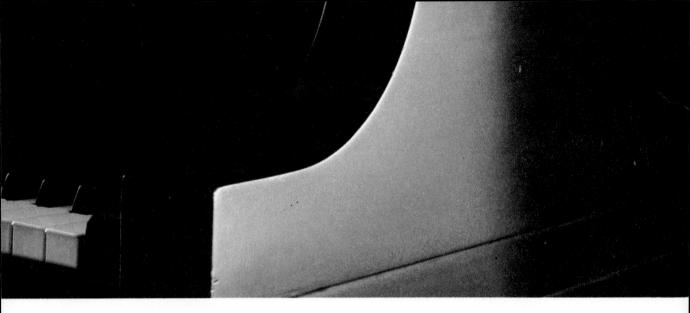

Try If there is not enough information given, write *too little information*. Otherwise, solve the problem.

a. Sue practices the piano for $1\frac{1}{2}$ hours a day, except on days that she has a lesson. Then she practices $\frac{1}{2}$ as long. How many hours does she practice in 5 days?

b. Sue played 3 songs in a recital. She had practiced for the recital for $20\frac{3}{4}$ hours. Each song was about $4\frac{1}{2}$ minutes long. What was the total time that Sue played in the recital?

Apply If there is not enough information given, write *too little information*. Otherwise, solve the problem.

1. Gerry has 2 accordion lessons a week. The lessons cost $8 an hour. What is the cost of a $\frac{3}{4}$-hour lesson?

2. Sue used $\frac{1}{3}$ of her earnings from 4 baby-sitting jobs to buy a book of music. What was the cost of the book?

3. Gerry made a $50 down payment on an accordion. An accordion costs about $\frac{1}{10}$ as much as a piano. What is the cost of an accordion?

4. There are 16 children in Gerry's accordion band. $\frac{3}{4}$ of them are boys and $\frac{1}{4}$ of them are girls. How many boys are in the band?

5. Jim practices the piano for $1\frac{1}{2}$ hours each school day and for $2\frac{1}{2}$ hours each day of the weekend. How long did he practice last weekend?

6. The accordion band has practiced $26\frac{3}{4}$ hours and given 6 concerts. What is the total number of hours they have played together?

Predicting Outcomes

Career Barbara Green is a teller at the bank. Since there are 7 tellers working, Barbara figures that she will serve about 1 out of 7 customers. There are 42 customers in the bank. How many of them is Barbara likely to serve?

Find $\frac{1}{7}$ of 42.

$$\frac{1}{7} \times 42$$

$$\frac{1}{7} \times \frac{42}{1} = \frac{1 \times \overset{6}{\cancel{42}}}{\underset{1}{\cancel{7}} \times 1} = 6$$

Barbara is likely to serve 6 customers.

Try Solve each problem.

a. If Barbara serves 1 out of 7 customers, how many will she serve if there are 35 customers?

b. About 3 out of 4 customers have a savings account at the bank. Out of 40 customers, how many have a savings account?

Practice Solve each problem.

If Barbara serves 1 out of 7 customers, how many will she serve if there are

1. 7 customers?

2. 28 customers?

3. 56 customers?

4. 84 customers?

If Barbara serves 1 out of 5 customers, how many will she serve if there are

5. 35 customers?

6. 50 customers?

7. 65 customers?

8. 80 customers?

Barbara found that about 2 out of 3 customers make only one transaction. How many customers make one transaction if there are

9. 24 customers?

10. 30 customers?

11. 36 customers?

12. 45 customers?

About 3 out of 4 customers have a savings account at the bank. How many customers have a savings account if there are

13. 24 customers?

14. 32 customers?

15. 48 customers?

16. 60 customers?

On every dollar bill there is a serial number. The last digit of the serial number can be any digit from 0 to 9. Barbara has 300 dollar bills in her cash drawer. How many of them are likely to have a last digit

17. of 5?   **★18.** of 5 or 0?   **★19.** that is an even number?

More Practice Set 89, page 397

Write each fraction in lowest terms.

1. $\frac{2}{6}$ **2.** $\frac{5}{10}$

3. $\frac{12}{16}$ **4.** $\frac{15}{24}$

5. $\frac{9}{18}$ **6.** $\frac{4}{10}$

7. $\frac{10}{15}$ **8.** $\frac{27}{30}$

9. $\frac{6}{9}$ **10.** $\frac{10}{16}$

11. $\frac{7}{14}$ **12.** $\frac{16}{20}$

13. $\frac{12}{18}$ **14.** $\frac{10}{15}$

15. $\frac{12}{24}$ **16.** $\frac{18}{27}$

17. $\frac{6}{18}$ **18.** $\frac{6}{30}$

19. $\frac{14}{35}$ **20.** $\frac{20}{30}$

21. $\frac{20}{24}$ **22.** $\frac{27}{36}$

23. $\frac{9}{21}$ **24.** $\frac{15}{40}$

25. $\frac{14}{24}$ **26.** $\frac{16}{18}$

27. $\frac{18}{24}$ **28.** $\frac{24}{36}$

29. $\frac{48}{60}$ **30.** $\frac{36}{100}$

31. $\frac{45}{100}$ **32.** $\frac{64}{100}$

NEW ACCOUNTS

Probability

A. Mr. Rogers has a 4-digit code number to use the automatic-teller machine at his bank. What is the probability that his code number ends in 3?

Each of the digits from 0 to 9 are *equally likely* outcomes for the last digit. Getting 3 is a *favorable outcome*. It is 1 of 10 *possible outcomes*. The *probability* of the number ending in 3 is $\frac{1}{10}$.

$\frac{1}{10}$ ← **Number of favorable outcomes**
   ← **Number of possible outcomes**

The probability of the code number ending in 3 is $\frac{1}{10}$.

B. What is the probability that Mr. Rogers's code number is an even number?

There are 10 equally likely outcomes. If the code number is even, it ends in 0, 2, 4, 6, or 8, so there are 5 favorable outcomes. The probability of getting an even number is $\frac{5}{10}$, or $\frac{1}{2}$.

When all outcomes are equally likely, the probability of a favorable outcome is given by the following formula:

$$probability = \frac{number\ of\ favorable\ outcomes}{number\ of\ possible\ outcomes}$$

Try Solve each problem.

What is the probability that Mr. Rogers's code number ends in

a. 5?   **b.** 5 or 0?

Practice Solve each problem.

The first digit of the code number for the automatic bank teller can be any digit from 1 to 9. What is the probability that it is

1. 6?   **2.** 5 or 6?   **3.** an odd number?   **4.** an even number?

The first digit of the extension number for a phone at the bank can be any digit from 2 to 8. What is the probability that it is

5. 2?   **6.** 1?   **7.** 3 or 4?   **8.** an even number?

The first digit of a special savings account can be any digit from 1 to 5. What is the probability that it is

9. 4?   **10.** 2 or 5?   **11.** an odd number?   **12.** an even number?

The first letter of a code to use the bank computer can be X, Y, or Z. What is the probability that it is

13. X?   **14.** A?   **15.** X or Y?   **16.** X, Y, or Z?

CHALLENGE

The product of two numbers is 1,000,000. Neither number has any zeros. What are the numbers?

Introduction to Division of Fractions

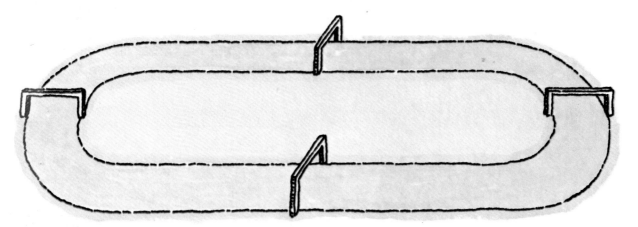

A. Della set up 4 hurdles on an oval track for a horse show. Each hurdle was $\frac{1}{4}$ mi. from two other hurdles. How long was the track?

Find $\frac{1}{4} \times 4$.

$$\frac{1}{4} \times 4$$

$$\frac{1}{4} \times \frac{4}{1} = \frac{1 \times \overset{1}{\cancel{4}}}{\underset{1}{\cancel{4}} \times 1} = 1$$

The track was 1 mi. long.

4 is the reciprocal of $\frac{1}{4}$.

Two numbers whose product is 1 are reciprocals of each other.

B. Here is a way to find $1\frac{1}{2} \div \frac{1}{6}$.

THINK How many sixths in $1\frac{1}{2}$?

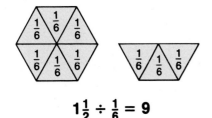

$$1\frac{1}{2} \div \frac{1}{6} = 9$$

Try Give the reciprocal for each number.

a. $\frac{1}{3}$ **b.** 2   **c.** $1\frac{3}{5}$

Use the picture to find the answer to Exercise d. Multiply to find the answer to Exercise e.

d. $1\frac{3}{4} \div \frac{1}{4}$

e. $1\frac{3}{4} \times \frac{4}{1}$

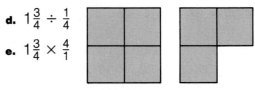

230

Practice Give the reciprocal for each number.

1. $\frac{3}{4}$ 2. $\frac{2}{5}$ 3. $\frac{4}{7}$ 4. $\frac{3}{8}$ 5. 6   6. 9   7. 7

8. 10   9. $2\frac{1}{4}$ 10. $1\frac{5}{9}$ 11. $3\frac{5}{8}$ 12. $2\frac{2}{5}$ 13. $1\frac{7}{10}$ 14. $2\frac{5}{12}$

Use the picture to find the answer to part a.
Multiply to find the answer to part b.

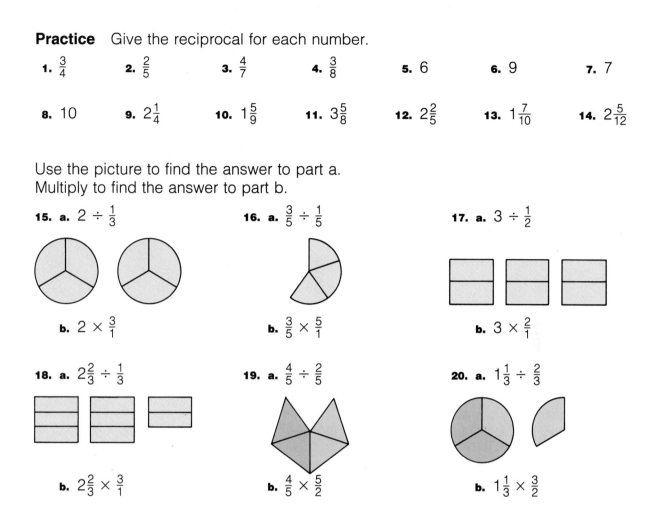

15. a. $2 \div \frac{1}{3}$

b. $2 \times \frac{3}{1}$

16. a. $\frac{3}{5} \div \frac{1}{5}$

b. $\frac{3}{5} \times \frac{5}{1}$

17. a. $3 \div \frac{1}{2}$

b. $3 \times \frac{2}{1}$

18. a. $2\frac{2}{3} \div \frac{1}{3}$

b. $2\frac{2}{3} \times \frac{3}{1}$

19. a. $\frac{4}{5} \div \frac{2}{5}$

b. $\frac{4}{5} \times \frac{5}{2}$

20. a. $1\frac{1}{3} \div \frac{2}{3}$

b. $1\frac{1}{3} \times \frac{3}{2}$

Apply Use the diagram to solve each problem.

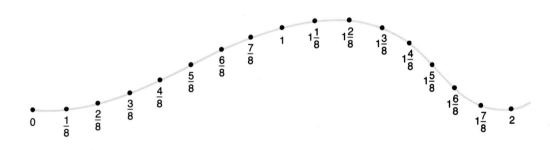

21. Part of the course of the cross-country event is shown above. A flag marks each $\frac{1}{8}$ mi. How many $\frac{1}{8}$ mi. are there in 2 mi.?

22. When Shining Star had completed $1\frac{5}{8}$ mi. of the event, how many $\frac{1}{8}$ mi. had she run?

Dividing Fractions and Whole Numbers

Dividing by a number is the same as multiplying by its reciprocal.

A. The distance around the deck of an oil-carrying supertanker is $\frac{3}{4}$ mile. The crew made a jogging track on the deck by marking it off in $\frac{1}{8}$-mile sections. How many sections were there?

Find $\frac{3}{4} \div \frac{1}{8}$.

$$\frac{3}{4} \div \frac{1}{8}$$ The reciprocal of $\frac{1}{8}$ is $\frac{8}{1}$.

$$\frac{3}{4} \times \frac{8}{1} = \frac{3 \times \overset{2}{\cancel{8}}}{\underset{1}{\cancel{4}} \times 1} = 6$$

There were 6 sections.

B. Find $\frac{4}{5} \div 12$.

$$\frac{4}{5} \div 12$$

$$\frac{4}{5} \times \frac{1}{12} = \frac{\overset{1}{\cancel{4}} \times 1}{5 \times \underset{3}{\cancel{12}}} = \frac{1}{15}$$

Try   Find the missing number.

a. $\frac{3}{4} \div \frac{5}{6} = \frac{3}{4} \times \frac{\blacksquare}{5}$

Divide.

b. $\frac{2}{3} \div \frac{3}{8}$ **c.** $2 \div \frac{3}{4}$

Practice Find each missing number.

1. $\frac{2}{3} \div \frac{5}{8} = \frac{2}{3} \times \frac{\blacksquare}{5}$ 2. $5 \div \frac{2}{9} = \frac{5}{1} \times \frac{9}{\blacksquare}$ 3. $\frac{3}{8} \div 4 = \frac{3}{8} \times \blacksquare$ 4. $\frac{4}{9} \div \frac{7}{8} = \blacksquare \times \blacksquare$

Divide.

5. $\frac{3}{8} \div \frac{2}{3}$ 6. $\frac{1}{2} \div \frac{4}{5}$ 7. $\frac{3}{4} \div \frac{4}{5}$ 8. $\frac{1}{3} \div \frac{5}{8}$ 9. $\frac{1}{4} \div \frac{3}{5}$

10. $\frac{3}{5} \div \frac{5}{6}$ 11. $\frac{3}{8} \div \frac{6}{7}$ 12. $\frac{2}{3} \div \frac{5}{6}$ 13. $6 \div \frac{3}{4}$ 14. $9 \div \frac{3}{5}$

15. $\frac{2}{3} \div 5$ 16. $\frac{3}{4} \div 2$ 17. $\frac{3}{5} \div 4$ 18. $2 \div \frac{1}{8}$ 19. $3 \div \frac{5}{8}$

20. $8 \div \frac{4}{5}$ 21. $10 \div \frac{5}{8}$ 22. $\frac{9}{10} \div 3$ 23. $\frac{2}{3} \div 6$ 24. $\frac{5}{6} \div \frac{7}{12}$

Apply Solve each problem.

25. George jogged the $\frac{3}{4}$-mile track in 6 minutes. How far did he jog in 1 minute?

26. George jogged around the $\frac{3}{4}$-mile track 3 times. How many miles did he jog?

More Practice Set 92, page 398

Dividing Mixed Numbers

A marathon is a race that covers a distance of about $26\frac{1}{4}$ miles. A runner completed a marathon in $2\frac{1}{4}$ hours. What was his average speed in miles per hour?

Find $26\frac{1}{4} \div 2\frac{1}{4}$.

$$26\frac{1}{4} \div 2\frac{1}{4}$$ Change each mixed number to a fraction.

$$\frac{105}{4} \div \frac{9}{4}$$ Then divide.

$$\frac{105}{4} \times \frac{4}{9} = \frac{\overset{35}{\cancel{105}} \times \overset{1}{\cancel{4}}}{\underset{1}{\cancel{4}} \times \underset{3}{\cancel{9}}} = \frac{35}{3} = 11\frac{2}{3}$$

The runner's average speed was $11\frac{2}{3}$ miles per hour.

Try Divide.

a. $2\frac{1}{4} \div 2$ b. $15 \div 1\frac{1}{2}$ c. $4\frac{1}{2} \div 1\frac{1}{5}$

234

Practice Divide.

1. $1\frac{2}{3} \div 2$
2. $1\frac{3}{5} \div 3$
3. $4 \div 2\frac{1}{2}$
4. $6 \div 1\frac{2}{3}$
5. $5 \div 1\frac{3}{4}$

6. $2\frac{2}{3} \div 1\frac{2}{5}$
7. $1\frac{3}{8} \div 2\frac{2}{5}$
8. $4\frac{1}{3} \div 6$
9. $3\frac{5}{8} \div 4$
10. $1\frac{7}{9} \div 3$

11. $5 \div 1\frac{2}{3}$
12. $2 \div 2\frac{2}{7}$
13. $2\frac{1}{5} \div 1\frac{5}{6}$
14. $2\frac{5}{6} \div 1\frac{3}{4}$
15. $2\frac{1}{2} \div 1\frac{5}{6}$

16. $2\frac{3}{4} \div \frac{2}{3}$
17. $3\frac{3}{5} \div \frac{1}{4}$
18. $3 \div 1\frac{4}{5}$
19. $10 \div 1\frac{1}{4}$
20. $9 \div 5\frac{1}{4}$

21. $\frac{5}{8} \div 3\frac{1}{2}$
22. $\frac{3}{4} \div 2\frac{1}{2}$
23. $\frac{5}{8} \div 1\frac{2}{3}$
24. $\frac{8}{9} \div 2\frac{1}{3}$
25. $12 \div 2\frac{1}{4}$

26. $5 \div 3\frac{1}{3}$
27. $3\frac{3}{4} \div 3\frac{1}{8}$
28. $2\frac{1}{2} \div \frac{5}{8}$
29. $4\frac{1}{5} \div \frac{7}{10}$
30. $3\frac{1}{3} \div 1\frac{2}{3}$

31. $3\frac{1}{9} \div 4\frac{2}{3}$
32. $8\frac{3}{4} \div 10$
33. $\frac{7}{8} \div 3\frac{3}{8}$
34. $4\frac{2}{5} \div 1\frac{1}{10}$
35. $8\frac{1}{3} \div 1\frac{2}{3}$

36. $24\frac{1}{2} \div \frac{1}{6}$
37. $90 \div 3\frac{1}{3}$
38. $56 \div 1\frac{3}{4}$
39. $60 \div 2\frac{1}{2}$
40. $100 \div 33\frac{1}{3}$

Apply Find the average speed of the winner of the marathon in each of the following Olympic Games. Use $26\frac{1}{4}$ miles for the length of a marathon.

	Year	Winner	Country	Time
41.	1900	Michael Teato	France	3 hours
42.	1924	Albin Stenroos	Finland	$2\frac{3}{4}$ hours
43.	1936	Kitei Son	Japan	$2\frac{1}{2}$ hours
44.	1968	Mamo Wolde	Ethiopia	$2\frac{1}{3}$ hours
45.	1976	Waldemar Cierpinski	East Germany	$2\frac{1}{6}$ hours

Practice: Multiplying and Dividing Mixed Numbers

Multiply or divide.

1. $5\frac{1}{3} \times 3\frac{4}{5}$ 2. $\frac{5}{6} \div \frac{5}{9}$ 3. $2\frac{5}{8} \div \frac{3}{4}$ 4. $\frac{3}{4} \times 1\frac{1}{3}$ 5. $\frac{2}{3} \times \frac{3}{4}$

6. $5 \div \frac{1}{4}$ 7. $4\frac{2}{5} \times 3\frac{5}{6}$ 8. $4\frac{3}{8} \div 4\frac{1}{6}$ 9. $\frac{5}{9} \div 4\frac{1}{6}$ 10. $\frac{1}{10} \times 5$

11. $\frac{5}{6} \times 1\frac{1}{5}$ 12. $6\frac{2}{5} \div \frac{8}{15}$ 13. $3\frac{5}{7} \div 2\frac{1}{4}$ 14. $8 \times \frac{2}{9}$ 15. $2 \div 1\frac{1}{5}$

16. $\frac{2}{3} \times \frac{3}{8}$ 17. $6 \div \frac{3}{8}$ 18. $1\frac{1}{7} \times 2\frac{4}{9}$ 19. $5\frac{2}{5} \div 2\frac{2}{9}$ 20. $\frac{8}{15} \times 3\frac{1}{3}$

21. $\frac{5}{8} \div \frac{3}{4}$ 22. $5\frac{1}{3} \times 2\frac{1}{4}$ 23. $1\frac{1}{8} \times \frac{1}{3}$ 24. $9 \div 2\frac{1}{4}$ 25. $5\frac{2}{3} \times 1\frac{4}{5}$

26. $1\frac{5}{9} \div 2\frac{1}{3}$ 27. $2\frac{1}{2} \div 3\frac{3}{4}$ 28. $1\frac{3}{7} \times 3\frac{3}{5}$ 29. $3\frac{1}{6} \times 1\frac{6}{7}$ 30. $\frac{4}{5} \div 1\frac{3}{5}$

Several pieces are missing from the puzzle. Work the
exercise on each missing piece and match the
answer with an answer on a piece at the right.

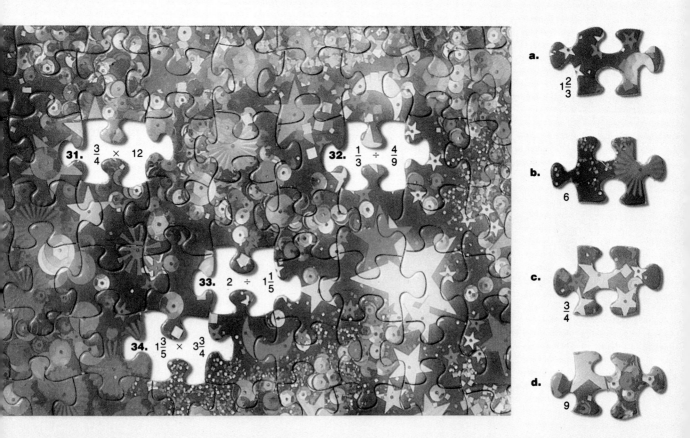

31. $\frac{3}{4} \times 12$

32. $\frac{1}{3} \div \frac{4}{9}$

33. $2 \div 1\frac{1}{5}$

34. $1\frac{3}{5} \times 3\frac{3}{4}$

a. $1\frac{2}{3}$

b. 6

c. $\frac{3}{4}$

d. 9

Apply Solve each problem.

35. Linda jogged a lap in $1\frac{1}{4}$ minutes. At this rate, how long would it take her to jog 10 laps?

36. There are about $365\frac{1}{4}$ days in a year. How many weeks is that?

37. John is $64\frac{1}{2}$ inches tall. Fred is $\frac{7}{8}$ as tall as John. How tall is Fred?

38. Martha is weaving a scarf. One row of the weaving is $\frac{1}{6}$ inch wide. How many rows are in $\frac{1}{2}$ inch?

39. A recipe for carrot cookies calls for 5 carrots. Masumi wants to make $2\frac{1}{2}$ times the recipe. How many carrots does she need?

40. A great white shark is about $\frac{1}{3}$ the length of a whale shark. A whale shark is 18 m long. How long is a great white shark?

41. A shark's liver is about $\frac{1}{4}$ of its weight. A whale shark weighs 14 metric tons. How much does a whale shark's liver weigh?

42. An office clerk has 126 transactions to record. Each one takes about $2\frac{1}{2}$ minutes to complete. How long will it take to record all the transactions?

BASIC: FOR . . . NEXT Loops

FOR and NEXT statements are used together to form a loop. The lines between these statements are done repeatedly.

Line 10 tells the computer to use 2 as the first value of X. Line 40 sends the computer back to line 10, and the computer uses 3 as the next value for X. The loop is completed after 5 is used for X.

A semicolon at the end of a PRINT statement causes the next output item to be printed on the same line going across the screen.

```
                                    Output
   ┌10 FOR X=2 TO 4     1.5 2.25 3
 g │ 20 LET N=3/4*X
 o │ 30 PRINT N;
 ol└40 NEXT X
    50 END
```

Give the output for each program.

1.
```
10 FOR X=1 TO 5
20 LET N=1/2*X
30 PRINT N;
40 NEXT X
50 END
```

2.
```
10 FOR A=10 TO 15
20 PRINT 3/5*A
30 NEXT A
40 END
```

3. Write a program using FOR and NEXT that multiplies the numbers from 5 to 20 by $\frac{3}{4}$. Print the output across the screen.

237

Problem Solving:
Write a Problem

Chicken Parmesan

2½ lb. frying chicken
⅛ teaspoon garlic powder
¾ cup bread crumbs
¼ cup parmesan cheese
⅓ cup margarine

1. Rinse chicken pieces in cold water and dry on paper towels.
2. Grease a large flat baking dish.
3. Dip each dried piece of chicken in the melted margarine and then in a mixture of garlic powder, bread crumbs, and parmesan cheese.
4. Sprinkle with salt and pepper.
5. Bake uncovered in a preheated 350°F oven for 1¼ hours.

Serves 4.

Pommes Salad

1 envelope unflavored gelatin
¼ cup cold water
1¾ cup cider
½ stick cinnamon
3 cloves
1 unpeeled apple, diced
½ cup celery, diced
½ cup drained crushed pineapple

1. Soften the gelatin in the water while you bring the cider to a boil with the cinnamon and cloves. Add the gelatin and stir. Put the cover on the pan and allow the cider to steep for 1 hour off the heat.
2. Remove the spices and add the other ingredients. Refrigerate and stir once or twice until the mixture begins to thicken.
3. Pour into molds and refrigerate.

Serves 6.

Tim wrote this multiplication problem. The recipe calls for 2½ lb. of frying chicken. How much chicken would be needed to make 1½ times the recipe?

Try

a. Write a problem about the amount of an ingredient needed to make ½ the Pommes Salad.

238

Apply Write a problem about

1. the amount of an ingredient needed to make 4 times the amount of Chicken Parmesan.

2. the amount of an ingredient needed to make $3\frac{1}{2}$ times the amount of Chicken Parmesan.

3. the amount of an ingredient needed to make $\frac{1}{3}$ the amount of Pommes Salad.

4. changing the recipe for Chicken Parmesan to serve a different number of people.

5. changing the recipe for Pommes Salad to serve a different number of people.

6. finding what part of a jug of cider is used for the Pommes Salad recipe.

7. comparing the amount of time the Chicken Parmesan bakes with the amount of time for a different recipe.

8. finding the cost of the apple.

9. finding the cost of the chicken.

10. finding the amount of change received when paying for the chicken.

To multiply or divide fractions on a calculator, you must remember the rules for the order of operations.

To multiply $\frac{3}{4} \times \frac{2}{5}$ on a calculator, which of the following key sequences are correct?

a. 3 $\boxed{\times}$ 2 $\boxed{\div}$ 4 $\boxed{\times}$ 5

b. 3 $\boxed{\div}$ 4 $\boxed{\times}$ 2 $\boxed{\div}$ 5

c. 3 $\boxed{\times}$ 2 $\boxed{\div}$ 4 $\boxed{\div}$ 5

Both b and c are correct.

Use your calculator to find each product or quotient. Use a key sequence like b or c above.

1. $\frac{4}{5} \times \frac{3}{8}$ 2. $\frac{5}{6} \times \frac{3}{4}$

3. $\frac{2}{3} \times \frac{3}{8}$ 4. $\frac{3}{8} \times \frac{5}{6}$

5. $\frac{5}{8} \times \frac{3}{10}$ 6. $\frac{9}{10} \times \frac{5}{12}$

7. $\frac{7}{8} \times \frac{6}{7}$ 8. $\frac{2}{3} \times \frac{5}{8}$

9. $\frac{5}{9} \times \frac{3}{7}$ 10. $\frac{5}{6} \times \frac{3}{10}$

11. $\frac{2}{3} \div \frac{5}{8}$ 12. $\frac{3}{8} \div \frac{4}{5}$

13. $\frac{5}{6} \div \frac{3}{4}$ 14. $\frac{7}{10} \div \frac{2}{5}$

15. $\frac{8}{9} \div \frac{4}{9}$ 16. $\frac{5}{8} \div \frac{5}{6}$

17. $\frac{9}{10} \div \frac{3}{5}$ 18. $\frac{5}{6} \div \frac{5}{9}$

More Practice Set 94, page 399

239

Chapter 8 Test

Multiply.

1. $\frac{3}{4} \times \frac{1}{4}$ **2.** $\frac{3}{5} \times \frac{3}{4}$

3. $\frac{5}{6} \times \frac{9}{10}$ **4.** $\frac{3}{4} \times 20$

5. $\frac{4}{9} \times 18$ **6.** $40 \times \frac{5}{6}$

7. $2\frac{1}{2} \times \frac{4}{5}$ **8.** $4\frac{5}{6} \times 2\frac{2}{5}$

Give the reciprocal for each number.

9. $\frac{2}{3}$ **10.** 5   **11.** $1\frac{3}{4}$

Use the picture to find each answer.

12. $2 \div \frac{1}{3}$

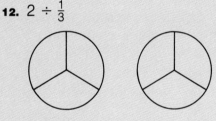

13. $1\frac{1}{2} \div \frac{1}{4}$

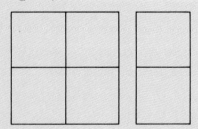

Divide.

14. $\frac{6}{7} \div \frac{2}{3}$ **15.** $\frac{3}{10} \div \frac{4}{5}$

16. $\frac{5}{8} \div 5$ **17.** $3\frac{2}{3} \div 1\frac{5}{8}$

18. $3 \div 1\frac{4}{5}$ **19.** $2\frac{1}{5} \div 1\frac{5}{6}$

If there is not enough information given, write *too little information*. Otherwise, solve the problem.

20. Adults' tickets for the concert cost $3 and children's tickets cost $1.50. Keiko sold 12 tickets. How much money did she collect for the tickets?

21. Mona has exercise class 2 times a week. Each class is $1\frac{1}{2}$ hours long and costs $5 per hour. How many hours does she spend in exercise class each week?

Solve each problem.

22. If Barbara serves 1 out of 6 customers, how many will she serve if there are 30 customers?

23. The first digit of a special savings account can be any digit from 1 to 5. What is the probability that it is 3 or 4?

Write a problem about

24. the amount of change received when paying for an item that costs $3.57.

25. the amount of an ingredient needed to make $1\frac{1}{2}$ times a recipe.

Greatest Possible Error

There is always a certain amount of error in any measurement.

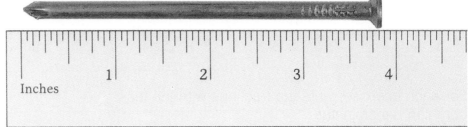

Kathy said the nail is $3\frac{7}{8}$ inches long. The unit used for measuring was $\frac{1}{8}$ inch. The *greatest possible error* between the measurement and the real length is $\frac{1}{2}$ of the unit, or $\frac{1}{2} \times \frac{1}{8}$, or $\frac{1}{16}$ inch. The real length is between $3\frac{13}{16}$ inches and $3\frac{15}{16}$ inches.

The allowance for error in measurement is called *tolerance*. The tolerance for the length of the nail is written as $3\frac{7}{8} \pm \frac{1}{16}$ in.

Find the greatest possible error for each measurement.

1. $6\frac{5}{6}$ hours   **2.** $10\frac{7}{8}$ lb.   **3.** 294 gal.   **4.** $4\frac{17}{32}$ in.

5. $7\frac{2}{3}$ yd.   **6.** 3 ft. 9 in.   **7.** $8\frac{1}{2}$ pt.   **8.** $10\frac{3}{16}$ in.

9. 1 lb. 3 oz.   **10.** $5\frac{7}{12}$ ft.   **11.** $22\frac{1}{2}$ mi.   **12.** $2\frac{3}{10}$ seconds

Find the tolerance for each measurement.

13. $5\frac{13}{16}$ in.   **14.** $7\frac{3}{5}$ hours   **15.** $2\frac{1}{2}$ pt.   **16.** $4\frac{3}{4}$ lb.

17. 6 ft. 2 in.   **18.** 75 yd.   **19.** $8\frac{9}{10}$ seconds   **20.** $3\frac{7}{8}$ in.

21. $4\frac{1}{3}$ yd.   **22.** $\frac{17}{32}$ in.   **23.** 2 lb. 10 oz.   **24.** $7\frac{11}{12}$ ft.

MAINTENANCE

For each exercise, give the least common denominator.

1. $\frac{1}{3}$ $\frac{5}{6}$

2. $\frac{5}{7}$ $\frac{1}{14}$

3. $\frac{3}{10}$ $\frac{2}{5}$

4. $\frac{2}{3}$ $\frac{3}{4}$

5. $\frac{4}{5}$ $\frac{1}{3}$

6. $\frac{2}{3}$ $\frac{1}{3}$ $\frac{3}{4}$

7. $\frac{3}{5}$ $\frac{1}{2}$ $\frac{4}{5}$

8. $\frac{5}{8}$ $\frac{1}{2}$ $\frac{3}{4}$

9. $\frac{2}{3}$ $\frac{7}{18}$ $\frac{5}{6}$

10. $\frac{1}{2}$ $\frac{3}{7}$ $\frac{5}{14}$

For each exercise, write the fractions with the least common denominator.

11. $\frac{3}{4}$ $\frac{1}{12}$

12. $\frac{1}{16}$ $\frac{3}{8}$

13. $\frac{20}{21}$ $\frac{2}{3}$

14. $\frac{1}{3}$ $\frac{7}{9}$

15. $\frac{5}{6}$ $\frac{19}{24}$

16. $\frac{1}{2}$ $\frac{5}{9}$

17. $\frac{3}{4}$ $\frac{1}{3}$

18. $\frac{1}{4}$ $\frac{5}{6}$

19. $\frac{6}{7}$ $\frac{1}{2}$

20. $\frac{5}{8}$ $\frac{1}{5}$

21. $\frac{1}{2}$ $\frac{1}{6}$ $\frac{2}{3}$

22. $\frac{2}{5}$ $\frac{1}{2}$ $\frac{7}{10}$

23. $\frac{1}{3}$ $\frac{3}{4}$ $\frac{5}{12}$

24. $\frac{11}{15}$ $\frac{2}{3}$ $\frac{3}{5}$

25. $\frac{4}{5}$ $\frac{3}{20}$ $\frac{3}{4}$

Solve each problem.

26. An airplane flies 8,624 km in 11 hours. What is its average speed?

27. A glacier moves about 12.7 km in one year. How far would it move in 20 years?

28. A pork chop has 21.3 g of protein. An egg has 3.7 g of protein. How much more protein does a pork chop have?

29. A movie camera with sound runs 1,440 frames per minute. How many frames are used in an 18-minute film?

30. Hank Aaron played baseball for 23 years. He was at bat 12,364 times. What was his average number of times at bat per year?

31. It takes Mars about 687 days to orbit the sun. It takes Venus about 225 days. How many days longer does it take Mars to orbit the sun?

32. In 1909, the average weekly wage for a factory worker was $9.84. By 1976, it was $198.28 more. What was the average weekly wage in 1976?

33. Sound travels at a rate of 332 meters per second. How far away is a train if you hear the whistle $1\frac{1}{4}$ seconds after it was blown?

Addition and Subtraction of Fractions

French horns

$$\frac{1}{30}$$

+

Rest of brass

$$\frac{1}{10}$$

=

Brass part of orchestra

$$\frac{2}{15}$$

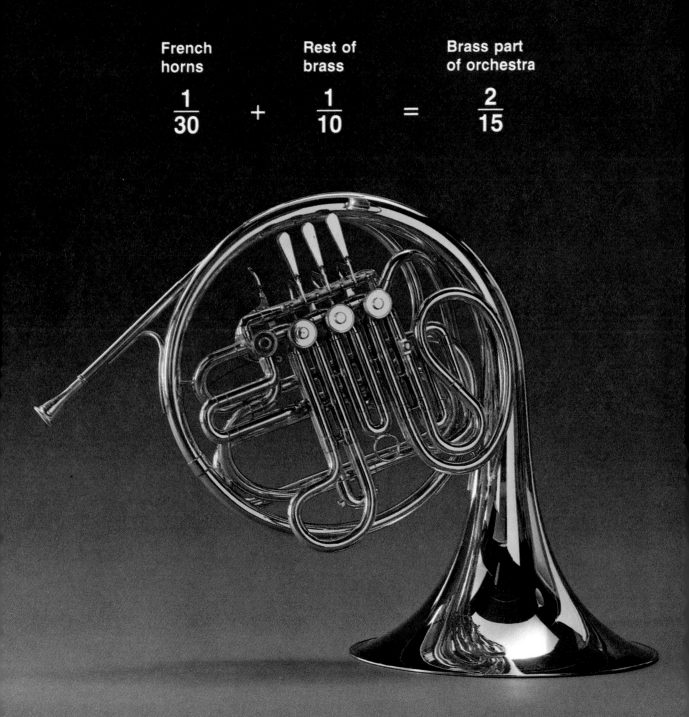

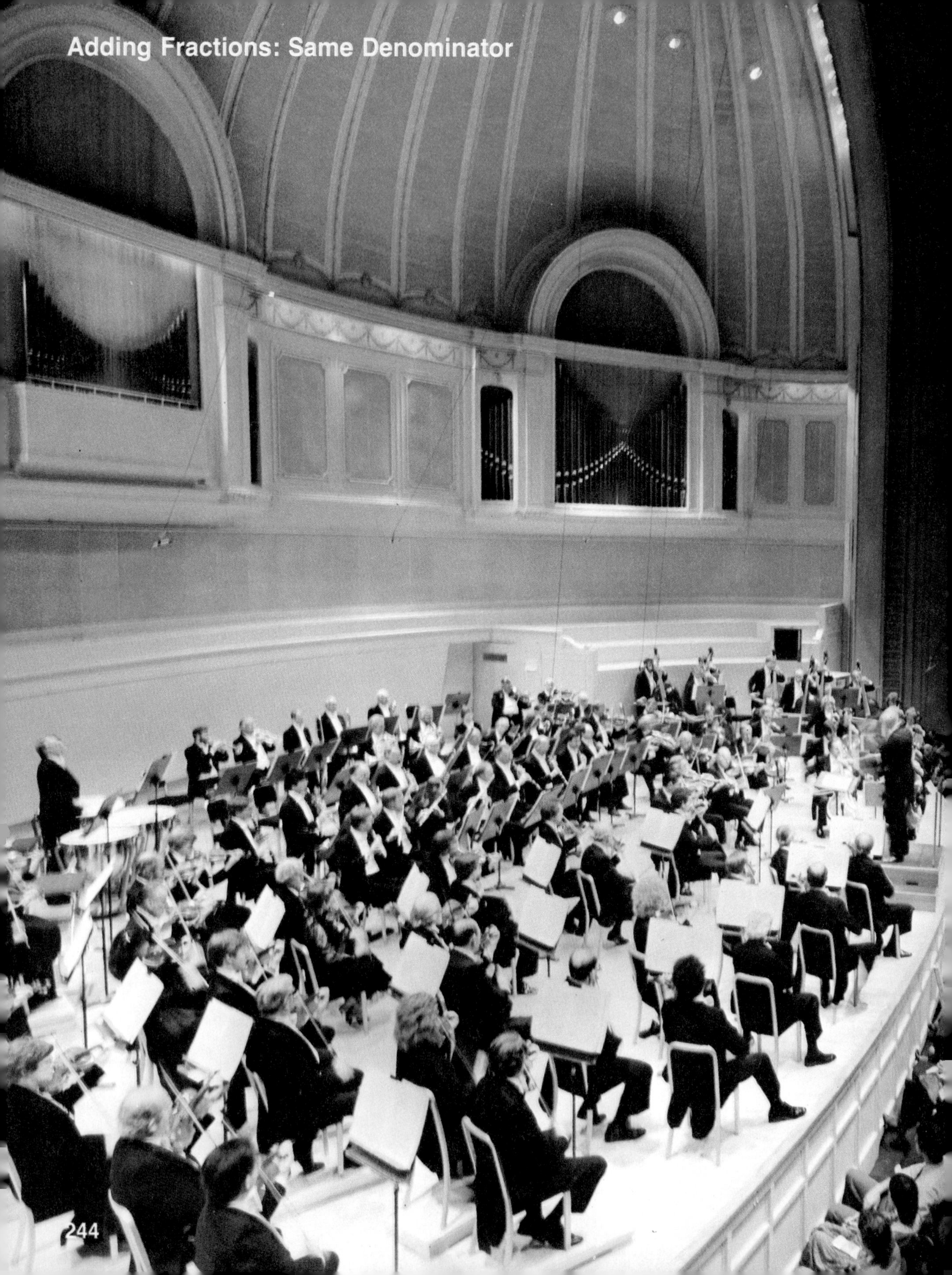

A. Violin players make up $\frac{2}{7}$ of the orchestra. The rest of the string section is another $\frac{2}{7}$ of the orchestra. What fraction of the orchestra is the string section?

Find $\frac{2}{7} + \frac{2}{7}$.

$$\frac{2}{7}$$
The fractions have the same denominator. Add the numerators. $2 + 2 = 4$.
$$+\frac{2}{7}$$
$$\overline{\frac{4}{7}}$$

The string section is $\frac{4}{7}$ of the orchestra.

B. Find $\frac{5}{8} + \frac{7}{8}$.

$$\frac{5}{8}$$
$$+\frac{7}{8}$$
$$\overline{\frac{12}{8}} = 1\frac{4}{8} = 1\frac{1}{2}$$

Try Add.

a. $\frac{2}{5} + \frac{1}{5}$

b. $\frac{1}{8} + \frac{3}{8}$

c. $\frac{7}{10} + \frac{4}{10}$

d. $\frac{1}{9} + \frac{4}{9} + \frac{5}{9}$

Practice Add.

1. $\frac{1}{4}$ $+\frac{2}{4}$

2. $\frac{2}{6}$ $+\frac{3}{6}$

3. $\frac{1}{5}$ $+\frac{3}{5}$

4. $\frac{2}{8}$ $+\frac{3}{8}$

5. $\frac{4}{9}$ $+\frac{2}{9}$

6. $\frac{5}{10}$ $+\frac{3}{10}$

7. $\frac{5}{12}$ $+\frac{3}{12}$

8. $\frac{2}{5}$ $+\frac{2}{5}$

9. $\frac{5}{9}$ $+\frac{7}{9}$

10. $\frac{9}{10}$ $+\frac{5}{10}$

11. $\frac{7}{8}$ $+\frac{3}{8}$

12. $\frac{11}{12}$ $+\frac{5}{12}$

13. $\frac{5}{8} + \frac{7}{8}$

14. $\frac{5}{12} + \frac{5}{12} + \frac{5}{12}$

15. $\frac{5}{16} + \frac{9}{16} + \frac{3}{16}$

16. $\frac{3}{8} + \frac{1}{8} + \frac{2}{8}$

Apply Solve each problem.

17. Of the musicians, $\frac{4}{9}$ have played for more than 10 years. $\frac{2}{9}$ have played between 5 and 10 years. What fraction of the musicians have played for at least 5 years?

18. The orchestra played 3 pieces of music. The first took $\frac{1}{5}$ hour, the next, $\frac{2}{5}$ hour, and the third, $\frac{3}{5}$ hour. How long did all three take together?

Adding Mixed Numbers: Same Denominator

A. A pianist played two Beethoven sonatas. She played the *Moonlight Sonata* in $15\frac{7}{12}$ minutes. She played the *Appassionata* in $24\frac{5}{12}$ minutes. How long did it take her to play both sonatas?

Find $15\frac{7}{12} + 24\frac{5}{12}$.

$$15\frac{7}{12}$$
$$+\,24\frac{5}{12}$$

Add the fractions.
Then add the whole numbers.

$$39\frac{12}{12} = 40$$

Rename $39\frac{12}{12}$. $39 + \frac{12}{12} = 39 + 1 = 40$.

It took her 40 minutes to play both sonatas.

B. Find $3\frac{4}{7} + 2\frac{5}{7}$.

$$3\frac{4}{7}$$
$$+\,2\frac{5}{7}$$

$$5\frac{9}{7} = 6\frac{2}{7}$$

Try Add.

a. $1\frac{4}{10}$
$+2\frac{7}{10}$

b. $2\frac{3}{4} + 3\frac{1}{4} + 5\frac{3}{4}$

Compare these decimals. Use <, >, or =.

1. 0.8 ● 0.9

2. 0.43 ● 0.28

Practice Add.

1. $2\frac{1}{3}$
$+3\frac{2}{3}$

2. $5\frac{4}{5}$
$+6\frac{3}{5}$

3. $4\frac{5}{9}$
$+2\frac{7}{9}$

4. $3\frac{3}{8}$
$+2\frac{5}{8}$

3. 0.472 ● 0.469

4. 0.926 ● 0.923

5. $3\frac{2}{3}$
$+4\frac{2}{3}$

6. $1\frac{7}{10}$
$+8\frac{8}{10}$

7. $5\frac{6}{8}$
$+4\frac{7}{8}$

8. $7\frac{3}{4}$
$+8\frac{3}{4}$

5. 0.40 ● 0.4

6. 0.032 ● 0.031

7. 1.056 ● 1.05

9. $2\frac{6}{12}$
$5\frac{11}{12}$
$+9\frac{7}{12}$

10. $3\frac{5}{6}$
$1\frac{1}{6}$
$+7\frac{1}{6}$

11. $5\frac{4}{7}$
$5\frac{4}{7}$
$+5\frac{4}{7}$

12. $4\frac{3}{15}$
$9\frac{8}{15}$
$+8\frac{11}{15}$

List the numbers in order from the least to the greatest.

8. 0.67   0.6   0.7

9. 0.25   0.52   0.052

13. $3\frac{5}{6} + 8\frac{3}{6}$

14. $5\frac{9}{10} + 16\frac{7}{10}$

10. 1.18   1.81   1.8

11. 9.76   9.67   96.7

15. $4\frac{7}{18} + 2\frac{7}{18} + 6\frac{5}{18}$

12. 5.7   5.77   5.07

13. 1.1   1.01   1.11

Apply Solve each problem.

16. In one piece for the violin, the first solo took $2\frac{5}{8}$ minutes to play. The second solo lasted for $4\frac{7}{8}$ minutes. How long did the two solos take to play?

14. 0.001   0.01   0.011

15. 2.23   2.43   2.21   2.4

17. The three movements of a symphony took $10\frac{5}{12}$, $11\frac{1}{12}$, and $14\frac{7}{12}$ minutes to play. How long did it take to play all three movements?

16. 0.678   0.6789   0.677   0.687

Adding Fractions: Different Denominators

Yesterday, Paul practiced on his violin by playing the scales for $\frac{1}{6}$ hour and musical compositions for $\frac{7}{12}$ hour. How long did he practice?

Find $\frac{1}{6} + \frac{7}{12}$.

$$\frac{1}{6} = \frac{2}{12}$$

Write the fractions with a common denominator.
12 is a common denominator.

$$+\frac{7}{12} = \frac{7}{12}$$
$$\frac{9}{12} = \frac{3}{4}$$

He practiced for $\frac{3}{4}$ hour.

Try Add.

a. $\dfrac{1}{2}$
  $+\dfrac{1}{4}$

b. $\dfrac{1}{3}$
  $+\dfrac{2}{5}$

c. $\dfrac{1}{5} + \dfrac{3}{10} + \dfrac{1}{2}$

Practice Add.

1. $\dfrac{1}{4}$
   $+\dfrac{2}{3}$

2. $\dfrac{1}{2}$
   $+\dfrac{3}{4}$

3. $\dfrac{2}{5}$
   $+\dfrac{3}{10}$

4. $\dfrac{1}{2}$
   $+\dfrac{5}{6}$

5. $\dfrac{1}{3}$
   $+\dfrac{4}{5}$

6. $\dfrac{2}{9}$
   $+\dfrac{1}{6}$

7. $\dfrac{5}{6}$
   $+\dfrac{3}{4}$

8. $\dfrac{1}{2}$
   $+\dfrac{5}{8}$

9. $\dfrac{5}{6}$
   $+\dfrac{2}{3}$

10. $\dfrac{5}{6}$
    $+\dfrac{5}{8}$

11. $\dfrac{3}{8}$
    $+\dfrac{1}{4}$

12. $\dfrac{9}{10}$
    $+\dfrac{1}{2}$

13. $\dfrac{1}{4}$
    $\dfrac{3}{4}$
    $+\dfrac{1}{8}$

14. $\dfrac{1}{6}$
    $\dfrac{1}{3}$
    $+\dfrac{5}{6}$

15. $\dfrac{2}{5}$
    $\dfrac{2}{3}$
    $+\dfrac{4}{5}$

16. $\dfrac{1}{2}$
    $\dfrac{3}{4}$
    $+\dfrac{5}{8}$

17. $\dfrac{5}{6}$
    $\dfrac{1}{3}$
    $+\dfrac{4}{9}$

18. $\dfrac{7}{12}$
    $\dfrac{7}{8}$
    $+\dfrac{2}{3}$

19. $\dfrac{5}{6} + \dfrac{1}{2} + \dfrac{1}{3}$

20. $\dfrac{5}{8} + \dfrac{9}{10} + \dfrac{3}{5}$

21. $\dfrac{2}{3} + \dfrac{5}{6} + \dfrac{7}{10}$

22. $\dfrac{5}{12} + \dfrac{1}{6} + \dfrac{3}{4}$

Apply Solve each problem.

23. A music teacher has 50 students. $\frac{1}{2}$ of them are 9 years old and $\frac{2}{5}$ of them are 10 years old. What fraction of the students are either 9 or 10 years old?

24. How many of the students in Problem 23 are 9 years old?

25. A music school has 560 students. $\frac{1}{2}$ of the students take only piano lessons. $\frac{1}{7}$ of the students take only violin lessons. What fraction of the students take either piano or violin lessons?

★26. How many students in Problem 25 do not take either piano or violin lessons?

Adding Mixed Numbers: Different Denominators

The body of Bill's guitar is $19\frac{5}{8}$ inches long. The neck of the guitar is $20\frac{3}{4}$ inches long. How long is the guitar?

Find $19\frac{5}{8} + 20\frac{3}{4}$.

$$19\frac{5}{8} = 19\frac{5}{8}$$
$$+\ 20\frac{3}{4} = 20\frac{6}{8}$$
$$\overline{\phantom{+\ 20\frac{3}{4} = {}}39\frac{11}{8} = 40\frac{3}{8}}$$

The least common denominator is 8.
Add the fractions.
Add the whole numbers.

The guitar is $40\frac{3}{8}$ inches long.

Try Add.

a. $1\frac{5}{6}$
$+3\frac{2}{5}$

b. $1\frac{5}{8}$
$7\frac{2}{3}$
$+4\frac{5}{6}$

c. $2\frac{1}{4} + 1\frac{3}{8}$

Practice Add.

1. $5\frac{1}{2}$
$+2\frac{3}{4}$

2. $6\frac{1}{4}$
$+2\frac{2}{3}$

3. $1\frac{2}{5}$
$+2\frac{3}{4}$

4. $5\frac{1}{2}$
$+2\frac{5}{6}$

5. $6\frac{1}{3}$
$+2\frac{4}{5}$

6. $8\frac{2}{9}$
$+4\frac{1}{6}$

7. $3\frac{5}{6}$
$+7\frac{3}{4}$

8. $6\frac{1}{2}$
$+3\frac{5}{8}$

9. $5\frac{5}{6}$
$+6\frac{2}{3}$

10. $6\frac{1}{2}$
$+3\frac{5}{8}$

11. $5\frac{5}{6}$
$+\ \frac{5}{8}$

12. $\frac{3}{8}$
$+5\frac{1}{4}$

13. $5\frac{5}{6}$
$+\ \frac{2}{3}$

14. $1\frac{1}{6}$
$+\ \frac{5}{8}$

15. $16\frac{3}{8}$
$+\ 5\frac{1}{4}$

16. $\frac{9}{10}$
$+8\frac{1}{2}$

17. 4
$+3\frac{4}{9}$

18. $2\frac{1}{2}$
$+3\frac{2}{7}$

19. $13\frac{2}{3}$
$+\ 7\frac{2}{9}$

20. $5\frac{1}{6}$
$+15\frac{3}{11}$

21. $5\frac{1}{4}$
$\frac{3}{4}$
$+6\frac{1}{8}$

22. $7\frac{1}{6}$
$2\frac{1}{3}$
$+\ \frac{5}{6}$

23. $2\frac{2}{5}$
$3\frac{2}{3}$
$+5\frac{1}{5}$

24. $11\frac{5}{6}$
$6\frac{1}{2}$
$+3\frac{1}{3}$

25. $1\frac{5}{8} + 2\frac{2}{3}$

26. $9\frac{7}{12} + 3\frac{5}{6}$

27. $3\frac{1}{3} + \frac{4}{5} + 6$

28. $\frac{4}{5} + 2\frac{3}{10} + \frac{1}{2}$

29. $7\frac{1}{2} + 3\frac{3}{8} + 6\frac{1}{4}$

30. $9\frac{5}{8} + \frac{9}{10} + 4\frac{3}{5}$

31. $5\frac{2}{3} + 6\frac{5}{6} + \frac{7}{10}$

32. $23\frac{5}{12} + 8\frac{1}{6} + 1\frac{5}{24}$

Apply Solve each problem.

33. Bill also has an electric guitar. It is $8\frac{1}{4}$ inches longer than the one described on page 250. How long is his electric guitar?

34. Bill practiced three days last week. He spent $2\frac{1}{2}$ hours practicing on Monday, $1\frac{3}{4}$ hours on Wednesday, and $1\frac{2}{3}$ hours on Friday. How many hours did he practice last week?

Subtracting Fractions and Mixed Numbers: Same Denominator

A. The rivet pictured is the type used to fasten parts of wings on airplanes. Find the missing dimension.

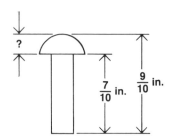

Find $\frac{9}{10} - \frac{7}{10}$.

$$
\begin{array}{r}
\dfrac{9}{10} \\[2mm]
-\ \dfrac{7}{10} \\[1mm]
\hline
\dfrac{2}{10} = \dfrac{1}{5}
\end{array}
$$

The fractions have the same denominators. Subtract the numerators.

The missing dimension is $\frac{1}{5}$ inch.

B. Find $9\frac{3}{8} - 6\frac{1}{8}$.

$$
\begin{array}{r}
9\frac{3}{8} \\[2mm]
-\ 6\frac{1}{8} \\[1mm]
\hline
3\frac{2}{8} = 3\frac{1}{4}
\end{array}
$$

The fractions have the same denominators. Subtract the fractions. Subtract the whole numbers.

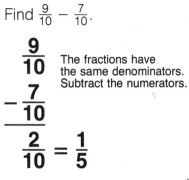

Try Subtract.

a. $\frac{4}{5}$
$-\frac{1}{5}$

b. $\frac{11}{12}$
$-\frac{7}{12}$

c. $3\frac{5}{9}$
$-1\frac{4}{9}$

d. $8\frac{5}{8}$
$-\frac{3}{8}$

Practice Subtract.

1. $\frac{7}{8}$
$-\frac{4}{8}$

2. $\frac{9}{10}$
$-\frac{6}{10}$

3. $\frac{4}{5}$
$-\frac{3}{5}$

4. $\frac{4}{9}$
$-\frac{2}{9}$

5. $\frac{7}{10}$
$-\frac{5}{10}$

6. $\frac{5}{12}$
$-\frac{1}{12}$

7. $9\frac{2}{3}$
$-9\frac{1}{3}$

8. $8\frac{3}{4}$
$-6\frac{3}{4}$

9. $6\frac{2}{3}$
$-3\frac{1}{3}$

10. $10\frac{3}{5}$
$-4\frac{1}{5}$

11. $15\frac{3}{4}$
$-9\frac{1}{4}$

12. $9\frac{4}{5}$
-8

13. $\frac{7}{9} - \frac{4}{9}$

14. $\frac{5}{6} - \frac{1}{6}$

15. $3\frac{5}{8} - \frac{3}{8}$

16. $5\frac{3}{4} - 3$

17. $1\frac{9}{10} - \frac{3}{10}$

18. $3\frac{7}{12} - 1\frac{4}{12}$

Solve each equation.

★19. $n + \frac{1}{4} = \frac{3}{4}$

★20. $3\frac{1}{8} + n = 6\frac{5}{8}$

Apply Solve each problem.

21. Last week, Samuel worked $40\frac{3}{4}$ hours. This week, he worked $39\frac{1}{4}$ hours. How much longer did he work last week?

22. Margaret cut a piece of metal $28\frac{3}{10}$ in. long from a piece that was $79\frac{7}{10}$ in. long. How long was the remaining piece?

$\frac{1}{4} + \frac{5}{8} = \frac{2}{8} + \frac{5}{8} = \frac{7}{8}$

Lynn checked the answer to the exercise above by changing each addend to a decimal, adding the decimals, and then comparing the answer to the decimal for $\frac{7}{8}$.

$0.25 + 0.625 = 0.875$

$\frac{7}{8} = 0.875$

The answers are the same.

Add. Then use your calculator to check.

1. $\frac{9}{10} + \frac{1}{2}$

2. $\frac{2}{5} + \frac{1}{2}$

3. $\frac{5}{8} + \frac{3}{5}$

4. $\frac{7}{10} + \frac{1}{4}$

5. $\frac{3}{4} + \frac{3}{8}$

6. $\frac{15}{16} + \frac{5}{8}$

7. $\frac{1}{3} + \frac{2}{3}$

8. $\frac{5}{6} + \frac{3}{8}$

9. $\frac{11}{12} + \frac{13}{15}$

Subtracting Mixed Numbers: Same Denominator with Renaming

A. The Wright brothers' *Model A* airplane was 29 feet long. The Wright brothers' *Flyer* was $21\frac{1}{12}$ feet long. How much longer was the *Model A* than the *Flyer*?

Find $29 - 21\frac{1}{12}$.

$$29$$
$$-21\frac{1}{12}$$

Before you can subtract you must rename 29.

$29 = 28 + 1$
$\quad = 28 + \frac{12}{12}$
$\quad = 28\frac{12}{12}$

$$29 \quad = 28\frac{12}{12}$$
$$-21\frac{1}{12} = 21\frac{1}{12}$$
$$7\frac{11}{12}$$

Subtract the fractions.
Subtract the whole numbers.

The *Model A* was $7\frac{11}{12}$ feet longer than the *Flyer*.

B. Find $12\frac{2}{5} - 4\frac{3}{5}$.

$$12\frac{2}{5} = 11\frac{7}{5}$$
$$-\ 4\frac{3}{5} = \ 4\frac{3}{5}$$
$$7\frac{4}{5}$$

Rename $12\frac{2}{5}$.
$12\frac{2}{5} = 12 + \frac{2}{5}$
$\quad = 11 + 1 + \frac{2}{5}$
$\quad = 11 + \frac{5}{5} + \frac{2}{5}$
$\quad = 11\frac{7}{5}$

Try First rename. Then subtract.

a. $7 = 6\frac{\blacksquare}{8}$
$-2\frac{1}{8} = 2\frac{1}{8}$

b. $12 = 11\frac{\blacksquare}{2}$
$-7\frac{1}{2} = 7\frac{1}{2}$

c. $9\frac{1}{4}$
$-8\frac{3}{4}$

d. $8\frac{1}{5}$
$-5\frac{4}{5}$

Practice Rename each number.

1. $3 = 2\frac{\blacksquare}{5}$

2. $5 = 4\frac{\blacksquare}{4}$

3. $4 = 3\frac{\blacksquare}{6}$

4. $7 = 6\frac{\blacksquare}{8}$

5. $1 = \frac{\blacksquare}{3}$

6. $5\frac{1}{4} = 4\frac{\blacksquare}{4}$

7. $2\frac{1}{8} = 1\frac{\blacksquare}{8}$

8. $4\frac{1}{3} = 3\frac{\blacksquare}{3}$

9. $1\frac{2}{6} = \frac{\blacksquare}{6}$

10. $7\frac{3}{10} = 6\frac{\blacksquare}{10}$

First rename. Then subtract.

11. $7 = 6\frac{\blacksquare}{4}$
$-3\frac{3}{4} = 3\frac{3}{4}$

12. $9\frac{3}{5} = 8\frac{\blacksquare}{5}$
$-2\frac{4}{5} = 2\frac{4}{5}$

13. $6 = 5\frac{\blacksquare}{3}$
$-2\frac{2}{3} = 2\frac{2}{3}$

14. $8\frac{5}{12} = 7\frac{\blacksquare}{12}$
$-6\frac{7}{12} = 6\frac{7}{12}$

15. $9\frac{1}{8}$
$-1\frac{5}{8}$

16. 10
$-6\frac{7}{10}$

17. $12\frac{1}{6}$
$-9\frac{5}{6}$

18. 6
$-\frac{3}{4}$

19. 9
$-6\frac{2}{3}$

20. 7
$-2\frac{5}{8}$

21. 8
$-7\frac{3}{10}$

22. $8\frac{2}{9}$
$-5\frac{5}{9}$

23. $6\frac{3}{8}$
$-2\frac{5}{8}$

24. $9\frac{1}{4}$
$-1\frac{3}{4}$

25. $1\frac{2}{5}$
$-\frac{4}{5}$

26. $17\frac{1}{6}$
$-14\frac{5}{6}$

27. $25\frac{3}{10}$
$-9\frac{7}{10}$

28. $9\frac{1}{10}$
$-8\frac{3}{10}$

29. $7\frac{1}{5}$
$-2\frac{3}{5}$

Apply Solve each problem.

30. The Wright brothers' *Flyer* was $21\frac{1}{12}$ feet long and had a wingspan of $40\frac{4}{12}$ feet. How much greater was its wingspan than its length?

31. A 747 airplane is $231\frac{1}{3}$ feet long and has a wingspan of $195\frac{2}{3}$ feet. How much greater is the length than the wingspan?

Subtracting Fractions and Mixed Numbers: Different Denominators

Career Bob Garden is a sheep shearer in New Zealand. From one sheep, he got $8\frac{3}{4}$ pounds of wool, and from another, he got $7\frac{1}{2}$ pounds. How much more wool did he get from the first sheep than from the second?

Find $8\frac{3}{4} - 7\frac{1}{2}$.

$$8\frac{3}{4} = 8\frac{3}{4}$$
$$\underline{-7\frac{1}{2} = 7\frac{2}{4}}$$
$$1\frac{1}{4}$$

Write the fractions with a common denominator.

He got $1\frac{1}{4}$ more pounds of wool from the first sheep.

Try Subtract.

a. $\dfrac{7}{8}$ b. $8\dfrac{4}{5}$ c. $17\dfrac{5}{6} - 12\dfrac{1}{9}$

    $-\dfrac{1}{2}$ $-2\dfrac{3}{10}$

Practice Subtract.

1. $\dfrac{1}{2}$ 2. $\dfrac{2}{3}$ 3. $\dfrac{7}{9}$ 4. $\dfrac{9}{10}$ 5. $\dfrac{2}{3}$ 6. $\dfrac{4}{5}$

   $-\dfrac{1}{8}$ $-\dfrac{1}{6}$ $-\dfrac{1}{3}$ $-\dfrac{1}{2}$ $-\dfrac{1}{2}$ $-\dfrac{1}{10}$

7. $\dfrac{3}{4}$ 8. $\dfrac{5}{6}$ 9. $\dfrac{3}{4}$ 10. $\dfrac{5}{6}$ 11. $\dfrac{1}{2}$ 12. $\dfrac{5}{6}$

   $-\dfrac{1}{6}$ $-\dfrac{3}{8}$ $-\dfrac{3}{8}$ $-\dfrac{2}{3}$ $-\dfrac{1}{10}$ $-\dfrac{4}{5}$

13. $4\dfrac{4}{5}$ 14. $7\dfrac{1}{2}$ 15. $9\dfrac{1}{4}$ 16. $8\dfrac{5}{6}$ 17. $5\dfrac{2}{3}$ 18. $6\dfrac{5}{8}$

  $-1\dfrac{1}{2}$ $-3\dfrac{1}{3}$ $-4\dfrac{1}{8}$ $-2\dfrac{1}{3}$ $-3\dfrac{1}{4}$ $-1\dfrac{1}{2}$

19. $6\dfrac{1}{4} - 3\dfrac{1}{5}$ 20. $9\dfrac{7}{8} - 4\dfrac{2}{5}$ 21. $10\dfrac{7}{8} - 3\dfrac{3}{4}$ 22. $9\dfrac{7}{10} - 2\dfrac{2}{5}$

23. $11\dfrac{7}{8} - 4\dfrac{1}{2}$ 24. $15\dfrac{2}{3} - 11\dfrac{4}{6}$ 25. $34\dfrac{3}{4} - 17\dfrac{11}{16}$ 26. $45\dfrac{5}{6} - 17\dfrac{3}{10}$

Apply Solve each problem.

27. Yesterday, Bob sheared 10 sheep and collected $97\dfrac{3}{4}$ pounds of wool. Today, he collected $87\dfrac{1}{3}$ pounds. How much more wool did he get yesterday?

28. Bob's helper sheared a sheep in $1\dfrac{1}{4}$ minutes. Bob sheared one in $1\dfrac{5}{8}$ minutes. How much slower was Bob than his helper?

If 2 robots made 2 welds in 2 seconds, how many welds will 10 robots make in 10 seconds?

Subtracting Mixed Numbers: Different Denominators with Renaming

The ferry trip from the North Island to the South Island of New Zealand took $3\frac{2}{3}$ hours. The return trip took $4\frac{1}{4}$ hours. How much longer was the return trip?

Find $4\frac{1}{4} - 3\frac{2}{3}$.

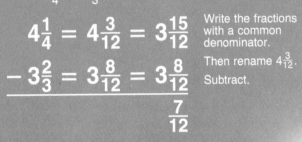

$$4\frac{1}{4} = 4\frac{3}{12} = 3\frac{15}{12}$$
$$-\,3\frac{2}{3} = 3\frac{8}{12} = 3\frac{8}{12}$$
$$\frac{7}{12}$$

Write the fractions with a common denominator. Then rename $4\frac{3}{12}$. Subtract.

The return trip was $\frac{7}{12}$ hour longer.

258

Try Subtract.

a. $7\frac{1}{8} = 7\frac{1}{8} = 6\frac{\blacksquare}{8}$

$-2\frac{1}{2} = 2\frac{\blacksquare}{8} = 2\frac{\blacksquare}{8}$

b. $5\frac{1}{4}$

$-3\frac{1}{2}$

c. 16

$-8\frac{3}{5}$

Practice Subtract.

1. $5\frac{1}{6} = 5\frac{1}{6} = 4\frac{\blacksquare}{6}$

$-2\frac{1}{3} = 2\frac{\blacksquare}{6} = 2\frac{\blacksquare}{6}$

2. $7\frac{1}{4} = 7\frac{\blacksquare}{12} = 6\frac{\blacksquare}{12}$

$-3\frac{1}{3} = 3\frac{\blacksquare}{12} = 3\frac{\blacksquare}{12}$

3. $9\frac{1}{2} = 9\frac{\blacksquare}{10} = 8\frac{\blacksquare}{10}$

$-4\frac{4}{5} = 4\frac{\blacksquare}{10} = 4\frac{\blacksquare}{10}$

4. $7\frac{1}{10}$

$-4\frac{4}{5}$

5. $3\frac{1}{4}$

$-\frac{1}{2}$

6. $9\frac{1}{3}$

$-5\frac{5}{6}$

7. $1\frac{1}{2}$

$-\frac{5}{6}$

8. $6\frac{3}{8}$

$-\frac{1}{2}$

9. $5\frac{1}{8}$

$-4\frac{3}{4}$

10. $10\frac{1}{3}$

$-3\frac{4}{9}$

11. $8\frac{1}{5}$

$-4\frac{7}{10}$

12. $4\frac{1}{3}$

$-2\frac{11}{12}$

13. $11\frac{2}{5}$

$-6\frac{1}{2}$

14. $9\frac{1}{3}$

$-\frac{1}{2}$

15. $12\frac{2}{5}$

$-7\frac{3}{4}$

16. $3\frac{2}{3}$

$-1\frac{4}{5}$

17. $9\frac{3}{4}$

$-6\frac{5}{6}$

18. $1\frac{2}{3}$

$-\frac{3}{4}$

19. $5\frac{1}{8}$

$-4\frac{5}{16}$

20. $16\frac{2}{3}$

$-8\frac{5}{6}$

21. $13\frac{5}{6}$

$-11\frac{9}{10}$

Solve each equation.

★22. $n + 1\frac{1}{3} = 6\frac{1}{5}$

★23. $4\frac{1}{4} + n = 7\frac{1}{10}$

★24. $n + 11\frac{1}{8} = 19$

Apply Solve each problem.

25. The total length of the ferry trip is about $63\frac{1}{4}$ miles. About $31\frac{7}{8}$ miles of the trip is in open water, where there is no protection from the wind. About how much of the trip is in protected water?

26. During one ferry crossing, the cafeteria served $47\frac{1}{4}$ gallons of juice. If they started with 55 gallons, how much did they have left at the end of the crossing?

Practice: Adding and Subtracting Fractions and Mixed Numbers

Add or subtract.

1. $\frac{3}{8}$
$+\frac{1}{8}$

2. $\frac{5}{10}$
$+\frac{3}{10}$

3. $\frac{7}{9}$
$-\frac{2}{9}$

4. $\frac{5}{6}$
$-\frac{2}{6}$

5. $\frac{2}{5}$
$+\frac{3}{5}$

6. $1\frac{1}{6}$
$-\frac{5}{6}$

7. $9\frac{1}{2}$
-3

8. 6
$-4\frac{1}{3}$

9. $\frac{2}{3}$
$+\frac{3}{5}$

10. $3\frac{3}{4}$
$+5\frac{2}{3}$

11. $9\frac{2}{3}$
$-4\frac{1}{6}$

12. $8\frac{1}{3}$
$-6\frac{3}{4}$

13. 12
$-7\frac{3}{8}$

14. $9\frac{1}{4}$
$-5\frac{3}{4}$

15. $\frac{3}{4}$
$+\frac{3}{4}$

16. $7\frac{5}{8}$
$+11\frac{7}{8}$

17. $2\frac{3}{5}$
$+6\frac{4}{5}$

18. 3
$-\frac{7}{9}$

19. $5\frac{1}{12}$
$-4\frac{3}{4}$

20. $4\frac{1}{3}$
$-2\frac{5}{9}$

21. $\frac{4}{9}$
$+\frac{3}{10}$

22. $2\frac{11}{16}$
$+2\frac{3}{8}$

23. $1\frac{5}{8}$
$-\frac{3}{4}$

24. $8\frac{1}{9}$
$+1\frac{5}{9}$

25. $6\frac{3}{4}$
$-2\frac{5}{8}$

26. $11\frac{2}{5}$
$-7\frac{3}{5}$

27. $7\frac{1}{6}$
$-3\frac{5}{8}$

28. $\frac{1}{8}$
$+\frac{2}{3}$

29. $10\frac{1}{2}$
$+1\frac{5}{12}$

30. $2\frac{2}{6}$
$+4\frac{5}{8}$

31. $6 + 8\frac{5}{8}$

32. $10\frac{1}{3} - 5\frac{2}{3}$

33. $15\frac{1}{6} - 9\frac{5}{6}$

34. $3\frac{7}{8} + 5\frac{3}{8}$

35. $9\frac{1}{2} - 2\frac{9}{10}$

36. $14\frac{2}{3} - 8\frac{3}{5}$

37. $4\frac{1}{3} + 9\frac{2}{3}$

38. $\frac{7}{8} + 3\frac{3}{10}$

39. $\frac{1}{2} + 1\frac{1}{4} + 3\frac{5}{8}$

40. $4\frac{1}{3} + 10\frac{2}{3} + \frac{1}{2}$

41. $21\frac{1}{2} + 3\frac{5}{8} + 1\frac{1}{4}$

260

Apply Solve each problem.

42. During their vacation in New Zealand, the Riedell family went fishing. They caught a salmon that weighed $28\frac{1}{4}$ pounds and a trout that weighed $8\frac{3}{4}$ pounds. What was the total weight of both fish?

43. The Riedells climbed Mount Cook. It took them $5\frac{1}{2}$ hours to reach the top. Climbing down took $3\frac{3}{4}$ hours. What was the total time?

44. Their tent and frame together weighed 30 pounds. The frame alone weighed $17\frac{1}{4}$ pounds. How much does the tent weigh?

45. The road to Sandalwood Park is $11\frac{1}{5}$ miles long. The distance by boat is $3\frac{3}{4}$ miles. How much less is the distance by boat?

46. The Riedells hiked $12\frac{3}{8}$ miles on Monday, $16\frac{1}{2}$ miles on Tuesday, and $10\frac{1}{2}$ miles on Wednesday. What was the total number of miles they hiked?

BASIC: Semicolons in PRINT Statements

This program adds two fractions with the same denominator. A and B are the numerators and D is the denominator. A<D and B<D. Semicolons in line 60 and 80 are for printing several items on one line.

```
10 REM ADD FRACTIONS
20 PRINT "ENTER A,B,D"
30 INPUT A,B,D
40 IF A+B<D THEN 80
50 LET N=A+B-D
60 PRINT "1 ";N;"/";D
70 GO TO 90
80 PRINT A+B;"/";D
90 END
```

To add $\frac{3}{5}$ and $\frac{4}{5}$, 3 is entered for A, 4 for B, and 5 for D.

Output

```
ENTER A,B,D
? 3,4,5
1 2/5
```

Use the program above to give the output for the following exercises.

1. $\frac{2}{7} + \frac{4}{7}$ **2.** $\frac{5}{8} + \frac{7}{8}$ **3.** $\frac{2}{3} + \frac{2}{3}$

★4. Write a program that will subtract two fractions with the same denominator.

★5. What lines would be taken out of the program above so that the sum would be written as an improper fraction?

261

Problem Solving: Choose the Operation

Read   Jay and Deanna went salmon fishing with their father. They caught 3 salmon. One salmon weighed $4\frac{1}{4}$ pounds, the second, $5\frac{1}{8}$ pounds, and the third, $11\frac{3}{4}$ pounds. How much did the three fish weigh together?

Plan   Add to find the total weight.
Find $4\frac{1}{4} + 5\frac{1}{8} + 11\frac{3}{4}$.

Solve

$$4\frac{1}{4} = 4\frac{2}{8}$$
$$5\frac{1}{8} = 5\frac{1}{8}$$
$$\underline{+ 11\frac{3}{4} = 11\frac{6}{8}}$$
$$20\frac{9}{8} = 21\frac{1}{8}$$

Answer   The three fish weighed $21\frac{1}{8}$ pounds.

Look Back   Adding the whole numbers 4, 5, and 11, you get 20. So the answer is reasonable.

Try   Tell which operation should be used to solve the problem. Then solve the problem.

a. Lynn caught a salmon that weighed $9\frac{1}{2}$ pounds. Beth caught one that was 3 times as heavy. How much did Beth's salmon weigh?

Apply Tell which operation should be used to solve each problem. Then solve each problem.

1. What was the average weight of the 3 salmon in the example on page 262?

2. Mr. Sherrill's old boat was $17\frac{3}{4}$ feet long. His new boat is $3\frac{1}{2}$ feet longer. How long is his new boat?

3. Jay caught a young salmon that was $8\frac{3}{4}$ inches long. It is illegal to keep a salmon that is less than 12 inches long. By how many inches was Jay's salmon too short?

4. On Friday, Mr. Sherrill caught a salmon that was 4 times heavier than the $7\frac{1}{8}$ pound salmon he caught on Tuesday. How much did the salmon that was caught on Friday weigh?

5. In last year's Salmon Derby, the biggest fish caught weighed $53\frac{1}{3}$ pounds. The next heaviest was $37\frac{5}{8}$ pounds. How much heavier was the winning salmon than the next heaviest salmon?

6. If the winning fisherman in Problem 5 got a prize of $5,000, how much per pound was his fish worth? Find your answer to the nearest dollar.

7. Mr. Sherrill purchased $73\frac{2}{5}$ gallons of gasoline for his boat on Monday and $67\frac{1}{10}$ gallons on Friday. How much gasoline did he purchase in all?

★8. Salmon sells in the supermarket for $3.50 per pound. How much would a salmon that weighed $11\frac{2}{5}$ pounds cost?

Chapter 9 Test

Add.

1. $\dfrac{1}{5}$
$+\dfrac{3}{5}$

2. $\dfrac{3}{8}$
$+\dfrac{7}{8}$

3. $\dfrac{3}{10}$
$+\dfrac{9}{10}$

4. $1\dfrac{3}{8}$
$+1\dfrac{3}{8}$

5. $9\dfrac{2}{3}$
$+1\dfrac{1}{3}$

6. $1\dfrac{7}{12}$
$+2\dfrac{5}{12}$

7. $\dfrac{1}{3}$
$+\dfrac{1}{6}$

8. $\dfrac{2}{3}$
$+\dfrac{2}{5}$

9. $\dfrac{3}{8}$
$+\dfrac{5}{6}$

10. $8\dfrac{1}{2}$
$+4\dfrac{1}{6}$

11. $7\dfrac{3}{8}$
$+6\dfrac{3}{4}$

12. $2\dfrac{1}{2}$
$+2\dfrac{3}{5}$

Subtract.

13. $\dfrac{5}{6}$
$-\dfrac{1}{6}$

14. $6\dfrac{7}{8}$
$-3\dfrac{3}{8}$

15. $5\dfrac{1}{8}$
$-3\dfrac{7}{8}$

16. $6\dfrac{1}{4}$
$-2\dfrac{3}{4}$

17. 23
$-\ 3\dfrac{1}{6}$

18. $\dfrac{5}{8}$
$-\dfrac{1}{4}$

19. $9\dfrac{3}{5}$
$-4\dfrac{1}{2}$

20. $2\dfrac{7}{12}$
$-2\dfrac{1}{3}$

21. $8\dfrac{1}{4}$
$-3\dfrac{5}{6}$

22. $6\dfrac{4}{9}$
$-1\dfrac{2}{3}$

23. $5\dfrac{1}{3}$
$-2\dfrac{4}{5}$

Solve each problem.

24. Joanne cut a piece of wood that was $23\dfrac{3}{8}$ inches long from a piece that was $45\dfrac{1}{4}$ inches long. How much of the wood was left?

25. It snowed $3\dfrac{1}{2}$ inches on Monday, $2\dfrac{3}{4}$ inches on Tuesday, and $1\dfrac{7}{8}$ inches on Wednesday. How much snow fell on the three days?

CHALLENGE

Order of Operations

A. To work exercises that have more than one operation, use the rules for the *standard order of operations*.

First multiply and divide in order from left to right.
Then add and subtract in order from left to right.

$$3 + 5 \times 5$$
$$3 + 25$$
$$28$$

$$36 \div 4 - 2$$
$$9 - 2$$
$$7$$

$$4 \times 3 + 8 \div 4$$
$$12 + 2$$
$$14$$

B. You can omit multiplication signs when parentheses are used.
6×4 can be written as 6(4), or (6)4, or (6)(4).

You can use a bar to indicate division.

$24 \div 4$ can be written $\frac{24}{4}$. $(7 + 3) \div 5$ can be written $\frac{7 + 3}{5}$.

When parentheses and division bars are involved in computation:

First do all operations within parentheses, using standard order. Next do all operations above and below division bars, using standard order. Finally, do all remaining operations, using standard order.

$$6 - \frac{9 + 4}{4} = 6 - \frac{13}{4} = 6 - 3\frac{1}{4} = 2\frac{3}{4}$$

Find each answer.

1. $2 + 6 \times 7$

2. $30 + 8 \times 2\frac{1}{2}$

3. $50 - 25 \div 5$

4. $3 \times 5 + 16 \div 6$

5. $24 \div 8 \times 3$

6. $6 \times 6 \div 9$

7. $5\left(3\frac{2}{5} + 7\frac{4}{5}\right)$

8. $7(9 - 6)$

9. $3(9) + 2(4)$

10. $\frac{8 + 7}{5}$

11. $\frac{9 + 9}{6 - 2}$

12. $\frac{5(6)}{10}$

13. $10 - \frac{4 + 5}{3}$

14. $\frac{10}{3} + 3\frac{2}{3}$

15. $\frac{5(8 - 2)}{4}$

MAINTENANCE

Multiply or divide.

1. $\frac{1}{3} \times \frac{4}{5}$ **2.** $\frac{1}{2} \div \frac{1}{3}$ **3.** $\frac{3}{4} \div \frac{2}{5}$ **4.** $\frac{3}{4} \times \frac{1}{2}$

5. $\frac{1}{6} \times \frac{3}{4}$ **6.** $\frac{3}{10} \times \frac{5}{8}$ **7.** $\frac{9}{10} \div \frac{1}{2}$ **8.** $\frac{1}{2} \div \frac{1}{8}$

9. $4 \times \frac{2}{3}$ **10.** $\frac{2}{3} \div 7$ **11.** $\frac{5}{8} \div 5$ **12.** $\frac{3}{8} \times 5$

13. $10 \div \frac{3}{4}$ **14.** $10 \times \frac{3}{5}$ **15.** $6 \div \frac{3}{5}$ **16.** $1\frac{1}{2} \div \frac{9}{10}$

17. $2\frac{1}{3} \div \frac{7}{10}$ **18.** $\frac{1}{2} \times 16$ **19.** $1\frac{1}{4} \times \frac{2}{3}$ **20.** $1\frac{2}{3} \div 2\frac{3}{4}$

21. $\frac{1}{10} \times 2\frac{1}{2}$ **22.** $2\frac{1}{3} \div 2\frac{4}{5}$ **23.** $1\frac{1}{4} \times 2\frac{1}{2}$ **24.** $4\frac{1}{2} \div 1\frac{1}{2}$

25. $2\frac{1}{3} \div 3\frac{1}{2}$ **26.** $3\frac{3}{4} \times 1\frac{3}{5}$ **27.** $4\frac{1}{2} \times 1\frac{3}{4}$ **28.** $8\frac{1}{4} \times 2\frac{2}{3}$

29. $3\frac{1}{2} \times \frac{2}{7} \times 4$ **30.** $5 \times 4\frac{2}{5} \times \frac{3}{11}$ **31.** $6\frac{1}{4} \times 2\frac{1}{5} \times 1\frac{3}{5}$ **32.** $7\frac{1}{2} \times 9\frac{3}{5} \times 1\frac{1}{12}$

Solve each problem.

33. Mike paid $16.50 for 6 tickets to a concert. Find the cost of each ticket.

34. Eva sleeps an average of 10 hours per day. How many hours is she awake each week? (1 day = 24 hours)

35. The odometer of a car read 45,874 kilometers at its last tune-up. The next tune-up is due at 55,000 kilometers. How far will the car have traveled between tune-ups?

36. Aiko bought two loaves of bread and two heads of lettuce for $2.40. If one head of lettuce and two loaves of bread cost $1.75, how much did one loaf of bread cost?

37. Julian bought 6 pounds of sliced turkey. $4\frac{1}{4}$ pounds of turkey was eaten. How much turkey was left?

38. For her party, Sara bought $1\frac{1}{4}$ pounds of potato salad, $2\frac{1}{2}$ pounds of cole slaw, and $2\frac{1}{3}$ pounds of macaroni salad. How many pounds did she buy in all?

Cumulative Test, Chapters 1–9

Give the letter for the correct answer.

1. Add.

   7,486
   + 1,249

   A 8,735
   B 8,625
   C 8,635
   D 8,725

2. Multiply.

   4,962
   ×   45

   A 222,280
   B 44,658
   C 223,290
   D 189,310

3. Divide.

   72)37,945

   A 527 R1
   B 624 R17
   C 520 R55
   D 527 R11

4. Choose the operation that should be used to solve this problem. Then solve the problem.

   If marigolds cost 15¢ each, how much would 385 marigolds cost?

   A Division; $25.66
   B Addition; $4.00
   C Subtraction; $3.70
   D Multiplication; $57.75

5. What is six tenths written as a decimal?

   A 10.6   C 0.610
   B 0.06   D 0.6

6. Which numbers are written in order from least to greatest?

   A 8.108   8.801   8.081
   B 8.081   8.108   8.801
   C 8.801   8.108   8.081
   D 8.801   8.081   8.108

7. Add.

   3.16
   + 4.88

   A 7.94
   B 8.04
   C 7.04
   D 8.94

8. Subtract.

   42.17
   − 1.29

   A 41.98
   B 40.88
   C 41.89
   D 40.98

9. Multiply.

   0.06
   × 0.4

   A 0.024
   B 0.24
   C 0.0024
   D 2.4

10. Divide.

    0.21)6.3

    A 3.0
    B 0.03
    C 0.30
    D 30

11. Choose the most sensible measure for the volume of a kitchen cabinet.

    A 6 sq. ft.
    B 6 ft.
    C 6 sq. in.
    D 6 cu. ft.

12. What fractions of the triangles are shaded?

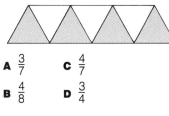

A $\frac{3}{7}$ **C** $\frac{4}{7}$

B $\frac{4}{8}$ **D** $\frac{3}{4}$

13. What is $\frac{8}{10}$ written in lowest terms?

A $\frac{4}{5}$ **C** $\frac{1}{2}$

B $\frac{3}{4}$ **D** $\frac{16}{20}$

14. What is the least common denominator of $\frac{1}{3}$ and $\frac{2}{5}$?

A 3   **C** 15

B 8   **D** 30

15. Which statement is true?

A $\frac{3}{10} < \frac{3}{13}$ **C** $\frac{3}{10} > \frac{7}{20}$

B $\frac{3}{10} > \frac{2}{5}$ **D** $\frac{3}{10} < \frac{3}{5}$

16. How many diamonds are shaded?

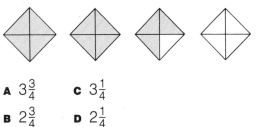

A $3\frac{3}{4}$ **C** $3\frac{1}{4}$

B $2\frac{3}{4}$ **D** $2\frac{1}{4}$

17. What is $\frac{17}{3}$ written as a mixed number?

A $2\frac{2}{3}$ **C** $7\frac{1}{3}$

B $5\frac{2}{3}$ **D** $14\frac{1}{3}$

18. What is $\frac{2}{5}$ written as a decimal?

A 2.5   **C** 0.25

B 0.4   **D** 0.5

19. Multiply.

$$2\frac{1}{3} \times \frac{6}{7}$$

A $2\frac{2}{7}$

B $2\frac{7}{18}$

C 2

D $2\frac{7}{10}$

20. Divide.

$$2 \div \frac{3}{8}$$

A $5\frac{1}{3}$

B $1\frac{5}{8}$

C $\frac{3}{4}$

D 6

21. Add.

$$\begin{aligned} 1\frac{3}{4} \\ + \ \frac{5}{8} \\ \hline \end{aligned}$$

A $2\frac{5}{8}$

B $2\frac{3}{8}$

C 2

D $3\frac{3}{8}$

22. Subtract.

$$\begin{aligned} 7\frac{1}{3} \\ - 2\frac{5}{9} \\ \hline \end{aligned}$$

A $5\frac{7}{9}$

B $5\frac{2}{9}$

C $4\frac{7}{9}$

D $4\frac{2}{3}$

Geometry

73 white triangles   36 black triangles   16 green rectangles

Basic Ideas of Geometry

A. Look for these geometric figures in the painting by Paul Klee.

Point P   • P

A point is an exact location in space.

Segment ST, or $\overline{ST}$

Points S and T are **endpoints** of the segment.

Line HK, or $\overleftrightarrow{HK}$

A line goes on without end in opposite directions.

Ray AB, or $\overrightarrow{AB}$

A ray has one endpoint and goes on without end in one direction. The endpoint is given first in the name of the ray.

B. A *plane* is a flat surface that extends without end in all directions.

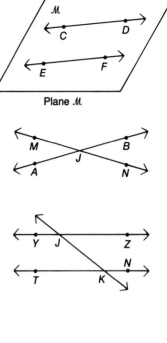

Lines in a plane that never meet are *parallel lines*. $\overleftrightarrow{CD}$ and $\overleftrightarrow{EF}$ are parallel.

Plane ℳ

Intersecting lines meet at a point. $\overleftrightarrow{MN}$ and $\overleftrightarrow{AB}$ intersect at point *J*.

Try Use the diagram at the right.

a. Name 3 points on the same line.

b. Name 3 segments on $\overleftrightarrow{YZ}$.

c. Name a pair of intersecting lines.

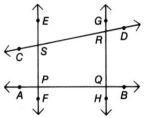

Practice Use the diagram at the right.

1. Which line appears to be parallel to $\overleftrightarrow{EF}$?

2. Which lines intersect at point *P*?

3. Name a point that is not on $\overleftrightarrow{EF}$.

4. Name 3 points on $\overleftrightarrow{CD}$.

5. Name 3 rays with endpoint *P*.

6. Which lines does $\overleftrightarrow{GH}$ intersect?

7. Give another name for $\overline{GH}$.

8. What is the endpoint of $\overrightarrow{CS}$?

9. Name 3 segments on $\overleftrightarrow{CD}$.

10. Name 2 rays on $\overleftrightarrow{CD}$.

11. Name 2 segments with endpoint *A*.

Apply Use the diagram at the right of a portion of the painting by Klee.

12. Name 3 segments on $\overline{KQ}$.

13. Name the intersection of $\overline{KQ}$ and $\overline{MN}$.

14. Give another name for $\overrightarrow{JK}$.

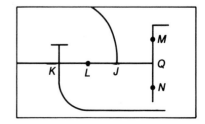

Congruence and Line Symmetry

A. Figures that have the same size and shape are *congruent*. In this painting by Pieter Mondrian, figure *a* is congruent to figure *b*.

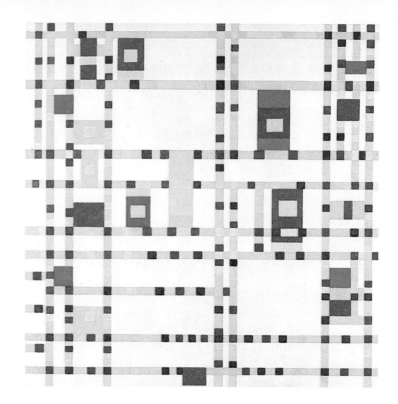

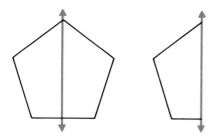

B. A *line of symmetry* divides a figure into two congruent parts.

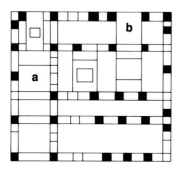

When this figure is folded on the blue line, the two parts match. The blue line is a line of symmetry.

When this figure is folded on the red line, the two parts do not match. The red line is not a line of symmetry.

Try Are the figures congruent?

a. 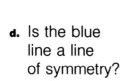 2 cm   2 cm

b.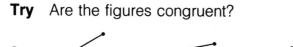

c.

d. Is the blue line a line of symmetry?

e. Tell how many lines of symmetry this figure has.

272

Practice   Are the figures congruent? Write *yes* or *no*.

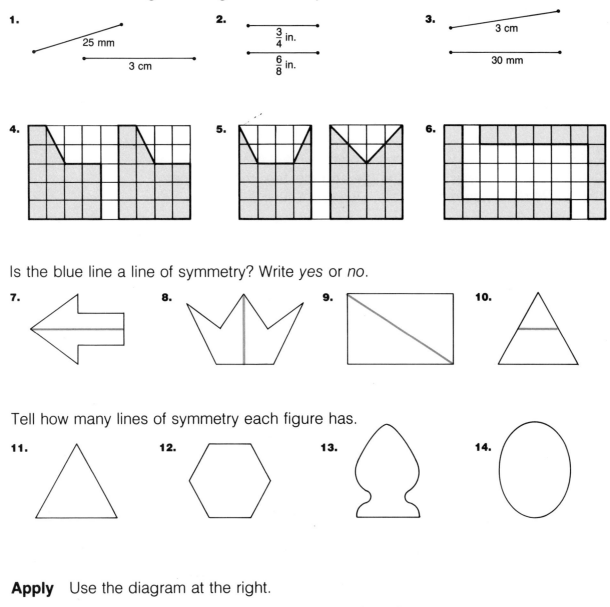

1.

25 mm

3 cm

2.

$\frac{3}{4}$ in.

$\frac{6}{8}$ in.

3.

3 cm

30 mm

4.

5.

6.

Is the blue line a line of symmetry? Write *yes* or *no*.

7.

8.

9.

10.

Tell how many lines of symmetry each figure has.

11.

12.

13.

14.

Apply   Use the diagram at the right.

15. Is figure *c* congruent to figure *d*?

*16. Is the blue line a line of symmetry for figure *e*?

*17. How many lines of symmetry does figure *e* have?

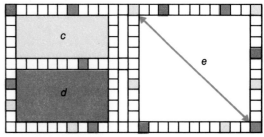

Angles and Angle Measurement

A. An *angle* is formed by two rays that have the same endpoint.

The rays are the *sides* of the angle. The endpoint of the rays is the *vertex* of the angle.

∠ABC is read "angle ABC." The name has the vertex letter in the middle.

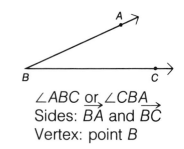

∠ABC or ∠CBA
Sides: $\overrightarrow{BA}$ and $\overrightarrow{BC}$
Vertex: point B

B. To measure an angle, place a *protractor* so that the center mark is on the vertex of the angle and the zero mark of one scale is on a side of the angle. Use that scale.

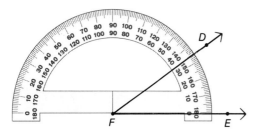

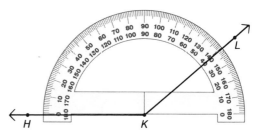

The measure of ∠DFE is 35°. ∠DFE is an *acute angle* because its measure is less than 90°.

The measure of ∠HKL is 140°. ∠HKL is an *obtuse angle* because its measure is between 90° and 180°.

C. Draw an angle that measures 90°.

Draw $\overrightarrow{CD}$.

Center a protractor on point C and put the zero mark of one scale on $\overrightarrow{CD}$. Mark point F at 90°.

Draw $\overrightarrow{CF}$. The measure of ∠FCD is 90°.

An angle that has a measure of 90° is a *right angle*. The sides of the angle are *perpendicular*.

Try

a. Name the angle.

b. Name the sides and the vertex of the angle.

c. Measure the angle. Then tell whether it is acute, right, or obtuse.

d. Draw an angle that measures 40°.

Practice Name each angle, its sides, and its vertex.

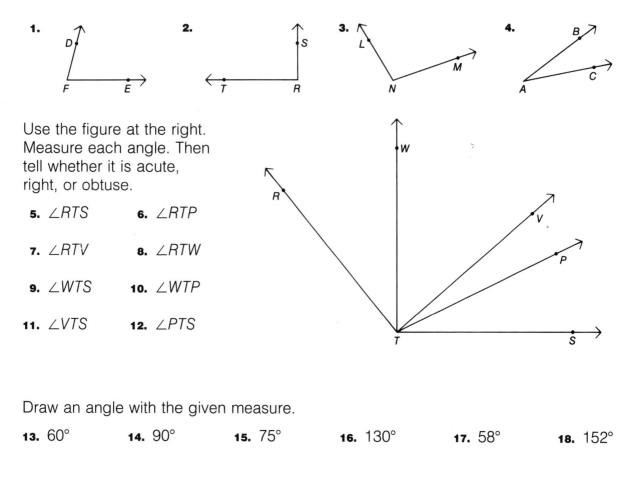

1.

2.

3.

4.

Use the figure at the right. Measure each angle. Then tell whether it is acute, right, or obtuse.

5. ∠RTS

6. ∠RTP

7. ∠RTV

8. ∠RTW

9. ∠WTS

10. ∠WTP

11. ∠VTS

12. ∠PTS

Draw an angle with the given measure.

13. 60° **14.** 90° **15.** 75° **16.** 130° **17.** 58° **18.** 152°

Apply Name something in your classroom that illustrates

19. an acute angle. **20.** a right angle. **21.** an obtuse angle.

Triangles

Parts of this stained glass window are *triangles*.
A triangle has three sides and three angles.

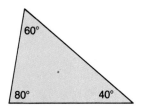

An *acute triangle* has
3 acute angles.

A *right triangle* has
1 right angle, marked
with the symbol, "⌐."

An *obtuse triangle* has
1 obtuse angle.

Notice that the sum of the measures of the three
angles in each triangle above is the same.

$40° + 60° + 80° = 180°$ $40° + 50° + 90° = 180°$ $25° + 35° + 120° = 180°$

In any triangle, the sum of the angle measures is 180°.

Try

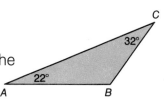

a. Find the third angle measure in the
triangle at the right.

b. Measure the angles of this triangle. Tell whether the triangle is acute, right, or obtuse.

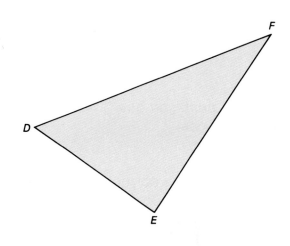

Practice   Trace each triangle and measure the angles. Tell whether the triangle is acute, right, or obtuse.

1. **2.** **3.**

Find the third angle measure in each triangle.

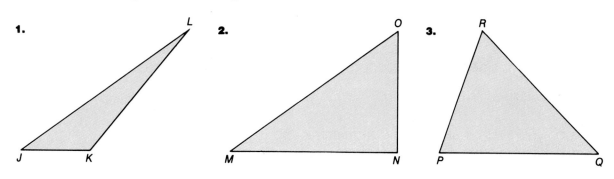

4. **5.** **6.** **7.**

Apply   Solve each problem.

8. Tell whether each green triangle on page 276 is acute, right, or obtuse.

9. Tell whether each yellow triangle on page 276 is acute, right, or obtuse.

Polygons

A. A *polygon* is a figure whose sides are all line segments.

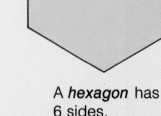

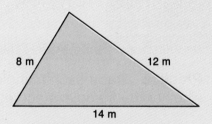

A *pentagon* has 5 sides.

A *hexagon* has 6 sides.

An *octagon* has 8 sides.

B. A triangle is a polygon with 3 sides.

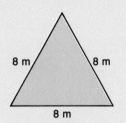

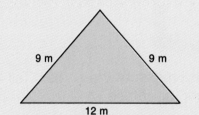

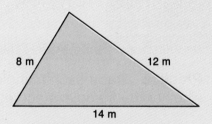

An *equilateral triangle* has 3 congruent sides.

An *isosceles triangle* has at least 2 congruent sides.

A *scalene triangle* has no congruent sides.

C. A polygon with 4 sides is a *quadrilateral*. Some quadrilaterals have special names.

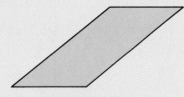

A *parallelogram* is a quadrilateral with opposite sides parallel.

A *rectangle* is a parallelogram with 4 right angles.

A *square* is a rectangle with 4 congruent sides.

Discuss   Is a square a parallelogram?

Try Use all terms that apply.

a. What kind of polygon is this figure?

b. Is the triangle equilateral, isosceles, or scalene?

16 m

8 m

16 m

c. Does the quadrilateral appear to be a square, a rectangle, or a parallelogram?

Practice What kind of polygon is each figure?

1.

2.

3.

4.

Is each triangle equilateral, isosceles, or scalene? Use all terms that apply.

5.

18 ft.

14 ft.

9 ft.

6.

25 mm

25 mm

25 mm

7.

6 in.

6 in.

4 in.

8.

30 m

25 m

20 m

Does each quadrilateral appear to be a square, a rectangle, or a parallelogram? Use all terms that apply.

9.

10.

11.

12.

★13. Draw a quadrilateral with four congruent sides that is not a square.

★14. Draw a quadrilateral with only one pair of parallel sides.

Perimeter

To find the distance around this sand castle, add the lengths of the walls.
The distance around a polygonal figure is its *perimeter*.

The walls form a pentagon and have lengths of 30 dm, 14 dm,
23 dm, 18 dm, and 8 dm.

Find $30 + 14 + 23 + 18 + 8$.

$$30 + 14 + 23 + 18 + 8 = 93$$

The perimeter of the
sand castle is 93 dm.

Try Find the perimeter of each polygon.

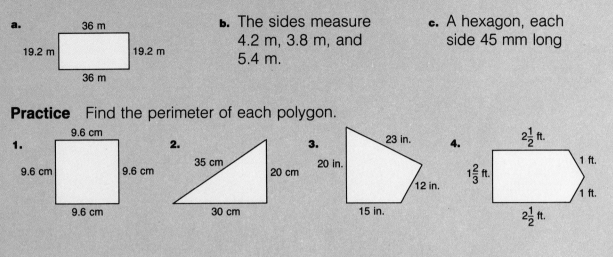

a.

36 m

19.2 m ___ 19.2 m

36 m

b. The sides measure 4.2 m, 3.8 m, and 5.4 m.

c. A hexagon, each side 45 mm long

Practice Find the perimeter of each polygon.

1.

9.6 cm

9.6 cm ___ 9.6 cm

9.6 cm

2.

35 cm

20 cm

30 cm

3.

23 in.

20 in.

12 in.

15 in.

4.

$2\frac{1}{2}$ ft.

$1\frac{2}{3}$ ft.

$1\frac{2}{3}$ ft.

1 ft.

1 ft.

$2\frac{1}{2}$ ft.

5. 8.3 m, 4.7 m, 5.1 m, 6.3 m

6. 10.3 m, 9.7 m, 3.9 m, 8.8 m

7. An octagon, each side 42 mm long

8. A pentagon, each side 12 ft. long

Apply Solve each problem.

9. Find the perimeter of a sand castle with sides measuring 186 mm, 213 mm, 215 mm, 240 mm, 200 mm, 240 mm, and 194 mm.

★10. The perimeter of a sand castle is 58 dm. The lengths of 3 sides are 16 dm, 18 dm, and 15 dm. Find the length of the fourth side.

Area of a Rectangle

A. Gloria is assembling a model of a castle. What is the area, in square inches, of the floor of a tower of the castle?

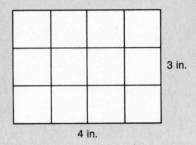

3 in.

4 in.

Count the squares to find the area.

The area is 12 sq. in.

Note that 12 = 4 × 3.

To find the area (A) of a rectangle, multiply the length (ℓ) and width (w).
$A = \ell \times w.$

B. Find the area of a rectangle 18 cm long and 15 cm wide.

$A = \ell \times w$

$A = 18 \times 15$

$A = 270$

The area is 270 cm².

Try Find the area of each rectangle.

a.

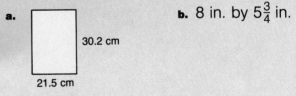

30.2 cm

21.5 cm

b. 8 in. by $5\frac{3}{4}$ in.

Practice Find the area of each rectangle.

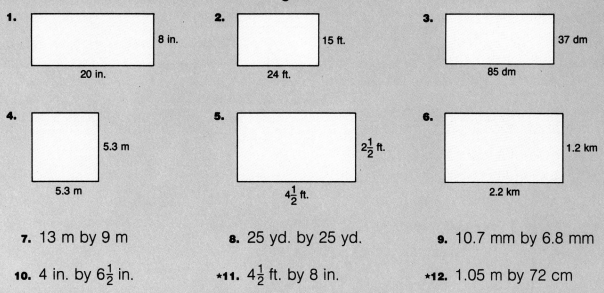

1. 8 in. / 20 in.

2. 15 ft. / 24 ft.

3. 37 dm / 85 dm

4. 5.3 m / 5.3 m

5. $2\frac{1}{2}$ ft. / $4\frac{1}{2}$ ft.

6. 1.2 km / 2.2 km

7. 13 m by 9 m

8. 25 yd. by 25 yd.

9. 10.7 mm by 6.8 mm

10. 4 in. by $6\frac{1}{2}$ in.

★11. $4\frac{1}{2}$ ft. by 8 in.

★12. 1.05 m by 72 cm

Apply Solve each problem.

13. The main room of the castle measures 12 in. by 9 in. What is the area of the main room?

14. A wall around the castle is in sections of 24 in., 4 in., 3 in., 18 in., 20 in., 20 in., 18 in., 4 in., and 3 in. Find the perimeter of the wall.

★15. The wall in Problem 14 is 4 in. high. Find the area of the wall.

★16. The area of the drawbridge is 8 sq. in. It is 4 in. long. How wide is it?

CHALLENGE

Here are some stamps left from a sheet of stamps. How many choices do you have if you want to select

1. 1 stamp?

2. 2 connected stamps?

3. 3 connected stamps?

4. 4 connected stamps?

5. 5 connected stamps?

6. 6 connected stamps?

Area of a Triangle

A. Pedro is making a model of a castle. One part of the roof of a tower is shaped like a triangle. Find the area of this part of the roof.

Base

Height

Draw a rectangle as long as the *base* of the triangle and as wide as the *height* of the triangle.

The area of a triangle is always half the area of the related rectangle.

The area of this rectangle is 12 cm².

The area of the triangular part of the roof is 6 cm².

The area (A) of a triangle is equal to one half the base (b) times the height (h). $A = \frac{1}{2} \times b \times h$

B. Find the area of a triangle with base 16 in. and height 10 in.

$A = \frac{1}{2} \times b \times h$

$A = \frac{1}{2} \times 16 \times 10$

$A = 80$

The area is 80 sq. in.

Try Find the area of each triangle.

a.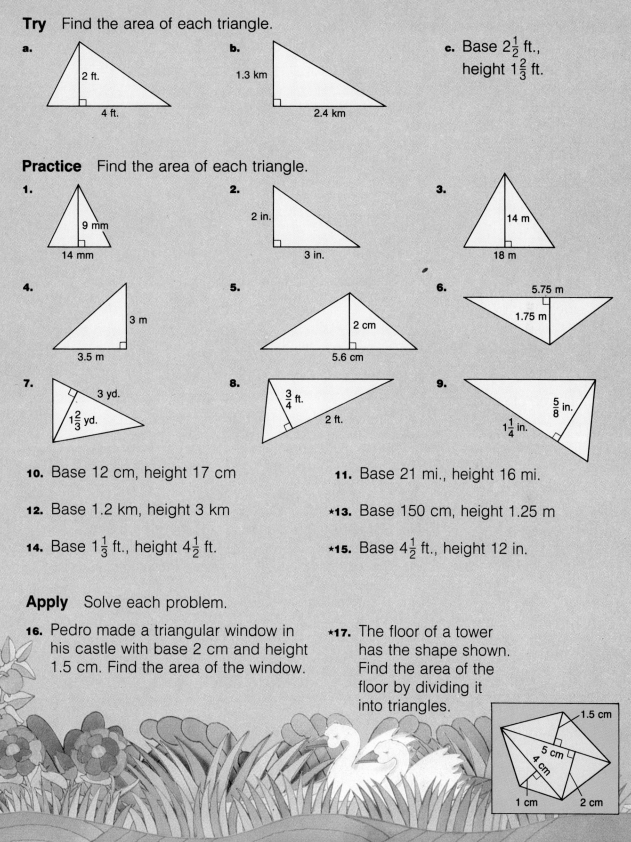
2 ft.
4 ft.

b.
1.3 km
2.4 km

c. Base $2\frac{1}{2}$ ft., height $1\frac{2}{3}$ ft.

Practice Find the area of each triangle.

1.
9 mm
14 mm

2.
2 in.
3 in.

3.
14 m
18 m

4.
3 m
3.5 m

5.
2 cm
5.6 cm

6.
5.75 m
1.75 m

7.
3 yd.
$1\frac{2}{3}$ yd.

8.
$\frac{3}{4}$ ft.
2 ft.

9.
$\frac{5}{8}$ in.
$1\frac{1}{4}$ in.

10. Base 12 cm, height 17 cm

11. Base 21 mi., height 16 mi.

12. Base 1.2 km, height 3 km

★13. Base 150 cm, height 1.25 m

14. Base $1\frac{1}{3}$ ft., height $4\frac{1}{2}$ ft.

★15. Base $4\frac{1}{2}$ ft., height 12 in.

Apply Solve each problem.

16. Pedro made a triangular window in his castle with base 2 cm and height 1.5 cm. Find the area of the window.

★17. The floor of a tower has the shape shown. Find the area of the floor by dividing it into triangles.

1.5 cm
5 cm
4 cm
1 cm
2 cm

Practice: Perimeter and Area

Find the perimeter of each polygon.

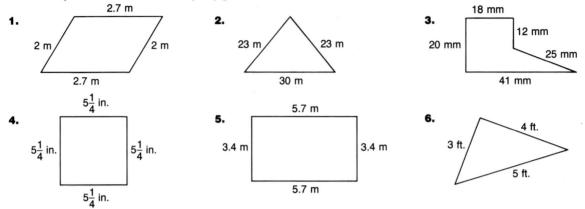

1. 2.7 m, 2 m, 2 m, 2.7 m

2. 23 m, 23 m, 30 m

3. 18 mm, 12 mm, 25 mm, 41 mm, 20 mm

4. $5\frac{1}{4}$ in., $5\frac{1}{4}$ in., $5\frac{1}{4}$ in., $5\frac{1}{4}$ in.

5. 5.7 m, 3.4 m, 3.4 m, 5.7 m

6. 4 ft., 3 ft., 5 ft.

Find the perimeter of a polygon with sides of the given lengths.

7. 5 sides, each 7.6 cm

8. 6.2 m, 8.3 m, 5.9 m, 7.1 m

9. 15 cm, 20 cm, 25 cm

10. 3 in., 5 in., 7 in., 6 in., 6 in.

Find the area of each rectangle.

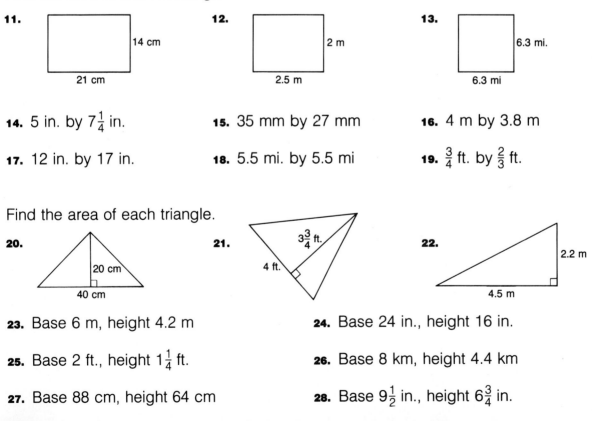

11. 21 cm, 14 cm

12. 2.5 m, 2 m

13. 6.3 mi, 6.3 mi.

14. 5 in. by $7\frac{1}{4}$ in.

15. 35 mm by 27 mm

16. 4 m by 3.8 m

17. 12 in. by 17 in.

18. 5.5 mi. by 5.5 mi

19. $\frac{3}{4}$ ft. by $\frac{2}{3}$ ft.

Find the area of each triangle.

20. 20 cm, 40 cm

21. $3\frac{3}{4}$ ft., 4 ft.

22. 2.2 m, 4.5 m

23. Base 6 m, height 4.2 m

24. Base 24 in., height 16 in.

25. Base 2 ft., height $1\frac{1}{4}$ ft.

26. Base 8 km, height 4.4 km

27. Base 88 cm, height 64 cm

28. Base $9\frac{1}{2}$ in., height $6\frac{3}{4}$ in.

Apply Solve each problem.

29. A stamp is 25 mm long and 21 mm wide. What is its area?

30. Find the area of a sheet of wall paneling that is 122 cm by 244 cm.

31. Find the perimeter of a square mirror that is 170 cm on a side.

32. Find the area of a square floor-tile that is 10 in. on a side.

33. Central Park is 4 km long and 0.8 km wide. Find the area of this rectangular park.

34. A dollar bill is 6 in. long and $2\frac{1}{2}$ in. wide. What is the area of a dollar bill?

35. Clyde wants to fence a horse pasture. The sides of the pasture are 35 m, 22 m, 56 m, 42 m, and 30 m long. How much fencing should he buy?

★36. *Estimation* Estimate the area of the state of Florida by finding the area of the triangle.

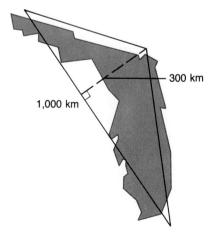

1,000 km

300 km

Logo: Arithmetic Computations

In Logo the Turtle is a small triangle on the computer screen. This Turtle can follow commands that make it do special things. Logo can also do arithmetic computations. The symbol / means divide.

REPEAT 4 [FD 50 RT 360/4] tells the Turtle to complete the following commands four times: move forward 50 steps and turn right 360/4.

REPEAT 4 FD 50 RT 360/4

number of sides

length of sides

360/number of angles = angle turned

360/4 = 90

REPEAT 4 [FD 50 RT 90] tells the Turtle to draw a square. The perimeter of this square is 200.

In any polygon, the number of sides will always equal the number of angles.

Give the computed angle size after each RT command. Name the polygon each series of commands will draw. Tell what the perimeter is for each polygon made by the REPEAT command.

1. REPEAT 6 [FD 50 RT 360/6]

2. REPEAT 5 [FD 10 RT 360/5]

3. REPEAT 3 [FD 25 RT 360/3]

4. REPEAT 8 [FD 40 RT 360/8]

Problem Solving: Use Estimation

Read　Naomi is remodeling her house. She is putting an arch between her living room and dining room. Estimate the area of the arch.

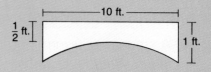

Plan　The arch fits inside a rectangle 10 ft. long and 1 ft. wide. Approximate the area "cut out" from the rectangle with a triangle and subtract the area of the triangle from the area of the rectangle.

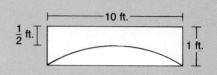

Solve

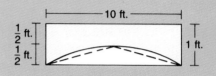

Area of rectangle	Area of triangle
$A = l \times w$	$A = \frac{1}{2} \times b \times h$
$A = 10 \times 1$	$A = \frac{1}{2} \times 10 \times \frac{1}{2}$
$A = 10$	$A = \frac{5}{2} = 2\frac{1}{2}$

Area of arch $\approx 10 - 2\frac{1}{2} \approx 7\frac{1}{2}$

Answer　The area of the arch is about $7\frac{1}{2}$ sq. ft.

Look Back　A rectangle 10 ft. long and $\frac{1}{2}$ ft. wide fits inside the arch. Since $7\frac{1}{2}$ sq. ft. is a little more than $10 \times \frac{1}{2} = 5$ sq. ft., the answer is reasonable.

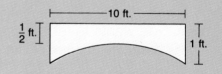

Try *Estimation* Give an estimate for the problem.

a. Naomi made a cut-out in the wall between the dining room and kitchen. Use the diagram at the right to estimate the area of the cut-out.

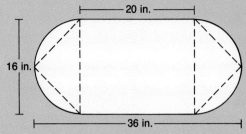

Apply *Estimation* Give an estimate for each problem.

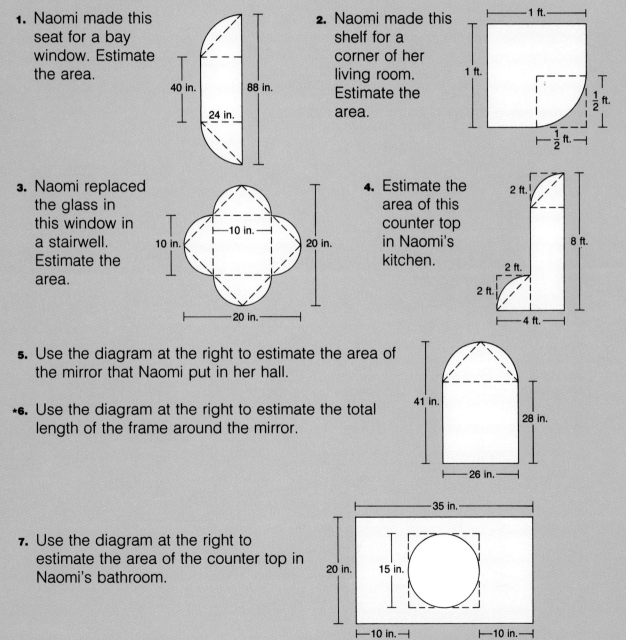

1. Naomi made this seat for a bay window. Estimate the area.

2. Naomi made this shelf for a corner of her living room. Estimate the area.

3. Naomi replaced the glass in this window in a stairwell. Estimate the area.

4. Estimate the area of this counter top in Naomi's kitchen.

5. Use the diagram at the right to estimate the area of the mirror that Naomi put in her hall.

6. Use the diagram at the right to estimate the total length of the frame around the mirror.

7. Use the diagram at the right to estimate the area of the counter top in Naomi's bathroom.

Circles

A. Naomi used a disc sander to refinish a table. The rim of the disc has the shape of a *circle*.

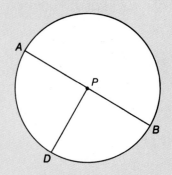

P is the *center* of the circle. All points of the circle are the same distance from P.

$\overline{PD}$ is a *radius* of the circle. A radius has the center and a point of the circle as endpoints.

$\overline{AB}$ is a *diameter* of the circle. A diameter has two points of the circle as endpoints and goes through the center.

B. A circle has a radius of 3 cm. Find the diameter.

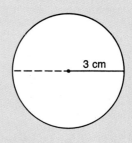

The diameter is twice the radius.

$3 \times 2 = 6$

The diameter is 6 cm.

In a circle, each radius is the same length, and each diameter is the same length.

The diameter of a circle is twice its radius.

Try

a. Name each radius. Point E is the center.

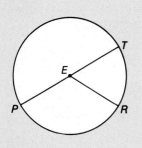

b. Name each diameter. Point K is the center.

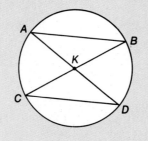

c. Give the missing measure.

Radius: 4 cm
Diameter: ▓ cm

Practice Name each radius. In each circle, point *E* is the center.

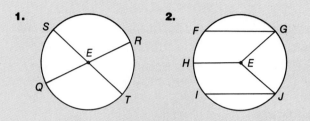

1.

2.

Name each diameter. In each circle, point *K* is the center.

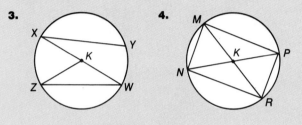

3.

4.

Give each missing measure.

5. Radius: 6 cm
   Diameter: ▦ cm

6. Radius: 10 cm
   Diameter: ▦ cm

7. Radius: ▦ cm
   Diameter: 8 cm

8. Radius: ▦ cm
   Diameter: 9 cm

Apply Solve each problem.

9. A sanding disc has a 10-inch diameter. What is the radius?

10. Will a lid with a $4\frac{1}{2}$-inch diameter fit on a can with a $2\frac{1}{2}$-inch radius?

The *circumference* of a circle is the distance around the circle. The circumference of a dime is about 56 mm. Its diameter is about 18 mm.

Divide the circumference by the diameter.

Press: 56 ÷ 18

Display: *3.11111111*

Use your calculator to divide the circumference of each object by its diameter. Round each answer to the nearest tenth.

	Object	Circumference	Diameter
1.	Record album	94 cm	30 cm
2.	Bicycle tire	207 cm	66 cm
3.	Quarter	75 mm	24 mm
4.	Clock	62.8 cm	20 cm
5.	Pie plate	72 cm	23 cm
6.	Nickel	6.6 cm	2.1 cm
7.	Ferris wheel	47 m	15 m

8. How would you estimate the circumference of a circle if you knew the diameter?

Circumference

Stonehenge is an ancient monument in England built about 3,500 years ago. It was built in the shape of a circle, but only part of it remains.

A. The *circumference* (C) of a circle is the distance around the circle. In any circle, the circumference divided by the diameter (d) is about 3.1.

$$C \div d \approx 3.1$$

The exact answer to $C \div d$ is the same for every circle and is a little more than 3.1. This quotient is given a special name, the Greek letter *pi* (π). Here is the value of π written with 10 decimal places.

$$C \div d = \pi \qquad \pi \approx 3.1415926536$$

Since the circumference divided by the diameter is π, you can multiply π and the diameter to get the circumference.

$$C = \pi \times d$$

B. Find the circumference of a circle with a diameter of 5 in. Use 3.14 for π.

$$C = \pi \times d$$

$$C \approx 3.14 \times 5$$

$$C \approx 15.70$$

The circumference is about 15.7 in.

Try Find the circumference of each circle. Use 3.14 for π.

a. 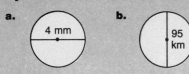 4 mm

b. 95 km

c. Diameter: 12 in.

Practice Find the circumference of each circle. Use 3.14 for π.

1. 5 m

2. 8 cm

3. 46 cm

4. 19.4 m

★5. 8 m

6. Diameter: 13 m

7. Diameter: 2.46 m

★8. Radius: 8.7 mi.

Apply Solve each problem. Use 3.14 for π.

9. In Stonehenge, 30 blocks of stone stood in a circle with a diameter of 30 m. Find the circumference of the circle.

10. An earth wall about 98 m in diameter surrounded Stonehenge. Find the circumference of the earth wall.

Polyhedrons

The Great Pyramid of Cheops was built about 4,500 years ago. It was made of 2 million stone blocks.

A. A *polyhedron* has *faces* that are shaped like polygons.

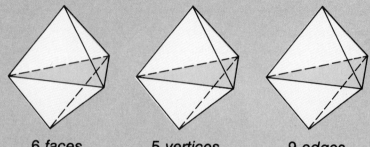

6 *faces*   5 *vertices*   9 *edges*

B. A *pyramid* is named for its base.

  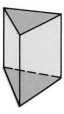

Triangular   Rectangular   Pentagonal
pyramid   pyramid   pyramid

C. *Prisms* have two congruent bases.

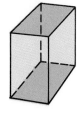 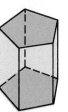

Triangular   Rectangular   Pentagonal
prism   prism   prism

Try   Is each figure a polyhedron?

a.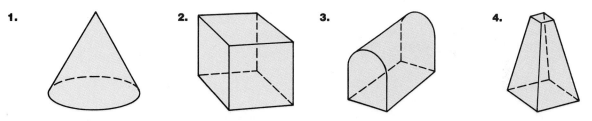

b.

c. How many faces, vertices, and edges does a pyramid with a 4-sided base have?

Practice   Is each figure a polyhedron? Write *yes* or *no*.

1.   **2.**   **3.**   **4.**

Find the number of faces, vertices, and edges in a pyramid if the base has

5. 5 sides.   **6.** 6 sides.   **7.** 8 sides.   **8.** 10 sides.   **9.** 15 sides.

Find the number of faces, vertices, and edges in a prism if the bases have

10. 5 sides.   **11.** 6 sides.   **12.** 8 sides.   **13.** 10 sides.   **14.** 15 sides.

Apply   Solve each problem.

15. The base of the Great Pyramid is a square that is 224 m on a side. What is the area of the base?

16. The height of the Great Pyramid was 147 m. It is now 10 m shorter because some of the upper stones are gone. How high is the Great Pyramid now?

Surface Area

A. To find the total surface area, add the areas of all the faces.

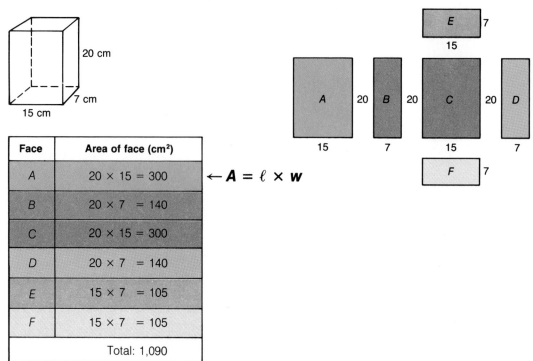

Face	Area of face (cm²)
A	20 × 15 = 300
B	20 × 7 = 140
C	20 × 15 = 300
D	20 × 7 = 140
E	15 × 7 = 105
F	15 × 7 = 105
	Total: 1,090

$\leftarrow A = \ell \times w$

The total surface area is 1,090 cm².

B. Find the total surface area.

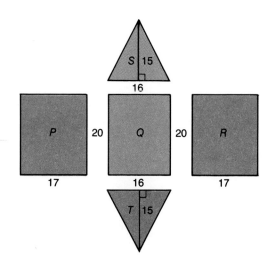

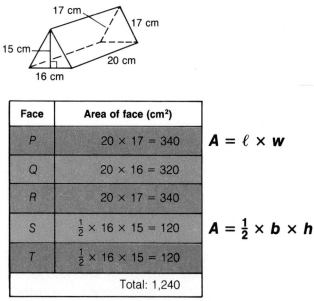

Face	Area of face (cm²)
P	20 × 17 = 340
Q	20 × 16 = 320
R	20 × 17 = 340
S	$\frac{1}{2}$ × 16 × 15 = 120
T	$\frac{1}{2}$ × 16 × 15 = 120
	Total: 1,240

$A = \ell \times w$

$A = \frac{1}{2} \times b \times h$

The total surface area is 1,240 cm².

Try Find the total surface area of each prism.

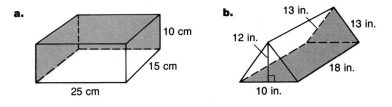

a.

10 cm
15 cm
25 cm

b.

13 in.
13 in.
12 in.
18 in.
10 in.

Practice Find the total surface area of each prism.

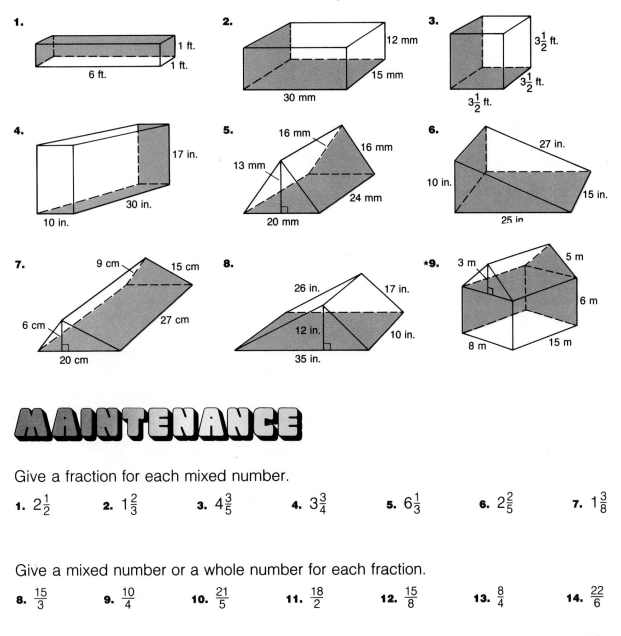

1.

1 ft.
1 ft.
6 ft.

2.

12 mm
15 mm
30 mm

3.

$3\frac{1}{2}$ ft.
$3\frac{1}{2}$ ft.
$3\frac{1}{2}$ ft.

4.

17 in.
30 in.
10 in.

5.

16 mm
16 mm
13 mm
24 mm
20 mm

6.

27 in.
10 in.
15 in.
25 in

7.

9 cm
15 cm
6 cm
27 cm
20 cm

8.

26 in.
17 in.
12 in.
10 in.
35 in.

★9.

3 m
5 m
6 m
8 m
15 m

MAINTENANCE

Give a fraction for each mixed number.

1. $2\frac{1}{2}$ **2.** $1\frac{2}{3}$ **3.** $4\frac{3}{5}$ **4.** $3\frac{3}{4}$ **5.** $6\frac{1}{3}$ **6.** $2\frac{2}{5}$ **7.** $1\frac{3}{8}$

Give a mixed number or a whole number for each fraction.

8. $\frac{15}{3}$ **9.** $\frac{10}{4}$ **10.** $\frac{21}{5}$ **11.** $\frac{18}{2}$ **12.** $\frac{15}{8}$ **13.** $\frac{8}{4}$ **14.** $\frac{22}{6}$

Volume

A. Kathy has a pet toad named Virgil. Virgil lives in a shoe box. Find the volume of the shoe box.

Think of filling the box with 1-inch-wide cubes.

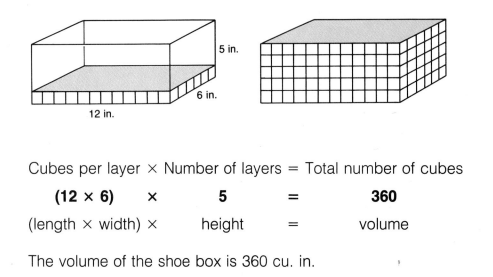

Cubes per layer × Number of layers = Total number of cubes

| **(12 × 6)** | **×** | **5** | **=** | **360** |
| (length × width) × | | height | = | volume |

The volume of the shoe box is 360 cu. in.

To find the volume (V) of a rectangular prism, multiply the length (l), the width (w), and the height (h).   **$V = \ell \times w \times h$**

B. Find the volume of this prism.

$V = \ell \times w \times h$

$V = 18 \times 5 \times 10$

$V = 900$

10 cm

5 cm

18 cm

The volume is 900 cm³.

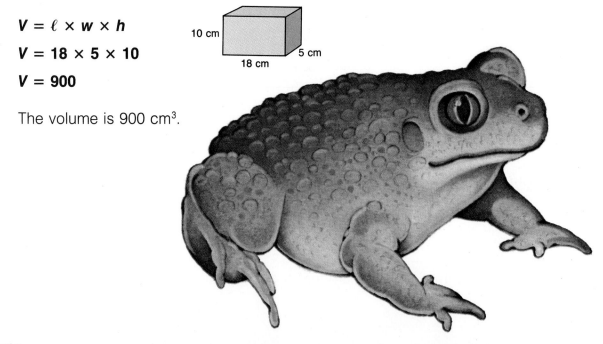

Try Find the volume of each rectangular prism.

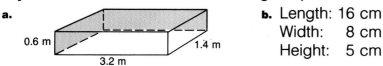

a. [diagram: 0.6 m, 3.2 m, 1.4 m]

b. Length: 16 cm
Width: 8 cm
Height: 5 cm

Practice Find the volume of each rectangular prism.

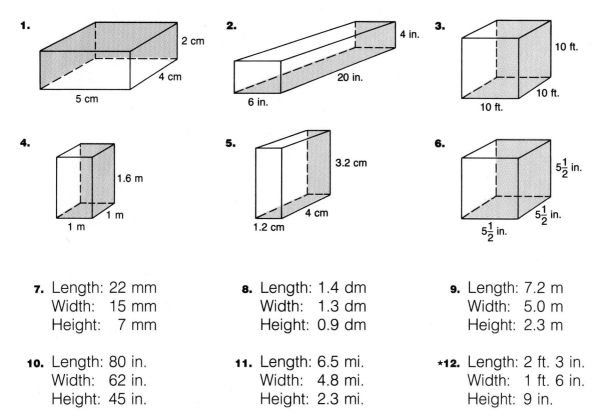

1. 2 cm, 4 cm, 5 cm

2. 4 in., 20 in., 6 in.

3. 10 ft., 10 ft., 10 ft.

4. 1.6 m, 1 m, 1 m

5. 3.2 cm, 4 cm, 1.2 cm

6. $5\frac{1}{2}$ in., $5\frac{1}{2}$ in., $5\frac{1}{2}$ in.

7. Length: 22 mm
Width: 15 mm
Height: 7 mm

8. Length: 1.4 dm
Width: 1.3 dm
Height: 0.9 dm

9. Length: 7.2 m
Width: 5.0 m
Height: 2.3 m

10. Length: 80 in.
Width: 62 in.
Height: 45 in.

11. Length: 6.5 mi.
Width: 4.8 mi.
Height: 2.3 mi.

★12. Length: 2 ft. 3 in.
Width: 1 ft. 6 in.
Height: 9 in.

Apply Solve each problem.

13. Kathy keeps Virgil's shoe-box house in her closet. Her closet is 4 ft. long, 2 ft. wide, and 6 ft. high. Find its volume.

14. A shelf in Kathy's closet is 4 ft. long and $1\frac{1}{2}$ ft. wide. What is the area of the shelf?

15. Kathy found Virgil in a dresser drawer. The drawer is 34 in. long, 22 in. wide, and 6 in. high. What is the volume of the drawer?

★16. If each shoe box is the size of Virgil's house, how many shoe boxes will fit in Kathy's closet?

Problem Solving: Use a Formula

Read   Alvin, a cricket, lives in a cage that has a volume of 640 cm². The cage is 10 cm long and 8 cm wide. How tall is the cage?

Plan   Use the formula for the volume of a rectangular prism. Divide to find the missing factor h.

Solve

$$V = \ell \times w \times h$$
$$640 = 10 \times 8 \times h$$
$$640 = 80 \times h$$
$$640 \div 80 = h$$
$$8 = h$$

Answer   The cage is 8 cm tall.

Look Back

$$V = \ell \times w \times h$$
$$640 \overset{?}{=} 10 \times 8 \times 8$$
$$640 = 640$$

The answer checks.

Try Use one of the formulas at the right to solve the problem.

a. Perky the parrot lives in a cage with a circular bottom. The diameter of the bottom is 18 in. What is the circumference?

Area of rectangle: $A = \ell \times w$

Area of triangle: $A = \frac{1}{2} \times b \times h$

Circumference of circle: $C = \pi \times d$

Volume of rectangular prism: $V = \ell \times w \times h$

Apply Use one of the formulas above to solve each problem.

1. A gerbil's cage should have at least 36 sq. in. of floor space. If the length of the floor is 6 in., what is the least the width should be?

2. Deedee and Donnie are flying squirrels. The volume of their cage is 30 cu. ft. It is 3 ft. long and 3 ft. wide. How tall is their cage?

3. A gerbil's cage has a section that is 6 in. long, 3 in. wide, and 3 in. high. What is the volume of this section?

4. Goldie the fish lives in a circular bowl. The circumference of the bottom is 15.7 in. What is the diameter of the bottom?

5. Tammy and Tommy are canaries. Their cage is 16 in. long and 12 in. wide. What is the area of the bottom of the cage?

6. Molly the rabbit lives in a hutch that is 3 ft. long, 2 ft. wide, and 2 ft. high. What is the volume of the hutch?

7. Sammy the shark lives in a tank with a volume of 1.62 m³. The width is 0.9 m and the height is 1.2 m. What is the length?

*8. A rectangular cage for white mice is 18 in. long and 8 in. wide. A wall goes between two opposite corners to separate a mother and her babies from the other mice. What is the floor area of one section?

Chapter 10 Test

1. Name 2 rays on $\overleftrightarrow{PR}$.

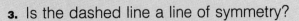
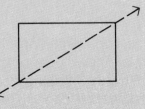

2. Which lines intersect at point Q?

3. Is the dashed line a line of symmetry?

4. Measure the angle and tell whether it is right, acute, or obtuse.

5. Draw an angle of 100°.

6. The angles of a triangle measure 30°, 40°, and 110°. Is the triangle right, acute, or obtuse?

7. Two angles of a triangle measure 50° and 70°. What is the measure of the third angle?

8. What kind of polygon does this appear to be? Use all terms that apply.

9. Is this triangle equilateral, isosceles, or scalene?

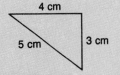

4 cm
5 cm   3 cm

10. Find the perimeter of a pentagon whose sides are 6 ft., 8 ft., 12 ft., 10 ft., and 12 ft. long.

11. Find the area of a rectangle 11 in. long and $8\frac{1}{2}$ in. wide.

12. Find the area of a triangle with base 31 cm and height 16 cm.

13. Estimate the area of the striped part of the flag of the Bahamas.

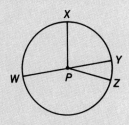

14. Name each radius in this circle. The center is P.

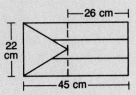

15. If the radius is 2 m, what is the diameter?

16. If the diameter of a circle is 6 in., what is the circumference? (Use 3.14 for π.)

17. A pyramid has a base with 7 sides. How many faces, edges, and vertices does it have?

18. Find the total surface area of this prism.

19. Find the volume of this prism.

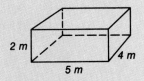

2 m   4 m
5 m

20. A baking dish has a circumference of 80 cm. To the nearest tenth, what is the diameter of the dish? (Use 3.14 for π in the formula $C = \pi \times d$.)

302

Area of a Circle

You can estimate the area of the circle at the right by counting the number of square centimeters that are shaded.

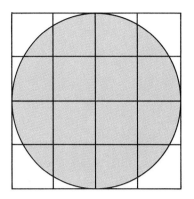

4	Completely shaded squares
8	Mostly shaded squares
+ 1	Partially shaded squares put together
13	

The area of the circle is about 13 cm².

You can also find the area by using the formula for the area (*A*) of a circle,

$$A = \pi \times r^2$$

where *r* is the radius of the circle,

Use 3.14 for π and 2 cm for the radius.

$$A = \pi \times r^2$$

$$A \approx 3.14 \times 2 \times 2$$

$$A \approx 12.56$$

The area of the circle is about 12.56 cm².

Find the area of each circle. Use 3.14 for π.

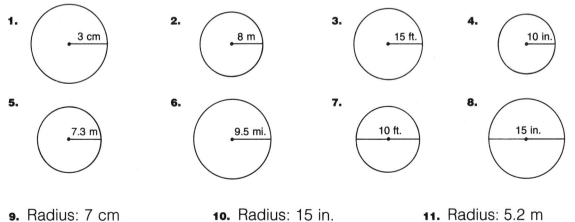

1. 3 cm

2. 8 m

3. 15 ft.

4. 10 in.

5. 7.3 m

6. 9.5 mi.

7. 10 ft.

8. 15 in.

9. Radius: 7 cm

10. Radius: 15 in.

11. Radius: 5.2 m

MAINTENANCE

Add or subtract.

1. $\frac{5}{8}$
  $+ 4\frac{1}{2}$

2. $6\frac{5}{8}$
  $+ 4\frac{3}{4}$

3. $\frac{1}{2}$
  $- \frac{1}{5}$

4. $\frac{5}{8}$
  $+ \frac{3}{8}$

5. $6\frac{3}{5}$
  $- 2\frac{1}{4}$

6. $6\frac{3}{8}$
  $+ 5\frac{1}{4}$

7. $9\frac{1}{3}$
  $- 8\frac{1}{4}$

8. $\frac{2}{3}$
  $- \frac{1}{5}$

9. $4\frac{1}{4}$
  $+ 3\frac{5}{6}$

10. $5\frac{4}{5}$
  $- 3\frac{1}{5}$

11. $7\frac{3}{8}$
  $+ 8\frac{3}{5}$

12. $17\frac{1}{4}$
  $- 8\frac{5}{8}$

13. $2\frac{3}{4}$
  $+ 5\frac{2}{5}$

14. $\frac{8}{9}$
  $- \frac{3}{4}$

15. $2\frac{5}{6}$
  $+ 9\frac{1}{3}$

16. $7\frac{3}{10}$
  $- 2\frac{4}{5}$

17. $\frac{3}{4}$
  $+ \frac{5}{6}$

18. $12\frac{4}{5}$
  $- 3\frac{1}{2}$

19. $\frac{2}{3} + 2\frac{1}{2} + \frac{5}{6}$

20. $6 - \frac{5}{8}$

21. $3\frac{3}{4} + \frac{5}{8} + 5\frac{1}{2}$

22. $5\frac{1}{3} - 2\frac{2}{3}$

23. $9 + 2\frac{3}{5} + \frac{5}{6}$

24. $5\frac{9}{10} + 2\frac{3}{5} + 6\frac{1}{2}$

Apply Solve each problem.

25. Mr. Kato has $9\frac{1}{3}$ yd. of fabric. He used 5 yd. to cover a chair. How much fabric did he have left?

26. A pitcher holds 6 c. of juice. How many $\frac{2}{3}$-c. servings can be poured?

27. A mouse weighs $\frac{7}{8}$ oz. Each day it eats $\frac{1}{2}$ as much as it weighs. How much does it eat each day?

28. It snowed $3\frac{1}{2}$ in. on Monday and $2\frac{3}{5}$ in. on Tuesday. How much snow fell on the two days?

29. Robin weighs 90 lb. $\frac{7}{10}$ of his body weight is water. How many pounds of his body weight are water?

30. Ms. Cohoe had $\frac{3}{4}$ c. of raisins. She used $\frac{1}{2}$ c. for a recipe. What part of a cup of raisins did she have left?

31. Elena had $5\frac{1}{2}$ yd. of rope. She cut it into 4 equal pieces to stake her tent. How long was each piece?

32. Five people each have a canteen full of water. Each canteen holds $1\frac{1}{2}$ qt. How much water do they have in all?

Ratio, Proportion, and Percent

95% water

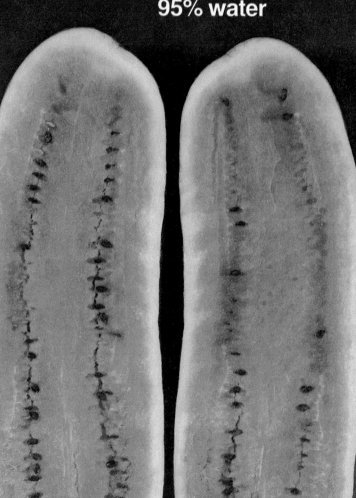

Ratio

A. Meg uses magnets to hang pictures in her locker. The *ratio* 2 for 3 can be used to describe the price per number of magnets.

Dollars ⟶ $\dfrac{2}{3}$
Magnets ⟶

Each of the *equal ratios* below describes the same price as 2 for 3.

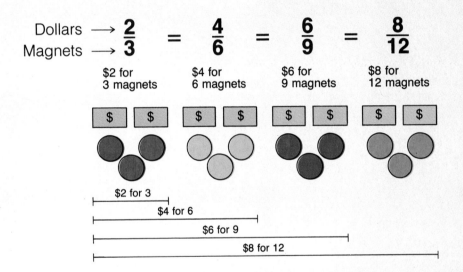

Dollars ⟶ $\dfrac{2}{3}$ = $\dfrac{4}{6}$ = $\dfrac{6}{9}$ = $\dfrac{8}{12}$
Magnets ⟶

$2 for 3 magnets $4 for 6 magnets $6 for 9 magnets $8 for 12 magnets

$2 for 3
$4 for 6
$6 for 9
$8 for 12

B. Four lockers take up 3 ft. of space. Write equal ratios until you find the number of lockers that will fit in 12 ft. of space.

$$\text{Lockers} \longrightarrow \frac{4}{3} = \overset{4\times2}{\underset{3\times2}{\frac{8}{6}}} = \overset{4\times3}{\underset{3\times3}{\frac{12}{9}}} = \overset{4\times4}{\underset{3\times4}{\frac{16}{12}}}$$
Feet ⟶

16 lockers will fit in 12 ft. of space.

You can multiply both numbers of a ratio by the same nonzero number to find an equal ratio.

306

Try Write a ratio for each situation.

a. 2 baskets in 5 tries   **b.** 55 miles per hour

c. Complete the list of equal ratios.

$$\frac{3}{39} = \frac{6}{\blacksquare} = \frac{\blacksquare}{117} = \frac{\blacksquare}{156}$$

Practice Write a ratio for each situation.

1. 5 boys to 6 girls   **2.** 3 wins to 5 losses

3. 7 days in 1 week   **4.** 7 red to 10 yellow

5. 3 for 89¢   **6.** 25 miles per hour

7. 1 run in 7 hits   **8.** 9 inches in 5 hours

9. 5 drums to 9 horns   **10.** 3 feet to 1 yard

Complete each list of equal ratios.

11. Lemons ⟶ $\frac{4}{49} = \frac{\blacksquare}{98} = \frac{\blacksquare}{147} = \frac{16}{\blacksquare} = \frac{20}{\blacksquare}$
Cents ⟶

12. Scoops cocoa ⟶ $\frac{5}{8} = \frac{10}{\blacksquare} = \frac{\blacksquare}{24} = \frac{20}{\blacksquare} = \frac{\blacksquare}{40}$
Ounces milk ⟶

13. British pounds ⟶ $\frac{8}{13} = \frac{\blacksquare}{26} = \frac{\blacksquare}{39} = \frac{\blacksquare}{52} = \frac{40}{\blacksquare}$
U.S. dollars ⟶

★14. Boys ⟶ $\frac{96}{80} = \frac{48}{\blacksquare} = \frac{\blacksquare}{20} = \frac{\blacksquare}{10} = \frac{6}{\blacksquare}$
Girls ⟶

Apply For each problem, write equal ratios until you find the answer.

15. Notebooks are priced at 3 for $4. What is the cost of 12 notebooks?

16. Five notebooks take up 7 in. of shelf space. How many notebooks would fit in 35 in. of space?

17. Five sheets of poster board cost 72¢. How much would 25 sheets cost?

★18. Four jars of poster paint cost $1.50. At this price, how many jars could Hal buy for $3.75?

Proerportion

A. Eduardo can buy 2 erasers for 39¢ or 10 for $1.95. Are the prices per eraser the same?

Write equal ratios for 2 for 39. If 10 for 195 is in the list, the prices are the same.

Erasers ⟶
Cents ⟶ $\frac{2}{39} = \frac{4}{78} = \frac{6}{117} = \frac{8}{156} = \frac{10}{195}$

The prices per eraser are the same.

2 for 39 and 10 for 195 are equal ratios.

$$\frac{2}{39} = \frac{10}{195}$$

2 × 195 and 39 × 10 are *cross-products* of these ratios.

2 × 195 = 390

39 × 10 = 390

The cross-products of equal ratios are equal.

When the cross-products of two ratios are equal, the ratios form a *proportion*.

$\frac{2}{39} = \frac{10}{195}$ is a proportion.

B. Do the ratios $\frac{8}{15}$ and $\frac{5}{12}$ form a proportion?

Find the cross-products.

$\frac{8}{15} \diagdown\!\!\!\!\diagup \frac{5}{12}$

8 × 12 = 96

15 × 5 = 75

No, because the cross-products are not equal.

Try For each proportion, show that the cross-products are equal.

a. $\frac{2}{6} = \frac{7}{21}$ b. $\frac{1.6}{3.2} = \frac{1}{2}$

Do the ratios form a proportion? Write *yes* or *no*.

c. $\frac{5}{10}$ $\frac{4}{8}$ d. $\frac{11}{27}$ $\frac{4}{9}$

Practice For each proportion, show that the cross-products are equal.

1. $\frac{2}{3} = \frac{8}{12}$ 2. $\frac{12}{9} = \frac{8}{6}$ 3. $\frac{4}{10} = \frac{10}{25}$

4. $\frac{10}{12} = \frac{15}{18}$ 5. $\frac{12}{15} = \frac{16}{20}$ 6. $\frac{24}{9} = \frac{16}{6}$

Do the ratios form a proportion? Write *yes* or *no*.

7. $\frac{2}{3}$ $\frac{10}{15}$ 8. $\frac{5}{9}$ $\frac{6}{10}$ 9. $\frac{12}{16}$ $\frac{15}{20}$

10. $\frac{20}{30}$ $\frac{14}{20}$ 11. $\frac{24}{16}$ $\frac{27}{18}$ 12. $\frac{8}{18}$ $\frac{10}{27}$

13. $\frac{40}{12}$ $\frac{45}{15}$ 14. $\frac{35}{28}$ $\frac{30}{24}$ 15. $\frac{24}{16}$ $\frac{32}{20}$

16. $\frac{0.6}{15}$ $\frac{0.9}{24}$ 17. $\frac{0.4}{12}$ $\frac{0.5}{20}$ 18. $\frac{15}{0.09}$ $\frac{30}{0.18}$

Apply For each problem, decide if the prices are the same. Write *the same* or *not the same*.

19. Pens

2 for 49¢
10 for $2.45

20. Pencils

10 for 85¢
16 for $1.35

21. Book covers

3 for 45¢
8 for $1.00

22. Notebook paper

200 sheets for $1.19
300 sheets for $1.89

Write each decimal in words.

1. 0.08   2. 0.003

3. 0.425   4. 0.87

5. 0.3   6. 0.302

Tell what each 6 means.

7. 5.06   8. 60.8

9. 0.0006   10. 4.62

11. 6.12   12. 7.906

Compare. Use <, >, or =.

13. 0.65 ● 0.48

14. 0.72 ● 0.711

15. 5.07 ● 5.070

16. 12.424 ● 12.461

17. 8.92 ● 12

18. 3.5 ● 3.05

Round to the nearest one.

19. 6.52   20. 42.3

21. 5.7   22. 0.83

23. $2.19   24. 59.6

Solving Proportions

Career Ed Williams is a photographer who takes pictures of students. If he takes 8 pictures every 15 minutes, how many minutes should he allow for 120 sixth-grade pictures?

You can use a proportion to find the answer.

Pictures $\longrightarrow$ $\dfrac{8}{15} = \dfrac{120}{n}$ Use *n* for the number of minutes it takes for 120 pictures.
Minutes $\longrightarrow$

$8 \times n = 15 \times 120$ Write the cross-products.

$8 \times n = 1,800$

$n = 1,800 \div 8$ Find *n*.

$n = 225$

He should allow 225 minutes.

Check/ $\dfrac{8}{15} \stackrel{?}{=} \dfrac{120}{225}$

$8 \times 225 \stackrel{?}{=} 15 \times 120$

$1,800 = 1,800$

Discuss Do you get the same answer using the proportion $\dfrac{15}{8} = \dfrac{n}{120}$?

Try Use cross-products to find n.

a. $\frac{6}{9} = \frac{n}{12}$ **b.** $\frac{8}{n} = \frac{14}{35}$

Practice Use cross-products to find n.

1. $\frac{n}{8} = \frac{10}{16}$ **2.** $\frac{5}{n} = \frac{20}{32}$ **3.** $\frac{n}{2} = \frac{45}{10}$ **4.** $\frac{4}{1} = \frac{28}{n}$ **5.** $\frac{3}{5} = \frac{n}{25}$

6. $\frac{20}{n} = \frac{8}{50}$ **7.** $\frac{18}{n} = \frac{12}{28}$ **8.** $\frac{16}{28} = \frac{n}{35}$ **9.** $\frac{45}{n} = \frac{18}{8}$ **10.** $\frac{n}{48} = \frac{21}{18}$

11. $\frac{21}{24} = \frac{n}{40}$ **12.** $\frac{12}{44} = \frac{9}{n}$ **13.** $\frac{6}{22} = \frac{9}{n}$ **14.** $\frac{n}{60} = \frac{15}{36}$ **15.** $\frac{28}{n} = \frac{12}{15}$

16. $\frac{5}{n} = \frac{40}{72}$ **17.** $\frac{n}{15} = \frac{16}{6}$ **18.** $\frac{27}{24} = \frac{36}{n}$ **19.** $\frac{15}{36} = \frac{n}{60}$ **20.** $\frac{45}{72} = \frac{5}{n}$

21. $\frac{35}{n} = \frac{14}{50}$ **22.** $\frac{27}{9} = \frac{n}{35}$ **23.** $\frac{15}{21} = \frac{n}{49}$ **24.** $\frac{n}{48} = \frac{7}{12}$ **25.** $\frac{12}{84} = \frac{56}{n}$

Apply Solve each problem.

26. Six wallet-size pictures cost $3.50. How much would 24 pictures cost?
HINT: $\frac{6}{3.50} = \frac{24}{n}$

★27. Mr. Williams spent 225 minutes taking the sixth-grade pictures. How many hours and minutes was this?

28. _Estimation_ If each of the 692 students in the school spends an average of $5.95 for pictures, estimate the total amount spent.

Similar Figures

Similar figures are figures that are the same shape. The ratios of the lengths of **corresponding sides** of similar figures are equal.

A. In the book *Gulliver's Travels*, the Lilliputians made a bed for Gulliver by sewing some of their own beds together. The shape of one of their beds was similar to the shape of Gulliver's bed.

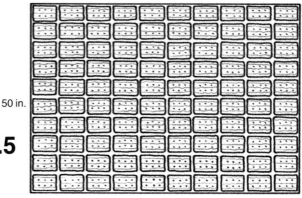

	Width	Length
Lilliputian's bed →	5	7.5
Gulliver's bed →	50	75

$$\frac{5}{50} = \frac{7.5}{75}$$

$$5 \times 75 = 50 \times 7.5$$

$$375 = 375$$

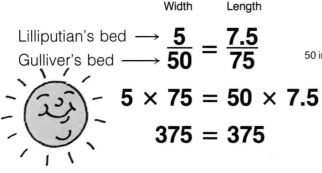

B. Gulliver and his shadow and a Lilliputian and her shadow form similar triangles. Use a proportion to find the height of the Lilliputian.

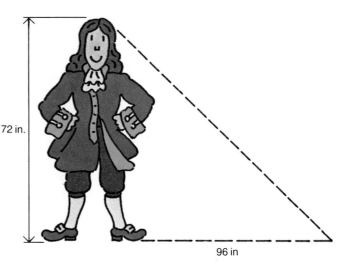

	Height	Shadow
Gulliver →	72	96
Lilliputian →	n	8

$$\frac{72}{n} = \frac{96}{8}$$

$$n \times 96 = 72 \times 8$$

$$n \times 96 = 576$$

$$n = 576 \div 96$$

$$n = 6$$

The Lilliputian was 6 in. tall.

Try For each pair of similar figures, find *n*. All measurements are in millimeters.

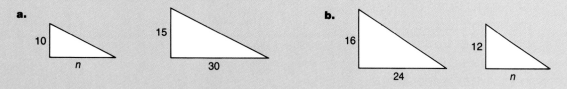

a.

10

15

n

30

b.

16

24

12

n

Practice For each pair of similar figures, find *n*. All measurements are in millimeters.

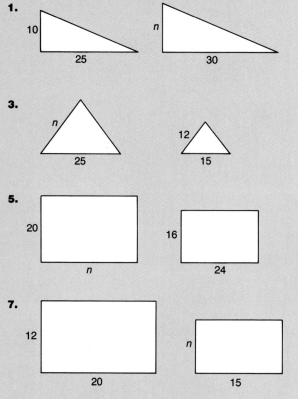

1.

10

25

n

30

2.

12

n

16

36

3.

n

25

12

15

4.

14

12

21

n

5.

20

n

16

24

6.

21

36

14

n

7.

12

20

n

15

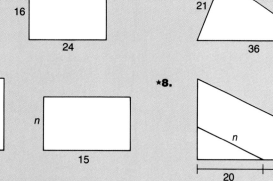

*8.

55

n

20

30

Apply Solve each problem.

9. The Lilliputians used a tablecloth that was 5 in. wide. The shape was similar to a tablecloth that is 60 in. wide and 84 in. long. How long was the Lilliputians' tablecloth?

*10. Gulliver also met some Brobdingnagians. The ratio of the heights of a Brobdingnagian and a human was 12 to 1. The ratio of the heights of a Lilliputian and a human was 1 to 12. Write a ratio that compares the heights of a Lilliputian and a Brobdingnagian.

Problem Solving: Use a Ratio

Read   This map, from the book *Treasure Island*, is a scale drawing. 3 mm on the map represents an actual distance of 250 m. On the map, the island is 168 mm long. What is the actual length?

Plan   From the scale we get the ratio 3 to 250. Use a proportion to find the actual length suggested by 168 mm.

Solve

$$\frac{3}{250} = \frac{168}{n} \quad \begin{array}{l} \leftarrow \text{ Millimeters} \\ \leftarrow \text{ Meters} \end{array}$$

$$3 \times n = 250 \times 168$$

$$3 \times n = 42{,}000$$

$$n = 42{,}000 \div 3$$

$$n = 14{,}000$$

Answer   The island is about 14,000 m long.

Look Back

$$\frac{3}{250} \overset{?}{=} \frac{168}{14{,}000}$$

$$3 \times 14{,}000 \overset{?}{=} 250 \times 168$$

$$42{,}000 = 42{,}000$$

Try   Solve the problem.

a. The treasure is supposed to be located west of the swamp and about 1,200 m from the coast. What is this distance on the map?

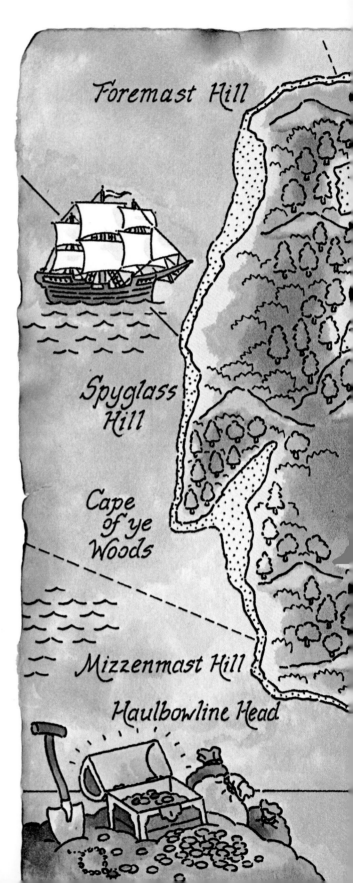

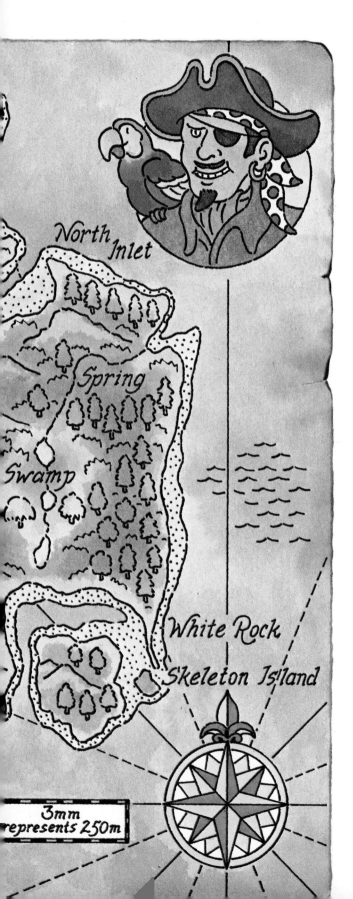

Apply Solve each problem.

1. Treasure Island is about 102 mm wide on the map. What is the actual width?

2. Skeleton Island is about 2,750 m wide. What is the width of this island on the map?

3. The distance around Skeleton Island on the map is about 120 mm. What is the actual distance around the island?

4. The treasure is supposed to be about 4,000 m southeast of Spyglass Hill. What is this distance on the map?

5. On the map, the location of the treasure is about 126 mm south of Foremast Hill. What is the actual distance?

★6. Make.a sketch of the map and put an X where you think the treasure is located. Use the clues in Problem a and Problems 4 and 5.

7. A guinea was an English coin worth 21 shillings. How many guineas were 378 shillings worth?

8. A shilling was worth 12 pence. How many pence were 378 shillings worth?

9. The value of 20 shillings was $2.40. What were 100 shillings worth?

★10. How many pence was a guinea worth?

Discuss 100% of the dots are how many *O*s?
0% are how many *O*s?

B. Write 4% as a decimal.

4% = 0.04

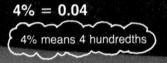

4% means 4 hundredths

c. Write 0.7 as a percent.

0.7 = 0.70 = 70%

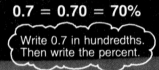

Write 0.7 in hundredths.
Then write the percent.

Try Write each percent as a decimal.　　Write each decimal as a percent.

a. 51%　　　**b.** 20%　　　**c.** 5%　　　　**d.** 0.37　　　**e.** 0.03　　　**f.** 0.9

Practice　Write each percent as a decimal.

1. 29%　　　　**2.** 46%　　　　**3.** 62%　　　　**4.** 81%　　　　**5.** 6%

6. 2%　　　　**7.** 1%　　　　**8.** 9%　　　　**9.** 10%　　　　**10.** 50%

11. 30%　　　**12.** 80%　　　**13.** 99%　　　**14.** 3%　　　　**15.** 7%

16. 18%　　　**17.** 40%　　　**18.** 60%　　　**★19.** 3.8%　　　**★20.** 0.4%

Write each decimal as a percent.

21. 0.42　　　**22.** 0.55　　　**23.** 0.67　　　**24.** 0.94　　　**25.** 0.04

26. 0.07　　　**27.** 0.06　　　**28.** 0.01　　　**29.** 0.8　　　　**30.** 0.3

31. 0.5　　　　**32.** 0.02　　　**33.** 0.2　　　　**34.** 0.6　　　　**35.** 0.06

36. 0.1　　　　**37.** 0.98　　　**38.** 0.05　　　**★39.** 0.125　　　**★40.** 1.25

Apply　Solve each problem.

41. What percent of the *O*s used to write FRAN on page 316 are in the letter *A*?

42. Brad used 100 dots to write his name. 26% of them were in the letter *B*. How many dots were used for the letter *B*?

43. Of the 100 students in the computer club, 46 are girls. What percent are girls?

44. Joe paid 5% sales tax on a computer magazine that cost $1.00 (100 cents). How many cents did he pay in tax?

★45. Linda made a picture on the computer using 100 letters. If 100% of the letters that she used were *X*s, how many *X*s did she use?

★46. Ramon's computer picture also used 100 letters, but 0% of them were *X*s. How many *X*s did he use?

Percents and Fractions

A. 80% of the students in Ravenswood School have learned to operate the computer. What fraction of the students is this?

80% is 80 hundredths. Write a fraction for 80 hundredths.

$$80\% = \frac{80}{100} = \frac{4}{5}$$

$\frac{4}{5}$ of the students can operate the computer.

B. Write $\frac{7}{20}$ as a percent.

Write an equal fraction for $\frac{7}{20}$ with a denominator of 100. Then write the percent.

$$\frac{7}{20} = \frac{35}{100} = 35\%$$

Since $\frac{7}{20}$ means $7 \div 20$, you can also find the answer by dividing.

$$\begin{array}{r} 0.3\,5 = 35\% \\ 20\overline{)7.0\,0} \\ \underline{6\,0} \\ 1\,0\,0 \\ \underline{1\,0\,0} \\ 0 \end{array}$$

Divide until the quotient is in hundredths. Then write the percent.

C. Write $\frac{1}{3}$ as a percent.

$$\begin{array}{r} 0.3\,3\frac{1}{3} = 33\frac{1}{3}\% \\ 3\overline{)1.0\,0} \\ \underline{9} \\ 1\,0 \\ \underline{9} \\ 1 \end{array}$$

Divide until the quotient is in hundredths. Write the remainder as a fraction. Then write the percent.

Try Write each percent as a fraction.

a. 50%   **b.** 45%

Write each fraction as a percent.

c. $\frac{8}{25}$ **d.** $\frac{5}{6}$

Practice Write each percent as a fraction.

1. 13%

2. 37%

3. 1%

4. 99%

5. 30%

6. 70%

7. 60%

8. 40%

9. 75%

10. 25%

11. 32%

12. 14%

13. 4%

14. 8%

★15. 125%

★16. 0.2%

Write each fraction as a percent.

17. $\frac{73}{100}$

18. $\frac{47}{100}$

19. $\frac{3}{100}$

20. $\frac{7}{100}$

21. $\frac{9}{10}$

22. $\frac{1}{10}$

23. $\frac{4}{5}$

24. $\frac{2}{5}$

25. $\frac{3}{4}$

26. $\frac{1}{4}$

27. $\frac{49}{50}$

28. $\frac{13}{20}$

29. $\frac{3}{25}$

30. $\frac{2}{3}$

31. $\frac{5}{6}$

32. $\frac{1}{6}$

33. $\frac{7}{8}$

34. $\frac{5}{8}$

★35. $\frac{5}{2}$

★36. $\frac{0.4}{20}$

Apply The computer room at Ravenswood School is shared among 6 grades. The table shows what fraction of the total time each grade gets. Write each fraction as a percent.

Grade	1	2	3	4	5	6
Fraction	$\frac{1}{20}$	$\frac{2}{25}$	$\frac{3}{25}$	$\frac{1}{5}$	$\frac{1}{4}$	$\frac{3}{10}$

37. Grade 1

38. Grade 2

39. Grade 3

40. Grade 4

41. Grade 5

42. Grade 6

★43. What percent represents the total computer time?

Find a Percent of a Number Using a Decimal

A. For her age, Jane needs 62 g of protein each day. A peanut butter sandwich and a glass of milk provide about 30% of this daily requirement. How many grams of protein are in the sandwich and milk?

Find 30% of 62.

What is 30% of 62?

$$n = 0.30 \times 62$$

$$\begin{array}{r} 62 \\ \times\, 0.3 \\ \hline 18.6 \end{array}$$

The sandwich and milk provide about 18.6 g of protein.

B. Find 48% of 75.

48% of 75 is what number?

$$0.48 \times 75 = n$$

$$36 = n$$

Try Find each number.

a. 5% of 4   **b.** 100% of 182

c. What is 18% of 52?

Practice Find each number.

1. 75% of 16
2. 25% of 88
3. 30% of 90
4. 60% of 20

5. 14% of 80
6. 16% of 40
7. 36% of 45
8. 65% of 84

9. 63% of 99
10. 28% of 72
11. 2% of 35
12. 5% of 180

13. 2% of 78
14. 6% of 82
15. 40% of 39
16. 1% of 34

17. 72% of 450
18. 21% of 800
19. 0% of 762
20. 100% of 925

21. What is 8% of 652?
22. What is 6% of 824?
23. What is 5% of 125?

24. What is 18% of 735?
25. What is 25% of 342?
26. What is 20% of 650?

★27. What is 125% of 90?
★28. What is 200% of 10?
★29. What is 0.5% of 50?

Apply Solve each problem.

30. In enriched white bread, about 9% of the weight is protein. About how many grams of protein are in a 28-g piece of bread?

31. About 31% of the weight of roasted chicken is protein. About how many grams of protein are in 144 g of roasted chicken?

32. One slice of bread contains 2.5 g of protein. How many grams are in a loaf containing 16 slices?

33. A 12-year-old girl needs 62 g of protein each day, while a 12-year-old boy needs 75 g. How much less protein does a girl need per day?

★34. Shelly needs 62 g of protein each day. She determined that she had 130% of her daily requirement on Tuesday. How many grams of protein did she have on Tuesday?

Finding a Percent of a Number Using a Fraction

Percent	10%	20%	25%	$33\frac{1}{3}$%	50%	$66\frac{2}{3}$%	75%	80%	90%
Fraction	$\frac{1}{10}$	$\frac{1}{5}$	$\frac{1}{4}$	$\frac{1}{3}$	$\frac{1}{2}$	$\frac{2}{3}$	$\frac{3}{4}$	$\frac{4}{5}$	$\frac{9}{10}$

A. About 90% of a pineapple's weight is water. Find the weight of the water in a 5-lb. pineapple.

Find 90% of 5.

What is 90% of 5?

$$n = \frac{9}{10} \times 5$$ Write 90% as a fraction.

$$n = 4\frac{1}{2}$$ Then multiply.

The water in the pineapple weighs $4\frac{1}{2}$ pounds.

Discuss Would you get the same answer if you had used $\frac{90}{100}$ for 90%? 0.9 for 90%?

B. Find $33\frac{1}{3}$% of 60.

$33\frac{1}{3}$% of 60 is what number?

$$\frac{1}{3} \times 60 = n$$

$$20 = n$$

Try Find each number using a fraction.

a. 25% of 36

b. $66\frac{2}{3}$% of 15

c. 45% of 50

Practice Find each number using a fraction. The fractions for the percents in Exercises 1–16 are given in the table on page 322.

1. 10% of 80
2. 20% of 80
3. 80% of 65

4. 80% of 15
5. 50% of 64
6. 50% of 38

7. 75% of 20
8. 25% of 52
9. 80% of 8

10. 90% of 60
11. 25% of 7
12. 75% of 9

13. $66\frac{2}{3}$% of 27
14. $33\frac{1}{3}$% of 24
15. $33\frac{1}{3}$% of 3

16. $66\frac{2}{3}$% of 3
17. 30% of 70
18. 15% of 80

19. 45% of 60
20. 4% of 75
21. 1% of 400

22. 2% of 100
★23. $12\frac{1}{2}$% of 16
★24. 125% of 5

Apply Solve each problem.

25. An apple is 80% water. What is the weight of the water in a 5-oz. apple?

26. Watermelon is about 95% water. What is the weight of the water in a 25-lb. watermelon?

Practice: Percent

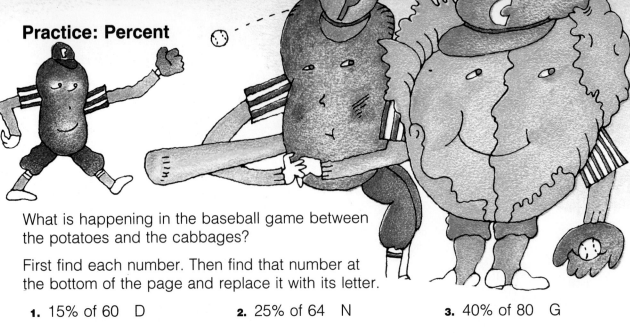

What is happening in the baseball game between the potatoes and the cabbages?

First find each number. Then find that number at the bottom of the page and replace it with its letter.

1. 15% of 60 D

2. 25% of 64 N

3. 40% of 80 G

4. 60% of 75 S

5. 75% of 32 A

6. 35% of 80 E

7. 45% of 40 E

8. 5% of 140 D

9. 8% of 125 H

10. 10% of 850 S

11. 1% of 300 E

12. 100% of 82 R

13. 42% of 50 A

14. 81% of 500 A

15. 75% of 124 I

16. 25% of 136 B

17. 16% of 125 A

18. 98% of 150 I

19. 48% of 25 A

20. 6% of 500 T

21. 14% of 600 S

22. 92% of 125 E

23. 50% of 88 O

24. 7% of 200 E

25. 100% of 49 A

26. 2% of 250 P

27. 0% of 72 E

28. 4% of 25 B

29. 8% of 475 T

30. 50% of 132 G

31. 18% of 150 N

32. 85% of 120 B

33. 68% of 175 O

34. 21% of 200 K

35. 37% of 200 N

36. 53% of 900 C

THE   <u> 5 </u> <u> 44 </u> <u> 38 </u> <u> 21 </u> <u> 30 </u> <u>119</u> <u> 18 </u> <u> 45 </u>   ARE   <u> 34 </u> <u> 3 </u> <u>147</u> <u> 27 </u> <u> 32 </u>

<u> 85 </u> <u> 42 </u> <u> 93 </u> <u> 16 </u> <u> 74 </u> <u>115</u> <u> 7 </u>   AND THE   <u>477</u> <u> 20 </u> <u> 1 </u> <u>102</u> <u>405</u> <u> 66 </u> <u> 28 </u> <u> 84 </u>

<u> 24 </u> <u> 82 </u> <u> 14 </u>   <u> 49 </u> <u> 10 </u> <u> 0 </u> <u> 12 </u> <u> 9 </u> .

Apply Solve each problem.

37. The Cabbages won 68% of their 25 games. How many games did they win?

38. Red Cabbage batted in 35% of the 20 runs his team scored. How many runs did Red bat in?

39. Of the players for the Potatoes, 50% are rotten hitters. What fraction of the players is this?

40. One third of the players for the Cabbages have big heads. What percent of the players is this?

41. Stuffed Cabbage got 4 hits in 10 times at bat. At this rate, how many hits will she get in 15 times at bat?

42. A season pass for 13 Vegetable-League games costs $9.75. What is the price per game?

The Vegetable-League baseball diamond is similar to a regular diamond, but smaller. 7 in. on the smaller diamond represents 15 ft. on a regular diamond.

43. It is 42 in. from home plate to first base on the smaller diamond. What is the distance on a regular diamond?

44. It is 60 ft. from home plate to the pitcher's mound on a regular diamond. What is the distance on the smaller diamond?

COMPUTER

Flow Charts

This flow chart of the program below shows a loop that counts to 10.

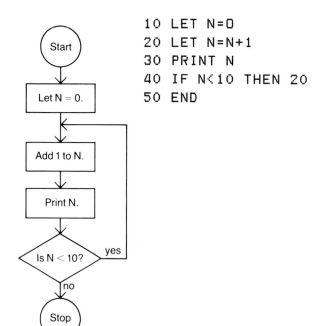

```
10 LET N=0
20 LET N=N+1
30 PRINT N
40 IF N<10 THEN 20
50 END
```

In line 20, the value stored in memory location N is increased by 1.

The "THEN 20" in line 40 means "THEN GO TO 20."

1. Make a flow chart for this program.

```
10 LET N=0
20 LET N=N+5
30 PRINT N
40 IF N<25 THEN 20
50 END
```

2. Make a flow chart that counts by twos to 30.

★3. Write a program for the flow chart you wrote for Exercise 2.

Problem Solving: Multiple-Step Problems

Read   Melissa is buying a tennis racket for $24.75 plus tax. The sales tax is 6%. What is the total cost of the racket?

Plan   Find the amount of the tax by finding 6% of $24.75. Round to the nearest cent. Then add the tax to the cost of the racket.

Solve   Find 6% of 24.75.

$$0.06 \times 24.75 = 1.485 \approx 1.49$$

Now add to find the total cost.

```
  24.75  ←— Cost of the racket
+  1.49  ←— Sales tax
  26.24  ←— Total cost
```

Answer   The total cost of the racket is $26.24.

Look Back   6% sales tax is 6¢ tax for each dollar spent. The racket costs about $25. 25 × 6 = 150, so the sales tax of $1.49 is reasonable.

Try

a. Melissa has $3.76 left. Does she have enough money left to buy tennis balls that cost $3.50 plus 6% tax?

Apply   Find the total cost of each item, including 4% sales tax.

1. Jogging shoes $18.50

2. Tube socks $1.25

3. Roller skates $23.25

4. Warm-up jacket $13.75

5. Croquet set $27.19

6. Surf mat $10.49

7. Table-tennis ball $ 0.39

8. Basketball backboard $89.99

Solve each problem.

9. Jerry has $25. Can he buy a jogging suit that costs $23.50 plus 5% sales tax?

10. Tim has $20. Can he buy a basketball that costs $19.95 plus 6% sales tax?

11. The Tabors are buying a canoe for $249.50 plus 5% sales tax. What is the total cost?

12. A table tennis set sells for $125.95 plus 3% sales tax. What is the total cost?

13. Laura bought a badminton set for $15 plus 7% sales tax. How much change did she get from $20?

14. Kenji bought a bat for $7 plus tax. He received $2.65 change from $10. How much was the tax?

15. Vern wants skis that cost $129 plus 6% sales tax. She has $125. How much more does she need?

16. Mona has $15. How much more does she need for ice skates that cost $19.95 plus 4% sales tax?

★17. A ski cap is marked $10, but the total cost with tax is $10.40. What is the percent of sales tax?

★18. Ski gloves are marked $14, but the total cost with tax is $14.84. What is the percent of sales tax?

CALCULATOR

A baseball costs $4.95 plus 6% sales tax. You can use the following key sequence to find the total cost.

Press: 4.95 $\boxed{\times}$ 1.06 $\boxed{=}$ 100% + 6% = 106%
106% = 1.06

Display: *5.247*

Rounded to the nearest cent, the baseball costs $5.25.

Use your calculator to find the total cost of each item. The sales tax is given in parentheses.

1. Duffle bag $9.99 (5%)

2. Water skis $159.50 (4%)

3. Golf ball $0.75 (6%)

4. Soccer ball $11.97 (7%)

5. Row boat $795.50 (3%)

6. Motor boat $3,295 (5%)

7. Sailboat $7,850 (6%)

8. Cabin cruiser $38,975 (4%)

Finding What Percent One Number Is of Another

A. During the season, the Emerson Eagles made 96 out of 160 free-throw attempts. What percent of the free-throw attempts did they make?

Find what percent 96 is of 160.

96 is what percent of 160?

$$96 = n \times 160$$
$$96 \div 160 = n$$
$$0.60 = n$$

The Eagles made 60% of the free-throw attempts.

B. 12 is what percent of 18?

What percent of 18 is 12?

$$n \times 18 = 12$$
$$n = 12 \div 18$$
$$n = 0.66\frac{2}{3} = 66\frac{2}{3}\%$$

Try Find each percent.

a. What percent of 75 is 15?

b. 8 is what percent of 400?

Practice Find each percent.

1. 5 is what percent of 20?

2. 6 is what percent of 25?

3. 6 is what percent of 40?

4. 7 is what percent of 14?

5. What percent of 40 is 4?

6. What percent of 60 is 3?

7. What percent of 16 is 12?

8. What percent of 20 is 19?

9. Find what percent 28 is of 40.

10. Find what percent 9 is of 18.

11. Find what percent 12 is of 36.

12. Find what percent 10 is of 15.

13. What percent of 50 is 2?

14. What percent of 75 is 6?

15. 24 is what percent of 150?

16. 72 is what percent of 800?

★17. What percent of 0.5 is 0.4?

★18. What percent of 15 is 18?

Apply Solve each problem.

During one game the Emerson Eagles scored 50 points. What percent of the 50 points did each of these Eagle players score?

19. Nancy, 7 points

20. Helen, 16 points

21. Roberta, 8 points

Here are eight purses.

Five contain paper money.
Three contain coins.
Two contain both paper money and coins.

How many of the purses contain neither paper money nor coins?

Problem Solving: Write an Equation

Read   The Jets won 13 out of 20 soccer games this year. What percent of the games did they win?

Plan   What percent of 20 is 13? Write an equation using n for the percent.

Solve $n \times 20 = 13$

$$n = 13 \div 20$$

$$n = 0.65 = 65\%$$

Answer   The Jets won 65% of their games.

Look Back   The Jets won more than half, or 50%, of their games. 65% is more than 50%.

Try   Write an equation. Then give the answer.

a. The Jets played 60% of the 20 games at home. How many games did they play at home?

Apply   Write an equation. Then give the answer.

1. A soccer ball costs $28.50 plus 4% sales tax. What is the amount of the sales tax?

2. Lee made 40% of his 30 field-goal attempts. How many field goals did he make?

3. In one game, Ralph made 30% of his free-throw attempts. He had 20 attempts. How many did he make?

4. The Long Grove football team won 60% of the 10 games they played. How many games did they win?

5. The Jets scored 56 goals last year and 66 goals this year. How many more goals did they score this year?

6. Seventy-five percent of the 24 players on the team are seniors. How many of the 24 players are seniors?

7. The Long Grove basketball team won 12 of their 18 games. What percent of the games did they win?

8. There are 600 students in Long Grove School. 18 of them are on the baseball team. What percent of the students are on the team?

9. Todd is the leading scorer for the Jets. He made 22 of the 66 goals this year. What percent of the goals did he make?

10. Jeff ran for 50 yards during one football game. 34 yards were on one play. This is what percent of the yards he ran that day?

11. This year, 96 students tried out for the Jets. Only 24 of them made the team. What percent of the students who tried out made the team?

12. There are 500 bleacher seats in the Long Grove stadium. During one game, 67% of the seats were filled. How many seats were filled?

13. A ticket to a basketball game costs $0.75. 275 tickets were sold for one game. How much money was taken in from the sale of these tickets?

14. The Booster Club is raising money for cheerleading outfits. Their goal is $250, and they have reached 72% of their goal. How much money have they raised?

*15. The Long Grove baseball team won 10 games and lost 20 games last season. What percent of the games did they win?

*16. During one game, Julio missed 6 out of 8 free-throw attempts. What percent of the free-throw attempts did he make?

Problem Solving: Multiple-Step Problems

Read   According to the newspaper ad, an electric guitar that regularly sells for $189 is on sale at a 25% discount. What is the sale price?

Plan   Find the amount of discount by finding 25% of $189. Then subtract the discount from the regular price to find the sale price.

Solve   Find 25% of 189.

$$0.25 \times 189 = 47.25$$

The discount is $47.25. Subtract to find the sale price.

$$
\begin{array}{rl}
\$189.00 & \longleftarrow \text{Regular price} \\
-\quad 47.25 & \longleftarrow \text{Discount} \\
\hline
\$141.75 & \longleftarrow \text{Sale price}
\end{array}
$$

Answer   The sale price is $141.75.

Look Back   The guitar regularly sells for about $200. 25% of $200 is $50, so the discount is reasonable.

Electric Guitar

Regular Price: $189
SALE
25% off

Flutes	Regularly $159	Now 15% off
Drums	Regularly $135	Now 15% off
Banjos	Regularly $98	Now 15% off
All records	10% off	
All tapes	25% off	
All albums	30% off	

Try Solve the problem.

a. A stereo is on sale for $225. The regular price was $250. What is the percent of discount?

Apply Use the newspaper ad on page 332. Find the sale price for each of these items.

1. Flute

2. Drums

3. Banjo

4. A $3 record

5. A $5.98 tape

6. A $14.50 album

Solve each problem.

7. A stereo radio that regularly sells for $180 is on sale for $153. What is the percent of discount?

8. A clarinet is on sale for $120. The regular price was $160. What is the percent of discount?

9. A snare-drum set is on sale for $60. The regular price was $75. What is the percent of discount?

10. A black-and-white television set is on sale for $66. The regular price was $75. What is the percent of discount?

11. A $1,200 piano is on sale for 22% off the regular price. What is the sale price of the piano?

12. A $2,850 organ is on sale for 30% off the regular price. What is the sale price of the organ?

13. The regular price of a video recorder was $740. This week it is on sale for 12% less. What is the sale price?

14. A cassette recorder is on sale for 18% off the regular price of $45. What is the sale price?

★15. Which television set is cheaper?

Brand X: Regular price $500
        On sale 25% off

Brand Y: Regular price $450
        On sale 15% off

★16. Which percent of discount is more?

Stereo A: Regular price $295
        Sale price $236

Stereo B: Regular price $250
        Sale price $195

Chapter 11 Test

1. Write a ratio for this situation.

   3 baskets in 7 tries

2. Complete the list of equal ratios.
   $$\frac{7}{9} = \frac{14}{\blacksquare} = \frac{\blacksquare}{27} = \frac{28}{\blacksquare}$$

For each proportion, show that the cross-products are equal.

3. $\frac{5}{8} = \frac{25}{40}$ 4. $\frac{9}{12} = \frac{15}{20}$

Do the ratios form a proportion? Write *yes* or *no*.

5. $\frac{12}{18}$ $\frac{14}{20}$ 6. $\frac{9}{21}$ $\frac{12}{28}$

Use cross-products to find *n*.

7. $\frac{8}{12} = \frac{n}{15}$ 8. $\frac{36}{40} = \frac{18}{n}$

9. For the pair of similar figures find *n*. All measurements are in millimeters.

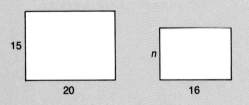

15   20   *n*   16

Write each percent as a decimal.

10. 47%   11. 80%   12. 7%

Write each decimal as a percent.

13. 0.23   14. 0.09   15. 0.4

Write each percent as a fraction.

16. 25%   17. 49%   18. 55%

Write each fraction as a percent.

19. $\frac{3}{4}$ 20. $\frac{7}{25}$ 21. $\frac{2}{3}$

22. Find 75% of 36.

23. Find 2% of 48.

24. Find $33\frac{1}{3}$% of 27.

25. Find 20% of 60.

26. What percent of 20 is 15?

Solve each problem.

27. A shilling was worth 12 pence. How many pence were 15 shillings worth?

28. Juanita has $20.85. Does she have enough to buy a sweater that costs $18.50 plus 5% sales tax?

29. A sleeping bag is on sale for $40. The regular price was $50. What is the percent of discount?

Write an equation. Then give the answer.

30. A record costs $8.75 plus a 6% sales tax. What is the amount of the sales tax?

CHALLENGE

Percents Greater Than 100% and Less Than 1%

The Jefferson School Band is trying to raise $200 for a new banner.

A. 1% of their goal is $2.

$$1\% = \frac{1}{100} = 0.01$$
$$0.01 \times 200 = 2$$

B. An amount less than $2 is less than 1% of the goal.

0.5% of the goal is $1.

$$0.5\% = \frac{0.5}{100} = \frac{5}{1,000} = 0.005$$
$$0.005 \times 200 = 1$$

C. 100% of the goal is $200.

$$100\% = \frac{100}{100} = 1$$
$$1 \times 200 = 200$$

D. An amount greater than $200 is more than 100% of the goal.

125% of the goal is $250.

$$125\% = \frac{125}{100} = 1.25$$
$$1.25 \times 200 = 250$$

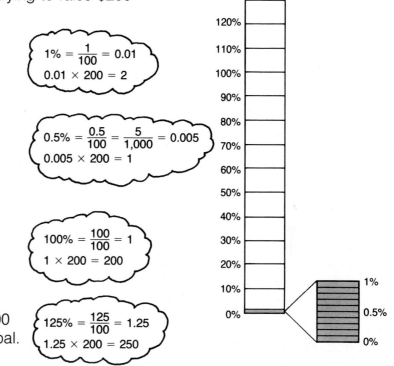

Does the statement make sense? Write *yes* or *no*.

1. The band reached 225% of its goal.

2. Brian made 200% of the points.

3. Karry ate 110% of the pizza.

4. The cup is filled to 125% capacity.

5. The bicycle is discounted 150%.

6. The price increased 150%.

Find each answer.

7. 140% of 6

8. 175% of 4

9. 300% of 18

10. 215% of 130

11. 480% of 96

12. $133\frac{1}{3}\%$ of 15

13. 0.5% of 800

14. 0.6% of 500

15. 0.2% of 80

16. 0.9% of 120

17. 0.08% of 900

18. 0.7% of 5,600

335

MAINTENANCE

Find each answer.

1. $24.3 + 18.9$
2. 6.2×4.8
3. $1.728 - 0.272$

4. $3.2 \div 8$
5. $1.207 + 5.702$
6. $47.34 \div 3$

7. $75.3 + 8.9$
8. 0.18×47.6
9. $0.064 + 0.12$

10. $29.07 - 22.3$
11. $58.4 - 28.63$
12. 0.031×100

13. 0.3×0.25
14. $8.12 - 2.3$
15. $6.5 - 1.236$

16. $0.42 \div 6$
17. $2.094 + 1.89$
18. $1,000 \times 4.5$

19. $0.134 \div 0.02$
20. $0.333 + 0.12$
21. $4.8 \div 0.32$

22. 0.2×0.0039
23. $6 - 3.195$
24. $75 \div 0.25$

Solve each problem.

25. Volleyball is played on a court 18 m long and 9 m wide. What is the area of the court?

26. A pike swims 11 m in 4 seconds. At this rate, how far can it swim in 60 seconds?

27. Heidi's scores on six math tests are 83, 76, 92, 82, 95, and 82. Find her average score.

28. Lyle had 48 problems correct out of 50. What percent of the problems did he have correct?

29. In a person who weighs 60 kg, the muscles weigh 30 kg. What percent of the body weight is muscles?

30. Kikuke weighs 100 lb. on Earth. She would weigh 38 lb. on Mars. Her father weighs 200 lb. on Earth. How much would he weigh on Mars?

31. The Innermost Treasury Room of King Tut's tomb is 5 m long, 4 m wide, and 2 m high. What is the volume of the room?

32. A pork chop has 21.3 g of protein. An egg has 3.7 g of protein. How much more protein does the pork chop have?

33. The earth's land area is about 150 million km². The area of Asia is about 45 million km². What percent of the earth's area is contained in Asia?

34. The singles tennis court is 75% as wide as the doubles tennis court. The doubles court is 11 m wide. How wide is the singles court?

Graphing and Integers

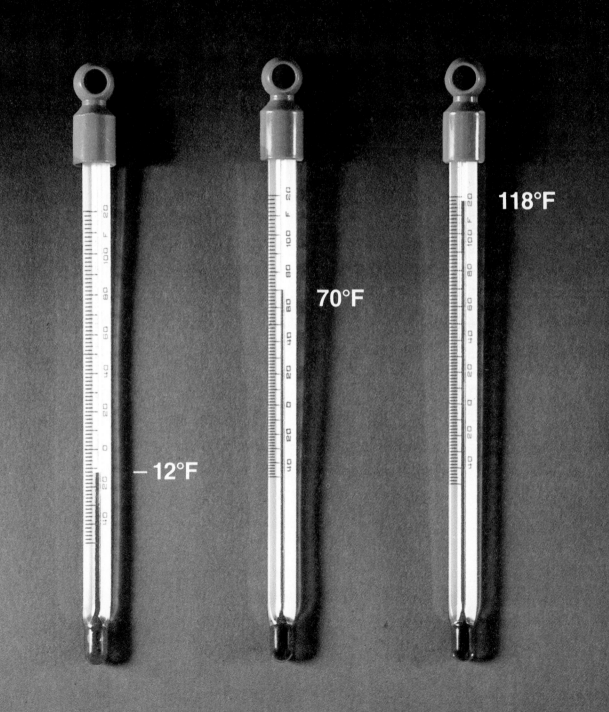

chapter 12

118°F

70°F

−12°F

Bar Graphs and Pictographs

Medals Won at 1980 Winter Olympics

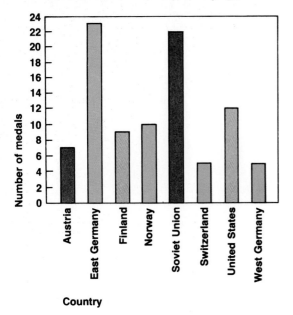

Gold Medals in 1980 Winter Olympics

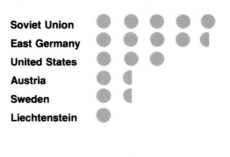

Each ⬤ represents 2 medals.
Each ◗ represents 1 medal.

A. The *bar graph* shows the number of medals won by the top winners during the 1980 Winter Olympics. How many medals did Norway win?

Go right on the horizontal scale to the bar for Norway. From the top of the bar, move back to the vertical scale.

Norway won 10 medals.

B. The *pictograph* shows the number of gold medals won by each country during the 1980 Winter Olympics. How many gold medals did East Germany win?

Because each ◯ represents 2 medals, 4 ◯s represent 8 medals. 1 ◖ represents 1 medal.

East Germany won 9 medals.

Try Use the graph in Example A on page 338.

a. How many medals did Austria win?

b. Which country won 9 medals?

Use the graph in Example B on page 338.

c. How many gold medals did Sweden win?

d. Which country won 6 gold medals?

Practice Use the graph in Example A on page 338.
How many medals did

1. the Soviet Union win?　**2.** East Germany win?　**3.** Finland win?

4. the United States win?　**5.** Switzerland win?　**6.** West Germany win?

Which country or countries won

7. 9 medals?　　**8.** 12 medals?　　**9.** 23 medals?　　**10.** 5 medals?

11. more than 20 rnedals?　　　　**12.** Less than 10 medals?

Use the graph in Example B on page 338. How many gold medals did

13. the United States win?　　　**14.** the Soviet Union win?

15. Austria win?　　　　　　　**16.** Liechtenstein win?

Which country or countries won

17. 6 medals?　　**18.** 2 medals?　　**19.** 3 medals?　　**20.** 5 medals?

Apply Use the data in the table.

21. Make a bar graph to show the data in the table.

22. Make a pictograph to show the data in the table. Let each symbol represent 2 medals.

Ice-Hockey Gold Medals

Country	Number of medals
Canada	6
Great Britain	1
Soviet Union	5
United States	2

Broken-Line Graphs

Olympic Winter Games

The Olympic Winter Games were first played in 1924. The *broken-line graph* shows the number of countries that participated each year.

How many countries participated in the Olympic Winter Games in 1924?

Find the dot above '24, follow the grid line to the left, and read the number.

16 countries participated in the Olympic Winter Games in 1924.

Try

a. How many countries participated in the Olympic Winter Games in 1928?

b. Which year did the most countries participate?

c. In which year(s) did 36 countries participate?

Practice Use the graph on page 340. How many countries participated in

1. 1936?   2. 1952?

3. 1960?   4. 1932?

5. 1968?   6. 1976?

In which year(s) did the following number of countries participate?

7. 32   8. 25

9. 30   10. 33

11. less than 20

12. more than 35

Apply Use the data in the table.

Olympic Winter Games

Year	Number of events
1924	16
1928	15
1932	19
1936	21
1948	24
1952	23

13. Make a broken-line graph from the data in the table.

Circle Graphs

The United States has 12,383 miles of coastline. The *circle graph* shows the amount of coastline on each shore.

U.S. Coastline

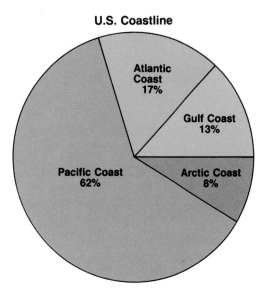

Atlantic Coast 17%

Gulf Coast 13%

Pacific Coast 62%

Arctic Coast 8%

A. How much coastline does the Atlantic coast have?

Find 17% of 12,383.

```
  1 2,3 8 3     Change 17% to a
×     0.1 7     decimal and multiply.
  8 6 6 8 1
1 2 3 8 3
2,1 0 5.1 1
```

The Atlantic coast has about 2,105 miles of coastline.

B. Which coast has the largest amount of coastline?

62% is the largest percent on the graph.

The Pacific coast has the largest amount of coastline.

Try Use the graph on the left.

a. How much coastline does the Gulf coast have?

b. Which coast has the smallest amount of coastline?

Practice Use the graph on the left. How much coastline does the

1. Pacific coast have?

2. Arctic coast have?

Use the graph at the right. The total area of the oceans is 131 million square miles. What is the area of the

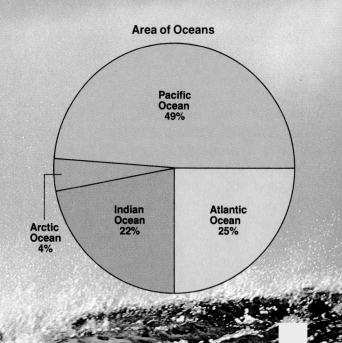

Area of Oceans

Pacific Ocean 49%

Indian Ocean 22%

Atlantic Ocean 25%

Arctic Ocean 4%

3. Arctic Ocean?

4. Atlantic Ocean?

5. Indian Ocean?

6. Pacific Ocean?

7. Which ocean has the largest area?

8. Which ocean has the smallest area?

Locating Points with Ordered Pairs

The location of the hurricane at Port au Prince can be given as the *ordered pair* (70, 20).

Two perpendicular lines, called the *horizontal axis* and the *vertical axis*, are used as reference lines. An ordered pair that gives the location of a point gives the distances from these axes. The intersection of the axes is called the *origin*. The ordered pair (0, 0) locates the origin.

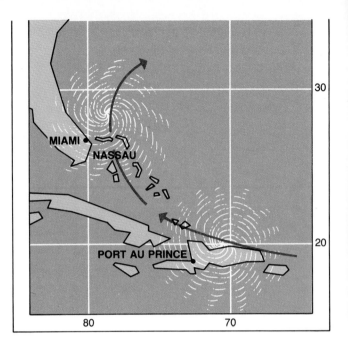

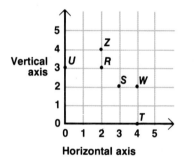

A. Name the point located by the ordered pair (4, 2).

The distance in the horizontal direction is given first in the ordered pair.

Start at the origin. Move right 4 units. Then move up 2 units.

W is the point located by the ordered pair (4, 2).

B. Give an ordered pair of numbers that locates point *R*.

For point *R*, the horizontal distance from the origin is 2 units, and the vertical distance is 3 units.

The ordered pair (2, 3) locates point *R*.

Try Use the grid above. Give the ordered pair that locates each point.

a. *Z*   **b.** *T*   **c.** *U*

On one grid, mark each point and label it with the given letter.

d. *A* (1, 4)   **e.** *B* (4, 1)

f. *C* (3, 0)   **g.** *D* (0, 2)

Practice Give the ordered pair that locates each point.

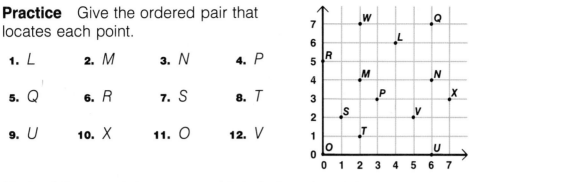

1. L
2. M
3. N
4. P

5. Q
6. R
7. S
8. T

9. U
10. X
11. O
12. V

Mark all these points on one grid. Label each point with the letter given.

13. A (2, 5)
14. B (5, 2)
15. C (4, 4)
16. D (1, 1)

17. E (3, 0)
18. F (0, 6)
19. G (0, 0)
20. H (3, 5)

Mark all these points on one grid. Then join the points in order.

21. (0, 1)
22. (3, 4)
23. (1, 7)
24. (3, 7)
25. (4, 5)
26. (6, 7)

27. (8, 7)
28. (5, 4)
29. (7, 1)
30. (5, 1)
31. (4, 3)
32. (2, 1)

CHALLENGE

Find each sum.

1. $1 + 2 + 3 + 4 + 5 + 6 + 7 + 8 + 9$
2. $11 + 22 + 33 + 44 + 55 + 66 + 77 + 88 + 99$
3. $111 + 222 + 333 + 444 + 555 + 666 + 777 + 888 + 999$

Guess the next two sums.

4. $1,111 + 2,222 + 3,333 + 4,444 + 5,555 + 6,666 + 7,777 + 8,888 + 9,999$
5. $11,111 + 22,222 + 33,333 + 44,444 + 55,555 + 66,666 + 77,777 + 88,888 + 99,999$

Line Graphs

Donna Whitewing's car averages 25 miles per gallon of fuel. The data in the table below can be used to make a *line graph*.

Use the table to write ordered pairs. Then use the ordered pairs to locate the points on a grid and join them. The line graph illustrates the data in the table.

Number of gallons	Number of miles	Ordered pairs
1	25	(1, 25)
2	50	(2, 50)
3	75	(3, 75)
4	100	(4, 100)
5	125	(5, 125)
6	150	(6, 150)

Fuel Consumption

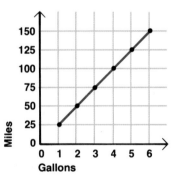

Try Complete the table, form ordered pairs, and make a line graph.

	n	$n - 5$
	5	0
	6	1
a.	7	
b.	8	
c.	9	

346

Practice Complete each table, form ordered pairs, and draw a line graph.

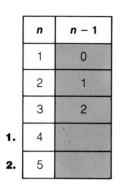

n	n − 1
1	0
2	1
3	2
1. 4	
2. 5	

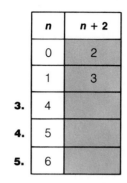

n	n + 2
0	2
1	3
3. 4	
4. 5	
5. 6	

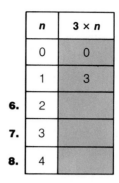

n	3 × n
0	0
1	3
6. 2	
7. 3	
8. 4	

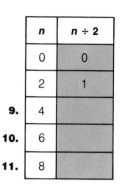

n	n ÷ 2
0	0
2	1
9. 4	
10. 6	
11. 8	

Apply Solve each problem.

12. The table at the right shows the average number of miles that Donna drove in a given number of hours. Make a line graph to illustrate this data.

Number of hours	Number of miles
1	50
2	100
3	150
4	200
5	250

The line graph shows what Donna paid for fuel. What was the cost of the following number of gallons of fuel?

13. 5   **14.** 10   **15.** 20   **16.** 25

How many gallons of fuel could Donna buy for

17. $15?   **18.** $22.50?   **19.** $30?

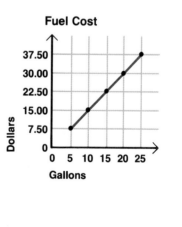

Fuel Cost

Compare. Use <, >, or =.

1. $\frac{5}{7}$ ⬤ $\frac{6}{7}$ **2.** $\frac{8}{9}$ ⬤ $\frac{7}{9}$ **3.** $\frac{3}{5}$ ⬤ $\frac{3}{5}$ **4.** $\frac{5}{6}$ ⬤ $\frac{3}{6}$

5. $2\frac{1}{4}$ ⬤ $2\frac{3}{4}$ **6.** $5\frac{2}{5}$ ⬤ $3\frac{2}{5}$ **7.** $6\frac{2}{3}$ ⬤ $7\frac{1}{3}$ **8.** $7\frac{3}{8}$ ⬤ $7\frac{5}{8}$

Problem Solving: Use a Graph

Read Joe and Elaine Phillips are pilots. They are both flying from Tucson to New York City. Joe leaves at 8 A.M., and Elaine leaves at 9 A.M. Joe averages 250 miles per hour, and Elaine averages 375 miles per hour. About what time will Elaine overtake Joe?

Plan Make two tables and draw two line graphs on the same grid. Each graph shows one pilot's distance from Tucson at a given time. When the two graphs intersect, Joe and Ellen are the same distance from Tucson.

Solve Make tables and draw the graphs.

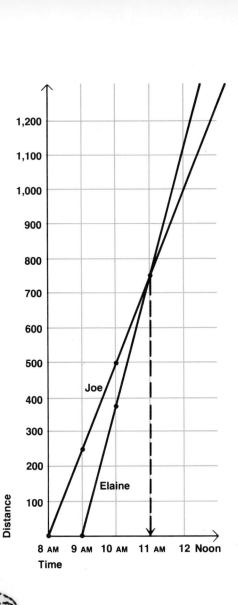

Joe

Time	Distance
8 A.M.	0
9 A.M.	250
10 A.M.	500

Elaine

Time	Distance
9 A.M.	0
10 A.M.	375
11 A.M.	750

Answer The graphs intersect at (11, 750). Elaine will overtake Joe at about 11 A.M.

Look Back Joe gets a 250-mile headstart. Elaine gains on Joe at the rate of 125 miles per hour. So, it will take Elaine about 2 hours to catch up.

348

Try Use a graph to solve each problem.

a. Colette started on a bicycle trail at 1 P.M. riding 10 miles per hour. One hour later, Jesse started on the same trail riding 15 miles per hour. About what time did Jesse overtake Colette?

b. How far from the beginning of the trail was each person at 3 P.M.?

Apply Use a graph to solve each problem.

1. Albert left Pine Corners at 7 A.M., driving at an average speed of 45 miles per hour. Darlene followed him one hour later, driving at an average speed of 55 miles per hour. About what time did Darlene overtake Albert?

2. Use your graph for Problem 1 to tell about how far from Pine Corners each person was at 11 A.M.

3. Rochelle and Jerome are both flying from Atlanta to Phoenix. Rochelle leaves at 10 A.M., flying at an average speed of 300 miles per hour. Jerome leaves at 11:30 A.M., flying at an average speed of 550 miles per hour. At what time will Jerome overtake Rochelle?

4. The distance from Atlanta to Phoenix is about 1,600 miles. Use your graph for Problem 3 to tell about what time each person arrived.

5. Dexter left White Sands at 4 P.M., traveling at an average speed of 40 miles per hour on a motorcycle. Barbara followed him one half hour later, traveling at an average speed of 50 miles per hour. About what time did Barbara overtake Dexter?

6. Use your graph for Problem 5 to determine about what time Dexter was 60 miles from White Sands.

★7. Craig left White Sands, following Dexter and Barbara at 5 P.M. If he traveled at an average speed of 55 miles per hour, would he overtake either of them by 7 P.M.?

★8. *Estimation* Tucson is about 2,200 miles from New York City. Give the approximate times that Elaine and Joe will each arrive in New York City.

Practice: Graphs

The graph at the right shows the number of times each country has won an Olympic gold medal for men's figure skating.

1. How many gold medals has Austria won?

2. Which country has won 2 gold medals?

3. Which countries have won 4 gold medals?

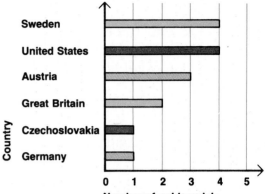

Olympic Gold Medals Men's Figure Skating

The graph at the right shows how the Bonomo family uses its monthly income of $2,200.

4. How much does the family spend on transportation?

5. How much does the family save?

6. On which item do the Bonomos spend the most money?

7. What is the total that the family spends on insurance and medical and dental bills?

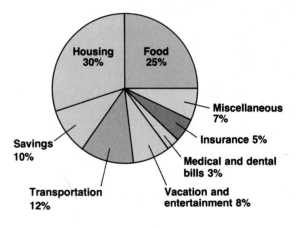

Bonomo Family Budget

Housing 30%
Food 25%
Miscellaneous 7%
Insurance 5%
Medical and dental bills 3%
Vacation and entertainment 8%
Transportation 12%
Savings 10%

The graph at the right shows the number of permits issued for single-family homes in El Paso.

About how many permits were issued in

8. March?   9. May?   10. July?

11. In which month were the most permits issued?

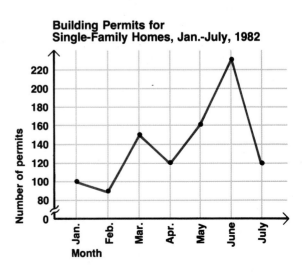

Building Permits for Single-Family Homes, Jan.-July, 1982

The graph shows how fast a computer can print. Tell how many lines the computer can print in

12. 2 minutes.   **13.** 8 minutes.

★14. 5 minutes.   **★15.** 9 minutes.

How long will it take the computer to print

16. 3,000 lines?   **17.** 7,000 lines?

18. 2,000 lines?   **19.** 8,000 lines?

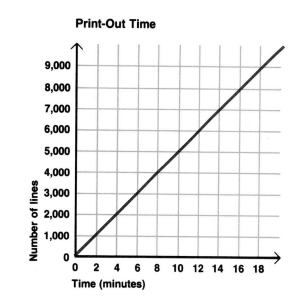

Print-Out Time

Number of lines / Time (minutes)

20. The table at the right gives the number of Olympic gold medals each country has won for women's figure skating. Make a bar graph to illustrate the data.

21. Chris and Pat are both flying from Seattle to Miami. Chris leaves at 8 A.M., and Pat leaves at 9:30 A.M. Chris averages 450 miles per hour, and Pat averages 550 miles per hour. About what time will Pat overtake Chris? Make a graph to solve the problem.

★22. Miami is about 2,700 miles from Seattle. Use your graph for Exercise 21 to determine what time (Seattle time) each person will arrive in Miami.

**Olympic Gold Medals
Women's Figure Skating**

Country	Number of Gold Medals
Austria	2
Canada	1
East Germany	1
Great Britain	2
Holland	1
Norway	3
Sweden	1
United States	4

Introduction to Integers

A. On *Columbia's* third space-shuttle mission, 3 seconds before liftoff the main engines were at 90 percent thrust. 126 seconds after liftoff, the solid rocket booster separated. You can use *integers* to represent these times.

$^-$**3**   Negative 3 represents 3 seconds before liftoff.

$^+$**126**   Positive 126 represents 126 seconds after liftoff.

B. What integer would you use to represent a profit of $15? What integer would you use to represent a loss of $15?

$^+$**15**   Positive 15 represents a profit of $15.

$^-$**15**   Negative 15 represents a loss of $15.

The integers $^+$15 and $^-$15 are called *opposites*.

Discuss What is the opposite of zero?

Try Represent each situation with an integer.

a. An increase in weight of 12 pounds

b. A temperature of 9 degrees below zero

Give the opposite of each integer.

c. $^+$8   **d.** $^-$10   **e.** $^-$5   **f.** $^+$1

Practice Write an integer to represent each situation.

1. Profit of $25

2. Loss of $85

3. Weight loss of 21 pounds

4. Weight gain of 13 pounds

5. Three flights of stairs down

6. Seven flights of stairs up

7. 10° below zero

8. 62° above zero

9. 1,012 feet above sea level

10. 635 feet below sea level

11. Forward 35 steps

12. Backward 26 steps

13. $65 savings deposit

14. $125 savings withdrawal

15. Eight minutes before the bell

16. Fifteen minutes after the bell

17. Sales decrease of $830

18. Sales increase of $250

19. Profit of $350

20. Loss of $625

★21. Altitude at sea level

★22. Time of liftoff

Give the opposite of each integer.

23. $^{+}1$

24. $^{-}3$

25. $^{+}9$

26. $^{-}8$

27. $^{-}15$

28. $^{+}20$

29. $^{-}62$

30. $^{+}34$

31. $^{+}160$

32. $^{-}183$

33. $^{-}211$

34. $^{+}235$

Apply Write an integer for each situation.

35. Eleven seconds after liftoff

36. Nine seconds before liftoff

37. At 117 seconds before liftoff, the flight crew begins pressurizing the liquid hydrogen tank.

38. At about 7 seconds before liftoff, the main engines are started.

39. In sunlight in space, the temperature can be as high as 200°C above zero.

40. On the night side of the orbit, the temperature is as cold as 100°C below zero.

Integers on the Number Line

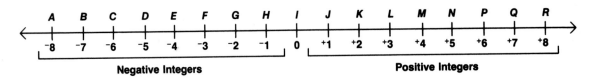

You can show integers on a number line. On a horizontal number line, positive integers are shown to the right of zero, and negative integers are shown to the left of zero. Zero is neither positive or negative.

A. Which is greater, ⁻2 or ⁻5?

The integer farther to the right on the number line is greater.

⁻2 is the greater integer.

⁻2 > ⁻5

B. Arrange the integers in order from least to greatest.

⁻1 ⁺4 ⁻3 0

List the integers as they appear from left to right on the number line.

⁻3 ⁻1 0 ⁺4

c. Name the integer for point *D* on the number line above.

⁻5 is point *D*.

Try Use the number line above to give an integer for each lettered point.

a. *A*   **b.** *I*   **c.** *M*

Compare the integers. Use < or >.

d. ⁺4 ● ⁺6   **e.** ⁻3 ● ⁺2   **f.** ⁻4 ● ⁻7   **g.** ⁻5 ● ⁺5

Arrange the integers in order from least to greatest.

h. ⁺3 ⁻6 ⁺2 ⁻4   **i.** ⁻7 ⁺5 ⁻8 ⁺1

Practice Use the number line below to give an integer for each lettered point.

```
      W    X    Y    Z    S    T    U    V    A    B    C    D
  ←───┼────┼────┼────┼────┼────┼────┼────┼────┼────┼────┼────┼───→
           ⁻4            ⁻1                                 ⁺6
```

1. T **2.** C **3.** Z **4.** V **5.** W **6.** Y **7.** U **8.** B **9.** A

Compare the integers. Use < or >.

10. ⁺40 ● ⁺2   **11.** ⁺30 ● ⁺8   **12.** ⁺54 ● ⁻3   **13.** ⁻17 ● ⁻5

14. ⁺90 ● ⁻9   **15.** ⁺25 ● ⁺6   **16.** ⁻34 ● ⁻1   **17.** ⁻18 ● ⁻3

18. ⁻85 ● ⁺62   **19.** ⁻57 ● ⁻14   **20.** ⁺18 ● ⁻18   **21.** ⁺61 ● ⁻60

Arrange the integers in order from least to greatest.

22. ⁺2 ⁺4 ⁻1   **23.** ⁺10 ⁻3 0   **24.** 0 ⁻2 ⁻7

25. ⁻5 ⁺3 ⁻2 ⁺1   **26.** ⁻7 ⁺8 ⁻6 ⁺1   **27.** ⁺2 ⁻3 ⁺7 ⁻5

Complete the following statements.

★28. Any positive integer is __?__ 0.   **★29.** Zero is less than any __?__.

★30. Any positive integer is __?__ any negative integer.

Apply This thermometer is an example of a vertical number line. The numbers get greater as you go from the bottom to the top.

Which temperature is warmer?

31. 32° or 80°   **32.** ⁻15° or 0°

33. ⁻18° or ⁻5°   **34.** ⁻22° or 45°

Adding Integers: Same Sign

A. In March, Erica made a savings withdrawal of $5 and a second withdrawal of $7. What is the total of these two withdrawals?

Use ⁻5 to represent a withdrawal of $5 and ⁻7 to represent a withdrawal of $7.

Find ⁻5 + ⁻7.

Use a number line. Start at zero and move 5 units to the left for ⁻5. Then move 7 units farther left for ⁻7.

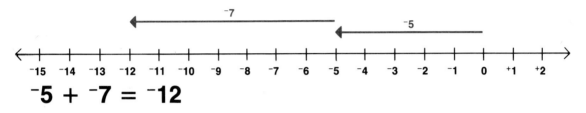

$$^-5 + {}^-7 = {}^-12$$

Erica's total withdrawals for March were $12.

B. Find ⁺6 + ⁺3.

Start at zero and move 6 units to the right for ⁺6. Then move 3 units farther right for ⁺3.

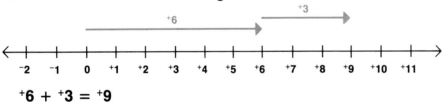

$$^+6 + {}^+3 = {}^+9$$

To add integers with the same sign, add without regard to the signs. Then use the sign of the numbers in your answer.

Try Add.

a. ⁺3 + ⁺6   **b.** ⁻9 + ⁻5   **c.** ⁻6 + ⁻6

356

Practice   Add.

1. $^{+}4 + {^{+}5}$ 2. $^{-}2 + {^{-}6}$

3. $^{+}1 + {^{+}7}$ 4. $^{-}8 + {^{-}3}$

5. $^{+}7 + {^{+}5}$ 6. $^{+}9 + {^{+}7}$

7. $^{-}10 + {^{-}4}$ 8. $^{-}5 + {^{-}11}$

9. $^{+}15 + {^{+}4}$ 10. $^{-}18 + {^{-}7}$

11. $^{-}13 + {^{-}6}$ 12. $^{+}14 + {^{+}2}$

13. $^{-}25 + {^{-}15}$ 14. $^{-}31 + {^{-}21}$

15. $^{+}38 + {^{+}17}$ ★16. $^{-}64 + 0$

Complete each statement.

★17. The sum of two positive integers is __?__.

★18. The sum of two negative integers is __?__.

Apply   Solve each problem.

19. During March, Erica made deposits of $35 and $20 to her savings account. What were Erica's total deposits for the month?

20. Rene made savings withdrawals of $85 and $45. What was the total of her withdrawals?

★21. On May 1, Erica had $545 in her savings account. During May she made deposits of $55 and $85. If she did not make withdrawals, how much did she have in her account on May 31?

Adding Integers: Different Signs

A. Juan works at a Junior Achievement company. He earned $15 ($^+$15). Then he spent $9 ($^-$9) for a record album. How much money does he have left?

Find $^+$15 + $^-$9.

Use a number line. Start at zero and move 15 units to the right for $^+$15. Then move 9 units to the left for $^-$9.

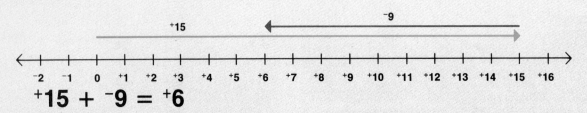

$$^+15 + {}^-9 = {}^+6$$

To add two integers with different signs, consider the distance each integer is from zero. Subtract the shorter distance from the longer distance. Then use the sign of the number farther from zero in your answer.

B. Find $^-$18 + $^+$12.

$18 - 12 = 6$ $\qquad$ $^-$18 is farther from zero than $^+$12.

$^-18 + {}^+12 = {}^-6$

C. Find $^-$4 + $^+$4.

$^-4 + {}^+4$ $\qquad$ $^-$4 and $^+$4 are the same distance from zero.

$^-4 + {}^+4 = 0$

Try Add.

a. $^-6 + ^+4$ b. $^+8 + ^-2$

c. $^-9 + ^+9$ d. $0 + ^-7$

Practice Add.

1. $^-4 + ^+1$ 2. $^-7 + ^+3$

3. $^+9 + ^-3$ 4. $^+5 + ^-5$

5. $^+3 + ^-5$ 6. $^+5 + ^-2$

7. $^-3 + ^+8$ 8. $^-1 + ^+10$

9. $^-3 + ^+3$ 10. $^+8 + ^-12$

11. $^+6 + ^-11$ 12. $^-4 + ^+13$

13. $^+12 + ^-7$ 14. $^+9 + ^-18$

15. $^+27 + ^-18$ 16. $^-35 + ^+14$

17. $^+13 + ^-45$ 18. $^-48 + ^+26$

19. $^-32 + ^+19$ 20. $^-65 + ^+17$

Apply Solve each problem.

21. One month, a Junior Achievement company had $125 in expenses and $185 in income. How much profit or loss did the company have that month?

22. It costs the company $4.17 to make one of its products. The product sells for $6.50. How much profit or loss does the company have on each item?

COMPUTER

BASIC: READ and DATA Statements

READ and DATA statements go together in a program. They provide another method to give values to memory locations. A READ statement looks for information from a DATA statement, which may be anywhere in a program. In the program below, X will have the value −5, Y will be 8, and Z will be 6.

```
10 READ X,Y,Z
20 LET T=X+Y+Z
30 LET A=T/3
40 PRINT "AVERAGE IS ";A
50 DATA -5, 8, 6
60 END
```
Output

```
AVERAGE IS 3
```

Give the output for the program above if line 50 were changed to the following.

1. 50 DATA 7, -9, 5

2. 50 DATA 2, -4, 8

Make the necessary changes in lines 10, 20, 30, and 50 to find the average for each set of numbers.

3. -3, 4, 7, -9, 6

4. 0, -1, 4, 8, 12, -5

5. Give the output for the programs in Exercises 3 and 4.

Subtracting Integers

Study these pairs of equations.

$5 - 2 = 3$	$9 - 2 = 7$	$7 - 3 = 4$
$^+5 + {}^-2 = {}^+3$	$^+9 + {}^-2 = {}^+7$	$^+7 + {}^-3 = {}^+4$

In each case, adding the opposite integer gives the same result as subtracting.

To subtract an integer, add its opposite.

A. The high temperature in Chicago during April was 21°C. The low temperature was ⁻3°C. How much warmer was the high temperature than the low?

Find $^+21 - {}^-3$.

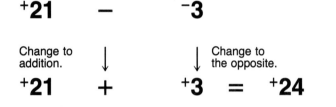

$$^+21 \qquad - \qquad {}^-3$$

Change to addition. $\downarrow$ $\qquad$ $\downarrow$ Change to the opposite.

$$^+21 \quad + \quad {}^+3 \quad = \quad {}^+24$$

The high temperature for April was 24 degrees warmer than the low.

B. Find $^+7 - {}^-5$.

$^+7 - {}^-5$ Change ⁻5 to ⁺5 and add.

$$^+7 + {}^+5 = {}^+12$$

C. Find $^-4 - {}^-9$.

$^-4 - {}^-9$ Change ⁻9 to ⁺9 and add.

$$^-4 + {}^+9 = {}^+5$$

Try Subtract.

a. $^+6 - {}^+4$ **b.** $^+5 - {}^+9$ **c.** $^-3 - {}^-8$ **d.** $^-7 - 0$

Practice Subtract.

1. $^+7 - {}^+1$ **2.** $^-9 - {}^-5$ **3.** $^+10 - {}^-7$ **4.** $^-2 - {}^+5$ **5.** $^+2 - {}^+4$

6. $^-1 - 0$ **7.** $^+6 - {}^+5$ **8.** $^-7 - {}^+2$ **9.** $^-5 - {}^-3$ **10.** $^-4 - {}^+5$

11. $^+2 - {}^-3$ **12.** $^-10 - {}^-3$ **13.** $^+4 - {}^-5$ **14.** $^+9 - {}^-1$ **15.** $^-2 - {}^-2$

16. $0 - {}^-8$ **17.** ${}^+6 - 0$ **18.** ${}^-9 - {}^-11$ **19.** ${}^+7 - {}^+7$

20. ${}^+12 - {}^+20$ **21.** ${}^-11 - {}^-30$ **22.** ${}^+18 - {}^-16$ **23.** ${}^+15 - {}^+5$

24. $0 - {}^+24$ **25.** ${}^-21 - {}^+15$ **26.** ${}^-15 - {}^-12$ **27.** ${}^+16 - {}^-38$

28. ${}^-5 - {}^+29$ **29.** ${}^-65 - {}^+28$ **30.** ${}^+43 - {}^-36$ **31.** ${}^+58 - {}^+16$

Apply Solve each problem.

32. At 3 P.M. the temperature was ${}^+20°C$. At 11 P.M., it was ${}^+7°C$. What was the difference between the two temperatures?

33. The temperature dropped from ${}^+15°C$ to ${}^-8°C$. What was the change in temperature?

34. The temperature changed from ${}^-22°C$ to ${}^+35°C$. How many degrees did the temperature rise?

35. The temperature dropped from ${}^-2°C$ to ${}^-25°C$. What was the change in temperature?

CALCULATOR

Positive integers are entered as counting numbers on your calculator. To enter a negative integer on the calculator, press ⌊+/-⌋.

Find ${}^+5 + {}^-17$.

Press: 5 ⌊+⌋ 17 ⌊+/-⌋ ⌊=⌋.

Display: $^-12$

Add or subtract.

1. ${}^+3 + {}^+8$ **2.** ${}^-4 + {}^-7$ **3.** ${}^-6 + {}^+9$ **4.** ${}^-23 + {}^+42$

5. ${}^-50 + {}^+134$ **6.** ${}^-6 - {}^-9$ **7.** ${}^+7 - {}^-8$ **8.** ${}^+28 - {}^+13$

9. ${}^+63 - {}^-15$ **10.** ${}^-121 + {}^+67$ **11.** ${}^+45 - {}^+67$ **12.** ${}^-89 + {}^-34$

13. ${}^-27 - {}^+13$ **14.** ${}^+12 + {}^+49$ **15.** ${}^-45 - {}^-19$ **16.** ${}^+16 - {}^+63$

Locating Points with Ordered Pairs of Integers

An ordered pair of integers can be used to locate a point on a grid.

Name the point located by the ordered pair (⁻3, ⁺2).

To find a point located by an ordered pair of integers, start at the origin (0, 0). The first number in the ordered pair tells how far to move to the right (+) or left (−). The second number in the ordered pair tells how far to move up (+) or down (−).

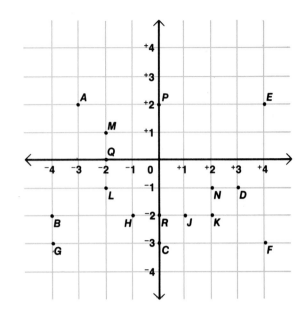

Point A is 3 units to the left of the origin, and 2 units above the origin. So the ordered pair (⁻3, ⁺2) locates point A.

Try Use the graph above. Name the point located by each ordered pair.

a. (⁻4, ⁻3)　　**b.** (⁺1, ⁻2)　　**c.** (⁻2, ⁺1)　　**d.** (0, ⁻2)

Give the ordered pair that locates each point.

e. B　　**f.** C　　**g.** D

Practice Use the graph at the right. Name the point located by each ordered pair.

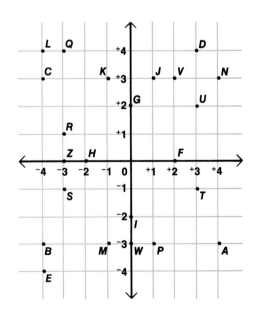

1. (⁺4, ⁺3)　　　　**2.** (⁻2, 0)

3. (⁻1, ⁻3)　　　　**4.** (⁻3, ⁺1)

5. (⁺3, ⁺2)　　　　**6.** (0, ⁻3)

7. (⁻4, ⁻4)　　　　**8.** (⁻4, ⁺4)

9. (⁺2, 0)　　　　**10.** (0, ⁺2)

Give the ordered pair that locates
each point.

11. *A*   **12.** *B*   **13.** *C*   **14.** *D*

15. *E*   **16.** *F*   **17.** *G*   **18.** *H*

19. *I*   **20.** *J*   **21.** *K*   **22.** *M*

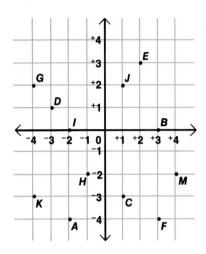

On a grid make a dot for each ordered pair. Join
the points in the order given, and identify the polygon.

23. (⁻4, ⁻3), (⁻4, ⁺2), (⁺1, ⁺2), (⁺1, ⁻3), (⁻4, ⁻3)

24. (⁺3, ⁺1), (⁻1, ⁺3), (⁻1, ⁻2), (⁺3, ⁻2), (⁺3, ⁺1)

25. (⁻3, ⁻1), (⁻3, ⁺3), (⁺1, ⁻1), (⁻3, ⁻1)

26. (⁺2, ⁺1), (⁺6, ⁺1), (⁺3, ⁻2), (⁻1, ⁻2), (⁺2, ⁺1)

27. (⁻3, ⁺1), (⁻1, ⁺3), (⁺1, ⁺1), (⁻1, ⁻1), (⁻3, ⁺1)

28. (⁺2, 0), (0, ⁺4), (⁻2, 0), (0, ⁻4), (⁺2, 0)

★29. (⁻3, 0), (⁻2, ⁺2), (⁺3, 0), (⁻2, ⁻2), (⁻3, 0)

★30. (⁻2, ⁻1), (⁺1, ⁺2), (⁺5, ⁻2), (⁻2, ⁻1)

Graphing with Ordered Pairs of Integers

A. Martin drew triangle *ABC* on a grid by joining the following points:

$$A(^-2, ^+1)\ B(^-5, ^+2)\ C(^-2, ^+4)$$

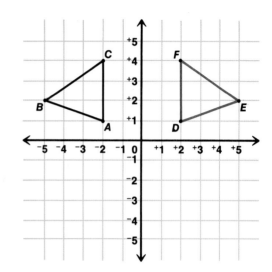

Then he changed the sign of the first number in each ordered pair. The new points were:

$$D(^+2, ^+1)\ E(^+5, ^+2)\ F(^+2, ^+4)$$

He drew triangle *DEF*, and folded his grid along the vertical axis. When he held the folded paper up to the light, he could see that the figures matched.

Triangle *DEF* is the **reflection** of triangle *ABC* over the vertical axis. The vertical axis is called the **reflection line**. Triangles *ABC* and *DEF* are congruent.

B. To draw a reflection of triangle *ABC* over the horizontal axis, Martin changed the second number in each of the original ordered pairs. The new points were:

$$G(^-2, ^-1)\ H(^-5, ^-2)\ I(^-2, ^-4)$$

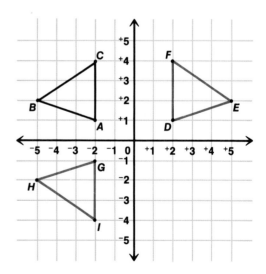

Triangle *GHI* is the reflection of triangle *ABC* over the horizontal axis. Triangle *ABC* and *GHI* are also congruent.

Discuss Are triangles *DEF* and *GHI* congruent?

Try

a. On a grid, draw the figure by joining the given points in order. Change the sign of the first number in each ordered pair. Then draw the new figure.

($^+$2, $^+$2), ($^+$5, $^+$2), ($^+$5, $^+$6), ($^+$2, $^+$6), ($^+$2, $^+$2)

Practice In each exercise, draw the figure by joining the given points in order. Change the sign of the first number in each ordered pair. Then draw the new figure.

1. ($^+$1, $^+$1), ($^+$7, $^+$1), ($^+$7, $^+$7), ($^+$1, $^+$1)

2. ($^-$1, $^+$2), ($^-$7, $^+$2), ($^-$7, $^+$5), ($^-$1, $^+$5), ($^-$1, $^+$2)

3. ($^+$1, $^+$2), ($^+$7, $^+$2), ($^+$9, $^+$5), ($^+$4, $^+$5), ($^+$1, $^+$2)

4. ($^-$4, $^-$1), ($^-$7, $^-$4), ($^-$4, $^-$7), ($^-$1, $^-$4), ($^-$4, $^-$1)

★5. (0, $^+$6), ($^-$3, $^+$2), ($^-$8, $^+$2), (0, $^+$6)

In each exercise, draw the figure by joining the given points in order. Change the sign of the second number in each ordered pair. Then draw the new figure.

6. ($^-$1, $^+$2), ($^-$4, $^+$4), ($^-$7, $^+$2), ($^-$4, $^+$7), ($^-$1, $^+$2)

7. ($^-$1, $^+$1), ($^-$1, $^+$4), ($^-$7, $^+$1), ($^-$7, $^+$4), ($^-$1, $^+$1)

8. ($^+$1, $^+$6), ($^+$4, $^+$1), ($^+$7, $^+$6), ($^+$5, $^+$6), ($^+$5, $^+$9), ($^+$3, $^+$9), ($^+$3, $^+$6), ($^+$1, $^+$6)

★9. ($^+$5, 0), ($^+$7, 0), ($^+$3, $^+$6), ($^+$1, $^+$6), ($^+$5, 0)

★10. Copy this figure on a grid. Write the ordered pairs for the vertices. Change the sign of the first number in each ordered pair. Then draw the new figure.

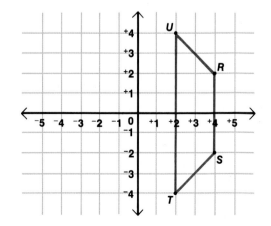

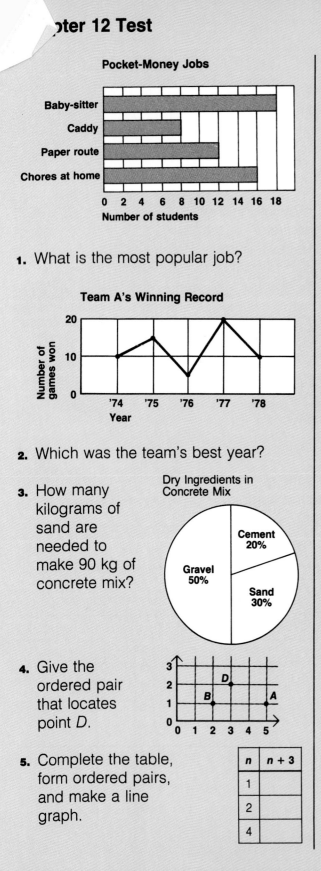

Pocket-Money Jobs

Number of students

1. What is the most popular job?

Team A's Winning Record

Number of games won

Year

2. Which was the team's best year?

3. How many kilograms of sand are needed to make 90 kg of concrete mix?

Dry Ingredients in Concrete Mix

Cement 20%

Gravel 50%

Sand 30%

4. Give the ordered pair that locates point *D*.

5. Complete the table, form ordered pairs, and make a line graph.

n	n + 3
1	
2	
4	

Give the opposite of each integer.

6. $^-3$ **7.** $^+2$ **8.** $^-7$

Compare the integers. Use < or >.

9. $^+1$ ● $^-4$ **10.** $^-3$ ● $^-1$

Add or subtract.

11. $^-3 + {}^-5$ **12.** $^+2 + {}^-7$

13. $^+6 + {}^-6$ **14.** $^+5 - {}^-2$

15. $^-8 - {}^-4$ **16.** $^+3 - {}^-1$

Give the ordered pair that locates each point.

17. *A*

18. *B*

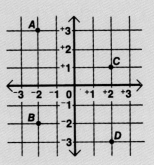

19. On a grid, draw the figure by joining the given points in order. Change the sign of the first number in each ordered pair. Then draw the new figure.

($^+2$, $^+1$), ($^+4$, $^+1$), ($^+4$, $^+3$), ($^+2$, $^+1$)

20. Dale started on a bicycle trail at 2 P.M., riding 12 miles per hour. Lisa started on the same trail at 3:30 P.M., riding 16 miles per hour. About what time did Lisa overtake Dale?

CHALLENGE

Translations of a Triangle

Draw triangle *ABC* by connecting the given points.

A($^-$7, $^-$2), *B*($^-$2, $^-$2), *C*($^-$2, $^-$6)

Add $^+$8 to the first number in each ordered pair. The new points are:

E($^+$1, $^-$2), *F*($^+$6, $^-$2), *G*($^+$6, $^-$6)

Draw triangle *EFG* by connecting the given points. Triangle *ABC* is *translated* 8 units to the right to triangle *EFG*.

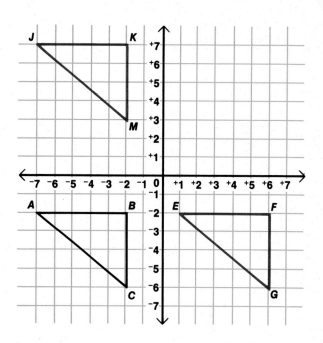

Add $^+$9 to the second number in each of the original ordered pairs. The new points are:

J($^-$7, $^+$7), *K*($^-$2, $^+$7), *M*($^-$2, $^+$3)

Draw triangle *JKM* by connecting the points. Triangle *ABC* is translated 9 units up to get triangle *JKM*.

For each exercise, draw the figure by connecting the given points. Add $^+$6 to the first number in each ordered pair. Then draw the new figure.

1. ($^-$1, $^+$1), ($^-$4, $^+$5), ($^-$7, $^+$2)

2. ($^-$5, $^-$1), ($^-$5, $^-$6), ($^-$2, $^-$4)

For each exercise, draw the figure by connecting the given points. Add $^-$5 to the second number in each ordered pair. Then draw the new figure.

3. ($^+$1, 0), ($^+$2, $^-$5), ($^+$6, $^-$2)

4. ($^-$7, $^-$4), (0, $^-$4), ($^-$4, 0)

5. ($^+$1, $^+$1), ($^+$2, $^+$1), ($^+$2, $^+$6), ($^+$1, $^+$6), ($^+$1, $^+$1)

MAINTENANCE

Find each answer.

1. $\frac{4}{10} + \frac{7}{10}$ 2. $\frac{4}{5} - \frac{2}{3}$ 3. $\frac{3}{5} \times \frac{2}{3}$ 4. $\frac{3}{8} \div \frac{2}{3}$ 5. $3\frac{2}{3} - 2\frac{1}{3}$

6. $3\frac{1}{4} + 5\frac{3}{4}$ 7. $\frac{3}{4} \div \frac{4}{5}$ 8. $\frac{5}{6} \times \frac{2}{3}$ 9. $6\frac{1}{5} + 4\frac{3}{10}$ 10. $5\frac{2}{5} - 3\frac{4}{5}$

11. $2\frac{1}{2} \times 1\frac{4}{5}$ 12. $3 \div 5\frac{1}{3}$ 13. $5 - 2\frac{1}{4}$ 14. $7\frac{9}{10} + 8\frac{1}{2}$ 15. $2\frac{3}{8} \times 6$

16. $1\frac{2}{3} \div 2$ 17. $\frac{3}{8} + 5\frac{1}{4}$ 18. $5\frac{2}{3} - 3$ 19. $4 \div 2\frac{1}{2}$ 20. $2\frac{3}{4} \times 4\frac{3}{8}$

21. $2\frac{5}{6} \times \frac{3}{4}$ 22. $7\frac{3}{4} \div \frac{2}{3}$ 23. $8\frac{2}{3} \div 4\frac{5}{6}$ 24. $3\frac{5}{6} + 7\frac{5}{6}$ 25. $9\frac{1}{4} - 4\frac{1}{2}$

26. $6\frac{4}{9} - 2\frac{1}{3}$ 27. $\frac{3}{7} \times \frac{1}{5}$ 28. $\frac{9}{10} \times \frac{2}{3}$ 29. $1\frac{4}{5} + 3\frac{5}{6}$ 30. $\frac{1}{8} \div 3$

31. $7 - 3\frac{1}{8}$ 32. $\frac{1}{4} + 2\frac{3}{8}$ 33. $6\frac{1}{4} - 2\frac{1}{2}$ 34. $4\frac{2}{3} - 3\frac{5}{8}$ 35. $6 - 2\frac{5}{6}$

36. $\frac{4}{5} \times 3$ 37. $\frac{7}{8} \div 6$ 38. $3\frac{1}{3} \div 10$ 39. $9\frac{1}{5} \div 2\frac{1}{2}$ 40. $4 \times 2\frac{3}{5}$

Solve each problem.

41. How many $\frac{1}{4}$-pound hamburgers can be made with $5\frac{3}{4}$ lb. of meat?

42. A recipe calls for $1\frac{1}{8}$ cups of water. How much water is needed to make 3 times the recipe?

43. Oranges cost $1.59 per dozen. How much will 6 dozen oranges cost?

44. Illinois sales-tax rate is 7%. How much sales tax would be charged on a $45.65 grocery bill?

45. Volleyball is played on a court that is 18 m long and 9 m wide. What is the area of the court?

46. Tim lost 2 kg in March. He lost 4 kg in April. What was his total loss or gain?

47. A pitcher holds 6 cups of juice. How many $\frac{2}{3}$-cup servings can be poured?

48. Every 2 weeks Tony saves $5. How much would he save in 6 weeks?

Cumulative Test, Chapters 1–12

Give the letter for the correct answer.

1. Round 47,639 to the nearest thousand.

    A 47,000   **C** 50,000
    B 48,000   **D** 40,000

2. Subtract.

$$\begin{array}{r} 35,127 \\ -\ \ 6,819 \\ \hline \end{array}$$

    A 28,308
    B 28,318
    C 29,308
    D 29,408

3. Multiply.

$$\begin{array}{r} 426 \\ \times\ \ 34 \\ \hline \end{array}$$

    A 18,318
    B 14,484
    C 14,364
    D 18,108

4. Divide.

$$33\overline{)7,082}$$

    A 202 R16
    B 214 R20
    C 236 R2
    D 211 R19

5. Choose the operation that should be used to solve this problem. Then solve the problem.

If daisies cost 12¢ each, how much would 992 daisies cost?

    A Division; $82.66
    B Addition; $10.04
    C Multiplication; $119.04
    D Subtraction; $9.80

6. Choose the equation that should be used to solve this problem. Then solve the problem.

An oil well yielded its owners $21,000 in 3 months. How much money did the oil well average per month?

    A $21,000 − 3 = x; $18,000
    B $21,000 × 3 = x; $63,000
    C $21,000 ÷ 3 = x; $7,000
    D $21,000 + 3 = x; $24,000

7. Which of the following numbers is greater than 1.3?

    A 1.05   **C** 1.36
    B 1.30   **D** 1.235

8. Subtract.

$$\begin{array}{r} 6.41 \\ -\ 1.63 \\ \hline \end{array}$$

    A 5.88
    B 4.78
    C 5.78
    D 4.88

9. Divide.

$$10\overline{)6.12}$$

    A 612
    B 61.2
    C 0.0612
    D 0.612

10. What is $\frac{6}{18}$ in lowest terms?

    A $\frac{1}{6}$ **C** $\frac{2}{3}$
    B $\frac{1}{3}$ **D** $\frac{5}{6}$

11. Add.

$$\frac{2}{3} + \frac{1}{6} + \frac{7}{12}$$

A $1\frac{5}{12}$

B $\frac{5}{6}$

C $1\frac{9}{24}$

D $1\frac{7}{12}$

12. What is the perimeter of the polygon shown below?

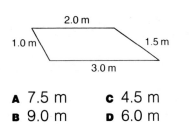

2.0 m

1.0 m 1.5 m

3.0 m

A 7.5 m   **C** 4.5 m
B 9.0 m   **D** 6.0 m

13. What is the area of a rectangle 7 mm long and 3 mm wide?

A 10 mm²   **C** 21 mm²
B 20 mm²   **D** 18 mm²

14. Which ratio comes next in the series below?

$$\frac{2}{7} = \frac{4}{14} = \frac{6}{21} = \blacksquare$$

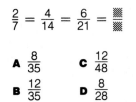

A $\frac{8}{35}$ **C** $\frac{12}{48}$

B $\frac{12}{35}$ **D** $\frac{8}{28}$

15. Which of these ratios form a proportion?

A $\frac{1}{3}$ $\frac{6}{9}$ **C** $\frac{2}{3}$ $\frac{3}{8}$

B $\frac{3}{8}$ $\frac{6}{16}$ **D** $\frac{3}{4}$ $\frac{8}{12}$

16. What is 42% written as a decimal?

A 4.2   **C** 42.0
B 0.042   **D** 0.42

17. What is $\frac{7}{20}$ written as a percent?

A 7%   **C** 14%
B 35%   **D** 27%

18. What is 4% of 32?

A 12.8   **C** 2.56
B 25.6   **D** 1.28

19. What is $66\frac{2}{3}\%$ of 45?

A 30   **C** 35
B 15   **D** 42

20. Choose the equation that should be used to solve the problem. Then solve the problem.

A book costs $7.80 plus 5% for sales tax. What is the amount of the tax?

A $7.80 - 0.05 = n$; $156.00
B $7.80 + 0.05 = n$; $7.85
C $7.80 - 0.05 = n$; $7.75
D $7.80 \times 0.05 = n$; $0.39

21. Add.

$$^-2 + {}^-5$$

A $^-3$
B 7
C 3
D $^-7$

22. Add.

$$^+14 + {}^-6$$

A $^-8$
B $^+20$
C $^+8$
D $^-20$

MORE PRACTICE

Set 1 *pages 2–3*   Write each number in words.

1. 2,640   **2.** 3,041   **3.** 67,456   **4.** 81,637   **5.** 92,892   **6.** 108,993   **7.** 70,019

Write each number in expanded form.

8. 5,341   **9.** 4,203   **10.** 20,735   **11.** 72,401   **12.** 73,250   **13.** 640,612   **14.** 67,036

Write each number in standard form.

15. 5,000 + 200 + 40 + 2   **16.** 7,000 + 600 + 50 + 1   **17.** 60,000 + 400 + 40 + 2

18. 40,000 + 300 + 50 + 7   **19.** 90,000 + 2,000 + 600   **20.** 900,000 + 500 + 10 + 5

21. Three thousand, four hundred twelve   **22.** Five hundred thousand, fifteen   **23.** Sixty-six thousand, three hundred twenty-five

Set 2 *pages 4–5*   Tell which digits are in the millions period in each number.

1. 52,384,621   **2.** 463,521,000   **3.** 6,724,520,000   **4.** 6,748,524,000

5. 921,432,501   **6.** 9,234,567,490   **7.** 576,327,621,000   **8.** 794,326,000,000

Tell what the 7 in each number means.

9. 8,167,432   **10.** 5,325,762   **11.** 87,462,000   **12.** 981,145,074   **13.** 64,702,303

Write each number in words.

14. 6,325,346   **15.** 755,000,000   **16.** 8,350,830,000   **17.** 25,685,446,251

Write each number in standard form.

18. 16 million, 205 thousand, 724   **19.** 720 million, 715 thousand, 502

20. 6 billion, 626 thousand, 305   **21.** 2 trillion, 45 million, 300 thousand

Set 3 *pages 6–7*   Compare. Use >, <, or =.

1. 2,435 ● 2,445   **2.** 1,201 ● 1,102   **3.** 3,443 ● 4,334   **4.** 15,261 ● 16,261

5. 17,025 ● 17,025   **6.** 50,263 ● 50,623   **7.** 640,321 ● 540,321   **8.** 302,200 ● 289,540

List these numbers in order from the least to the greatest.

9. 4,618   3,250   4,520   **10.** 6,151   5,616   6,515   **11.** 1,000   1,010   1,001

12. 24,521   25,241   24,251   **13.** 43,283   43,823   43,238   **14.** 35,000   35,005   30,500

15. 63,782   36,827   83,276   **16.** 26,456   25,654   26,654   **17.** 25,521   25,255   52,125

Set 4 *pages 8–9* Round to the nearest hundred.

1. 548　　**2.** 653　　**3.** 743　　**4.** 892　　**5.** 6,934　　**6.** 7,582　　**7.** 8,421

8. 4,354　　**9.** 1,221　　**10.** 2,154　　**11.** 5,273　　**12.** 8,761　　**13.** 9,442　　**14.** 7,663

Round to the nearest thousand.

15. 6,172　　**16.** 9,540　　**17.** 3,416　　**18.** 4,623　　**19.** 7,230　　**20.** 7,531

21. 29,345　　**22.** 29,545　　**23.** 80,732　　**24.** 214,400　　**25.** 112,521　　**26.** 341,225

Round to the nearest ten-thousand.

27. 68,845　　**28.** 37,134　　**29.** 21,562　　**30.** 63,351　　**31.** 59,640　　**32.** 47,634

33. 394,567　　**34.** 706,602　　**35.** 808,305　　**36.** 298,633　　**37.** 482,564　　**38.** 672,128

Set 5 *pages 10–11* Estimate each sum or difference. First round each number to the nearest hundred.

1. 436 + 293　　**2.** 376 − 218　　**3.** 328 + 587　　**4.** 498 + 835　　**5.** 627 − 432

6. 654 − 275　　**7.** 775 − 423　　**8.** 478 + 440　　**9.** 807 − 562　　**10.** 573 + 284

Estimate each sum or difference. First round each number to the nearest thousand.

11. 4,730 + 6,234　　**12.** 8,965 − 2,003　　**13.** 3,947 − 3,047　　**14.** 4,967 + 2,542

15. 7,452 − 4,227　　**16.** 2,541 + 2,341　　**17.** 34,731 + 3,876　　**18.** 29,421 − 1,001

Set 6 *pages 12–13*

1. $\begin{array}{r} 25 \\ + 47 \\ \hline \end{array}$
2. $\begin{array}{r} 38 \\ + 29 \\ \hline \end{array}$
3. $\begin{array}{r} 59 \\ + 36 \\ \hline \end{array}$
4. $\begin{array}{r} 34 \\ + 48 \\ \hline \end{array}$
5. $\begin{array}{r} 26 \\ + 37 \\ \hline \end{array}$
6. $\begin{array}{r} 47 \\ + 18 \\ \hline \end{array}$
7. $\begin{array}{r} 46 \\ + 34 \\ \hline \end{array}$

8. $\begin{array}{r} 372 \\ + 92 \\ \hline \end{array}$
9. $\begin{array}{r} 575 \\ + 74 \\ \hline \end{array}$
10. $\begin{array}{r} 382 \\ + 64 \\ \hline \end{array}$
11. $\begin{array}{r} 437 \\ + 547 \\ \hline \end{array}$
12. $\begin{array}{r} 472 \\ + 356 \\ \hline \end{array}$
13. $\begin{array}{r} 651 \\ + 294 \\ \hline \end{array}$
14. $\begin{array}{r} 845 \\ + 126 \\ \hline \end{array}$

15. $\begin{array}{r} 5,742 \\ + 3,631 \\ \hline \end{array}$
16. $\begin{array}{r} 3,736 \\ + 2,248 \\ \hline \end{array}$
17. $\begin{array}{r} 7,262 \\ + 1,186 \\ \hline \end{array}$
18. $\begin{array}{r} 3,724 \\ + 5,180 \\ \hline \end{array}$
19. $\begin{array}{r} 1,724 \\ + 5,311 \\ \hline \end{array}$
20. $\begin{array}{r} 3,161 \\ + 4,453 \\ \hline \end{array}$

21. 2 + 5 + 8　　　**22.** 7 + 8 + 6 + 3　　　**23.** 4 + 6 + 3 + 8　　　**24.** 18 + 25 + 14

25. 19 + 3 + 17　　　**26.** 54 + 12 + 28　　　**27.** 29 + 6 + 37　　　**28.** 46 + 28 + 15

29. 47 + 9 + 33　　　**30.** 66 + 14 + 19　　　**31.** 48 + 8 + 26　　　**32.** 45 + 33 + 19

MORE PRACTICE

Set 7 *pages 14–15*

1.	2.	3.	4.	5.	6.
3,476 + 865	6,585 + 188	7,783 + 888	8,483 + 967	9,597 + 4,828	7,472 + 8,868

7.	8.	9.	10.	11.	12.
37,424 + 25,749	57,389 + 74,368	47,496 + 85,387	286,193 + 315,457	423,568 + 194,547	803,645 + 197,286

13.	14.	15.	16.	17.	18.
638 473 + 566	187 284 + 555	4,237 3,528 + 967	63,333 4,444 + 8,888	6,767 8,686 + 7,777	1,858 12,401 + 456,823

19. 8,765 + 2,345   **20.** 2,567 + 3,876   **21.** 8,872 + 3,478   **22.** 906,445 + 32,670

Set 8 *pages 16–17*

1.	2.	3.	4.	5.	6.	7.	8.
32 − 19	53 − 44	24 − 17	60 − 13	46 − 28	88 − 39	74 − 29	91 − 38

9.	10.	11.	12.	13.	14.	15.	16.
247 − 119	317 − 193	408 − 295	209 − 153	306 − 184	643 − 283	195 − 147	592 − 282

17.	18.	19.	20.	21.	22.
4,708 − 136	7,352 − 236	9,563 − 5,538	6,037 − 5,136	6,583 − 2,931	4,436 − 2,191

23. 426 − 293   **24.** 7,984 − 4,736   **25.** 1,060 − 32   **26.** 8,392 − 168   **27.** 6,088 − 59

Set 9 *pages 18–19*

1.	2.	3.	4.	5.	6.
517 − 249	723 − 365	308 − 149	635 − 567	5,348 − 3,662	5,013 − 4,678

7.	8.	9.	10.	11.	12.
3,108 − 389	5,076 − 995	5,700 − 2,453	3,701 − 1,468	6,050 − 2,397	3,030 − 1,673

13.	14.	15.	16.	17.	18.
10,203 − 8,888	10,000 − 9,999	62,901 − 48,058	93,021 − 84,722	90,000 − 35,327	225,045 − 167,836

19. 500 − 243   **20.** 6,000 − 5,555   **21.** 1,305 − 777   **22.** 6,000 − 3,291

Set 10 *pages 20–21*   Tell what operation you would use to solve each problem.
Then solve each problem.

1. Don's pack contains an insect repellent weighing 28 grams and a first-aid kit weighing 225 grams. What is the total weight of these items?

2. On Friday, at Cleveland Hopkins Airport, 1,258 planes landed and 1,569 planes took off. Find the total number of landings and takeoffs for that day.

3. The stadium at Wayside College has 30,000 seats. 19,437 people attended a basketball game at Wayside. How many seats were empty?

4. Pam has 178 books. Paul has 49 books. How many more books has Pam than Paul?

5. Ms. Frost ordered 104 new books. 59 of the books have been delivered. How many of the new books have not arrived?

6. Kathy made 79 new cards for the library. Ms. Frost made 152 new cards. How many cards did they make altogether?

Set 11 *pages 24–25*   Find *n*.

1. $83 + n = 121$
2. $n + 67 = 114$
3. $n + 24 = 39$
4. $19 + n = 31$
5. $80 = 21 + n$

6. $42 = n + 21$
7. $29 + n = 57$
8. $50 = n + 18$
9. $n + 19 = 78$
10. $94 = n + 28$

11. $887 = n + 146$
12. $862 = 457 + n$
13. $369 + n = 500$
14. $n + 910 = 1,333$

15. $266 + n = 300$
16. $323 + n = 540$
17. $n + 125 = 700$
18. $285 + n = 606$

19. $2,163 + n = 5,000$
20. $807 + n = 1,016$
21. $1,000 = n + 98$
22. $2,388 = n + 754$

23. $2,002 + n = 4,000$
24. $3,054 = 1,827 + n$
25. $n + 99 = 1,717$
26. $n + 174 = 2,350$

27. $n + 4,706 = 5,550$
28. $8,037 + n = 9,013$
29. $2,020 = n + 49$
30. $9,008 = n + 879$

Set 12 *pages 26–27*   Write an equation. Then find the answer.

1. Debbie read 4 of the 12 books she took with her on vacation. How many of these books did she not read?

2. There are 350 students at Lakeside Junior High. If 120 of these students are girls, how many are boys?

3. Of those students who took the arithmetic test, 24 passed and 5 did not pass. How many students took the test?

4. There are 150 boys and 175 girls at Holmes Elementary. How many students are there at Holmes?

5. Zachary worked 24 hours in the library. Marla worked 16 hours. How many more hours did Zachary work than Marla?

6. The library can seat 62 people. When 33 of the chairs are empty, how many people are sitting in the library?

MORE PRACTICE

Set 13 *pages 32–33*   Write two multiplication equations with these numbers.

1. 24 6 4   **2.** 15 3 5   **3.** 2 8 16   **4.** 9 54 6   **5.** 4 32 8

6. 3 4 12   **7.** 2 7 14   **8.** 4 20 5   **9.** 7 42 6   **10.** 7 8 56

11. 3 27 9   **12.** 2 6 12   **13.** 45 9 5   **14.** 5 40 8   **15.** 7 35 5

Set 14 *pages 34–35*

1. 6×10 **2.** 9×100 **3.** $1{,}000 \times 10$ **4.** 80×5 **5.** $6 \times 7{,}000$

6. 40×30 **7.** 60×95 **8.** 80×400 **9.** 700×20 **10.** $60 \times 4{,}000$

11. $27 \times 1{,}000$ **12.** $270 \times 1{,}000$ **13.** 30×60 **14.** 90×40 **15.** $300 \times 2{,}000$

16. 900×700 **17.** $6{,}000 \times 60$ **18.** $800 \times 7{,}000$ **19.** $6{,}000 \times 6{,}000$ **20.** $8{,}000 \times 500$

21. 800×400 **22.** $700 \times 2{,}000$ **23.** $900 \times 3{,}000$ **24.** $7{,}000 \times 7{,}000$ **25.** $5{,}000 \times 700$

Set 15 *pages 36–37*   Estimate each product.

1. 85×43 **2.** 63×39 **3.** 55×72 **4.** 72×36 **5.** 29×31

6. 42×749 **7.** 56×821 **8.** 83×391 **9.** 74×576 **10.** 66×529

11. 517×139 **12.** 762×253 **13.** 328×943 **14.** 211×111 **15.** 425×198

16. $38 \times 13 \times 47$ **17.** $21 \times 42 \times 86$ **18.** $57 \times 19 \times 12$ **19.** $27 \times 33 \times 46$

Set 16 *pages 38–39*

1. 34×6 **2.** 78×3 **3.** 80×4 **4.** 70×6 **5.** 136×2 **6.** 436×4 **7.** 537×2 **8.** 617×6

9. 640×8 **10.** 261×4 **11.** 623×3 **12.** 214×5 **13.** 724×3 **14.** 160×7 **15.** 560×9 **16.** 362×6

17. $9{,}746 \times 5$ **18.** $8{,}004 \times 7$ **19.** $6{,}720 \times 8$ **20.** $1{,}276 \times 9$ **21.** $7{,}272 \times 6$ **22.** $2{,}565 \times 4$

23. 8×25 **24.** 6×72 **25.** 7×87 **26.** 5×643 **27.** 4×612

28. $2 \times 2{,}729$ **29.** $4 \times 4{,}325$ **30.** $3 \times 2{,}567$ **31.** $6 \times 6{,}541$ **32.** $5 \times 2{,}728$

Set 17 *pages 40–41*

1. 23
    × 30

2. 39
    × 40

3. 47
    × 30

4. 63
    × 20

5. 55
    × 40

6. 624
    × 80

7. 564
    × 40

8. 873
    × 20

9. 743
    × 50

10. 2,724
     × 30

11. 4,800
     × 60

12. 7,204
     × 80

13. 6,542
     × 70

14. 8,765
     × 90

15. 65 × 30

16. 48 × 50

17. 3,007 × 40

18. 2,125 × 60

19. 6,324 × 70

Set 18 *pages 42–43*

1. 34
    × 21

2. 71
    × 42

3. 68
    × 29

4. 45
    × 23

5. 74
    × 55

6. 82
    × 34

7. 94
    × 34

8. 58
    × 39

9. 463
    × 75

10. 341
     × 86

11. 106
     × 47

12. 305
     × 83

13. 639
     × 82

14. 417
     × 58

15. 507
     × 49

16. 859
     × 67

17. 8,247
     ×   83

18. 8,316
     ×   94

19. 4,278
     ×   45

20. 3,967
     ×   53

21. 8,437
     ×   61

22. 3,096
     ×   82

23. 36 × 85

24. 27 × 346

25. 18 × 360

26. 35 × 536

27. 56 × 2,680

28. 72 × 3,571

29. 53 × 90,175

30. 38 × 90,034

31. 35 × 22 × 12

32. 44 × 10 × 11

33. 67 × 43 × 72

34. 85 × 73 × 34

Set 19 *pages 44–45*

1. 597
    × 486

2. 570
    × 845

3. 409
    × 832

4. 480
    × 906

5. 254
    × 362

6. 847
    × 600

7. 636
    × 408

8. 705
    × 318

9. 748
    × 302

10. 821
     × 613

11. 207
     × 340

12. 747
     × 340

13. 396
     × 800

14. 639
     × 409

15. 466
     × 729

16. 657
     × 387

17. 2,375
     ×   400

18. 6,178
     ×   900

19. 5,346
     ×   803

20. 1,809
     ×   509

21. 2,750
     ×   306

22. 4,703
     ×   562

23. 618 × 203

24. 459 × 761

25. 1,251 × 720

26. 6,367 × 488

27. 5,834 × 604

MORE PRACTICE

Set 20 *pages 46–47*   Tell which operation you would use to solve the problem. Then find the answer.

1. Chris works in the shop 4 days every week for 8 hours each day. How many hours does he work each week?

2. At Midtown College, 117 freshmen tried out for varsity sports. 72 of them were trying out for football. How many were trying out for other sports?

3. The zoo had 125 porpoise shows this summer. There were 250 people at each show. How many people saw the shows?

4. Of 738 runners who began a marathon, only 446 finished the race. How many dropped out along the way?

5. Tony collects sports magazines. Randi gave him 23 magazines. His collection had 52 magazines. How many magazines does Tony have now?

6. The band students sold 4 kinds of school pennants at the games. They had 225 pennants of each kind. How many pennants did the band have?

Set 21 *pages 50–51*   Solve each problem.

1. Angelo is shopping for a new bike. He can choose from 3 models and 4 colors. List the different choices Angelo has for his new bike.

2. The bike shop sells 2 styles of handlebars. How many different ways can Angelo choose one model, one color, and one style of handlebars for his new bike?

3. Angelo can choose from 2 lights, 3 reflectors, and 2 horns. How many different ways can Angelo choose one light, one reflector, and one horn?

4. The bike shop sells 3 styles and 2 colors for the saddle of a bike. How many choices does Angelo have for the saddle?

5. Angelo can choose from 2 kinds of brakes and 4 kinds of tires for his bike. How many choices does he have?

6. Angelo has 4 ways to get from his home to school. He has 6 ways to get from school to the park. How many ways can Angelo get from his home to the park by way of the school?

Set 22 *pages 52–53*   Write each number in standard form.

1. 2^5 2. 4^2 3. 3^5 4. 5^4 5. 7^3 6. 9^3

7. $2^3 \times 3$ 8. $3^3 \times 2$ 9. $3^3 \times 4^4$ 10. $2^3 \times 3^3$ 11. $2^3 \times 3^5$ 12. $2^5 \times 5^2$

Write each product with exponents.

13. 2×2 14. $4 \times 4 \times 4$ 15. $4 \times 4 \times 4 \times 4$ 16. $2 \times 2 \times 4 \times 4$ 17. $3 \times 3 \times 5 \times 5$

18. $2 \times 2 \times 2 \times 7 \times 7$ 19. $3 \times 3 \times 3 \times 5 \times 5$ 20. $5 \times 5 \times 5 \times 6 \times 6$

21. $8 \times 8 \times 8 \times 4 \times 4$ 22. $9 \times 9 \times 9 \times 9 \times 9$ 23. $5 \times 5 \times 3 \times 3 \times 3 \times 3 \times 3$

Set 23 *pages 54–55*   List the first 8 multiples of each number.

1. 4   **2.** 10   **3.** 14   **4.** 30   **5.** 16   **6.** 21   **7.** 18   **8.** 40   **9.** 50   **10.** 60

Find two common multiples of each pair of numbers.

11. 3 and 4   **12.** 6 and 7   **13.** 3 and 9   **14.** 5 and 7   **15.** 2 and 6   **16.** 3 and 7

17. 5 and 10   **18.** 3 and 10   **19.** 4 and 16   **20.** 6 and 12   **21.** 4 and 12   **22.** 7 and 14

Find the least common multiple.

23. 2 and 7   **24.** 5 and 6   **25.** 3 and 5   **26.** 4 and 5   **27.** 7 and 8

28. 7 and 14   **29.** 8 and 16   **30.** 6 and 15   **31.** 10 and 20   **32.** 20 and 30

33. 9 and 15   **34.** 6 and 8   **35.** 4 and 14   **36.** 12 and 15   **37.** 25 and 30

Set 24 *pages 56–57*   Solve each problem.

1. How many games are there in a round-robin tournament with 7 teams?

2. How many games are there in a round-robin tournament with 9 teams?

3. What is the tenth triangular number?

4. Twelve people all shake hands with each other. How many handshakes are there?

Set 25 *pages 62–63*

1. $3\overline{)16}$ **2.** $4\overline{)21}$ **3.** $2\overline{)17}$ **4.** $5\overline{)34}$ **5.** $4\overline{)23}$ **6.** $5\overline{)26}$ **7.** $7\overline{)44}$ **8.** $9\overline{)49}$

9. $5\overline{)42}$ **10.** $6\overline{)39}$ **11.** $3\overline{)14}$ **12.** $8\overline{)71}$ **13.** $7\overline{)20}$ **14.** $5\overline{)33}$ **15.** $6\overline{)47}$ **16.** $8\overline{)39}$

17. $7\overline{)16}$ **18.** $5\overline{)13}$ **19.** $4\overline{)26}$ **20.** $9\overline{)75}$ **21.** $5\overline{)41}$ **22.** $6\overline{)58}$ **23.** $4\overline{)38}$ **24.** $9\overline{)55}$

25. $17 \div 3$ **26.** $19 \div 9$ **27.** $22 \div 5$ **28.** $60 \div 8$ **29.** $62 \div 7$ **30.** $25 \div 4$

31. $56 \div 6$ **32.** $39 \div 4$ **33.** $15 \div 2$ **34.** $31 \div 5$ **35.** $22 \div 6$ **36.** $43 \div 7$

37. $15 \div 4$ **38.** $18 \div 5$ **39.** $36 \div 7$ **40.** $47 \div 5$ **41.** $73 \div 8$ **42.** $46 \div 5$

List two divisors of each number.

43. 24   **44.** 15   **45.** 20   **46.** 28   **47.** 56   **48.** 18   **49.** 12   **50.** 30   **51.** 45

52. 64   **53.** 40   **54.** 42   **55.** 72   **56.** 96   **57.** 84   **58.** 48   **59.** 36   **60.** 27

List four numbers that are divisible by the given number.

61. 5   **62.** 3   **63.** 2   **64.** 6

RE PRACTICE

Set 26 *pages 64-65*

1. $6\overline{)73}$ **2.** $9\overline{)93}$ **3.** $2\overline{)91}$ **4.** $5\overline{)96}$ **5.** $4\overline{)64}$ **6.** $4\overline{)72}$ **7.** $8\overline{)97}$

8. $6\overline{)391}$ **9.** $5\overline{)423}$ **10.** $3\overline{)189}$ **11.** $8\overline{)728}$ **12.** $7\overline{)209}$ **13.** $5\overline{)579}$ **14.** $9\overline{)840}$

15. $7\overline{)2,340}$ **16.** $8\overline{)6,755}$ **17.** $4\overline{)9,740}$ **18.** $9\overline{)5,620}$ **19.** $5\overline{)8,355}$ **20.** $3\overline{)8,505}$

21. $750 \div 8$ **22.** $423 \div 5$ **23.** $189 \div 3$ **24.** $736 \div 2$ **25.** $794 \div 4$ **26.** $368 \div 6$

27. $9,863 \div 3$ **28.** $8,528 \div 6$ **29.** $8,405 \div 5$ **30.** $6,711 \div 4$ **31.** $7,992 \div 7$

Set 27 *pages 66-67*

1. $3\overline{)122}$ **2.** $8\overline{)164}$ **3.** $7\overline{)425}$ **4.** $8\overline{)247}$ **5.** $5\overline{)538}$ **6.** $7\overline{)740}$

7. $7\overline{)2,114}$ **8.** $9\overline{)1,845}$ **9.** $5\overline{)3,504}$ **10.** $8\overline{)2,406}$ **11.** $4\overline{)2,680}$ **12.** $3\overline{)2,462}$

13. $9,274 \div 9$ **14.** $7,496 \div 7$ **15.** $9,001 \div 3$ **16.** $6,035 \div 5$ **17.** $3,248 \div 8$

18. $15,468 \div 7$ **19.** $70,201 \div 5$ **20.** $16,321 \div 8$ **21.** $24,243 \div 4$ **22.** $12,452 \div 3$

23. $20,754 \div 9$ **24.** $24,096 \div 8$ **25.** $49,742 \div 7$ **26.** $31,860 \div 6$ **27.** $21,672 \div 9$

Set 28 *pages 68-69* Find the average for each set of numbers.

1. 5 12 14 16 18 **2.** 11 13 15 **3.** 45 46 47 **4.** 2 4 6 8 10

5. 15 20 25 24 1 **6.** 24 26 28 **7.** 213 103 **8.** 71 91 91 79 81 157

9. 17 19 21 23 **10.** 52 53 54 **11.** 480 102 **12.** 56 53 66 68 84 75

Set 29 *pages 70-71* Solve each problem.

1. There are 178 pirates on a sinking ship. How many 7-person rowboats are needed to save all the pirates?

2. The pirates had 215 meters of rope. They cut as many 8-meter pieces as they could. How many meters of rope were left over?

3. The cook on the pirate ship made 330 cups of soup. How many 4-cup bowls can be filled with soup?

4. If 8 pirates share 950 gold coins equally, how many coins will be left over?

5. The pirates need 110 boards to fix the deck of the ship. They can make 9 boards from each tree they cut down. How many trees must they cut?

6. The pirates had 492 jewels. They put the jewels in bags that each hold 9 jewels. How many bags do they need to hold all the jewels?

Set 30 *pages 72–73*

1. 21)79 **2.** 23)98 **3.** 12)49 **4.** 12)28 **5.** 40)285 **6.** 30)273

7. 60)181 **8.** 90)362 **9.** 80)483 **10.** 51)172 **11.** 62)258 **12.** 33)198

13. 436 ÷ 44 **14.** 512 ÷ 52 **15.** 206 ÷ 23 **16.** 312 ÷ 36 **17.** 208 ÷ 29 **18.** 159 ÷ 26

19. 122 ÷ 14 **20.** 114 ÷ 15 **21.** 103 ÷ 13 **22.** 115 ÷ 18 **23.** 546 ÷ 74 **24.** 697 ÷ 76

25. 149 ÷ 23 **26.** 632 ÷ 71 **27.** 824 ÷ 92 **28.** 736 ÷ 84 **29.** 523 ÷ 62 **30.** 426 ÷ 51

Set 31 *pages 74–75*

1. 55)304 **2.** 39)285 **3.** 18)140 **4.** 19)103 **5.** 19)150 **6.** 16)108

7. 18)161 **8.** 28)144 **9.** 37)306 **10.** 27)216 **11.** 57)179 **12.** 49)372

13. 431 ÷ 78 **14.** 495 ÷ 85 **15.** 529 ÷ 88 **16.** 443 ÷ 48 **17.** 569 ÷ 89 **18.** 361 ÷ 79

19. 218 ÷ 37 **20.** 288 ÷ 48 **21.** 129 ÷ 16 **22.** 136 ÷ 17 **23.** 226 ÷ 68 **24.** 484 ÷ 65

25. 232 ÷ 25 **26.** 541 ÷ 62 **27.** 323 ÷ 56 **28.** 645 ÷ 72 **29.** 168 ÷ 25 **30.** 136 ÷ 15

Set 32 *pages 76–77*

1. 32)842 **2.** 21)721 **3.** 28)941 **4.** 43)739 **5.** 38)837 **6.** 42)739

7. 79)858 **8.** 66)957 **9.** 15)326 **10.** 35)643 **11.** 23)571 **12.** 42)697

13. 5,014 ÷ 88 **14.** 2,923 ÷ 34 **15.** 6,065 ÷ 67 **16.** 2,379 ÷ 26 **17.** 3,173 ÷ 63

18. 3,951 ÷ 43 **19.** 2,327 ÷ 28 **20.** 1,217 ÷ 17 **21.** 1,129 ÷ 14 **22.** 1,363 ÷ 16

23. 1,154 ÷ 81 **24.** 2,458 ÷ 25 **25.** 2,426 ÷ 27 **26.** 2,215 ÷ 23 **27.** 2,871 ÷ 32

Set 33 *pages 78–79*

1. 60)8,133 **2.** 70)8,632 **3.** 30)9,347 **4.** 32)4,555 **5.** 26)6,343

6. 19)8,241 **7.** 70)8,591 **8.** 38)8,556 **9.** 27)7,893 **10.** 38)8,475

11. 23)78,591 **12.** 53)93,651 **13.** 37)83,352 **14.** 57)87,534 **15.** 27)53,873

16. 47)27,403 **17.** 54)24,135 **18.** 81)34,124 **19.** 66)15,312 **20.** 40)17,661

MORE PRACTICE

Set 34 *pages 80–81*

1. $43\overline{)3,044}$ 2. $54\overline{)3,248}$ 3. $21\overline{)1,069}$ 4. $92\overline{)3,683}$ 5. $89\overline{)1,832}$ 6. $22\overline{)8,816}$

7. $78\overline{)2,405}$ 8. $59\overline{)7,716}$ 9. $34\overline{)6,834}$ 10. $68\overline{)8,905}$ 11. $27\overline{)9,995}$ 12. $38\overline{)9,138}$

13. $18\overline{)9,720}$ 14. $19\overline{)6,085}$ 15. $80\overline{)48,072}$ 16. $71\overline{)36,180}$ 17. $93\overline{)19,241}$

18. $56\overline{)28,542}$ 19. $90\overline{)18,602}$ 20. $55\overline{)27,885}$ 21. $73\overline{)59,057}$ 22. $54\overline{)11,275}$

23. $86\overline{)26,098}$ 24. $79\overline{)31,658}$ 25. $76\overline{)23,408}$ 26. $39\overline{)16,000}$ 27. $63\overline{)18,924}$

Set 35 *pages 82–83*   Tell what operation you would use to solve the problem. Then solve the problem.

1. A color TV is on sale for $400. A black-and-white set at the same store sells for $100. How much more does the color TV cost?

2. The Kagins bought a new TV. They paid $600 for the set, $60 for the antenna, and $130 for the remote-control device. What was the total cost?

3. The television show *Lassie* ran for 17 years. If there was a show every week, how many shows were there?
(1 year = 52 weeks)

4. In 30 days, a total of 8,100 people attended the music festival. What was the average daily attendance?

5. Laura watches TV an average of 2 hours per day. John watches TV an average of 1 hour per day. How much longer does Laura watch TV each day?

6. Ramon practiced piano 25 minutes on Monday, 36 minutes on Tuesday, and 50 minutes on Wednesday. What was the total number of minutes that he practiced?

7. The price for cassette tapes is $4 each. What is the cost of 12 cassette tapes?

8. Mack received a total of $6,960 for selling 58 car radios. What was the average price of each radio sold?

Set 36 *pages 86–87*

1. $8 \times n = 120$ 2. $n \times 4 = 856$ 3. $192 = 6 \times n$ 4. $2 \times n = 298$ 5. $350 = n \times 7$

6. $n \times 3 = 195$ 7. $225 = n \times 5$ 8. $7 \times n = 343$ 9. $n \times 8 = 512$ 10. $5 \times n = 625$

11. $663 = n \times 13$ 12. $16 \times n = 512$ 13. $n \times 35 = 525$ 14. $289 = n \times 17$

15. $5,840 = 80 \times n$ 16. $n \times 40 = 3,680$ 17. $21 \times n = 1,827$ 18. $2,244 = n \times 33$

19. $50 \times n = 7,500$ 20. $1,150 = 46 \times n$ 21. $92 \times n = 3,128$ 22. $1,720 = 20 \times n$

23. $n \times 38 = 1,596$ 24. $60 \times n = 2,880$ 25. $2,700 = 90 \times n$ 26. $36 \times n = 1,620$

Set 37 *pages 88–89*   Write an equation. Then find the answer.

1. John weighs about 12 times his weight at birth. He weighs 96 pounds. How much did John weigh at birth?

2. Ed spent $36 to fill his car with gas. His car holds 18 gallons. What was the cost of gas per gallon?

3. 5 members of the Spruce family bought tickets to an amusement park for a total cost of $30. What was the price per ticket?

4. The house that cost $35,000 in 1950, cost 5 times that amount in 1980. How much did the house cost in 1980?

5. Iromie spent $125 on a suit and $50 on a pair of shoes. How much more did Iromie spend for the suit?

6. Raoul's suit cost about 9 times as much as his shirt. His shirt cost $20. How much did Raoul's suit cost?

7. Property taxes that were $325 in 1950, increased to $2,400 in 1980. How much more were property taxes in 1980?

8. Matt earned a total of $615 in 3 months. How much did Matt earn per month?

Set 38 *pages 90–91*   Answer *yes* or *no*.

1. Is 8 a factor of 72?
2. Is 7 a factor of 34?
3. Is 6 a factor of 3?
4. Is 5 a factor of 40?
5. Is 3 a factor of 23?
6. Is 9 a factor of 81?
7. Is 4 a factor of 24?
8. Is 5 a factor of 52?
9. Is 6 a factor of 18?

List all the factors of each number.

10. 3   11. 24   12. 4   13. 36   14. 9   15. 17   16. 21   17. 26   18. 19

19. 29   20. 16   21. 54   22. 31   23. 60   24. 27   25. 33   26. 44   27. 99

28. 37   29. 93   30. 25   31. 22   32. 5   33. 51   34. 41   35. 6   36. 23

Find the common factors of each pair of numbers. Circle the greatest common factor.

37. 6; 15   38. 7; 13   39. 10; 25   40. 5; 11   41. 20; 28   42. 24; 40

43. 14; 21   44. 6; 10   45. 8; 8   46. 5; 35   47. 16; 20   48. 18; 38

49. 6; 20   50. 9; 36   51. 5; 30   52. 7; 56   53. 5; 50   54. 35; 45

Set 39 *pages 92–93*   List all the factors of each number. Then tell if the number is prime, or composite, or neither.

1. 22   2. 12   3. 7   4. 51   5. 16   6. 57   7. 36   8. 8   9. 48

10. 64   11. 20   12. 33   13. 50   14. 75   15. 66   16. 13   17. 96   18. 19

MORE PRACTICE

Set 40 *pages 100–101*   Write each decimal in words.

1. 0.6   **2.** 0.12   **3.** 0.008   **4.** 0.09   **5.** 0.015   **6.** 0.825   **7.** 0.932

8. 0.3   **9.** 0.75   **10.** 0.235   **11.** 0.007   **12.** 0.057   **13.** 0.209   **14.** 0.063

Write the decimal.

15. six tenths   **16.** eight tenths   **17.** three hundredths

18. three thousandths   **19.** twelve hundredths   **20.** eighteen thousandths

21. forty-nine thousandths   **22.** nine hundred two thousandths

23. five hundred seventy-one thousandths   **24.** eighty-five hundredths

Set 41 *pages 102–103*   Tell what each 3 means.

1. 2.13   **2.** 8.2635   **3.** 21.308   **4.** 32.978   **5.** 129.438   **6.** 0.75431

7. 6.45973   **8.** 2,352.6   **9.** 43.761   **10.** 49.346   **11.** 732.97   **12.** 1.608003

Tell how many decimal places are in each number.

13. 5.4   **14.** 8.0072   **15.** 9.272   **16.** 3.45   **17.** 3.82043   **18.** 1.706002

In each exercise place a decimal point to show 3 decimal places.

19. 845   **20.** 3124   **21.** 7168   **22.** 504   **23.** 23457   **24.** 617432

Write each decimal.

25. 6 ones 2 hundredths   **26.** 5 hundred thousand five millionths

27. thirty-three ten-thousandths   **28.** twelve and twenty thousandths

Set 42 *pages 104–105*   Write each number in hundredths.

1. 0.8   **2.** 0.2   **3.** 8.8   **4.** 4   **5.** 7.6   **6.** 12.500   **7.** 3.7   **8.** 5.6

Write each number in thousandths.

9. 0.48   **10.** 0.2   **11.** 5.85   **12.** 3.92   **13.** 5   **14.** 0.75   **15.** 16.32   **16.** 24.04

Compare. Use <, =, >.

17. 0.08 ● 0.9   **18.** 0.43 ● 0.28   **19.** 0.751 ● 0.739   **20.** 0.83 ● 0.830

List these numbers in order from least to greatest.

21. 0.15   1.5   5.1   **22.** 1.18   1.81   1.8   **23.** 97.6   96.7   97.06

Set 43 *pages 106–107* Round to the nearest one.

1. 5.4   **2.** 2.5   **3.** 21.2   **4.** 27.7   **5.** 32.6   **6.** 51.1   **7.** 63.3   **8.** 70.4

9. 3.87   **10.** 6.15   **11.** 1.58   **12.** 4.50   **13.** 6.05   **14.** 8.49   **15.** 1.11   **16.** 50.7

Round to the nearest tenth.

17. 0.27   **18.** 0.77   **19.** 2.25   **20.** 6.19   **21.** 3.42   **22.** 8.94   **23.** 6.78   **24.** 7.09

25. 7.03   **26.** 5.98   **27.** 9.97   **28.** 6.14   **29.** 7.25   **30.** 1.15   **31.** 8.73   **32.** 5.02

Round to the nearest hundredth.

33. 7.107   **34.** 2.055   **35.** 4.603   **36.** 8.432   **37.** 2.727   **38.** 7.876   **39.** 9.804

Round to the nearest thousandth.

40. 6.2178   **41.** 9.7543   **42.** 5.2135   **43.** 6.7002   **44.** 7.8597   **45.** 4.2198

Set 44 *pages 108–109* Estimate each sum or difference. Round to the nearest one.

1. 6.23 + 8.81   **2.** 4.93 + 6.87   **3.** 7.75 − 2.25   **4.** 20.2 + 15.1   **5.** 9.36 + 5.77

6. 9.23 − 3.75   **7.** 6.714 + 2.17   **8.** 15.4 − 10.1   **9.** 8.63 + 4.31   **10.** 18.3 − 8.99

11. $12.25 + $13.74   **12.** $2.75 − $1.25   **13.** $35.52 + $16.45   **14.** $18.47 − $16.51

15. $23.12 + $14.53 + $6.74   **16.** $125.75 + $63.45 + $20.13   **17.** $86.44 + $18.52 + $1.96

Set 45 *pages 110–111*

1. 5.3
    + 7.8

2. 6.5
    + 8.9

3. 64.7
    + 8.3

4.   2.6
    + 35.7

5. 9.28
    + 5.74

6. 7.83
    + 8.17

7.   8.31
   47.008
   + 1.235

8. 12.63
     8.497
   + 23.2

9.   4.35
    76.8
   + 2.10

10. 53.02
      9.8
   + 6.43

11. 5.484
     7.391
   + 62.2

12. 9.25
    83.007
   + 61.0723

13. 27.63 + 82.97   **14.** 43.21 + 8.37   **15.** 5.684 + 37.43   **16.** 14.53 + 6.38

17. 83.5 + 2.634   **18.** 381.4 + 1.654   **19.** 189.167 + 28.03   **20.** 216.7 + 2.309

21. 9.07 + 7.3 + 18.4   **22.** 96.8 + 23.9 + 56.35   **23.** 64.23 + 71.49 + 9.68

24. 34.56 + 45.4 + 345.6   **25.** 125.6 + 32.8 + 2.16   **26.** 26.7 + 19.3 + 45.8

27. 42.78 + 66.5 + 108.4   **28.** 139.4 + 28.6 + 3.99   **29.** 88.9 + 16.6 + 77.2

MORE PRACTICE

Set 46 pages 112–113

1. 4.63 − 1.22		**2.** 7.35 − 4.88		**3.** 16.59 − 8.72		**4.** 23.29 − 6.83		**5.** 67.18 − 25.09		**6.** 29.18 − 15.12	

7. 53.4 − 26.358		**8.** 72.916 − 36.25		**9.** 76.824 − 48.273		**10.** 84.26 − 51.288		**11.** 35.8 − 16.953		**12.** 42.713 − 6.835	

13. $0.24 - 0.17$ **14.** $0.5 - 0.29$ **15.** $63 - 49.53$ **16.** $14.24 - 12.56$

17. $145.3 - 37.604$ **18.** $236.4 - 20.002$ **19.** $6.751 - 3.245$ **20.** $163.73 - 45.928$

21. $257.62 - 134.7$ **22.** $670.68 - 245.72$ **23.** $9.891 - 8.59$ **24.** $354.72 - 222.83$

Set 47 pages 114–115   Make a table to solve each problem.

1. On Hay's farm, there were 17 hens and cows. If he counted a total of 54 legs, how many of each kind of animal were on the farm?

2. Mr. Post bought some fifteen-cent stamps and some ten-cent stamps. If he paid $3.10 for 24 stamps, how many of each kind did he buy?

3. Tara spent $12.70 for 14 fish for her aquarium. She bought goldfish for $0.65 each and angelfish for $1.25 each. How many of each kind of fish did she buy?

4. One day 21 coins were collected from a parking meter. The meter takes only nickels and dimes. If the coins totaled $1.75, how many of each kind of coin were collected?

5. Curtis has 17 coins in his pocket. The coins are dimes and quarters. He has $2.75. How many of each kind of coin does he have in his pocket?

6. The school bookstore sells pencils for $0.20 each and pens for $0.39 each. Jane spent $1.78 on a total of 7 pencils and pens. How many of each did she buy?

Set 48 pages 118–119   Try and check to solve each problem.

1. The sum of two numbers is 48 and their difference is 16. What are the two numbers?

2. The difference of two numbers is 4.8 and their sum is 12. What are the two numbers?

3. The book cost $18 less than the cassette tape. The two together cost $51. How much was the cassette tape?

4. One number is 5.7 more than another number. The sum of the two numbers is 20.7. What are the two numbers?

5. The sum of two numbers is 18. One number is 2 times the other. What are the two numbers?

6. The jacket cost $21 more than the shirt. The two together cost $63. How much was the shirt?

Set 49 *pages 124-125*   Place a decimal point correctly in each circled number.

1. 4.2 × 33 = (1386)   **2.** 0.54 × 9.01 = (48654)   **3.** 8.004 × 1.2 = (96048)

4. 6.4 × 2.7 = (1728)   **5.** 2.7 × 1.83 = (4941)   **6.** 3.15 × 2.001 = (630315)

Multiply.

7. 12.5   **8.** 1.25   **9.** 1.25   **10.** 0.218   **11.** 21.8   **12.** 3.27   **13.** 6.48
   × 9   × 0.9   × 9   × 0.6   × 0.6   × 0.5   × 0.3

14. 4.2 × 3.8   **15.** 9 × 2.4   **16.** 0.58 × 0.36   **17.** 0.077 × 2.9   **18.** 0.0284 × 9.31

Set 50 *pages 126-127*

1. 0.4   **2.** 0.04   **3.** 0.004   **4.** 0.004   **5.** 0.0004   **6.** 0.08   **7.** 0.06
   × 0.9   × 0.9   × 0.9   × 0.09   × 0.09   × 0.6   × 0.03

8. 0.007   **9.** 0.018   **10.** 0.053   **11.** 1.001   **12.** 0.356   **13.** 0.028   **14.** 0.18
   × 0.05   × 0.2   × 0.6   × 0.047   × 0.124   × 0.36   × 0.02

15. 0.3 × 0.01 × 0.5   **16.** 0.008 × 0.09 × 0.7   **17.** 0.012 × 0.63 × 1.5

Set 51 *pages 128-129*

1. 10 × 0.3   **2.** 100 × 0.3   **3.** 1,000 × 0.3   **4.** 10 × 0.29

5. 100 × 0.29   **6.** 1,000 × 0.29   **7.** 10 × 5.03   **8.** 100 × 5.03

9. 10 × 0.006   **10.** 100 × 4.316   **11.** 1,000 × 9.065   **12.** 2.904 × 1,000

13. 82.613 × 100   **14.** 8.446 × 1,000   **15.** 1,000 × 941.80   **16.** 100 × 427.6345

Set 52 *pages 130-131*

1. 8)5.6   **2.** 2)0.70   **3.** 3)8.7   **4.** 6)7.8   **5.** 9)72.9   **6.** 5)7.0

7. 8)25.6   **8.** 4)0.492   **9.** 3)0.771   **10.** 9)4.86   **11.** 6)5.10   **12.** 7)9.17

13. 83)41.5   **14.** 74)29.6   **15.** 32)51.2   **16.** 21)58.8   **17.** 19)17.1   **18.** 25)62.5

19. 8.4 ÷ 7   **20.** 7.2 ÷ 4   **21.** 229.6 ÷ 4   **22.** 3.85 ÷ 5   **23.** 0.75 ÷ 5

24. 91.8 ÷ 27   **25.** 98.9 ÷ 43   **26.** 68.08 ÷ 37   **27.** 544.5 ÷ 33   **28.** 9.828 ÷ 27

MORE PRACTICE

Set 53 *pages 132–133*

1. $9\overline{)0.108}$ **2.** $7\overline{)0.182}$ **3.** $9\overline{)0.315}$ **4.** $33\overline{)2.31}$ **5.** $42\overline{)3.78}$ **6.** $28\overline{)1.568}$

7. $52\overline{)3.12}$ **8.** $74\overline{)3.034}$ **9.** $85\overline{)1.105}$ **10.** $26\overline{)0.234}$ **11.** $37\overline{)0.185}$ **12.** $63\overline{)3.087}$

13. $0.64 \div 8$ **14.** $0.63 \div 9$ **15.** $0.54 \div 6$ **16.** $0.072 \div 9$ **17.** $0.84 \div 14$

18. $0.65 \div 13$ **19.** $0.065 \div 13$ **20.** $0.06 \div 2$ **21.** $0.08 \div 4$ **22.** $0.096 \div 8$

Set 54 *pages 134–135*   Solve each problem.

1. Barry ran in three marathons. He completed distances of 6.8 miles, 9.3 miles, and 8.2 miles. What is the average distance he ran?

2. Peter ran in a charity race. He took pledges of $0.10, $0.15, $0.20, $0.10, $0.20, $0.05, and $0.25. What is the average pledge?

3. Marie received a pledge from her mother of $0.10 per mile plus a bonus of $2 for running at least 5 miles. Marie ran 7 miles. How much did her mother pay?

4. Sandra took pledges of $0.08, $0.16, $0.20, and $0.15. Donna took pledges of $0.05, $0.08, and $0.12. What was their combined average pledge?

Set 55 *pages 136–137*   Place the decimal point correctly in each quotient.

1. $0.7\overline{)2.8}^{\;4}$ **2.** $0.7\overline{)0.28}^{\;04}$ **3.** $0.7\overline{)0.028}^{\;004}$ **4.** $0.09\overline{)0.72}^{\;8}$ **5.** $0.09\overline{)0.072}^{\;08}$

Divide.

6. $0.8\overline{)0.48}$ **7.** $0.02\overline{)1.74}$ **8.** $0.03\overline{)1.68}$ **9.** $0.51\overline{)17.34}$ **10.** $0.05\overline{)3.95}$

11. $2.8\overline{)9.52}$ **12.** $0.52\overline{)18.72}$ **13.** $0.61\overline{)29.28}$ **14.** $0.12\overline{)9.36}$ **15.** $0.83\overline{)1.577}$

16. $0.45\overline{)8.55}$ **17.** $0.39\overline{)9.75}$ **18.** $7.5\overline{)35.25}$ **19.** $0.025\overline{)0.625}$ **20.** $0.72\overline{)1.656}$

Set 56 *pages 138–139*

1. $0.4\overline{)72}$ **2.** $0.3\overline{)78}$ **3.** $6.2\overline{)248}$ **4.** $0.6\overline{)18}$ **5.** $0.05\overline{)23}$ **6.** $0.9\overline{)81}$

7. $0.82\overline{)12.3}$ **8.** $0.95\overline{)13.3}$ **9.** $0.16\overline{)4}$ **10.** $0.25\overline{)9}$ **11.** $0.45\overline{)15.3}$ **12.** $0.25\overline{)6}$

13. $0.32\overline{)20.8}$ **14.** $0.18\overline{)365.4}$ **15.** $3.4\overline{)102}$ **16.** $0.25\overline{)8}$ **17.** $0.16\overline{)8}$ **18.** $4.2\overline{)21}$

19. $874 \div 0.38$ **20.** $874 \div 3.8$ **21.** $105 \div 0.15$ **22.** $27.2 \div 0.32$ **23.** $17 \div 0.34$

24. $144 \div 0.6$ **25.** $29.4 \div 0.35$ **26.** $189.9 \div 0.45$ **27.** $16.8 \div 0.42$ **28.** $135 \div 4.5$

Set 57 *pages 140–141*   Divide. Round each quotient to the nearest one.

1. 180 ÷ 7   **2.** 241 ÷ 6   **3.** 42 ÷ 6.1   **4.** 87 ÷ 3.4   **5.** 94 ÷ 3.3

Divide. Round each quotient to the nearest tenth.

6. 5)2.95   **7.** 2)0.5   **8.** 0.7)1.57   **9.** 0.06)0.23   **10.** 0.04)0.17

Divide. Round each quotient to the nearest hundredth.

11. 2)8.906   **12.** 5)0.386   **13.** 0.5)0.316   **14.** 1.5)0.107   **15.** 1.2)0.113

16. 7 ÷ 23   **17.** 4.53 ÷ 6   **18.** 3.1 ÷ 0.09   **19.** 7 ÷ 27   **20.** 0.23 ÷ 0.06

21. 9 ÷ 23   **22.** 8.16 ÷ 7   **23.** 6.2 ÷ 0.3   **24.** 83 ÷ 15   **25.** 77 ÷ 12

Set 58 *pages 142–143*

1. 291 ÷ 10   **2.** 291 ÷ 100   **3.** 294 ÷ 1,000   **4.** 82.5 ÷ 10   **5.** 0.32 ÷ 10

6. 82.5 ÷ 100   **7.** 82.5 ÷ 1,000   **8.** 2.8 ÷ 10   **9.** 2.8 ÷ 100   **10.** 9.7 ÷ 100

11. 2.8 ÷ 1,000   **12.** 93 ÷ 1,000   **13.** 1.7 ÷ 100   **14.** 4.8 ÷ 1,000   **15.** 75 ÷ 1,000

Set 59 *pages 150–151*   Would you use millimeters, centimeters, meters, or kilometers to measure the

1. length of a dog?   **2.** height of a boy?   **3.** width of a calculator?

4. distance of a marathon race?   **5.** width of a boat?   **6.** width of a toothpick?

Choose the best measure.

7. Length of a ski   **8.** The length of a garden fence   **9.** The length of a flower petal

    1 km   1 m   1 cm   10 km   10 m   10 cm   30 mm   30 cm   30 m

Set 60 *pages 152–153*   Give each measure in meters.

1. 132 cm   **2.** 56 mm   **3.** 3,500 mm   **4.** 330 dm   **5.** 18.4 km   **6.** 21 hm

Give each measure in centimeters.

7. 21.3 m   **8.** 160 mm   **9.** 32 km   **10.** 6 m   **11.** 172 dm   **12.** 5.4 km

Give each measure in millimeters.

13. 24 m   **14.** 14 cm   **15.** 6 km   **16.** 8.6 m   **17.** 39 cm   **18.** 6.6 m

19. 46 cm   **20.** 9 m   **21.** 17 m   **22.** 2.5 m   **23.** 193 m   **24.** 27.15 cm

MORE PRACTICE

Set 61 *pages 154–155*   Give the length of each segment to the nearest millimeter.

1. ├──────┤   **2.** ├────────────┤   **3.** ├───┤   **4.** ├─────┤

Give the length of each segment to the nearest centimeter.

5. ├──────────────┤   **6.** ├───────────┤   **7.** ├──┤

Draw a segment for each of the following lengths.

8. 6 cm   **9.** 36 mm   **10.** 48 mm   **11.** 12.6 cm   **12.** 17 cm   **13.** 40 mm   **14.** 18 cm

Set 62 *pages 156–157*   Find the area of each figure by counting.

1.   **2.**   **3.**

Would you use square millimeters, square centimeters, or square meters to measure the area of

4. a ceiling?   **5.** a garden?   **6.** a sheet of notebook paper?   **7.** a tile floor?

Set 63 *pages 158–159*   Give the volume of each box. The volume of each cube is 1 cm³.

1.   **2.**   **3.**

Set 64 *pages 160–161*   Choose the better measure.

1. Dog
35 g   35 kg

2. Pencil
6 g   6 kg

3. TV set
50 g   50 kg

4. A pail
12 L   12 mL

Give each measure in liters.

5. 7,400 mL   **6.** 6,000 mL   **7.** 12,000 mL   **8.** 752 mL   **9.** 19,200 mL   **10.** 405 mL

Give each measure in milliliters.

11. 7 L   **12.** 28.2 L   **13.** 375 L   **14.** 0.25 L   **15.** 0.8 L   **16.** 13.5 L

Give each measure in kilograms.

17. 7,500 g   **18.** 200 g   **19.** 1,930 mg   **20.** 850 g   **21.** 50 mg   **22.** 14,500 mg

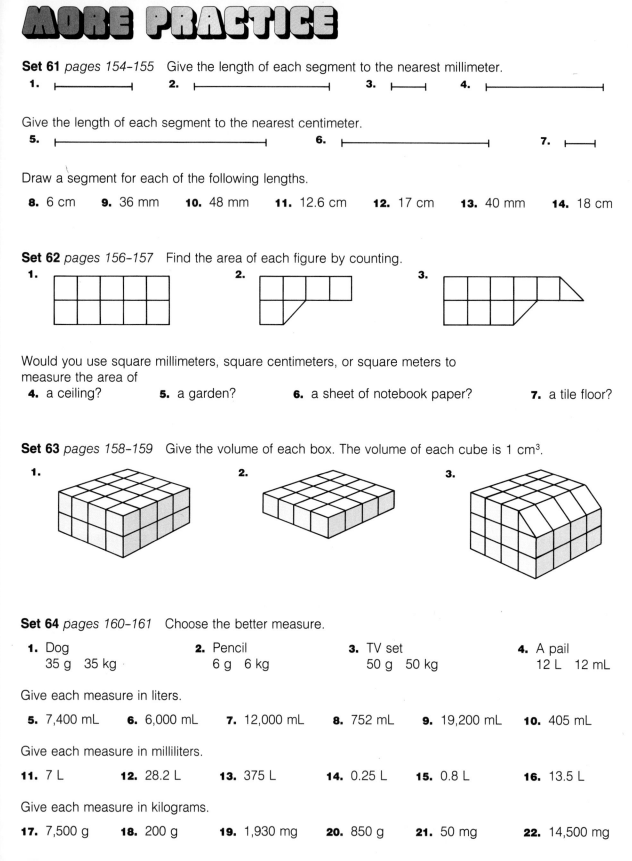

Set 65 *pages 164–165* Choose the best measure.

1. Length of a pencil
   6 in.   6 ft.   6 yd.

2. Width of a door
   2 in.   2 ft.   2 yd.

3. Length of a cane
   3 in.   3 ft.   3 yd.

Give each measure as inches.

4. 4 ft.   **5.** 8 ft.   **6.** 3 yd.   **7.** 3 yd. 1 ft.   **8.** 2 ft. 9 in.   **9.** 4 yd. 11 in.

Give each measure as feet, inches.

10. 19 in.   **11.** 37 in.   **12.** 98 in.   **13.** 125 in.   **14.** 200 in.   **15.** 69 in.

Give each measure as yards, feet, inches.

16. 8 ft. 3 in.   **17.** 11 ft. 2 in.   **18.** 4 ft. 8 in.   **19.** 7 ft. 1 in.   **20.** 78 in.

Set 66 *pages 166–167* Find the area of each figure. Each square represents 1 sq. in.

1.   **2.**   **3.**   **4.**

Find the volume of each box. Each cube represents 1 cu. in.

5.   **6.**   **7.**

Set 67 *pages 168–169* Choose the better measure.

1. Weight of an infant
   7 oz.   7 lb.

2. Glass of milk
   1 c.   1 qt.

3. Box of cereal
   8 oz.   8 lb.

4. A gelatin mold
   4 c.   4 gal.

Give each measure as pints.

5. 3 qt.   **6.** 3 gal.   **7.** 20 c.   **8.** 7 qt. 3 pt.   **9.** 12 qt. 1 pt.

Give each measure as gallons, quarts, pints.

10. 32 pt.   **11.** 6 qt.   **12.** 20 qt.   **13.** 8 qt.   **14.** 40 qt.   **15.** 31 qt.

Give each measure as pounds, ounces.

16. 5 T.   **17.** 95 oz.   **18.** 74 oz.   **19.** 144 oz.   **20.** 100 oz.   **21.** 59 oz.

22. 110 oz.   **23.** 41 oz.   **24.** 62 oz.   **25.** 29 oz.   **26.** 350 oz.   **27.** 5,000 oz.

MORE PRACTICE

Set 68 *pages 172–173*   Add or subtract.

1. 9 ft. 3 in.
  + 6 ft. 2 in.

2. 8 ft. 5 in.
  − 3 ft. 2 in.

3. 7 ft. 6 in.
  − 2 ft. 8 in.

4. 10 gal. 3 qt.
  + 6 gal. 2 qt.

5. 6 lb. 2 oz.
  −   6 oz.

6. 5 lb. 14 oz.
  + 3 lb. 9 oz.

7. 14 gal. 1 qt.
  −   3 qt.

8. 17 ft. 5 in.
   6 ft. 4 in.
  + 7 ft. 6 in.

Set 69 *pages 174–175*   Choose the most sensible answer.

1. Jane is buying tile for the basement and kitchen. The basement has an area of 1,210 sq. ft. and the kitchen has an area of 150 sq. ft. Estimate the total number of square feet of tile she should buy.

   140 sq. ft.   400 sq. ft.   1,400 sq. ft.

2. Sue's house has an area of 2,320 sq. ft. Jan's house has an area of 3,230 sq. ft. Estimate how much larger Jan's house is.

   9 sq. ft.   90 sq. ft.   900 sq. ft.

3. Ed paid $72.49 for 8 ft. 6 in. of fencing. Estimate the cost per foot.

   $0.85 $8.50 $85

4. Upholstery fabric sells for $15 a square yard. Estimate the cost of 57 sq. yd. of upholstery fabric.

   $86 $750 $860

Set 70 *pages 176–177*   Use the map on pages 176–177. Would you set your watch ahead or back when flying from

1. Jackson to Phoenix?   2. Omaha to Detroit?   3. Dallas to Denver?

When it is 5:30 P.M. in Reno, what time is it in

4. Atlanta?   5. Denver?   6. Vancouver?   7. St. Louis?   8. Memphis?

When it is 4:00 A.M. in Phoenix, what time is it in

9. Miami?   10. Eugene?   11. Charleston?   12. Boise?   13. Toronto?

14. Houston?   15. Fairbanks?   16. Louisville?   17. Houston?   18. Pittsburgh?

Set 71 *pages 178–179*   Choose the more sensible temperature.

1. Cold juice
   4°C   40°C

2. Classroom
   22°C   70°C

3. Hot soup
   20°C   80°C

4. Ice cream
   9°C   −5°C

5. Steam
   9°F   212°F

6. Arctic waters
   30°C   1°C

7. Spring day
   20°C   65°C

8. Drinking water
   10°C   70°C

9. Ice cube
   0°C   32°C

10. A cave
   55°F   90°F

Set 72 *pages 186–187*   Write each fraction.

1. one half   **2.** three fourths   **3.** zero sixths   **4.** seven ninths   **5.** six tenths

The vowels are *A, E, I, O, U*. For each word, tell what fraction of the letters are vowels.

6. SKI   **7.** SKATE   **8.** BOAT   **9.** TRACK   **10.** BASEBALL   **11.** SOCCER   **12.** LACROSSE

For each word, tell what fraction of the letters are not vowels.

13. SPORT   **14.** HURDLES   **15.** CHAMPION   **16.** DECATHLON   **17.** WRESTLER   **18.** FIELD

Set 73 *pages 188–189*   Give the missing numbers.

1. $\frac{2}{3} = \frac{\blacksquare}{15}$ **2.** $\frac{1}{3} = \frac{\blacksquare}{9}$ **3.** $\frac{1}{9} = \frac{\blacksquare}{36}$ **4.** $\frac{5}{9} = \frac{\blacksquare}{27}$ **5.** $\frac{5}{7} = \frac{\blacksquare}{35}$ **6.** $\frac{3}{4} = \frac{\blacksquare}{24}$

7. $\frac{7}{8} = \frac{21}{\blacksquare}$ **8.** $\frac{5}{6} = \frac{25}{\blacksquare}$ **9.** $\frac{1}{8} = \frac{4}{\blacksquare}$ **10.** $\frac{9}{10} = \frac{36}{\blacksquare}$ **11.** $\frac{7}{15} = \frac{14}{\blacksquare}$ **12.** $\frac{4}{9} = \frac{8}{\blacksquare}$

13. $\frac{4}{4} = \frac{8}{\blacksquare} = \frac{\blacksquare}{12} = \frac{16}{\blacksquare}$ **14.** $\frac{5}{7} = \frac{10}{\blacksquare} = \frac{\blacksquare}{21} = \frac{20}{\blacksquare}$ **15.** $\frac{4}{5} = \frac{8}{\blacksquare} = \frac{\blacksquare}{15} = \frac{16}{\blacksquare}$ **16.** $\frac{3}{10} = \frac{6}{\blacksquare} = \frac{\blacksquare}{30}$

Set 74 *pages 190–191*   Tell whether the fraction is in lowest terms. Write *yes* or *no*.

1. $\frac{3}{6}$ **2.** $\frac{6}{9}$ **3.** $\frac{3}{4}$ **4.** $\frac{4}{5}$ **5.** $\frac{1}{3}$ **6.** $\frac{4}{8}$ **7.** $\frac{4}{5}$ **8.** $\frac{10}{20}$ **9.** $\frac{8}{28}$ **10.** $\frac{11}{17}$

Write each fraction in lowest terms.

11. $\frac{5}{10}$ **12.** $\frac{4}{6}$ **13.** $\frac{2}{12}$ **14.** $\frac{2}{8}$ **15.** $\frac{3}{12}$ **16.** $\frac{6}{9}$ **17.** $\frac{6}{15}$ **18.** $\frac{14}{35}$ **19.** $\frac{28}{32}$

20. $\frac{7}{14}$ **21.** $\frac{16}{20}$ **22.** $\frac{12}{18}$ **23.** $\frac{10}{15}$ **24.** $\frac{12}{24}$ **25.** $\frac{18}{27}$ **26.** $\frac{6}{30}$ **27.** $\frac{9}{21}$ **28.** $\frac{16}{48}$

Set 75 *pages 192–193*   For each exercise, give the least common denominator.

1. $\frac{3}{4}$ $\frac{7}{8}$ **2.** $\frac{1}{6}$ $\frac{3}{4}$ **3.** $\frac{4}{5}$ $\frac{3}{10}$ **4.** $\frac{1}{2}$ $\frac{5}{6}$ **5.** $\frac{2}{3}$ $\frac{4}{7}$ **6.** $\frac{4}{7}$ $\frac{5}{14}$ **7.** $\frac{5}{6}$ $\frac{5}{8}$

For each exercise, write the fractions with the least common denominator.

8. $\frac{3}{4}$ $\frac{4}{5}$ **9.** $\frac{1}{8}$ $\frac{1}{4}$ **10.** $\frac{4}{15}$ $\frac{11}{30}$ **11.** $\frac{5}{8}$ $\frac{4}{9}$ **12.** $\frac{6}{7}$ $\frac{3}{8}$

13. $\frac{1}{4}$ $\frac{1}{3}$ $\frac{1}{12}$ **14.** $\frac{1}{9}$ $\frac{2}{3}$ $\frac{5}{18}$ **15.** $\frac{5}{6}$ $\frac{1}{2}$ $\frac{3}{4}$ **16.** $\frac{2}{5}$ $\frac{8}{15}$ $\frac{7}{30}$ **17.** $\frac{1}{6}$ $\frac{5}{12}$ $\frac{2}{3}$

18. $\frac{1}{6}$ $\frac{9}{10}$ **19.** $\frac{1}{5}$ $\frac{2}{3}$ $\frac{3}{4}$ **20.** $\frac{1}{2}$ $\frac{5}{7}$ $\frac{3}{4}$ **21.** $\frac{4}{5}$ $\frac{7}{8}$ $\frac{7}{10}$ **22.** $\frac{9}{12}$ $\frac{5}{9}$ $\frac{1}{6}$

23. $\frac{5}{8}$ $\frac{2}{3}$ $\frac{5}{12}$ **24.** $\frac{5}{6}$ $\frac{4}{9}$ $\frac{1}{2}$ **25.** $\frac{5}{8}$ $\frac{5}{6}$ $\frac{1}{3}$ **26.** $\frac{3}{4}$ $\frac{7}{9}$ $\frac{5}{12}$ **27.** $\frac{5}{10}$ $\frac{4}{5}$ $\frac{1}{4}$

28. $\frac{1}{6}$ $\frac{3}{5}$ $\frac{8}{15}$ **29.** $\frac{7}{8}$ $\frac{1}{4}$ $\frac{2}{16}$ **30.** $\frac{4}{7}$ $\frac{2}{3}$ $\frac{5}{6}$ **31.** $\frac{3}{4}$ $\frac{4}{5}$ $\frac{7}{10}$ **32.** $\frac{8}{9}$ $\frac{4}{6}$ $\frac{2}{3}$

MORE PRACTICE

Set 76 *pages 194–195*   Compare the fractions. Use <, >, or =.

1. $\frac{3}{10} \bullet \frac{7}{10}$ **2.** $\frac{4}{7} \bullet \frac{4}{7}$ **3.** $\frac{2}{3} \bullet \frac{5}{6}$ **4.** $\frac{5}{9} \bullet \frac{2}{3}$ **5.** $\frac{3}{8} \bullet \frac{1}{4}$ **6.** $\frac{3}{5} \bullet \frac{4}{15}$

7. $\frac{3}{8} \bullet \frac{1}{24}$ **8.** $\frac{3}{4} \bullet \frac{7}{8}$ **9.** $\frac{1}{3} \bullet \frac{2}{7}$ **10.** $\frac{4}{8} \bullet \frac{2}{4}$ **11.** $\frac{6}{7} \bullet \frac{12}{14}$ **12.** $\frac{3}{7} \bullet \frac{1}{6}$

List these fractions in order from least to greatest.

13. $\frac{3}{4}$ $\frac{7}{8}$ $\frac{2}{3}$ **14.** $\frac{3}{4}$ $\frac{4}{5}$ $\frac{1}{5}$ **15.** $\frac{5}{12}$ $\frac{3}{4}$ $\frac{2}{3}$ **16.** $\frac{1}{12}$ $\frac{1}{4}$ $\frac{1}{6}$ **17.** $\frac{1}{2}$ $\frac{1}{6}$ $\frac{1}{8}$

18. $\frac{3}{8}$ $\frac{1}{2}$ $\frac{1}{4}$ **19.** $\frac{2}{9}$ $\frac{1}{3}$ $\frac{4}{9}$ **20.** $\frac{1}{3}$ $\frac{3}{5}$ $\frac{4}{15}$ **21.** $\frac{3}{5}$ $\frac{2}{5}$ $\frac{1}{10}$ **22.** $\frac{1}{7}$ $\frac{2}{3}$ $\frac{1}{2}$

Set 77 *pages 196–197*   Write each as a mixed number.

1. seven and one half   **2.** eight and two thirds   **3.** nine and three fourths

Compare the numbers. Use <, >, or =.

4. $3\frac{2}{5} \bullet 2\frac{2}{5}$ **5.** $4\frac{2}{3} \bullet 5\frac{1}{3}$ **6.** $6\frac{3}{8} \bullet 6\frac{1}{2}$ **7.** $2\frac{6}{10} \bullet 2\frac{3}{5}$ **8.** $5\frac{1}{2} \bullet 5\frac{2}{3}$

9. $6\frac{1}{5} \bullet 6\frac{2}{10}$ **10.** $2\frac{5}{7} \bullet 1\frac{5}{6}$ **11.** $7\frac{3}{8} \bullet 7\frac{2}{3}$ **12.** $5\frac{2}{5} \bullet 5\frac{4}{10}$ **13.** $3\frac{2}{3} \bullet 3\frac{7}{12}$

Set 78 *pages 198–199*   Draw a segment to show each length.

1. $\frac{7}{8}$ inch   **2.** $3\frac{1}{4}$ inches   **3.** $4\frac{1}{8}$ inches   **4.** $5\frac{6}{8}$ inches   **5.** $3\frac{3}{8}$ inches

6. $6\frac{6}{8}$ inches   **7.** $2\frac{1}{2}$ inches   **8.** $2\frac{3}{4}$ inches   **9.** $1\frac{2}{8}$ inches   **10.** $2\frac{1}{8}$ inches

Set 79 *pages 200–201*   Give each answer as a fraction in lowest terms.

1. $2 \div 12$ **2.** $3 \div 6$ **3.** $7 \div 14$ **4.** $5 \div 25$ **5.** $4 \div 36$ **6.** $7 \div 49$

7. $48 \div 64$ **8.** $12 \div 72$ **9.** $21 \div 63$ **10.** $36 \div 72$ **11.** $13 \div 39$ **12.** $15 \div 75$

Give each answer as a mixed number.

13. $4\overline{)85}$ **14.** $5\overline{)73}$ **15.** $3\overline{)61}$ **16.** $6\overline{)77}$ **17.** $4\overline{)27}$ **18.** $8\overline{)86}$

19. $10\overline{)105}$ **20.** $26\overline{)72}$ **21.** $45\overline{)110}$ **22.** $24\overline{)430}$ **23.** $15\overline{)624}$ **24.** $25\overline{)735}$

25. $18\overline{)392}$ **26.** $14\overline{)276}$ **27.** $15\overline{)410}$ **28.** $16\overline{)308}$ **29.** $48\overline{)630}$ **30.** $28\overline{)490}$

Set 80 *pages 202–203* Solve each problem.

1. Fran picked 27 pounds of pecans to fill 4 baskets. She used the same amount for each basket. How many pounds of pecans did she use for each basket?

2. Each boy scout can carry 25 pounds. How many boy scouts would be needed to carry 220 pounds of supplies?

3. Each van carries 8 people. How many vans would be needed for 53 people?

4. Each boat holds 4 people. How many boats are needed for 63 people?

5. Tolinis Catering Service served 360 ounces of cheese to a party of 75 people. How many ounces of cheese were served per person?

6. Tolinis served 14 salads. If 91 tomatoes were used, how many tomatoes were in each salad?

Set 81 *pages 204–205* Give each missing number.

1. $5 = \frac{\blacksquare}{3}$
2. $8 = \frac{\blacksquare}{2}$
3. $3 = \frac{\blacksquare}{4}$
4. $2 = \frac{\blacksquare}{6}$
5. $1 = \frac{\blacksquare}{8}$
6. $5 = \frac{\blacksquare}{3}$
7. $4 = \frac{\blacksquare}{9}$

Give a fraction for each mixed number.

8. $4\frac{1}{5}$
9. $3\frac{1}{4}$
10. $2\frac{5}{8}$
11. $3\frac{2}{7}$
12. $4\frac{2}{3}$
13. $5\frac{1}{4}$
14. $9\frac{4}{7}$

15. $8\frac{3}{10}$
16. $5\frac{7}{8}$
17. $4\frac{7}{12}$
18. $9\frac{3}{5}$
19. $7\frac{1}{4}$
20. $6\frac{1}{2}$
21. $5\frac{1}{3}$

Give a mixed number or a whole number for each fraction.

22. $\frac{8}{7}$
23. $\frac{15}{4}$
24. $\frac{19}{2}$
25. $\frac{16}{5}$
26. $\frac{11}{2}$
27. $\frac{56}{8}$
28. $\frac{34}{7}$

29. $\frac{50}{4}$
30. $\frac{40}{4}$
31. $\frac{21}{2}$
32. $\frac{74}{10}$
33. $\frac{34}{6}$
34. $\frac{84}{9}$
35. $\frac{99}{11}$

Set 82 *pages 208–209* Write each decimal as a fraction.

1. 0.5
2. 0.7
3. 0.4
4. 0.75
5. 0.99
6. 0.6
7. 0.04

8. 0.63
9. 0.25
10. 0.29
11. 0.34
12. 0.125
13. 0.001
14. 0.015

Write each fraction as a decimal.

15. $\frac{1}{10}$
16. $\frac{2}{10}$
17. $\frac{6}{10}$
18. $\frac{3}{4}$
19. $\frac{1}{5}$
20. $\frac{3}{5}$
21. $\frac{17}{20}$
22. $\frac{17}{50}$

23. $\frac{16}{25}$
24. $\frac{3}{50}$
25. $\frac{7}{20}$
26. $\frac{16}{50}$
27. $\frac{31}{100}$
28. $\frac{25}{100}$
29. $\frac{325}{1,000}$
30. $\frac{5}{8}$

31. $\frac{7}{16}$
32. $\frac{7}{25}$
33. $\frac{27}{50}$
34. $\frac{13}{20}$
35. $\frac{67}{100}$
36. $\frac{9}{20}$
37. $\frac{37}{1,000}$
38. $\frac{9}{50}$

MORE PRACTICE

Set 83 *pages 210–211*   Write 6 digits of each decimal.

1. $0.0\overline{6}$ **2.** $0.\overline{60}$ **3.** $0.4\overline{3}$ **4.** $0.\overline{26}$ **5.** $0.7\overline{34}$ **6.** $0.8\overline{33}$ **7.** $0.1\overline{66}$

Write each decimal with a bar over the digit or digits that repeat.

8. $0.888\ldots$ **9.** $0.6222\ldots$ **10.** $0.7272\ldots$ **11.** $0.04333\ldots$ **12.** $0.033\ldots$

Write each fraction as a repeating decimal. Use the bar over
the digit or digits that repeat.

13. $\frac{1}{3}$ **14.** $\frac{1}{11}$ **15.** $\frac{1}{7}$ **16.** $\frac{2}{7}$ **17.** $\frac{1}{9}$ **18.** $\frac{3}{11}$ **19.** $\frac{5}{9}$ **20.** $\frac{1}{15}$ **21.** $\frac{6}{11}$

22. $\frac{4}{15}$ **23.** $\frac{7}{12}$ **24.** $\frac{2}{11}$ **25.** $\frac{7}{18}$ **26.** $\frac{19}{22}$ **27.** $\frac{7}{9}$ **28.** $\frac{3}{22}$ **29.** $\frac{2}{15}$ **30.** $\frac{5}{12}$

Set 84 *pages 216–217*

1. $\frac{1}{2} \times \frac{1}{3}$ **2.** $\frac{3}{4} \times \frac{1}{4}$ **3.** $\frac{7}{8} \times \frac{1}{3}$ **4.** $\frac{3}{5} \times \frac{3}{4}$ **5.** $\frac{1}{3} \times \frac{3}{4}$ **6.** $\frac{3}{5} \times \frac{2}{3}$

7. $\frac{9}{11} \times \frac{5}{6}$ **8.** $\frac{3}{8} \times \frac{4}{9}$ **9.** $\frac{5}{6} \times \frac{9}{10}$ **10.** $\frac{5}{12} \times \frac{9}{10}$ **11.** $\frac{6}{7} \times \frac{7}{12}$ **12.** $\frac{2}{5} \times \frac{5}{6}$

13. $\frac{3}{4} \times \frac{1}{6} \times \frac{2}{5}$ **14.** $\frac{4}{5} \times \frac{3}{8} \times \frac{5}{6}$ **15.** $\frac{2}{3} \times \frac{3}{4} \times \frac{3}{5}$ **16.** $\frac{5}{6} \times \frac{2}{3} \times \frac{4}{5}$ **17.** $\frac{3}{7} \times \frac{3}{8} \times \frac{1}{9}$

18. $\frac{1}{2} \times \frac{2}{3} \times \frac{6}{9}$ **19.** $\frac{8}{9} \times \frac{3}{4} \times \frac{1}{6}$ **20.** $\frac{7}{8} \times \frac{1}{7} \times \frac{3}{14}$ **21.** $\frac{6}{7} \times \frac{2}{3} \times \frac{6}{8}$ **22.** $\frac{5}{9} \times \frac{1}{4} \times \frac{3}{7}$

Set 85 *pages 218–219*

1. $\frac{1}{2} \times 6$ **2.** $\frac{1}{2} \times 9$ **3.** $\frac{1}{3} \times 11$ **4.** $\frac{1}{4} \times 12$ **5.** $\frac{1}{3} \times 18$ **6.** $\frac{1}{6} \times 14$

7. $63 \times \frac{2}{9}$ **8.** $54 \times \frac{1}{6}$ **9.** $90 \times \frac{2}{3}$ **10.** $56 \times \frac{4}{7}$ **11.** $36 \times \frac{4}{9}$ **12.** $52 \times \frac{1}{2}$

13. $150 \times \frac{4}{5}$ **14.** $633 \times \frac{2}{3}$ **15.** $729 \times \frac{3}{9}$ **16.** $100 \times \frac{5}{6}$ **17.** $432 \times \frac{5}{8}$ **18.** $256 \times \frac{3}{4}$

Set 86 *pages 220–221*

1. $3 \times 3\frac{1}{4}$ **2.** $4 \times 1\frac{2}{5}$ **3.** $\frac{3}{5} \times 1\frac{2}{5}$ **4.** $\frac{1}{2} \times 5\frac{1}{2}$ **5.** $\frac{5}{6} \times 3\frac{1}{3}$ **6.** $\frac{8}{9} \times 7\frac{1}{8}$

7. $3\frac{1}{6} \times 4\frac{2}{3}$ **8.** $5\frac{1}{4} \times 6\frac{1}{2}$ **9.** $4\frac{2}{7} \times 3\frac{1}{3}$ **10.** $7\frac{1}{2} \times 3\frac{1}{3}$ **11.** $4\frac{1}{5} \times 3\frac{1}{7}$ **12.** $2\frac{3}{4} \times 8\frac{1}{2}$

13. $5\frac{3}{4} \times 2\frac{1}{8}$ **14.** $4\frac{5}{6} \times 2\frac{2}{5}$ **15.** $6\frac{1}{7} \times 3\frac{1}{2}$ **16.** $2\frac{5}{8} \times 7\frac{2}{3}$ **17.** $8\frac{3}{4} \times 2\frac{5}{7}$ **18.** $8\frac{1}{9} \times 2\frac{1}{4}$

Set 87 *pages 222–223*

1. $\frac{1}{2} \times \frac{2}{5}$ 2. $\frac{3}{4} \times \frac{4}{7}$ 3. $4 \times 1\frac{3}{8}$ 4. $2\frac{2}{3} \times \frac{3}{8}$ 5. $1\frac{1}{5} \times 3\frac{1}{3}$

6. $\frac{5}{9} \times \frac{3}{8}$ 7. $\frac{5}{6} \times \frac{3}{10}$ 8. $6 \times 3\frac{2}{3}$ 9. $3\frac{1}{2} \times \frac{6}{7}$ 10. $1\frac{5}{7} \times 3\frac{1}{2}$

11. $\frac{2}{3} \times \frac{9}{10}$ 12. $\frac{4}{5} \times \frac{5}{8}$ 13. $1\frac{5}{9} \times 3$ 14. $2\frac{2}{5} \times 3\frac{1}{3}$ 15. $4\frac{1}{5} \times 1\frac{3}{7}$

16. $\frac{3}{5} \times \frac{5}{6} \times \frac{2}{15}$ 17. $\frac{7}{10} \times \frac{5}{7} \times \frac{1}{5}$ 18. $\frac{2}{3} \times \frac{5}{8} \times \frac{9}{10}$ 19. $1\frac{1}{5} \times \frac{2}{3} \times \frac{3}{4}$ 20. $1\frac{7}{8} \times 1\frac{1}{3} \times \frac{2}{5}$

Set 88 *pages 224–225* If there is not enough information given, write *too little information*. Otherwise, solve the problem.

1. Mr. Wong carves a whistle in about $1\frac{1}{4}$ hours. How long does it take him to carve 50 whistles?

2. Chris is mailing 6 copies of a book that weighs $2\frac{1}{2}$ pounds. What is the weight of all the books?

3. John wants to make 8 columns on a sheet of paper. How many inches should each column be?

4. Luis jogs at a speed of one lap every $6\frac{1}{2}$ minutes. How long will it take him to complete $2\frac{1}{2}$ laps?

5. Debbie rides her bicycle at a speed of one lap every $1\frac{3}{4}$ minutes. How long will it take her to complete 8 laps?

6. Anita gave away $\frac{2}{3}$ of her posters. She kept the rest of the posters. How many posters did she have to begin with?

Set 89 *pages 226–227* Solve each problem.

If Barbara serves 1 out of 9 customers, how many will she serve if there are

1. 9 customers?   2. 36 customers?   3. 63 customers?   4. 81 customers?

About 5 out of 6 customers have a charge card at the department store. How many customers have a charge card if there are

5. 72 customers?   6. 48 customers?   7. 60 customers?   8. 216 customers?

About 2 out of 5 customers pay cash. How many customers pay cash if there are

9. 25 customers?   10. 45 customers?   11. 65 customers?   12. 200 customers?

About 7 out of 8 customers at Randalls are women. How many customers are women if there are

13. 64 customers?   14. 96 customers?   15. 120 customers?   16. 160 customers?

MORE PRACTICE

Set 90 *pages 228–229* Solve each problem.

The first digit of the code number for the automatic bank teller can be any digit from 1 to 7. What is the probability that it is

1. 4?   **2.** 3 or 4?   **3.** an odd number?   **4.** an even number?   **5.** 3, 4, 5, 6, or 7?

The first digit of a checking account can be any digit from 0 to 7. What is the probability that it is

6. 2?   **7.** 8?   **8.** 0?   **9.** an odd number?   **10.** 9?   **11.** 0, 1, or 2?

The first letter of a code to use the store computer can be A, B, or C. What is the probability that it is

12. A?   **13.** X?   **14.** B or C?   **15.** A, B, or C?   **16.** A or H?   **17.** A, B, C, or D?

Set 91 *pages 230–231* Give the reciprocal for each number.

1. $\frac{6}{7}$ **2.** 5   **3.** $\frac{2}{7}$ **4.** $\frac{8}{9}$ **5.** 3   **6.** $\frac{4}{9}$ **7.** $\frac{11}{12}$ **8.** $13\frac{2}{9}$ **9.** 15

10. $1\frac{3}{8}$ **11.** $3\frac{2}{3}$ **12.** $1\frac{8}{11}$ **13.** $2\frac{5}{12}$ **14.** $1\frac{4}{5}$ **15.** $2\frac{7}{8}$ **16.** $8\frac{3}{4}$ **17.** $1\frac{4}{9}$ **18.** $6\frac{5}{6}$

Use the picture to find the answer to part a. Multiply to find the answer to part b.

19. **a.** $2 \div \frac{1}{5}$ **20.** **a.** $\frac{3}{4} \div \frac{1}{8}$ **21.** **a.** $2 \div \frac{1}{4}$

b. $2 \times \frac{5}{1}$ **b.** $\frac{3}{4} \times \frac{8}{1}$ **b.** $2 \times \frac{4}{1}$

Set 92 *pages 232–233* Find each missing number.

1. $\frac{5}{9} \div \frac{3}{4} = \frac{5}{9} \times \frac{▦}{3}$ **2.** $6 \div \frac{2}{7} = \frac{6}{1} \times \frac{7}{▦}$ **3.** $\frac{1}{2} \div 7 = \frac{1}{2} \times \frac{▦}{▦}$ **4.** $\frac{3}{10} \div \frac{4}{5} = \frac{▦}{▦} \times \frac{▦}{▦}$

Divide.

5. $\frac{3}{10} \div \frac{3}{4}$ **6.** $\frac{6}{7} \div \frac{2}{3}$ **7.** $\frac{3}{4} \div 6$ **8.** $\frac{8}{9} \div \frac{8}{9}$ **9.** $\frac{5}{8} \div \frac{1}{4}$ **10.** $\frac{9}{10} \div 3$ **11.** $\frac{4}{5} \div 8$

12. $8 \div \frac{3}{4}$ **13.** $\frac{3}{10} \div \frac{4}{5}$ **14.** $\frac{5}{8} \div 5$ **15.** $4 \div \frac{1}{9}$ **16.** $\frac{1}{12} \div \frac{5}{6}$ **17.** $5 \div \frac{3}{5}$ **18.** $12 \div \frac{6}{7}$

Set 93 *pages 234–235*

1. $1\frac{5}{8} \div 3$ 2. $3\frac{1}{6} \div 4$ 3. $7 \div 1\frac{3}{8}$ 4. $9 \div 1\frac{3}{4}$ 5. $1\frac{5}{8} \div 2\frac{1}{3}$ 6. $1\frac{2}{5} \div 2\frac{1}{4}$

7. $2\frac{2}{5} \div \frac{3}{4}$ 8. $1\frac{3}{5} \div \frac{2}{3}$ 9. $1\frac{5}{6} \div 2\frac{1}{3}$ 10. $1\frac{7}{9} \div 1\frac{1}{3}$ 11. $1\frac{4}{5} \div 12$ 12. $1\frac{7}{9} \div 8$

13. $\frac{5}{8} \div 7\frac{1}{2}$ 14. $\frac{8}{9} \div 2\frac{1}{3}$ 15. $12 \div 3\frac{3}{5}$ 16. $5 \div 3\frac{1}{8}$ 17. $3\frac{3}{4} \div 4\frac{2}{7}$ 18. $4\frac{1}{2} \div 2\frac{5}{8}$

19. $2\frac{1}{2} \div \frac{5}{8}$ 20. $6\frac{2}{5} \div \frac{3}{10}$ 21. $3\frac{1}{3} \div 4\frac{4}{9}$ 22. $3\frac{1}{9} \div 2\frac{1}{3}$ 23. $5\frac{1}{3} \div 8$ 24. $8\frac{3}{4} \div 7$

25. $2\frac{3}{4} \div 4$ 26. $3\frac{5}{6} \div \frac{2}{3}$ 27. $2\frac{3}{8} \div 1\frac{4}{5}$ 28. $3 \div 1\frac{3}{4}$ 29. $15 \div 1\frac{1}{2}$ 30. $3\frac{1}{4} \div \frac{1}{10}$

Set 94 *pages 238–239*

Spaghetti Sauce

$\frac{3}{4}$ cup mushrooms   1 bay leaf

2 cans tomato paste $2\frac{1}{2}$ teaspoons parsley

5 cans water   flakes

$\frac{1}{2}$ teaspoon salt $3\frac{1}{2}$ tablespoons celery

1 teaspoon pepper   flakes

1 teaspoon oregano $\frac{1}{2}$ cup green pepper,

4 garlic cloves   chopped

Mix all the ingredients together in a large saucepan and cook on low heat for 2 hours.   Serves 4

Write a problem about

1. the amount of tomato paste needed to make enough sauce for $2\frac{1}{2}$ times as many people.

2. the amount of mushrooms needed to make enough sauce for 2 people.

3. the amount of celery flakes needed for three times the recipe.

4. the cost of the tomato paste.

Set 95 *pages 244–245*

1. $\frac{5}{8}$ $+\frac{1}{8}$ 2. $\frac{3}{5}$ $+\frac{2}{5}$ 3. $\frac{4}{6}$ $+\frac{2}{6}$ 4. $\frac{2}{4}$ $+\frac{3}{4}$ 5. $\frac{5}{8}$ $+\frac{6}{8}$ 6. $\frac{4}{10}$ $+\frac{2}{10}$ 7. $\frac{3}{12}$ $+\frac{6}{12}$ 8. $\frac{5}{9}$ $+\frac{1}{9}$

9. $\frac{6}{16}$ $+\frac{2}{16}$ 10. $\frac{4}{6}$ $+\frac{3}{6}$ 11. $\frac{8}{12}$ $+\frac{6}{12}$ 12. $\frac{4}{7}$ $+\frac{2}{7}$ 13. $\frac{3}{9}$ $+\frac{2}{9}$ 14. $\frac{1}{11}$ $+\frac{8}{11}$ 15. $\frac{2}{15}$ $+\frac{8}{15}$ 16. $\frac{3}{10}$ $+\frac{9}{10}$

17. $\frac{3}{10} + \frac{2}{10} + \frac{1}{10}$ 18. $\frac{2}{16} + \frac{4}{16} + \frac{6}{16}$ 19. $\frac{2}{9} + \frac{4}{9} + \frac{3}{9}$ 20. $\frac{1}{8} + \frac{5}{8} + \frac{2}{8}$ 21. $\frac{3}{11} + \frac{5}{11} + \frac{8}{11}$

MORE PRACTICE

Set 96 *pages 246–247*

1. $3\frac{1}{5}$
$+\,6\frac{2}{5}$

2. $2\frac{2}{9}$
$+\,3\frac{5}{9}$

3. $5\frac{3}{10}$
$+\,6\frac{7}{10}$

4. $4\frac{5}{12}$
$+\,2\frac{11}{12}$

5. $3\frac{2}{5}$
$+\,1\frac{4}{5}$

6. $1\frac{3}{8}$
$+\,2\frac{7}{8}$

7. $4\frac{3}{4}$
$+\,3\frac{3}{4}$

8. $5\frac{1}{7}$
$+\,4\frac{6}{7}$

9. $1\frac{3}{13}$
$+\,8\frac{11}{13}$

10. $6\frac{7}{10}$
$+\,2\frac{9}{10}$

11. $2\frac{5}{12}$
$+\,6\frac{7}{12}$

12. $4\frac{4}{9}$
$+\,6\frac{8}{9}$

13. $6\frac{2}{15}$
$+\,1\frac{14}{15}$

14. $1\frac{8}{9}$
$+\,1\frac{7}{9}$

15. $9\frac{13}{18}$
$+\,8\frac{11}{18}$

16. $6\frac{13}{21}$
$+\,3\frac{11}{21}$

17. $4\frac{1}{8} + 2\frac{3}{8} + 3\frac{7}{8}$

18. $6\frac{4}{11} + 15\frac{5}{11} + 20\frac{7}{11}$

19. $4\frac{11}{15} + 21\frac{2}{15} + 9\frac{8}{15}$

20. $5\frac{7}{12} + 9\frac{5}{12} + 8\frac{11}{12}$

Set 97 *pages 248–249*

1. $\frac{3}{5}$
$+\,\frac{1}{2}$

2. $\frac{3}{4}$
$+\,\frac{2}{3}$

3. $\frac{5}{6}$
$+\,\frac{7}{8}$

4. $\frac{4}{5}$
$+\,\frac{4}{9}$

5. $\frac{2}{9}$
$+\,\frac{1}{2}$

6. $\frac{1}{6}$
$+\,\frac{3}{5}$

7. $\frac{2}{7}$
$+\,\frac{1}{2}$

8. $\frac{5}{7}$
$+\,\frac{1}{3}$

9. $\frac{3}{8}$
$+\,\frac{7}{10}$

10. $\frac{4}{9}$
$+\,\frac{2}{3}$

11. $\frac{3}{4} + \frac{1}{2} + \frac{5}{6}$

12. $\frac{1}{6} + \frac{3}{8} + \frac{5}{12}$

13. $\frac{3}{4} + \frac{2}{7} + \frac{1}{8}$

14. $\frac{3}{5} + \frac{1}{10} + \frac{4}{7}$

15. $\frac{1}{2} + \frac{1}{8} + \frac{3}{4}$

Set 98 *pages 250–251*

1. $2\frac{1}{2}$
$+\,3\frac{5}{6}$

2. $2\frac{3}{5}$
$+\,3\frac{1}{2}$

3. $5\frac{3}{4}$
$+\,3\frac{2}{3}$

4. $5\frac{5}{6}$
$+\,2\frac{1}{3}$

5. $9\frac{2}{3}$
$+\,1\frac{4}{5}$

6. $7\frac{4}{9}$
$+\,3\frac{1}{6}$

7. $6\frac{3}{8}$
$+\,2\frac{1}{4}$

8. $6\frac{7}{10}$
$+\,4\frac{3}{4}$

9. $7\frac{7}{8}$
$+\,2\frac{4}{5}$

10. $8\frac{5}{12} + 2\frac{2}{3}$

11. $2\frac{5}{7} + 3\frac{2}{3}$

12. $6\frac{1}{2} + 3\frac{7}{9}$

13. $\frac{6}{7} + 2\frac{7}{10} + \frac{3}{5}$

14. $6\frac{2}{3} + 3\frac{4}{5} + 4\frac{9}{10}$

Set 99 *pages 252–253*

1. $\frac{7}{9}$
$-\,\frac{2}{9}$

2. $\frac{5}{6}$
$-\,\frac{1}{6}$

3. $5\frac{2}{3}$
$-\,1\frac{1}{3}$

4. $8\frac{3}{4}$
$-\,4\frac{1}{4}$

5. $2\frac{7}{10}$
$-\,\frac{3}{10}$

6. $5\frac{7}{8}$
$-\,3$

7. $8\frac{4}{5}$
$-\,4\frac{1}{5}$

8. $6\frac{7}{8}$
$-\,2\frac{3}{8}$

9. $12\frac{11}{12}$
$-\,4\frac{5}{12}$

10. $8\frac{5}{9}$
$-\,7$

11. $16\frac{3}{8}$
$-\,2\frac{1}{8}$

12. $9\frac{7}{12}$
$-\,3\frac{1}{12}$

13. $15\frac{4}{5}$
$-\,1\frac{2}{5}$

14. $7\frac{7}{10}$
$-\,5\frac{1}{10}$

15. $4\frac{11}{18}$
$-\,2\frac{5}{18}$

16. $21\frac{14}{15}$
$-\,1\frac{11}{15}$

17. $\frac{6}{7} - \frac{3}{7}$

18. $6\frac{7}{8} - \frac{3}{8}$

19. $8\frac{11}{12} - 2\frac{1}{12}$

20. $5\frac{9}{10} - \frac{3}{10}$

21. $9\frac{8}{9} - 7\frac{2}{9}$

22. $8\frac{5}{6} - 5\frac{1}{6}$

Set 100 *pages 254–255* Rename each number.

1. $4 = 3\frac{\blacksquare}{4}$ **2.** $7 = 6\frac{\blacksquare}{5}$ **3.** $8 = 7\frac{\blacksquare}{8}$ **4.** $1 = \frac{\blacksquare}{7}$ **5.** $6 = 5\frac{\blacksquare}{9}$ **6.** $9 = 8\frac{\blacksquare}{6}$

First rename. Then subtract.

7. $\begin{array}{r} 6 = 5\frac{\blacksquare}{3} \\ -4\frac{1}{3} = 4\frac{1}{3} \\ \hline \end{array}$ **8.** $\begin{array}{r} 8 = 7\frac{\blacksquare}{5} \\ -2\frac{4}{5} = 1\frac{4}{5} \\ \hline \end{array}$ **9.** $\begin{array}{r} 7\frac{5}{12} = 6\frac{\blacksquare}{12} \\ -1\frac{11}{12} = 1\frac{11}{12} \\ \hline \end{array}$ **10.** $\begin{array}{r} 9\frac{1}{4} = 8\frac{\blacksquare}{4} \\ -5\frac{3}{4} = 5\frac{3}{4} \\ \hline \end{array}$ **11.** $\begin{array}{r} 12 = 11\frac{\blacksquare}{8} \\ -7\frac{3}{8} = 7\frac{3}{8} \\ \hline \end{array}$

Set 101 *pages 256–257*

1. $\begin{array}{r} \frac{5}{8} \\ -\frac{1}{2} \\ \hline \end{array}$ **2.** $\begin{array}{r} \frac{8}{9} \\ -\frac{2}{3} \\ \hline \end{array}$ **3.** $\begin{array}{r} \frac{5}{6} \\ -\frac{4}{9} \\ \hline \end{array}$ **4.** $\begin{array}{r} 3\frac{3}{5} \\ -1\frac{1}{3} \\ \hline \end{array}$ **5.** $\begin{array}{r} 8\frac{3}{5} \\ -6\frac{3}{10} \\ \hline \end{array}$ **6.** $\begin{array}{r} 9\frac{2}{3} \\ -4\frac{1}{6} \\ \hline \end{array}$ **7.** $\begin{array}{r} 6\frac{4}{5} \\ -3\frac{1}{3} \\ \hline \end{array}$ **8.** $\begin{array}{r} 6\frac{3}{4} \\ -2\frac{5}{8} \\ \hline \end{array}$

9. $10\frac{1}{2} - 7\frac{1}{3}$ **10.** $14\frac{2}{3} - 8\frac{3}{5}$ **11.** $18\frac{5}{6} - 12\frac{3}{8}$ **12.** $18\frac{3}{4} - 14\frac{5}{8}$ **13.** $20\frac{5}{7} - 6\frac{1}{2}$

Set 102 *pages 258–259*

1. $\begin{array}{r} 7\frac{1}{6} = 7\frac{\blacksquare}{24} = 6\frac{\blacksquare}{24} \\ -3\frac{5}{8} = 3\frac{\blacksquare}{24} = 3\frac{\blacksquare}{24} \\ \hline \end{array}$ **2.** $\begin{array}{r} 9\frac{1}{2} = 9\frac{\blacksquare}{10} = 8\frac{\blacksquare}{10} \\ -2\frac{9}{10} = 2\frac{\blacksquare}{10} = 2\frac{\blacksquare}{10} \\ \hline \end{array}$ **3.** $\begin{array}{r} 10\frac{3}{8} = 10\frac{\blacksquare}{8} = 9\frac{\blacksquare}{8} \\ -6\frac{1}{2} = 6\frac{\blacksquare}{8} = 6\frac{\blacksquare}{8} \\ \hline \end{array}$ **4.** $\begin{array}{r} 5\frac{1}{12} = 5\frac{\blacksquare}{12} = 4\frac{\blacksquare}{12} \\ -4\frac{3}{4} = 4\frac{\blacksquare}{12} = 4\frac{\blacksquare}{12} \\ \hline \end{array}$

5. $\begin{array}{r} 8\frac{1}{3} \\ -6\frac{3}{4} \\ \hline \end{array}$ **6.** $\begin{array}{r} 7\frac{3}{10} \\ -2\frac{4}{5} \\ \hline \end{array}$ **7.** $\begin{array}{r} 5\frac{1}{4} \\ -1\frac{5}{6} \\ \hline \end{array}$ **8.** $\begin{array}{r} 9\frac{1}{2} \\ -\frac{3}{5} \\ \hline \end{array}$ **9.** $\begin{array}{r} 3\frac{1}{2} \\ -1\frac{3}{4} \\ \hline \end{array}$ **10.** $\begin{array}{r} 4\frac{1}{3} \\ -2\frac{5}{9} \\ \hline \end{array}$ **11.** $\begin{array}{r} 3\frac{1}{3} \\ -2\frac{5}{12} \\ \hline \end{array}$ **12.** $\begin{array}{r} 12\frac{5}{6} \\ -8\frac{9}{10} \\ \hline \end{array}$

Set 103 *pages 262–263* Tell which operation should be used to solve each problem. Then, solve each problem.

1. Breakaway can clear a $4\frac{1}{3}$-foot hurdle. Capital Gaines can clear a $3\frac{3}{4}$-foot hurdle. How much higher can Breakaway jump?

2. A mouse weighs $\frac{7}{8}$ ounce. Each day, it eats $\frac{1}{2}$ as much as it weighs. How much does it eat each day?

3. Gene glued together wood which had thicknesses of $3\frac{1}{16}$ inches, $\frac{4}{16}$ inch, and $\frac{4}{8}$ inch. What was the total thickness?

4. On a 10-mile hike, Dean's bike got a flat tire after he had ridden $4\frac{6}{7}$ miles. How many miles were left on the hike?

MORE PRACTICE

Set 104 *pages 270–271* Use the diagram at the right.

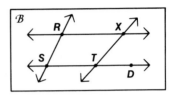

1. Which line appears to be parallel to $\overleftrightarrow{RX}$?

2. Which lines intersect at point *S*?

3. What is the endpoint of $\overrightarrow{TS}$?

4. Name 3 line segments on $\overleftrightarrow{ST}$.

5. Name two rays on $\overleftrightarrow{RX}$.

6. Name a point that is not on $\overleftrightarrow{ST}$.

7. Give another name for $\overleftrightarrow{ST}$.

Set 105 *pages 272–273* Tell whether the figures are congruent. Write *yes* or *no*.

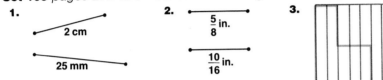

1. 2 cm / 25 mm

2. $\frac{5}{8}$ in. / $\frac{10}{16}$ in.

3.

4.

5. Tell if the blue line is a line of symmetry. Write *yes* or *no*.

6. Tell how many lines of symmetry the figure has.

Set 106 *pages 274–275* Measure each angle at the right. Then tell whether it is acute, right, or obtuse.

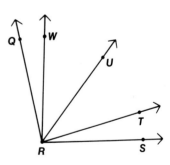

1. ∠QRS 2. ∠WRS 3. ∠URS 4. ∠TRS

5. ∠WRT 6. ∠URT 7. ∠QRW 8. ∠QRU 9. ∠QRT

Draw an angle with the given measure.

10. 45° 11. 145° 12. 135° 13. 22° 14. 68°

Set 107 *pages 274–275* Find the third angle measure in each triangle. Then tell whether the triangle is acute, right, or obtuse.

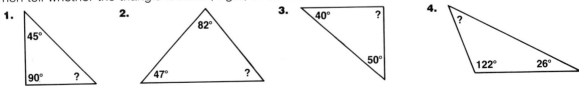

1. 45°, 90°, ?

2. 82°, 47°, ?

3. 40°, ?, 50°

4. ?, 122°, 26°

Set 108 *pages 278–279*   Is each triangle equilateral, isosceles, or scalene? Use all terms that apply.

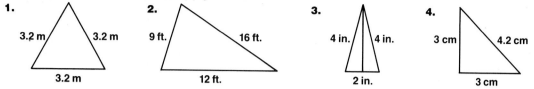

1. 3.2 m 3.2 m 3.2 m

2. 9 ft. 16 ft. 12 ft.

3. 4 in. 4 in. 2 in.

4. 3 cm 4.2 cm 3 cm

Use as many of the classifications as possible. Tell whether each quadrilateral is a parallelogram, a rectangle, or a square.

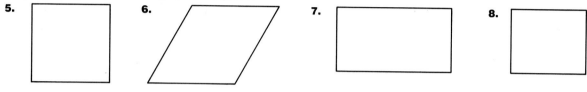

5.

6.

7.

8.

Set 109 *pages 280–281*   Find the perimeter of each polygon.

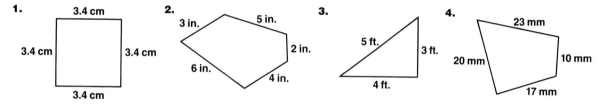

1. 3.4 cm 3.4 cm 3.4 cm 3.4 cm

2. 3 in. 5 in. 2 in. 4 in. 6 in.

3. 5 ft. 3 ft. 4 ft.

4. 23 mm 20 mm 10 mm 17 mm

Set 110 *pages 282–283*   Find the area of each rectangle.

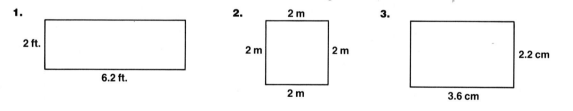

1. 2 ft. 6.2 ft.

2. 2 m 2 m 2 m 2 m

3. 2.2 cm 3.6 cm

Set 111 *pages 284–285*   Find the area of each triangle.

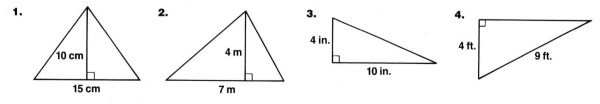

1. 10 cm 15 cm

2. 4 m 7 m

3. 4 in. 10 in.

4. 4 ft. 9 ft.

MORE PRACTICE

Set 112 *pages 288–289* Give an estimate for each problem.

1. Use the diagram below to estimate the area of the step.

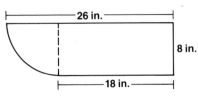

2. Use the diagram below to estimate the area of the stained-glass window.

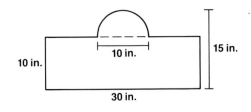

Set 113 *pages 290–291* Name each radius. Then name each diameter. In each circle, point *P* is the center.

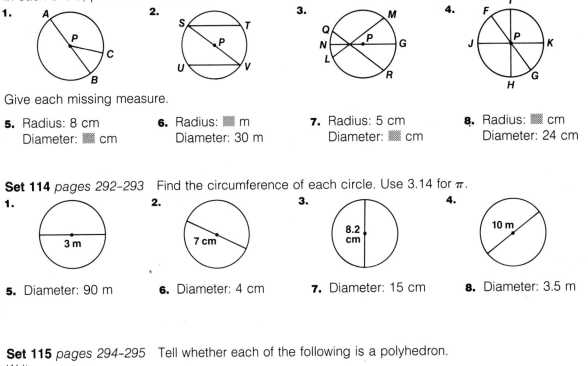

Give each missing measure.

5. Radius: 8 cm
   Diameter: ▓ cm

6. Radius: ▓ m
   Diameter: 30 m

7. Radius: 5 cm
   Diameter: ▓ cm

8. Radius: ▓ cm
   Diameter: 24 cm

Set 114 *pages 292–293* Find the circumference of each circle. Use 3.14 for π.

1. 3 m

2. 7 cm

3. 8.2 cm

4. 10 m

5. Diameter: 90 m

6. Diameter: 4 cm

7. Diameter: 15 cm

8. Diameter: 3.5 m

Set 115 *pages 294–295* Tell whether each of the following is a polyhedron. Write *yes* or *no*.

1.

2.

3.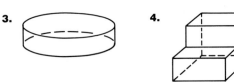

4.

Name the number of faces, vertices, and edges for a

5. pyramid with a 3-sided base.

6. prism with 3-sided bases.

7. pyramid with a 7-sided base.

8. prism with 7-sided bases.

Set 116 *pages 296–297* Find the total surface area of each prism.

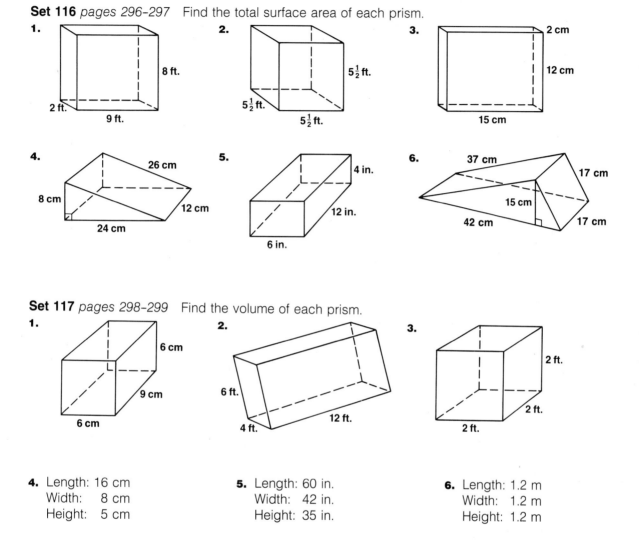

1.
8 ft.
2 ft.
9 ft.

2.
$5\frac{1}{2}$ ft.
$5\frac{1}{2}$ ft.
$5\frac{1}{2}$ ft.

3.
2 cm
12 cm
15 cm

4.
26 cm
8 cm
12 cm
24 cm

5.
4 in.
12 in.
6 in.

6.
37 cm
17 cm
15 cm
42 cm
17 cm

Set 117 *pages 298–299* Find the volume of each prism.

1.
6 cm
9 cm
6 cm

2.
6 ft.
12 ft.
4 ft.

3.
2 ft.
2 ft.
2 ft.

4. Length: 16 cm
Width: 8 cm
Height: 5 cm

5. Length: 60 in.
Width: 42 in.
Height: 35 in.

6. Length: 1.2 m
Width: 1.2 m
Height: 1.2 m

Set 118 *pages 300–301* Use one of the formulas to solve each problem.

Area of rectangle: $A = \ell \times w$

Area of triangle: $A = \frac{1}{2} \times b \times h$

Circumference of circle: $C = \pi \times d$

Volume of prism: $V = \ell \times w \times h$

1. Five congruent triangles form the roof of a gazebo. The base of each triangle measures 1.2 m. The height of each triangle is 1.1 m. What is the area of one of the triangles?

2. Joe Venturi used 3 m³ of concrete for the sidewalk in his backyard. The sidewalk is 5 m wide and 0.1 m thick. What is the length of the sidewalk?

3. Maggie, the dog, lives in a pen that is 4 ft. long, 3 ft. wide, and 3 ft. high. What is the volume of the pen?

4. The planet Earth has a diameter of 12,756 km. What is the circumference? Use 3.14 for π.

MORE PRACTICE

Set 119 *pages 306-307*   Write a ratio for each situation.

1. 12 inches to 1 foot

2. 8 girls to 12 boys

3. 6 teachers for 150 students

4. 4 for 24¢

5. 5 houses for 25 people

6. 3 books to 5 magazines

7. 12 months in 1 year

8. 1 planet to 10 stars

9. 14 sunny days to 10 rainy days

Complete each list of equal ratios.

10. dimes → cents $\dfrac{2}{50} = \dfrac{\text{▨}}{100} = \dfrac{6}{\text{▨}} = \dfrac{8}{\text{▨}} = \dfrac{10}{\text{▨}}$

11. reds → blues $\dfrac{5}{2} = \dfrac{10}{\text{▨}} = \dfrac{\text{▨}}{6} = \dfrac{20}{\text{▨}} = \dfrac{\text{▨}}{10}$

12. minutes → hours $\dfrac{60}{1} = \dfrac{120}{\text{▨}} = \dfrac{\text{▨}}{3} = \dfrac{240}{\text{▨}} = \dfrac{\text{▨}}{5}$

13. months → days $\dfrac{1}{30} = \dfrac{\text{▨}}{60} = \dfrac{3}{\text{▨}} = \dfrac{\text{▨}}{120} = \dfrac{5}{\text{▨}}$

Set 120 *pages 308-309*   For each proportion, show that the cross-products are equal.

1. $\dfrac{4}{6} = \dfrac{2}{3}$

2. $\dfrac{4}{5} = \dfrac{12}{15}$

3. $\dfrac{6}{7} = \dfrac{24}{28}$

4. $\dfrac{9}{10} = \dfrac{90}{100}$

5. $\dfrac{2}{7} = \dfrac{14}{49}$

6. $\dfrac{20}{60} = \dfrac{1}{3}$

7. $\dfrac{16}{18} = \dfrac{8}{9}$

8. $\dfrac{24}{12} = \dfrac{72}{36}$

9. $\dfrac{13}{16} = \dfrac{52}{64}$

10. $\dfrac{12}{3.6} = \dfrac{1}{0.3}$

11. $\dfrac{3}{6.2} = \dfrac{1.5}{3.10}$

12. $\dfrac{0.5}{0.7} = \dfrac{1}{1.4}$

13. $\dfrac{5.4}{12} = \dfrac{10.8}{24}$

14. $\dfrac{0.2}{12} = \dfrac{1.2}{72}$

15. $\dfrac{1.3}{0.6} = \dfrac{13}{6}$

Do the ratios form a proportion? Write *yes* or *no*.

16. $\dfrac{4}{5}$ $\dfrac{8}{3}$

17. $\dfrac{6}{8}$ $\dfrac{3}{4}$

18. $\dfrac{9}{10}$ $\dfrac{90}{99}$

19. $\dfrac{7}{6}$ $\dfrac{14}{12}$

20. $\dfrac{24}{26}$ $\dfrac{12}{14}$

21. $\dfrac{20}{54}$ $\dfrac{4}{9}$

22. $\dfrac{6}{7}$ $\dfrac{18}{21}$

23. $\dfrac{5}{20}$ $\dfrac{20}{30}$

24. $\dfrac{3}{7}$ $\dfrac{6}{14}$

25. $\dfrac{12}{18}$ $\dfrac{6}{9}$

26. $\dfrac{10}{14}$ $\dfrac{2}{3}$

27. $\dfrac{33}{20}$ $\dfrac{3}{2}$

Set 121 *pages 310-311*   Use cross products to find *n*.

1. $\dfrac{3}{4} = \dfrac{n}{20}$

2. $\dfrac{24}{n} = \dfrac{6}{5}$

3. $\dfrac{n}{5} = \dfrac{20}{10}$

4. $\dfrac{1}{6} = \dfrac{5}{n}$

5. $\dfrac{3}{7} = \dfrac{n}{21}$

6. $\dfrac{2}{5} = \dfrac{12}{n}$

7. $\dfrac{10}{9} = \dfrac{n}{27}$

8. $\dfrac{8}{3} = \dfrac{32}{n}$

9. $\dfrac{60}{n} = \dfrac{4}{1}$

10. $\dfrac{n}{6} = \dfrac{1}{6}$

11. $\dfrac{9}{12} = \dfrac{3}{n}$

12. $\dfrac{20}{25} = \dfrac{n}{100}$

13. $\dfrac{21}{12} = \dfrac{7}{n}$

14. $\dfrac{6}{8} = \dfrac{n}{4}$

15. $\dfrac{3}{n} = \dfrac{12}{20}$

16. $\dfrac{n}{2} = \dfrac{18}{12}$

17. $\dfrac{7}{n} = \dfrac{14}{8}$

18. $\dfrac{n}{7} = \dfrac{48}{42}$

19. $\dfrac{45}{50} = \dfrac{n}{10}$

20. $\dfrac{n}{4} = \dfrac{24}{32}$

21. $\dfrac{10}{35} = \dfrac{2}{n}$

22. $\dfrac{54}{n} = \dfrac{9}{8}$

23. $\dfrac{n}{27} = \dfrac{10}{18}$

24. $\dfrac{24}{9} = \dfrac{n}{6}$

25. $\dfrac{8}{5} = \dfrac{n}{25}$

26. $\dfrac{2}{15} = \dfrac{n}{75}$

27. $\dfrac{n}{96} = \dfrac{3}{16}$

28. $\dfrac{24}{88} = \dfrac{15}{n}$

29. $\dfrac{54}{81} = \dfrac{n}{6}$

30. $\dfrac{n}{30} = \dfrac{15}{9}$

31. $\dfrac{27}{72} = \dfrac{n}{8}$

32. $\dfrac{n}{3} = \dfrac{48}{18}$

33. $\dfrac{63}{90} = \dfrac{7}{n}$

34. $\dfrac{8}{36} = \dfrac{12}{n}$

35. $\dfrac{13}{20} = \dfrac{65}{n}$

36. $\dfrac{48}{9} = \dfrac{n}{6}$

Set 122 *pages 312-313* For each pair of similar figures, find *n*. All measurements are in feet.

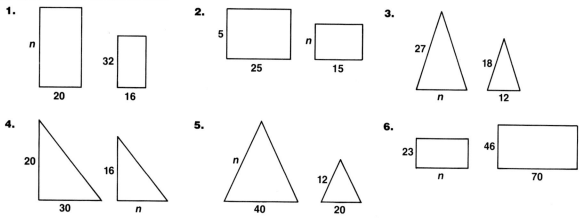

Set 123 *pages 314-315* Solve each problem.

1. Three teaspoons of mix make 24 ounces of iced tea. How much mix is needed to make 40 ounces of iced tea?

2. Shirts are sale priced at 3 for $12.99. At that rate, how much will 4 shirts cost?

3. If it takes 12 hours to drive 660 miles, how long does it take to drive 880 miles?

4. The Kleins spent $270 the first 4 days of their vacation. At this rate, how much will they spend in 10 days?

5. If a car uses 12 gallons of gas for every 168 miles, how many gallons of gas will it use for 14 miles?

6. Marla walked 4 blocks in 9 minutes. At this speed, how many minutes did it take her to walk 56 blocks?

Set 124 *pages 316-317* Write each percent as a decimal.

1. 37%   **2.** 64%   **3.** 8%   **4.** 70%   **5.** 34%   **6.** 17%   **7.** 44%   **8.** 98%

9. 4%   **10.** 53%   **11.** 26%   **12.** 90%   **13.** 27%   **14.** 39%   **15.** 52%   **16.** 13%

17. 25%   **18.** 73%   **19.** 96%   **20.** 83%   **21.** 28%   **22.** 69%   **23.** 41%   **24.** 19%

Write each decimal as a percent.

25. 0.24   **26.** 0.15   **27.** 0.11   **28.** 0.09   **29.** 0.78   **30.** 0.38   **31.** 0.96   **32.** 0.4

33. 0.7   **34.** 0.52   **35.** 0.34   **36.** 0.11   **37.** 0.08   **38.** 0.25   **39.** 0.43   **40.** 0.69

41. 0.9   **42.** 0.85   **43.** 0.17   **44.** 0.58   **45.** 0.62   **46.** 0.22   **47.** 0.99   **48.** 0.79

49. 0.41   **50.** 0.36   **51.** 0.21   **52.** 0.33   **53.** 0.81   **54.** 0.48   **55.** 0.44   **56.** 0.97

MORE PRACTICE

Set 125 *pages 318–319*   Write each percent as a fraction.

1. 11%   **2.** 9%   **3.** 67%   **4.** 3%   **5.** 42%   **6.** 12%   **7.** 72%   **8.** 58%

9. 5%   **10.** 2%   **11.** 36%   **12.** 88%   **13.** 24%   **14.** 10%   **15.** 98%   **16.** 55%

17. 47%   **18.** 51%   **19.** 89%   **20.** 62%   **21.** 16%   **22.** 20%   **23.** 90%   **24.** 48%

Write each fraction as a percent.

25. $\frac{11}{50}$ **26.** $\frac{9}{100}$ **27.** $\frac{1}{50}$ **28.** $\frac{7}{10}$ **29.** $\frac{9}{20}$ **30.** $\frac{1}{50}$ **31.** $\frac{4}{25}$ **32.** $\frac{1}{25}$

33. $\frac{3}{5}$ **34.** $\frac{3}{20}$ **35.** $\frac{19}{20}$ **36.** $\frac{1}{5}$ **37.** $\frac{7}{20}$ **38.** $\frac{17}{20}$ **39.** $\frac{12}{25}$ **40.** $\frac{19}{25}$

41. $\frac{33}{50}$ **42.** $\frac{13}{100}$ **43.** $\frac{6}{25}$ **44.** $\frac{18}{25}$ **45.** $\frac{3}{8}$ **46.** $\frac{3}{10}$ **47.** $\frac{1}{20}$ **48.** $\frac{7}{25}$

Set 126 *pages 320–321*   Find each number.

1. 15% of 80   **2.** 36% of 253   **3.** 18% of 40   **4.** 16% of 10   **5.** 49% of 83

6. 75% of 56   **7.** 50% of 44   **8.** 20% of 85   **9.** 5% of 18   **10.** 6% of 92

11. 1% of 37   **12.** 4% of 20   **13.** 11% of 200   **14.** 12% of 36   **15.** 25% of 116

16. 7% of 115   **17.** 30% of 600   **18.** 47% of 345   **19.** 0% of 672   **20.** 100% of 845

21. 19% of 80   **22.** 5% of 350   **23.** 38% of 400   **24.** 92% of 90   **25.** 100% of 51

Set 127 *pages 322–323*   Find each number using a fraction.
The fractions for the percents in Exercises 1–20 are given in the table below.

Percent	10%	20%	25%	$33\frac{1}{3}$%	50%	$66\frac{2}{3}$%	75%	80%	90%
Fraction	$\frac{1}{10}$	$\frac{2}{5}$	$\frac{1}{4}$	$\frac{1}{3}$	$\frac{1}{2}$	$\frac{2}{3}$	$\frac{3}{4}$	$\frac{4}{5}$	$\frac{9}{10}$

1. 10% of 60   **2.** 20% of 25   **3.** 75% of 32   **4.** 50% of 72   **5.** $66\frac{2}{3}$% of 6

6. 80% of 50   **7.** 75% of 12   **8.** 25% of 160   **9.** 90% of 50   **10.** $33\frac{1}{3}$% of 9

11. $66\frac{2}{3}$% of 75   **12.** 10% of 70   **13.** 20% of 40   **14.** 25% of 76   **15.** 90% of 130

16. 80% of 40   **17.** 75% of 24   **18.** $33\frac{1}{3}$% of 33   **19.** 25% of 9   **20.** 50% of 50

21. 1% of 400   **22.** 3% of 500   **23.** 60% of 700   **24.** 35% of 80   **25.** 5% of 120

26. 12% of 150   **27.** 4% of 100   **28.** 95% of 20   **29.** 7% of 100   **30.** 51% of 400

Set 128 *pages 326–327*   Solve each problem.

1. Wayne bought a down jacket for $85 plus 6% sales tax. How much change did he get from $100?

2. Sally wants skates that cost $68 plus 5% sales tax. She has $70. How much more does she need?

3. Leslie has $80. Can she buy a tennis racket that costs $75 plus 5% sales tax?

4. Justin bought a football for $18 plus sales tax. He received $0.92 change from a $20 bill. How much was the tax?

Set 129 *pages 328–329*   Find each percent.

1. 6 is what percent of 20?

2. 8 is what percent of 16?

3. 3 is what percent of 15?

4. 19 is what percent of 20?

5. What percent of 50 is 33?

6. What percent of 40 is 32?

7. What percent of 25 is 9?

8. What percent of 80 is 12?

9. Find what percent 21 is of 60.

10. Find what percent 6 is of 24.

11. Find what percent 22 is of 25.

12. Find what percent 69 is of 75.

13. 17 is what percent of 50?

14. What percent of 90 is 27?

Set 130 *pages 330–331*   Write an equation. Then give the answer.

1. During the baseball season, Juan had 14 hits in 50 times at bat. What percent of his times at bat were hits?

2. Sheri scored 60% on a test that had a total of 125 problems. How many problems did she answer correctly?

3. Twenty-five percent of the 28 players on the team are freshmen. How many of the 28 players are freshmen?

4. There are 1,600 books in the library. 18% are reference books. How many are reference books?

Set 131 *pages 332–333*   Solve each problem.

1. Charles bought a watch on sale at 30% off the regular price. The regular price was $90. What was the sale price?

2. Ling bought a bicycle for $150. She sold it for $45 less than she had paid for it. By what percent had the value of the bicycle decreased?

3. A $28 shirt is on sale for 20% off the regular price. What is the sale price of the shirt?

4. A guitar is on sale for $100. The regular price was $150. What is the percent of discount?

MORE PRACTICE

Set 132 *pages 338–339*   Use the data in the graph.

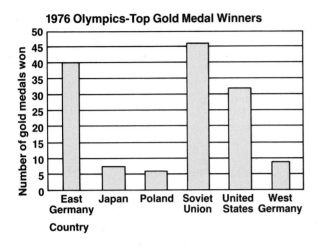

1976 Olympics-Top Gold Medal Winners

Which countries won

1. more than 30 gold medals?

2. fewer than 20 gold medals?

3. more than 5 gold medals?

Which country won more gold medals?

4. East Germany or the Soviet Union?

5. Poland or Japan?

6. Which country won more than 30 but fewer than 40 gold medals?

Set 133 *pages 340–341*   Use the graph to answer these questions.

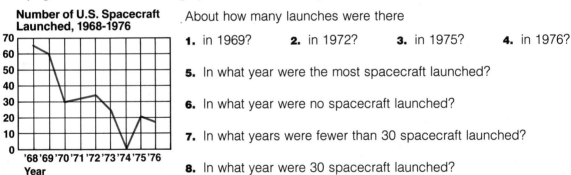

Number of U.S. Spacecraft Launched, 1968-1976

About how many launches were there

1. in 1969?   **2.** in 1972?   **3.** in 1975?   **4.** in 1976?

5. In what year were the most spacecraft launched?

6. In what year were no spacecraft launched?

7. In what years were fewer than 30 spacecraft launched?

8. In what year were 30 spacecraft launched?

Set 134 *pages 342–343*   Use the graph.

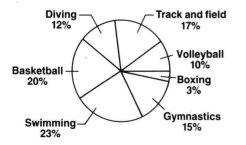

Favorite Olympic Sport at Carisbrooke School

Diving 12%
Track and field 17%
Volleyball 10%
Boxing 3%
Basketball 20%
Gymnastics 15%
Swimming 23%

The 600 students in Carisbrooke School chose their favorite Olympic sport. The results are shown on this circle graph.

How many students chose

1. boxing?   **2.** swimming?   **3.** track and field?

4. diving?   **5.** gymnastics?   **6.** basketball?

7. volleyball?

Set 135 *pages 344–345* Give the ordered pair that locates each point on the grid below.

1. *A*   2. *B*   3. *C*   4. *D*   5. *E*   6. *F*

7. *G*   8. *H*   9. *I*   10. *J*   11. *K*   12. *L*

Mark all these points on one grid. Label each point with the letter given.

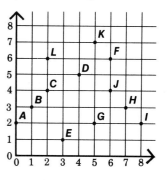

13. *S* (3, 2)   14. *M* (5, 6)   15. *N* (8, 5)

16. *P* (7, 5)   17. *Q* (0, 4)   18. *R* (1, 3)

Mark all these points on one grid. Then join the points in order.

19. (4, 0)   20. (0, 7)   21. (3, 7)   22. (4, 5)   23. (5, 7)   24. (8, 7)

Set 136 *pages 346–347* Complete each table, form ordered pairs, and draw a line graph.

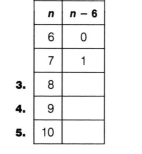

n	n + 4
0	4
1	5
2	6
1. 3	
2. 4	

n	n − 6
6	0
7	1
3. 8	
4. 9	
5. 10	

n	2 × n
0	0
1	2
6. 2	
7. 3	
8. 4	

n	n ÷ 3
3	1
6	2
9. 9	
10. 12	
11. 15	

Set 137 *pages 348–349* Use a graph to solve each problem.

1. Roberto left Meadow Valley at 8 A.M., driving at an average speed of 50 kilometers per hour. Lucy followed him one hour later, driving at an average speed of 70 kilometers per hour. About what time did Lucy overtake Roberto?

2. Use your graph for Problem 1 to tell about how far from Meadow Valley each person was at 12 P.M.

3. A bat left the forest at 1 A.M., flying at an average speed of 25 kilometers per hour. At 3 A.M. a raven left the forest, flying after the bat at an average speed of 45 kilometers per hour. About what time will the raven catch up with the bat?

4. Use your graph for Problem 3 to tell about how far apart the raven was from the bat at 4 A.M.

5. Joan started the bicycle trail at 1 P.M., riding at an average speed of 9 kilometers per hour. Sue started one hour later, riding at an average speed of 15 kilometers per hour. About when will Sue overtake Joan?

6. Use your graph for Problem 5 to tell about how far apart Joan and Sue were at 3 P.M.

411

MORE PRACTICE

Set 138 *pages 352–353* Write an integer to represent each situation.

1. Profit of $12

2. Loss of $93

3. 2 floors below ground level

4. 8 floors above ground level

5. 3 steps forward

6. 5 steps backward

7. Loss of 8 points

8. Gain of 4 points

9. 12° above zero

10. 8° below zero

Give the opposite of each integer.

11. $^+5$ **12.** $^-4$ **13.** $^+6$ **14.** $^-7$ **15.** $^-12$ **16.** $^+14$ **17.** $^-32$ **18.** $^+36$

19. $^-60$ **20.** $^+25$ **21.** $^-43$ **22.** $^+152$ **23.** $^-112$ **24.** $^+136$ **25.** $^-250$ **26.** $^+143$

Set 139 *pages 354–355* Use number line below to given an integer for each lettered point.

```
    R   S   T   U   V   W   X   Z   A   B   C
  <-+---+---+---+---+---+---+---+---+---+---+->
        -6                  -1              +3
```

1. A **2.** Z **3.** B **4.** R **5.** T **6.** V **7.** U **8.** W

Compare the integers. Use < or >.

9. $^+36$ ⬤ $^+4$ **10.** $^+11$ ⬤ $^+12$ **11.** $^-90$ ⬤ $^+9$ **12.** $^+22$ ⬤ $^-26$ **13.** $^-32$ ⬤ $^-6$

14. $^-24$ ⬤ $^-18$ **15.** $^+14$ ⬤ $^-14$ **16.** $^+12$ ⬤ $^+15$ **17.** $^-24$ ⬤ $^+12$ **18.** $^-63$ ⬤ $^-36$

Arrange the integers in order from the least to the greatest.

19. $^+3$ $^+6$ $^-4$ **20.** $^+9$ 0 $^-2$ **21.** $^-8$ $^-4$ $^+2$ **22.** $^+1$ $^-4$ $^+9$ $^-8$

Set 140 *pages 356–357*

1. $^+6 + {}^+7$ **2.** $^-4 + {}^-5$ **3.** $^+5 + {}^+1$ **4.** $^-7 + {}^-2$ **5.** $^+8 + {}^+2$

6. $^-8 + {}^-17$ **7.** $^+6 + {}^+13$ **8.** $^-14 + {}^-5$ **9.** $^+8 + {}^+6$ **10.** $^+12 + {}^+3$

11. $^-17 + {}^-6$ **12.** $^-14 + {}^-4$ **13.** $^+13 + {}^+3$ **14.** $^-24 + {}^-13$ **15.** $^+33 + {}^+25$

16. $^-22 + {}^-15$ **17.** $^-63 + {}^-15$ **18.** $^+44 + {}^+18$ **19.** $^-64 + {}^-32$ **20.** $^+13 + {}^+16$

21. $^-25 + {}^-22$ **22.** $^+43 + {}^+25$ **23.** $^-17 + {}^-11$ **24.** $^-38 + {}^-32$ **25.** $^+15 + {}^+24$

26. $^-14 + {}^-26$ **27.** $^+17 + {}^+24$ **28.** $^+12 + {}^+15$ **29.** $^-43 + {}^-56$ **30.** $^+65 + {}^+33$

Set 141 *pages 358–359*

1. $^+3 + {}^-5$
2. $^+5 + {}^-2$
3. $^-3 + {}^+8$
4. $^-1 + {}^+10$
5. $^+6 + {}^-7$

6. $^-8 + {}^+2$
7. $^-9 + {}^+12$
8. $^-3 + {}^+3$
9. $^+6 + {}^-11$
10. $^+4 + {}^-13$

11. $^-15 + {}^+15$
12. $^-4 + {}^+16$
13. $^+6 + {}^-20$
14. $^+12 + {}^-12$
15. $^-14 + {}^+7$

16. $^+11 + {}^-7$
17. $^-13 + {}^+8$
18. $^+3 + {}^-19$
19. $^+15 + {}^-3$
20. $^-8 + {}^+7$

21. $^-65 + {}^+33$
22. $^+24 + {}^-22$
23. $^-72 + {}^+12$
24. $^+4 + {}^-59$
25. $^-42 + {}^+16$

Set 142 *pages 360–361*

1. $^+9 - {}^+3$
2. $^-8 - {}^-4$
3. $^-3 - {}^+7$
4. $^+10 - {}^-2$
5. $^+7 - {}^+3$

6. $^-12 - {}^-4$
7. $^+4 - {}^+2$
8. $^-4 - {}^-3$
9. $^+9 - {}^-3$
10. $^-3 - 0$

11. $^+6 - {}^+6$
12. $0 - {}^-4$
13. $^+14 - {}^+3$
14. $^-16 - {}^-11$
15. $^+18 - {}^-20$

16. $^+8 - 0$
17. $^-6 - {}^+32$
18. $^-72 - {}^+45$
19. $^+46 - {}^-12$
20. $^+84 - {}^+15$

Set 143 *pages 362–363* Name the point which is located by each ordered pair.

1. $(^-1, 0)$
2. $(^+2, {}^+1)$
3. $(0, {}^+3)$

4. $(^-2, {}^+1)$
5. $(^+3, {}^-2)$
6. $(^-4, {}^-3)$

Give the ordered pair which locates each point.

7. *R*
8. *S*
9. *T*

10. *U*
11. *V*
12. *W*

Set 144 *pages 364–365* Draw the figure by joining the given points in order. Change the sign of the first number in each ordered pair. Then draw the new figure.

1. $(^+2, {}^+4), (^+4, {}^+2), (^+4, {}^-2), (^+2, {}^-4), (^+2, {}^+4)$

2. $(^-1, {}^-1), (^-2, {}^-4), (^-5, {}^-3), (^-1, {}^-1)$

Draw the figure by joining the given points in order. Change the sign of the second number in each ordered pair. Then draw the new figure.

3. $(^+1, {}^+1), (^+1, {}^+4), (^+3, {}^+1), (^+1, {}^+1)$

4. $(^-1, {}^+1), (^-1, {}^+4), (^-3, {}^+4), (^-3, {}^+1), (^-1, {}^+1)$

Tables

Metric System

Length

10 millimeters (mm) = 1 centimeter (cm)

10 centimeters }
100 millimeters } = 1 decimeter (dm)

10 decimeters }
100 centimeters } = 1 meter (m)

1,000 meters = 1 kilometer (km)

Area

100 square millimeters (mm^2) = 1 square centimeter (cm^2)

10,000 square centimeters = 1 square meter (m^2)

100 square meters = 1 are (a)

10,000 square meters = 1 hectare (ha)

Volume

1,000 cubic millimeters (mm^3) = 1 cubic centimeter (cm^3)

1,000 cubic centimeters = 1 cubic decimeter (dm^3)

1,000,000 cubic centimeters = 1 cubic meter (m^3)

Mass (weight)

1,000 milligrams (mg) = 1 gram (g)

1,000 grams = 1 kilogram (kg)

1,000 kilograms = 1 metric ton (t)

Capacity

1,000 milliliters (mL) = 1 liter (L)

Customary System

Length

12 inches (in.) = 1 foot (ft.)

3 feet }
36 inches } = 1 yard (yd.)

1,760 yards }
5,280 feet } = 1 mile (mi.)

6,076 feet = 1 nautical mile

Area

144 square inches (sq. in.) = 1 square foot (sq. ft.)

9 square feet = 1 square yard (sq. yd.)

4,840 square yards = 1 acre (A.)

Volume

1,728 cubic inches (cu. in.) = 1 cubic foot (cu. ft.)

27 cubic feet = 1 cubic yard (cu. yd.)

Weight

16 ounces (oz.) = 1 pound (lb.)

2,000 pounds = 1 ton (T.)

Capacity

8 fluid ounces (fl. oz.) = 1 cup (c.)

2 cups = 1 pint (pt.)

2 pints = 1 quart (qt.)

4 quarts = 1 gallon (gal.)

Time

60 seconds = 1 minute

60 minutes = 1 hour

24 hours = 1 day

7 days = 1 week

365 days }
52 weeks } = 1 year
12 months }

366 days = 1 leap year

Addition-Subtraction Table

+	0	1	2	3	4	5	6	7	8	9
0	0	1	2	3	4	5	6	7	8	9
1	1	2	3	4	5	6	7	8	9	10
2	2	3	4	5	6	7	8	9	10	11
3	3	4	5	6	7	8	9	10	11	12
4	4	5	6	7	8	9	10	11	12	13
5	5	6	7	8	9	10	11	12	13	14
6	6	7	8	9	10	11	12	13	14	15
7	7	8	9	10	11	12	13	14	15	16
8	8	9	10	11	12	13	14	15	16	17
9	9	10	11	12	13	14	15	16	17	18

Multiplication-Division Table

×	1	2	3	4	5	6	7	8	9
1	1	2	3	4	5	6	7	8	9
2	2	4	6	8	10	12	14	16	18
3	3	6	9	12	15	18	21	24	27
4	4	8	12	16	20	24	28	32	36
5	5	10	15	20	25	30	35	40	45
6	6	12	18	24	30	36	42	48	54
7	7	14	21	28	35	42	49	56	63
8	8	16	24	32	40	48	56	64	72
9	9	18	27	36	45	54	63	72	81

Glossary

Acute angle   An angle that has a measure less than 90°.

Addition property of zero   The sum of zero and a number is that number.

Adjacent angles   Angles *ABC* and *CBD* are adjacent.

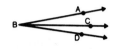

Alternate interior angles   See transversal.

Altitude of a triangle   A segment that extends from one vertex of the triangle to the opposite side and is perpendicular to that side.

altitude

Angle (∠)   The figure formed by two rays with the same endpoint.

vertex
side

Arc   Part of a circle.

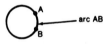

arc AB

Area   A number indicating the size of the inside of a plane figure.

Associative property of addition   The way in which addends are grouped does not affect the sum. For example,
(7 + 2) + 5 = 7 + (2 + 5)

Associative property of multiplication   The way in which factors are grouped does not affect the product. For example,
(7 × 2) × 5 = 7 × (2 × 5)

Average   A number obtained by dividing the sum of two or more addends by the number of addends.

BASIC   A simple language used to give instructions to computers.

Binary numbers   Base two numbers which are used to store numbers in a computer.

Central angle   An angle with its vertex at the center of a circle.

Chord   A segment whose endpoints are on a circle. A diameter is a special chord.

Circle   A plane figure with all of its points the same distance from a given point called the center.

Circumference   The distance around a circle.

Common denominator   A common multiple of two or more denominators. A common denominator for $\frac{1}{6}$ and $\frac{3}{8}$ is 48.

Common factor   A number that is a factor of two or more numbers. A common factor of 6 and 12 is 3.

Common multiple   A number that is a multiple of two or more numbers. A common multiple of 4 and 6 is 12.

Commutative property of addition   The order in which numbers are added does not affect the sum. For example,
4 + 6 = 6 + 4.

Commutative property of multiplication   The order in which numbers are multiplied does not affect the product. For example,
4 × 6 = 6 × 4.

Composite number   A whole number, greater than 0, that has more than two factors.

Computer program   A set of instructions that tells the computer how to do a certain job.

Concentric circles   Circles in the same plane that have the same center but different radii.

Cone   A space figure formed by connecting a circle to a point not in the plane of the circle.

Congruent   Having the same size and the same shape.

Consecutive angles   In this quadrilateral, angles *J* and *K* are consecutive.

consecutive angles

Cosine   For a given acute angle in a right triangle, the ratio:
$$\frac{\text{length of adjacent side}}{\text{length of hypotenuse}}$$

Cross-products   For the ratios $\frac{3}{4}$ and $\frac{9}{12}$, the cross-products are 3 × 12 and 4 × 9.

Cube   A prism with all square faces.

Cylinder   A space figure shaped like this.

Degree (of an angle)   A unit for measuring angles.

Diagonal   In a polygon, a segment that connects one vertex to another vertex but is not a side of the polygon.

Diameter   In a circle, a segment that passes through the center and has its endpoints on the circle.

Distributive property   The general pattern of numbers of which the following is an example.
4 × (7 + 3) = (4 × 7) + (4 × 3)

Dividend A number that is divided by another number. In 48 ÷ 6 = 8, the dividend is 48.

Divisor A number that divides another number. In 48 ÷ 6 = 8, the divisor is 6.

Edge In a space figure, a segment where two faces meet.

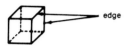

END The last line in a BASIC computer program.

Endpoint The point at the end of a segment or ray.

Equation A mathematical sentence that uses the = symbol.
14 − 7 = 7.

Equilateral triangle A triangle with all three sides congruent.

Even number A whole number with a factor of 2.

Exponent In 4^3, the exponent is 3. It tells that 4 is to be used as a factor three times.
$4^3 = 4 \times 4 \times 4$

Exponential form The form that the computer uses to print very large or very small numbers.

Face A flat surface that is part of a polyhedron.

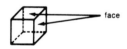

Factor (1) A number to be multiplied. (2) A number that divides evenly into a given second number is a factor of that number.

Factorial The product of a whole number and every whole number less than itself.
$4! = 4 \times 3 \times 2 \times 1 = 24$.

Flow chart A diagram illustrating the steps used to solve a problem.

FOR . . . NEXT BASIC statements in a computer program that tell the computer to do something a certain number of times.

FORWARD (FD) A LOGO command that tells the turtle to move forward a certain number of steps.

Fraction A number written in the form $\frac{a}{b}$, such as $\frac{2}{3}$, or $\frac{11}{5}$, or $\frac{4}{1}$.

Frequency table In statistics, a listing of the data and how many times each item of data occurred.

GO TO A BASIC statement in a computer program that tells the computer to go to another line in the program.

Greatest common factor The greatest number that is a factor of two or more numbers. The greatest common factor of 8 and 12 is 4.

Hexadecimal numbers Base sixteen numbers used for storage in a computer.

Hexagon A six-sided polygon.

Hypotenuse In a right triangle, the side opposite the right angle.

IF . . . THEN A BASIC statement used to test certain conditions and act on the results of the test.

Improper fraction A fraction, such as $\frac{15}{2}$ or $\frac{2}{1}$, that can be written as a mixed number or as a whole number greater than zero.

INPUT A BASIC statement in a computer program that allows information to be entered into the program by the program user.

Inscribed angle An angle whose vertex is on a circle and whose sides cut off an arc of the circle.

Inscribed polygon A polygon inside a circle with its vertices on the circle.

INT (N) A BASIC function used on the computer to find the greatest integer less than or equal to N.

Integers The whole numbers and their opposites. Some integers are +2, −2, +75, and −75.

Intersecting lines Two lines that meet at exactly one point.

Isosceles triangle A triangle with at least two sides congruent.

Least common multiple The smallest number that is a common multiple of two given numbers. The least common multiple for 6 and 8 is 24.

LET A BASIC statement that allows a value to be assigned to a memory location named by a letter.

LOGO A simple language used to give instructions to a computer.

Loop A set of instructions that a computer carries out more than once.

Lowest terms A fraction is in lowest terms if 1 is the only number that will divide both the numerator and the denominator.

Mean Another name for "average." The mean of the set 2, 4, 5, 6, 6 is 23 ÷ 5, or 4.6.

Median The middle number in a set of numbers when the numbers are in order. The median of the set 2, 4, 5, 6, 6 is 5.

Midpoint The point in a segment that divides it into two equal parts.

Mixed number A number that has a whole number part and a fraction part, such as $3\frac{1}{4}$ and $6\frac{7}{8}$.

Mode The number that occurs most often in a set of numbers. The mode of 2, 4, 5, 6, 6 is 6.

Multiple A multiple of a number is the product of that number and a whole number. Some multiples of 3 are 3, 6, and 9.

Multiplication property of one The product of a number and one is that number.

Negative integer An integer less than 0, such as −1, −5, −7, or −10.

Obtuse angle An angle that has a measure greater than 90° and less than 180°.

Octagon An eight-sided polygon.

Odd number A whole number that does not have 2 as a factor.

Opposite angles In this quadrilateral, angles *J* and *L* are opposite angles.

Opposites Two numbers whose sum is 0. +5 and −5 are opposites because +5 + (−5) = 0.

Ordered pair A number pair, such as (3, 5), in which 3 is the first number and 5 is the second number.

Origin On a coordinate grid, the point, (0, 0), where the two number lines, or axes, intersect.

Output Any information that is produced by a computer.

Parallel lines Lines in the same plane that do not meet.

Parallelogram A quadrilateral with opposite sides parallel and equal.

Pentagon A five-sided polygon.

Percent (%) A word indicating "hundredths" or "out of 100." 45 percent (45%) means 0.45 or $\frac{45}{100}$.

Perimeter The sum of the lengths of the sides of a polygon.

Permutations The ordered arrangements of a set of objects or numbers. The permutations of the set A, B, C are:
  ABC BAC CAB
  ACB BCA CBA

Perpendicular lines Two intersecting lines that form right angles.

Pi (π) The number obtained by dividing the circumference of any circle by its diameter. A common approximation for π is 3.14.

Polygon A plane figure made up of segments called its *sides*, each side intersecting two other sides, one at each of its endpoints.

Polyhedron A space figure with all flat surfaces. The outline of each surface is a polygon.

Positive integer An integer greater than 0, such as +1, +2, +10, or +35.

Power 3^4 is read "3 to the fourth power." $3^4 = 3 \times 3 \times 3 \times 3 = 81$. The fourth power of 3 is 81. 4^2 is read "4 to the second power" or "4 squared." *See* Exponent.

Precision A property of measurement that depends upon the size of the unit of measure. The smaller the unit, the more precise the measurement.

Prime factor A factor that is a prime number. The prime factors of 10 are 2 and 5.

Prime number A whole number, greater than 1, that has exactly two factors: itself and 1. 17 is a prime number.

PRINT An instruction to the computer to give certain output on the screen.

Prism A polyhedron with two parallel, congruent faces, called *bases*. All other faces are parallelograms.

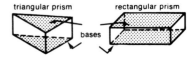

Probability A number that tells how likely it is that a certain event will happen.

Program *See* Computer program

Proportion A statement that two ratios are equal.
$$\frac{2}{5} = \frac{12}{30}$$

Pyramid The space figure formed by connecting points of a polygon to a point not in the plane of the polygon. The polygon and its interior is the *base*.

Quadrant One of the four parts into which a plane is divided by two perpendicular lines.

Quadrilateral A four-sided polygon.

Quotient The answer to a division problem. In 48 ÷ 6 = 8, the quotient is 8.

Radius (1) In a circle, a segment that connects the center of the circle with a point on the circle. (2) In a circle, the distance from the center to a point of the circle.

Ratio A pair of numbers that expresses a rate or a comparison.

Rational number   Any number that can be expressed as either a terminating decimal or a repeating decimal.
$4\frac{3}{4} = 4.75$ $\frac{1}{3} = 0.333\ldots$

Ray   Part of a line that has one endpoint and goes on and on in one direction.

READ . . . DATA   Statements that go together in a computer program to assign values to memory locations.

Reciprocals   Two numbers whose product is 1. $\frac{3}{4}$ and $\frac{4}{3}$ are reciprocals because $\frac{3}{4} \times \frac{4}{3} = 1$.

Rectangle   A parallelogram with four right angles.

Rectangular prism   *See* Prism.

Rectangular pyramid   *See* Pyramid.

Regular polygon   A polygon with all sides congruent and all angles congruent.

REM   A remark in a program that is intended to be read by someone who lists the program, but it does not affect the logic of the program.

REPEAT   A LOGO command that causes a list of commands to be done many times.

Repeating decimal   A decimal in which one or more digits keep repeating. 0.518181818 . . .

Rhombus   A parallelogram whose sides are congruent.

RIGHT (RT)   A LOGO command that directs the turtle to turn right a specified number of turtle turns.

Right angle   An angle that has a measure of 90°.

Right triangle   A triangle with one right angle.

Scalene triangle   A triangle with no two sides congruent.

Scientific notation   A method of expressing a number as a product so that:
• the first factor is a number greater than or equal to 1, and less than 10, and
• the second factor is a power of 10.

Segment   Part of a line, including the two endpoints.

Semicircle   An arc that is one half of a circle.

Significant digits   The number of digits in a measurement that have meaning in the measure and are not just estimates. The measurement 7.60 meters has three significant digits: 7, 6, and 0.

Similar figures   Figures with the same shape but not necessarily the same size.

Sine   For a given acute angle in a right triangle, the ratio:
length of opposite side
length of hypotenuse

Sphere   A space figure with all of its points the same distance from a given point called the *center.*

Square   A rectangle with all four sides congruent.

Square root   A number a is the square root of a number b if $a \times a = b$. 3 is the square root of 9.

Surface area   The sum of the areas of all the surfaces of a space figure.

TAB (N)   A BASIC function that is used with PRINT to place output at column N on the screen.

Tangent   For a given acute angle in a right triangle, the ratio:
length of opposite side
length of adjacent side

Terminating decimal   A decimal with a limited number of nonzero digits. Examples are 0.5 and 0.0082.

Transversal   A line that intersects two or more other lines in the same plane. In the drawing below, t is a transversal and angles 4 and 6 are alternate interior angles.

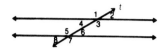

Trapezoid   A quadrilateral with one pair of parallel sides.

Triangle   A three-sided polygon.

Triangular prism   *See* Prism.

Triangular pyramid   *See* Pyramid.

Trigonometric ratios   *See* Cosine, Sine, and Tangent.

Variable   In an expression or an equation, a letter that represents a number.

Vertex   (1) The common endpoint of two rays that form an angle. (2) The point of intersection of two sides of a polygon. (3) The point of intersection of the edges of a polyhedron.

Volume   A number, measured in cubic units, indicating the size of the inside of a space figure.

Index